The Determinants and Effects of Mergers

PUBLICATION OF THE SCIENCE CENTER BERLIN
Volume 24

General Editor: Priv. doz. Dr. Hans-Jürgen Ewers

Editorial Board

Prof. Dr. Karl W. Deutsch
Prof. Dr. Meinolf Dierkes
Prof. Dr. Frieder Naschold
Prof. Dr. Fritz W. Scharpf

International Institute of Management

The Determinants and Effects of Mergers

An International Comparison

Edited by
Dennis C. Mueller
University of Maryland

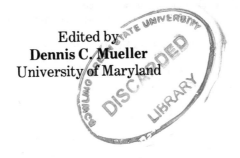

International Standard Book Number. 0-89946-045-3 (U.S.A.)

3-445-12080-3 (Germany)

Library of Congress Catalog Card Number: 80-19381

Printed in the United States of America

Contents

List of Figures

List of Tables

Preface

The study reported in this book began in the spring of 1974, when I was searching for a topic that would fit the international, comparative research objectives of the International Institute of Management (IIM) of the Science Center Berlin. Mergers seemed a "natural" topic, since outside of the United States and the United Kingdom, there was not a great deal of literature about mergers. Given the peculiarities of data sources in different countries, institutional differences in the environments in which mergers occur, and language barriers, it seemed essential that the research be undertaken by scholars from the seven different countries to be covered in the study. Thus, the first year of the project was spent enlisting an international team of researchers, each member of which was responsible for researching the determinants and effects of mergers in his own country.

Although we worked under the auspices of the IIM, each team member received most of his financial support—faculty time, computer funds, and so on—from his home institution. In addition, the Anglo/German Foundation contributed funds to the United Kingdom and German projects, and the Swedish study received financial help from the Stockholm Savings Bank Foundation for Scientific Research and from the Torsten and Rangar Söderberg Foundations. The IIM provided research assistant, summer salary, and travel support for all project teams—i.e., the oil to keep the wheels turning.

The project started in 1974, and was first projected to require three years. But it was not until five years later that we were ready to finalize the reports. This underlines the fact that a large, international comparative study is not to be taken up lightly. Fortunately, our study was blessed with a group of capable and cooperative scholars who were willing to start work immediately, and yet it still required five years to complete.

The study is different from others in a number of ways. Each country report has been individually and independently written. Thus, the reader will encounter slightly different formats and styles of presentation from chapter to chapter. Yet in spite of the differences that fourteen authors can impart to a manuscript, the chapters are tied together by an underlying set of hypotheses and methodological homogeneity that have existed since the study's outset. All country reports present results from a common set of tests comparing the characteristics of merging companies and determinants and effects of mergers in the seven countries. In this respect, the book is truly a team effort.

So many people have contributed to this project through the years that it is impossible to thank them all. Thanks must go first to the International Institute of Management of the Science Center Berlin and to its former director, Walter Goldberg, who for much of the project's history was responsible for the IO group. He never wavered in his support for the project, and without this support it probably never would have been completed. Thanks are also due to Jürgen Ewers, who succeeded Walter Goldberg as acting director of the Institute and who helped the project through its final stages. A special note of thanks is due to Manfred Fleischer for his efforts on behalf of the project throughout the years. Finally, I should like to thank my colleagues and coauthors in this endeavor for being such a congenial group with which to work.

Dennis C. Mueller

Foreword

When the International Institute of Management of the Science Center Berlin developed and implemented its research program for the seventies, research into industrial structures and their determinants and efficiency was chosen as a focal area. Later, the emphasis gradually shifted from a descriptive to an instrumental phase, i.e., into the question of how to initiate necessary or desirable changes in structures of industries in order to meet new economic and societal conditions.

Under the direction of Professor F. M. Scherer in the initial phase, and of Professor Dennis C. Mueller during the period 1975–1978, the question of growth (and nongrowth) of industries, as well as of firms within industries, and its consequences regarding competitiveness and overall efficiencies was approached in a number of ways.

Upon the initiative of Dennis Mueller, research teams were set up in some of the highly industrialized countries of Europe (Belgium, Federal Republic of Germany, France, the Netherlands, Sweden, and the United Kingdom) as well as in the United States. Their goal was to investigate the reasons for growth by merger and the modes chosen, as well as the efficiency of a merger and its consequences for concerned parties and for the industry.

A joint scheme and methodology of research was developed and applied. Several aspects of the results from the country studies, as well as from the comparative analysis, are most interesting and intriguing. As far as merger theory is concerned, the conclusions overthrow a number of well-established myths and beliefs regarding the objectives and consequences of mergers—e.g., their supposed improved efficiency, higher gains, lower prices, expanded markets, and benefits both to the customer as well as to the shareholder. As far as merger policy (as a subset of national or international competition policy) is concerned, the findings of the study have already both induced and influenced reforms in competition laws in several countries.

It is a delight to present this study in a condensed version to scientists, legislators, and policymakers and it is a pleasure to thank the members of a successful team for their deliberations and achievement. This volume will stimulate both policy discussion and further research.

The authors assume the responsibility for their contributions.

Walter Goldberg
Director (1977–1979)
International Institute of Management
Science Center Berlin

Mergers, Concentration, and Competition in Advanced Capitalist Economies: An International Perspective

Alan Hughes and Ajit Singh

INTRODUCTION

In purely material terms, the two decades preceding the oil price rise of 1973 could properly be called the golden age of world capitalist development. Most of the leading industrial countries achieved historically unprecedented rates of growth of output and consumption, as well as sustained high levels of employment. However, the period was also attended by another extremely important phenomenon—a merger wave that occurred more or less simultaneously in several countries and that in a number of them, again by past standards, was immense.

In the postwar period, the first increases in merger activity on a sizable scale took place in the 1950s in the United Kingdom and in the United States. For example, in the United Kingdom nearly 2000 manufacturing companies were quoted on the stock market in the mid-1950s. Of these, nearly 500 "died" or disappeared from the list six years later—more than 400 through the process of merger. In other words, a quoted manufacturing company had a one in five chance of "dying" through merger over a six-year period. As the merger movement gained momentum, a typical quoted company in the mid-1960s—and these are the relatively large firms—had a one in three chance of dying through merger over a similar period. During the peak merger years, 1967–1969, the assets of the manufacturing companies that were acquired comprised 14 percent of the total assets of manufacturing industry.

Similarly, in the United States at the height of the merger wave, 1966–1968, 462 large manufacturing and mining companies were acquired, accounting for 10 percent of the total assets of all large companies in 1964.[1] In West Germany the annual average percentage of equity capital disappearing through merger among AG (i.e., large incorporated) companies in 1967–1972 was 2.3 percent. In the same way in France, the value of net assets acquired more than quadrupled between the early and late 1960s, while the annual average number of mergers among companies listed on the stock market rose from 69 in 1953–1957 to a peak of 226 in 1967–1970. When the magnitude of merger activity is considered in terms of the labor force employed, in Sweden employment in the manufacturing companies acquired in 1967 and 1968 alone amounted to 7 percent of total industrial employment; in the Netherlands in 1971 and 1972, employment in merging firms was around 10 percent of the total employed population in both years.[2]

Not surprisingly, merger activity on this scale has produced great interest among academics and policymakers alike, and a considerable amount of research on mergers has developed. (For some recent surveys of this literature, see Hindley 1972; and Mueller 1977.) This has concentrated to an overwhelming extent, however, on the Anglo-Saxon economies. With a few notable exceptions (McGowan 1971; Jenny and Weber 1974; Rydén 1972; and de Jong 1971), it has left the European scene largely unexplored and has in the main analyzed the causes and effects of mergers within a purely national framework.

The lack of an international perspective in the existing merger literature was one of the main reasons for producing this book. The explanation of the simultaneous expansion of merger activity during the 1960s in the major industrial economies requires, at the very least, systematic and comparable accounts of the waves in each country. Thus one of the main objectives of this volume is to make available detailed accounts of merger activity in the major Western industrial nations. It reports the individual and collective research efforts of seven international teams of economists coordinated under the auspices of the International Institute of Management of the Science Center, Berlin. The countries analyzed are Belgium, France, the Netherlands, Sweden, the United Kingdom, the United States, and West Germany. Each is the subject of a separate chapter that explains the historical and institutional backgrounds to merger activity and sets out the results of an investigation of the microeconomic causes and effects of mergers. These results derive from a set of statistical tests common to all the research teams. (These are set out in Chapter 2.)

The common economic and statistical methodology makes possible the

second objective of the volume, which is to adopt an international comparative approach to mergers to shed some light on the important questions of
whether similar forces lay behind the growth of merger activity in each
country, whether particular institutional factors influenced the causes and
in particular the effects of the merger activity, and what implications
follow for economic theory. It is well known that important institutional
differences in the nature of capital markets, in the nature of ownership and
control patterns, and in government interventionist agencies exist among
the European economies and between them and the United States
economy. It is less obvious that these necessarily produce important
differences in economic performance. A cross-country comparison of
standardized results on the causes and effects of mergers may add to our
knowledge in these areas. In addition to the individual country chapters,
therefore, the book also includes a cross-country analysis of our main
results and conclusions about issues that are central to the current debate
on the theory of the firm.

The third and final objective of this book is to examine the national and
international policy implications of the merger waves in the various
countries. This chapter is designed to put the main individual country
chapters of the book in an international perspective. It sets out the historical and international context of the merger movement, the interconnec-
tions between the individual merger waves, and the possible reasons for
their simultaneous occurrences. It also studies the effects of mergers on
concentration and competition in the world economy.

THE INTERNATIONAL MERGER MOVEMENT: 1955-1975

In considering the most recent merger wave in a historical and
international perspective, we should find it useful first to examine mergers
in the United States and the United Kingdom. This is partly because there
are important institutional similarities in the conduct and legal organization of businesses in the two countries—for example the legal basis of the
joint stock company and the existence of highly developed and active stock
markets. Further, because of the stricter disclosure requirements for the
companies listed on the stock markets, as well as those of the respective
company laws, there are much more reliable data on companies available in
these two countries than in many continental ones.[3] In addition, there exist
important quantitative historical studies of mergers for the United States
and the United Kingdom.

Producing comparable series of merger deaths covering long periods is
very difficult. All the existing series for the United Kingdom and the

United States have important breaks in them, which suggest that the figures for the earliest years of this century are likely to be understated. The most widely accepted series for the United States and the United Kingdom are nevertheless shown in Figures 1–1 and 1–2. They suggest— even allowing for substantial downward reporting biases in earlier times— that in terms of the absolute numbers of firms involved, the waves of the late 1960s and early 1970s were unprecedented. For both the United States and the United Kingdom, the data suggest that the number of firms disappearing through merger was twice as high as ever before.[4]

Neither of these series is normalized, however, by the size of respective total company populations, which of course have changed considerably over the course of the past century. For the United Kingdom, long-run normalized merger death rates are available only for quoted companies. These confirm the impression given by Figure 1–1. In the 1960s the rate of disappearance of quoted companies was more than twice that recorded during 1885–1907, previously the most important merger movement period in the United Kingdom economy (see Singh 1975).

It is also significant that whereas up to 1950 the main cause of company disappearance in the United Kingdom was liquidations, during the past two decades, it has overwhelmingly been mergers and takeovers. Hart and Prais's (1956) analysis of the causes of death of a large sample of companies, quoted on the London stock market, that died during the period 1885–1950, showed that 34 percent of the deaths were caused by amalgamation (takeover-merger), 37 percent by liquidation, and 29 percent by other causes. However, a more complete examination of the data for quoted company disappearances during the period since the middle 1950s shows that more than 80 percent of these are due to takeovers and mergers,[5] 10 percent due to liquidation, and about 10 percent due to other causes. Singh (1971) has suggested that, inter alia, there are two main reasons for this major change in the mode of firm disappearances. First, a relatively higher and more stable rate of growth of economic activity in the postwar period has meant that the incidence of liquidation of quoted companies is much lower than it used to be. Second, with the growth in the absolute size of companies and the consequent dispersal of share owner- ship that has occurred, merger by means of takeover or a tender offer has become much more feasible than when companies were more or less family controlled (see also Hannah 1974a).

There is no long-run normalized merger series for the United States comparable to that for the United Kingdom quoted company sector men- tioned above. There is, however, some information on the percentage of the total assets of mining and manufacturing industry that the assets of the acquired companies constitute for the period since the First World War. These data suggest that the percentage of assets acquired, like the total

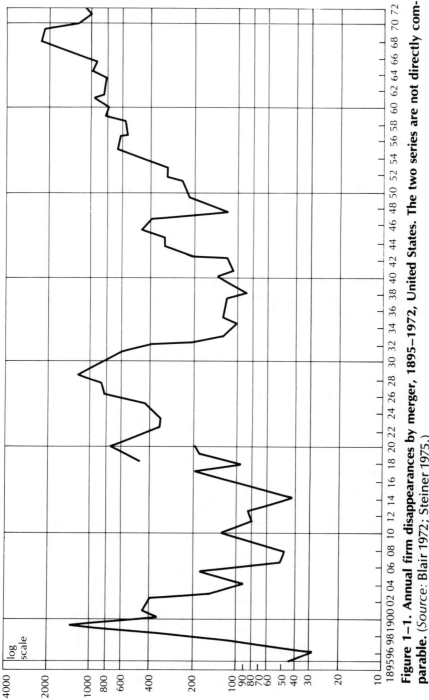

Figure 1–1. Annual firm disappearances by merger, 1895–1972, United States. The two series are not directly comparable. (*Source:* Blair 1972; Steiner 1975.)

Number of mergers

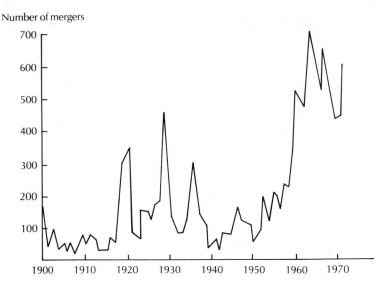

Figure 1–2. Annual firm disappearances by merger, 1900–1972, United Kingdom. There are important breaks in comparability in the series in 1919, 1938, and 1968. (*Source:* Hannah 1976a.)

number of firm disappearances, was greater in the merger boom of the 1960s than in the interwar period. For example, in the peak years of 1967 and 1968, 2.6 and 3.3 percent of assets were acquired as against the previously highest recorded figure of 2.5 percent in 1929 (see FTC 1969).

As far as the percentage of numbers of companies acquired is concerned, the data cover only the period since World War II. Acquisition rates for the large manufacturing and mining corporations (firms with assets greater than $10 million) show that there was a much greater incidence of mergers in the middle and late 1960s than during the 1950s: 1950, 0.3 percent; 1954, 1.8 percent; 1958, 1.7 percent; 1960, 2.6 percent; 1964, 3.4 percent; 1967, 5.1 percent; 1968, 5.7 percent (Gort and Hogarty 1970). Data for the subsequent period (see Chapter 9) show some decline in the acquisition rate in the earlier 1970s and in the subsequent recession, but it is still higher than that recorded during the 1950s.

Among the continental economies, the Netherlands and Sweden are probably the two countries whose institutional framework for the conduct of business activity comes closest to that of the Anglo-Saxon nations. Table 1–1 provides information on changes in merger activity in these two countries in the 1950s and 1960s. The Swedish data are normalized by employment; as in the case of the United Kingdom and the United States, they unambiguously show a big upsurge in merger activity in that country after the middle 1960s compared with the period before. Although the data

Table 1–1.   Indicators of Merger Activity in Sweden and the Netherlands, 1950–1970

	Sweden: employment in acquired industrial firms as percent of total industrial employment	Netherlands: index of number of mergers 1962 = 100
1950	0.78	
1955	0.75	
1958		25.0
1960	1.50	32.7
1965		127.1
1967	2.35	158.3
1968	4.38	352.1
1969		533.3
1972		
1976		

Source: For Sweden, Rydén (1972); for the Netherlands, de Jong (1971a) as quoted in Hughes (1976).

for the Netherlands in Table 1–1 give indexes only for the number of mergers, there clearly was a large increase in the incidence of merger activity in the Netherlands after 1965.

In comparing merger activity in West Germany with that in other countries, it is important to bear in mind certain institutional and historical differences. First, historically, Germany (like Japan) has been a country with traditionally high levels of economic concentration. However, immediately after World War II, the United States occupation authorities made some attempts—subsequently abandoned—to break up large combines and to discourage concentration in both countries (see further Scherer 1970). Second, as Cable, Palfrey, and Runge show in Chapter 4, the concept of a "merger" and the method of carrying out mergers are rather different in West Germany than in the United Kingdom and the United States. Third, there are a number of breaks in the information available on postwar mergers in West Germany. Nevertheless, it is generally agreed that there probably was a very large increase in merger activity in Germany in the late 1960s and early 1970s, at least comparable with that experienced, for instance, in the United Kingdom.

There are also serious gaps in the information available on merger activity in France and Belgium, as well as important differences in the institutional arrangements. These issues for France and Belgium are discussed in Chapters 3 (Belgium) and 5 (France). However, for our present purposes we note that both countries experienced a much higher level of merger activity in the 1960s than in the previous decade (see further Jenny and Weber, Chapter 5, and Kumps and Wtterwulghe, Chapter 3, this volume).

To sum up, a brief review of mergers in the leading industrial countries shows that most of them experienced a large merger wave during the 1960s. The dates for the peak levels of merger activity were of course somewhat different in the different countries. This, and other empirical material discussed above, raises the following issues:

1. Why did merger activity on such a vast scale take place?
2. Why was such activity more or less simultaneous during the 1960s in the various countries?
3. What factors explain intercountry differences in merger rates?

These clearly are large questions that by themselves would require a whole book for a proper answer. Nevertheless, in view of their importance, some tentative hypotheses concerning these issues will be outlined below, in particular relating to questions 1 and 2.

INTERNATIONAL TRADE, CAPITAL MOVEMENTS, GOVERNMENT POLICY, AND MERGER ACTIVITY

Two major forces shaping the world economy during the post–World War II period have been the rapid growth of international trade and of capital movements. As a consequence of the protectionist measures adopted by the nations of the world following the Great Depression, as well as the low level of economic activity, world trade in manufactures in 1939 was still below its peak level of 1929 (Neild 1979). However, during the 1950s and 1960s there was a fourfold increase in the world exports of manufactures. The growth in international capital movements—particularly in the form of investment abroad by the so-called multinational companies—was, if anything, even more rapid. According to the U.N. statistics, by 1971 the value of international production—that is, production carried on abroad by multinational companies—was greater than that of international trade. Although it is the Third World countries that have expressed the greatest public concern about the activities of the multinational companies, about three-quarters of the total direct investment abroad in the period 1950–1970 has taken place within the advanced countries themselves. However, both in the Third World and in the advanced countries the American multinational companies have played the leading role in foreign investment (U.N. 1974).

In principal, such large increases in international trade and capital movements should have an important influence on merger activity. Thus,

Table 1–2. Profitability Advantage of U.S. Firms in British Industries and Enterprise Rate of Merger Activity, 1950–1965

Industry	U.S. Advantage	Enterprise Rate
Food, drink, and tobacco	15.6	1.333
Electrical engineering	13.3	1.177
Metal manufacturing	6.6	1.400
Nonelectrical engineering	4.4	1.153
Other manufacturing	3.9	1.200
Vehicles	2.7	1.295
Paper, printing, etc.	1.8	0.862
Chemicals	1.0	1.103
Textiles, clothing, footwear	−2.0	1.025

Source: McGowan (1971).

Note: The enterprise rate of merger activity gives the annual average percentage of companies acquired in the industry concerned.

if an oligopolistic equilibrium—in the sense of stable market shares of the largest firms—exists in a typical manufacturing industry within the national economy, increased imports or entry by multinationals would lead to disequilibrium; inter alia, this may induce the existing firms to merge in the face of increased competition. There is some direct evidence that a process of this kind may have occurred in the European economies. For example, studies have shown that United States subsidiaries in the United Kingdom are more profitable than domestic firms in the same industry (Dunning 1967). McGowan (1971) found in a sample of United Kingdom industries that interindustry differences in merger rates during the period 1950–1965 were positively related to industrial differences in the profitability advantage of United States firms over the domestic firms (see Table 1–2). The two variables had a statistically significant rank correlation coefficient of 0.54. Similarly, for a sample of French industries, McGowan discovered that industrial merger rates were positively related (Kendall's rank correlation coefficient = 0.714) to a measure of the domestic market, which the French firms lost to foreign competitors as a consequence of France's entry into the EEC (see also Auguier and Caves 1979).

However, neither increased international trade nor new entry by subsidiaries of American multinationals would have provided such a significant or rapid stimulus to merger activity in Europe were it not for another extremely important related factor—the role of the government. The governments (as well as the public) in the European countries became very concerned with what they saw to be the increasing control of their economies by the American companies. This concern is perhaps best expressed in the French writer Servan-Schreiber's famous book of the period, *The American Challenge* (1967). Servan-Schreiber wrote: "Most striking of all is the strategic character of American industrial penetration. One by one United States corporations capture those sectors of the economy most technologically advanced, most adaptable to change, and with the highest growth rates." He went on to observe: "Starting with a rather matter of fact examination of American investment in Europe, we find an economic system which is in a state of collapse. It is our own. We see a foreign challenger breaking down the political and psychological framework of our societies. We are witnessing the prelude to our own historical bankruptcy" (quoted in Rowthorn 1971).

All this may sound rather strange today given the serious problems faced by the American economy and the increasing European and Japanese investment in the United States. However, although exaggerated, there indeed was some factual basis for the fears expressed by Servan-Schreiber. Between 1950 and 1967, the United States manufacturing and petroleum investment in Europe had increased tenfold, from $1358 million to $14,185 million (Rowthorn 1971). Further, the growth rate of American subsidiaries in Europe *(gas)* was considerably greater than that of the European companies *(ge)*. However, it was not realized at the time that because of the relatively slow postwar growth of the United States economy, the growth rates of the American parent companies *(gap)* were lower than those of the European companies. As researches by Rowthorn and Hymer (1971) subsequently showed, the actual situation was as follows:

$$gas > ge > gap$$

Nevertheless, in most European countries, to meet the "American" challenge and that of increased competition from abroad, the governments encouraged mergers of domestic companies. For example, in the United Kingdom the government established the Industrial Reorganisation Corporation specifically to promote some mergers. As one of its members put it: "The Corporation's principal purpose was to bring about mergers which otherwise would not have taken place . . . the case for the IRC stands or falls on the propositions that in many sectors British companies were not large enough, and that without intervention, they would not become large enough soon enough" (McCelland, 1972, quoted in Meeks 1977). Further, in relation to mergers in general, the philosophy and policy of the United Kingdom government then in power were best expressed by the president of the Board of Trade: "In general, mergers are desirable if they lead to better management or genuine economies of scale without eliminating workable competition. In my view, more often than not in Britain mergers will fulfil this condition" (cited in Meeks 1977). Under the monopolies and mergers act (1965), the government did indeed have statutory powers to investigate and prohibit large mergers; however, these powers were very little used (see further, Chapter 8).

A number of other European governments had a similar attitude toward mergers. In France, the industry minister declared: "The consolidation of French industry has become a national priority . . . we must form enterprises that are capable of standing up to foreign groups"[6]. Similar encouragement or a benign policy toward mergers was found in Sweden, Italy, and elsewhere (Rydén 1972).

It is necessary at this stage to call attention to three caveats or exceptions to the above analysis of the European merger wave of the 1960s. First, although we have stressed the role of increased international trade, foreign investment, and government interventionist policy as the main common causal elements in this process, this is not to deny in any way the importance of financial or other factors in any specific national context. For example, the relatively favorable tax treatment of mergers introduced in France in the mid-1960s has been cited as a factor in increased merger activity at that time.[7] One important reason why the merger movement in the United Kingdom preceded that in other countries may have been the large undervaluation of shares on the United Kingdom stock market in the early 1950s (see Wright 1962; Singh 1971; and Chapter 8). Further, apart from trade and foreign entry, legislation abolishing restrictive trade practices (cartels and other types of pricing agreements) in 1956 in the United Kingdom would also have provided some impetus toward mergers. In addition, once a few mergers have taken place in an industry in any country, this in itself could either cause or exacerbate a disequilibrium in the product markets and lead to defensive mergers by other firms.

Second, perhaps contrary to expectations, there have been relatively few intercountry mergers—that is, those involving firms of more than one country—in the six original EEC member countries. Table 1–3 shows that the number of international mergers in the EEC countries during the period 1966–1973 was miniscule compared with those between firms in the individual countries themselves. As Jacquemin and de Jong (1977) point out, such mergers evidently encounter a number of legal, institutional, and psychological obstacles.

Third and most important, we note that the above factors cannot directly explain the merger wave of the 1960s in the United States. In that country, neither the role of foreign subsidiaries nor that of increased imports was as important in the 1950s and 1960s as it has been subsequently or as it was in the European countries. Further, the public policy and philosophy toward mergers was diametrically opposite to that in Europe. As is well known, the United States has long had a strong structural antitrust policy (as embodied, for example, in the Sherman Act); this policy was strengthened with the passage of the Cellar-Kefauver Act in 1950 and certain Supreme Court decisions (e.g., the Bethlehem-Youngstown decision) and FTC rulings in the late 1950s and in the early

Table 1–3.   International Mergers in the EEC, 1966–1973

	West Germany	France	Italy	Netherlands	Belgium	Luxembourg
1966	22	19	13	16	24	6
1970	24	22	12	13	22	7
1971	22	24	11	12	24	7
1973	16	26	7	13	22	16

Source: Jacquemin and de Jong (1977).

1960s. Although the effect of these antitrust laws on reducing the overall degree of merger activity in the United States is still a matter of some controversy, two points are beyond dispute: (1) the United States antitrust measures cannot be deemed to have increased merger activity (as happened in the European economies); and (2) these measures, as Table 1–4 shows, have undoubtedly affected the direction of merger activity (Stigler 1966). As a consequence of the increasingly severe restrictions against horizontal mergers, the number of such mergers dropped dramatically during the 1960s, while the nonhorizontal, nonvertical conglomerate types correspondingly increased.

Although there is evidence that the nationalistic prodomestic sentiment, for example in France, may have provoked some United States multinationals to increase and widen their domestic base by acquisition in the face of European uncertainty,[8] the explanation for the huge United States merger wave must clearly include some factors other than those discussed earlier. It seems to us that certain institutional developments related to the operations and control of the large United States corporations are likely to have played a major role in initiating and sustaining the United States merger wave of the 1960s coincidental to that in Europe. As was mentioned earlier in the case of the United Kingdom, with the growth in the size of the large corporations, there is progressive diminution of family control, dispersal of share ownership, and an increasing degree of management control—a process that not surprisingly has gone very much further in the United States than in the United Kingdom.[9] These developments have both made it possible for the managers to indulge in predatory acquisitions and provided them with the means of doing so—through the device of a takeover bid or a tender offer. There is a great deal of evidence that indicates that the "empire building" or "growth" motive has played a leading role in the drive toward conglomerate mergers in the United States. This evidence is reviewed in Mueller (1977); it is also discussed further in Chapter 10. However, it is unlikely that a merger movement based on such factors would have gone far without, as well, certain technical innovations in the field of management and organization that enable

Table 1–4. U.S. Mergers of Large Firms by Type of Merger, 1951–1968 (percentage of all assets acquired in period)

	1951–1954	*1963–1966*	*1967–1968*
Horizontal mergers	40	14	8
Vertical mergers	9	15	7
Product extension merger	43	43	46
Market extension merger	4	13	4
Pure conglomerates	5	16	35

Source: Scherer (1970).

very large multiproduct, multicountry firms to be run with a reasonable degree of efficiency (Williamson 1970; Singh 1976b).[10]

Finally, turning to the last question, that of intercountry differences in merger rates, we should like to offer two comments. As mentioned earlier, there are data and conceptual difficulties in comparing merger rates between countries. For example, in West Germany a merger does not normally involve takeover—a complete absorption of one firm by another, rather, it is common for a firm to effect a "merger" by acquiring say a 25 to 30 percent stake in the other firm. Second, notwithstanding these difficulties, to the extent that such differences in merger rates between countries have been studied, there is little support for any simple hypotheses. For example, merger studies in the United States have shown that in general merger activity increases during periods of economic boom and declines when there is a downturn in the economy. Translating this into a hypothesis at the international level, McGowan (1971) did not find any relationship between the rates of growth of GDP and the national merger rates in the four countries he studied. Casual evidence suggests that a relationship between merger activity and indexes of share prices on an intercountry basis is also unlikely.

MERGERS AND CONCENTRATION

Among the most important policy questions related to mergers are those concerned with their effects on concentration and on competition. These issues will be examined in this and the following section in a comparative international context.

With respect to concentration, we shall first consider the broad changes in the aggregate concentration of industrial activity that have occurred in the various countries. There are three reasons why the phenomenon of aggregate concentration—the proportion of economic activity controlled by the largest firms in the economy—deserves attention. First, there is often a close connection between market and aggregate concentration.

For example, in the United Kingdom it was found that in 1963, the one hundred largest manufacturing firms were also among the leading four firms in about half the individual product markets (Utton 1974b). Further, seventy of the one hundred largest were among the four leaders in four or more industries (George 1972). In the United States, it has been argued that large conglomerate firms are able to exert influence in the individual product markets far beyond their size in those markets (Blair 1972).

The second reason for the importance of aggregate concentration, particularly in the European context, has been aptly put by Jacquemin and de Jong:

> Today in Europe, extra market power is probably more important than market power. This situation arises from the institutionalisation of the market economy. Our system is no longer a delicate self-regulating mechanism but a set of institutions open to manipulation by the participants. In this view, the large corporation becomes more and more a "body politic" for the accumulation and use of power. Reciprocally, there is a tendency for the European governments to develop policies which use large enterprises to solve specific problems, as if they were agencies of the state. (Jacquemin and de Jong 1977: 97)

Third, from a theoretical point of view, the concept of aggregate concentration per se plays a crucial role in the Marxist analysis of the dynamics of capitalist economies (see Hughes and Singh 1974; Singh 1976b).

As in the analysis of the merger waves presented earlier, it is useful first to examine the recent changes in aggregate concentration in the United States and the United Kingdom economies in a historical perspective. Table 1–5 shows the percentage of manufacturing value added accounted for by the one hundred largest firms in the two countries since 1909. Several points deserve notice. First, in both countries there has been a large increase in aggregate concentration since the end of World War II. In the United Kingdom in the forty years between 1909 and 1949, the share of the one hundred largest firms in net output increased only from about 16 to 22 percent. Over the next twenty years, the share nearly doubled. In the United States, there was little increase in concentration between 1906 and 1947; over the next quarter century the share of the one hundred largest firms increased by 10 percentage points. Second, whereas up to the early 1950s the level of concentration in the United Kingdom was lower than in the United States, it is now considerably higher. Third, concentration in the United States has remained constant during the years 1963–1970, the period that saw the peak of the postwar United States merger wave.

Table 1–5. Percent Share of the 100 Largest Enterprises in Manufacturing Net Output, the United Kingdom and the United States, 1909–1970

	United Kingdom	United States
1909	16[a]	22
1924	22[a]	25
1935	24	26
1949	22	23[d]
1953	27	30[e]
1958	32	30
1963	36.5[b]	33
1968	41	33[f]
1970	40[c]	33[b]

Source: Prais (1976).
[a] Approximate figures.
[b] Excludes steel companies.
[c] Provisional figures.
[d] Refers to 1947.
[e] Refers to 1954.
[f] Refers to 1967 and excludes steel companies.

However, in relation to the last two points, it is important to bear in mind that the Table 1–5 figures pertain only to domestic manufacturing activity. To the extent that the large United States and United Kingdom firms have increasingly been investing abroad during the last two decades, the level and changes in concentration would be understated.[11] However, a study of the share of total manufacturing assets held by the 200 largest United States corporations shows that measured in terms of control over assets, aggregate concentration in the United States increased appreciably during the 1960s in the manufacturing sector:[12] 1929, 45.8; 1933, 49.5; 1939, 48.7; 1949, 47.1; 1953, 48.7; 1956, 52.8; 1960, 55.2; 1964, 55.8; 1968, 60.4 (FTC 1969).

There were also significant increases in concentration in the 1960s in countries other than the United States and the United Kingdom. This is indicated by Table 1–6 which gives the shares of the largest EEC firms in the gross output of extractive and manufacturing industries in the community. As the individual country chapters show, there have been similar kinds of increases in aggregate concentration in most countries.

Although it is a minor digression from the main theme of this chapter, it is also appropriate at this stage to consider aggregate concentration at the level of the plant rather than the firm or enterprise. A comparison of plant and firm level concentration bears on the question of economies of scale as a possible motive for mergers and concentration—an important issue in the following chapters.

Table 1–6. Percentage Share of the Sales of the Largest EEC Firms in Industrial Output

Rank	1960	1965	1970	1976
1–4	2.6	2.0	3.6	4.5
5–8	2.0	2.2	2.9	3.4
9–20	4.6	4.7	6.4	7.2
21–50	6.3	5.5	7.4	9.4
1–50	15.4	15.4	20.3	24.5

Source: Locksley and Ward (1979).

Table 1–7 shows changes in the share of the one hundred largest plants in the net manufacturing output and employment in the United Kingdom since 1930.

A comparison of the above data with the analogous figures for the share of the one hundred largest United Kingdom companies shows that whereas since the 1930s the latter has risen dramatically, the share of the one hundred largest plants, in both net output and employment, has remained more or less constant. This strongly suggests, although by itself it by no means proves,[13] that increased company concentration is due not to a more than proportional increase in the size of large plants, but to the large firms controlling a greater number of plants than before. Prais (1976) provides direct evidence that there has in recent years been a sharp increase in the number of plants operated by large companies. Between 1958 and 1972, the average number of plants run by the one hundred largest United Kingdom companies rose from twenty-seven to seventy-two. During the same period, the size of the average plant operated by these companies fell

Table 1–7. Percentage Share of the 100 Largest Manufacturing Establishments[a] in Net Output and Employment in the United Kingdom, 1930–1968

	Net Output	Employment
1930	10.8	8.2[b]
1935	11.2	8.4
1948	9.0	9.5
1951	9.4	9.3
1954	10.1	9.6
1958	10.3[c]	9.9
1963	11.1	10.1
1968	10.8	9.2

Source: Prais (1976).
[a] On ranking by employment in each establishment.
[b] Approximate figures.
[c] Share in sales (net output was not available for this year).

in terms of employment from 750 workers to 430, although in terms of output it probably did not alter much.

The picture for the United States appears to be very similar. It has been estimated that the share of the one hundred largest plants in manufacturing employment has remained more or less steady since 1930 (at about 9 percent; Prais 1976), while as Table 1–5 showed, corporate concentration has greatly increased. There is also evidence of a large increase in the number of United States plants operated by the giant firms (Blair 1972). More detailed comparative information on plant and enterprise concentration within individual United States industries also points to the same conclusion (see Shepherd 1967; Nelson 1964; Blair 1972)—namely, the rise in concentration is almost entirely due to an increase in the number of plants per giant corporation, rather than an increase in the relative average plant size in such corporations. If this inference from the United Kingdom and the United States evidence is correct, it indicates that increased enterprise concentration is unlikely to be due to economies of scale, unless such economies are associated with multiplant operations. (For a discussion of the multiplant economies, see Scherer et al., 1975.)

Turning now to industry or market level concentration, we find that along with aggregate concentration, there was also a significant increase in market concentration during the 1960s in most countries, with the United States being a notable exception. For example, in the United Kingdom the average (five firms) sales concentration ratio rose by 8.27 percent during 1958–1963, and by a further 8.66 percent in the following five years (1963–1968). By 1968, 50 percent of United Kingdom sales were in industries with a five-firm sales concentration ratio of over 75 percent (Aaronovitch and Sawyer 1974). In West Germany, according to the Federal Cartel Office report for 1973, out of about eighty industrial branches and subbranches, concentration increased between 1962 and 1970 in forty-six cases and declined in twenty-five (Jacquemin and de Jong 1977). In the Netherlands, the entropy measure of concentration, or the Thiel coefficient, declined from 13.17 in 1950 to 12.51 in 1963 and to 11.65 in 1971—indicating an acceleration in the rate of increase of concentration in the later period (see Chapter 6). There was also a mild rise in concentration in France; the sales-weighted average four-firms concentration ratio for forty-eight two-digit French manufacturing industries increased from 20.08 in 1961 to 22.10 in 1969. However, most of this two percentage point rise occurred between 1965 and 1969 (Jacquemin and de Jong 1977). On the other hand, in the United States, despite an appreciable increase in aggregate concentration, the antitrust laws appear to have contained any general rise in market concentration (Hamm and Mueller 1974).

With respect to the question of intercountry differences in concentration ratios, there are even greater difficulties involved in such a comparison than in the case of intercountry differences in the merger rates, discussed earlier in the chapter. Nevertheless, comparing the United Kingdom and the United States, which are institutionally similar, the statistics in Table 1–5 showed that by the early 1960s the level of aggregate concentration in the United Kingdom was greater than in the United States. Moreover, during the 1960s concentration rose faster in the United Kingdom than in the United States.[14] In a comparison of West Germany and the United Kingdom, it is estimated that the one hundred largest industrial undertakings accounted for 43 percent of West German sales in 1968–1970, with the comparable figure for the United Kingdom being 62 percent in 1968 (Prais 1976). However, to the extent that there is a greater degree of interlocking directorships and control of industrial activity by the banks in West Germany, aggregate concentration might well be regarded as being higher in that country than in the United Kingdom.

In relation to the intercountry comparison of market concentration, the most striking point is the similarities between countries in this respect. Various studies (Bain 1966; Horowitz 1970; HMG 1978; Hughes 1976; Pryor 1972) show that concentrated sectors tend to be the same in most countries, which perhaps indicates the importance of the common technological and consumer demand factors over that of institutional and economic differences. George and Ward's (1975) recent study for four Common Market countries has suggested that the average level of market concentration is greater in the United Kingdom than in West Germany, France, or Italy. However, part of this difference could be due to inconsistencies in the definitions of the enterprises between countries (Hughes 1976; HMG 1978).

Finally, we come to the important issue: To what extent, if any, can the observed increase in concentration in the industrial countries in the 1960s be ascribed to mergers? Changes in concentration depend on a complex of interacting factors involving the growth of firms, their births, and their deaths. More specifically, such changes depend on: (1) variations in firm growth rates; (2) the relationship between size and growth of firms; (3) that between size and birth rates; and (4) that between size and death rates of firms. At the simplest level, other things being equal, the higher the birth rate and the lower the death rate of firms, the lower will be the concentration level; similarly, ceteris paribus, if small firms have a higher growth rate than large firms, concentration will decrease over time. Mergers not only cause deaths but also lead to different growth rates for firms of various sizes—for instance, when the merger propensity of large firms is greater than that of small firms. Also, because of the way that company statistics are recorded, mergers may simultaneously increase nominal

Table 1–8. The Industrial Direction of Merger Activity in Five European Nations

Country	Time Period	Industrial Coverage	Number of Mergers	Percent Horizontal	Percent Vertical	Percent Other
Sweden	1946–1969	Mining and manufacturing	1800	79.8	7.6	12.6
France	1950–1972	Manufacturing and distribution	565	48.3	24.7	27.4
West Germany	1970–1977	All industrial and nonindustrial	2091	72.3	15.2	12.5
United Kingdom[a]	1965–1977	All industrial and nonindustrial	1562	74.0	4.0	21.0
Netherlands	1958–1970	Manufacturing	1021	62.4	11.6	26.0

Sources: Rydén (1972); Jenny and Weber (Chapter 5, this volume); Cable, Palfrey, and Runge (Chapter 4, this volume); HMSO (1978); de Jong (1971).

[a] Data refer to mergers examined by the interdepartmental Mergers Panel.

"births" if two companies join together to form a new company with a different name. Moreover, as is well known, even if there were no mergers, concentration could increase due to the variation in the firm growth rates caused by the normal accumulation process. In view of these considerations, it becomes a difficult task to isolate the influence of mergers in the concentration process from those of normal "births" and "deaths" and of "normal" growth that firms of different sizes would in any case achieve in the absence of mergers (see further, Singh 1976b; Singh and Whittington 1975; Steindl 1965; Hannah and Kay 1977; Prais 1976).

Nevertheless, there are fortunately a number of studies for both the United Kingdom and the United States economies that have attempted to measure the relative contribution of mergers to the concentration process. Despite differences in methodology, there is general agreement in these studies that mergers have been the primary cause of increased aggregate concentration during the 1960s in both countries (see, for example, Hannah and Kay 1977; Prais 1976; Preston 1973; FTC 1969; McGowan 1965). As far as market concentration is concerned, we might expect the impact of mergers upon concentration to be higher the greater the incidence of merger and the greater the proportion of them that are horizontal in direction. We have already seen that in the United States mergers were overwhelmingly conglomerate and that at the market level concentration changed only slightly during the merger wave. In the European economies, experience was rather different, as Table 1–8 suggests. The data shown there are not directly comparable between countries since they cover different time periods and utilize definitions of "horizontal" and "vertical" that are not necessarily consistent. However, the broad picture that emerges is of a relative predominance of horizontal mergers compared to the United States, although an examination of the evidence over time suggests some growth in the importance of nonhorizontal mergers in the

Table 1-9. Import Penetration in Manufactures in Advanced Industrial Countries, 1961-1978 (ratio of manufactured imports to GNP)

	1961	1965	1969	1973	1978
United States	1.5	2.1	3.4	4.0	4.5
United Kingdom	4.6	6.7	8.0	11.7	14.2
Rest of EEC	6.1	7.6	10.1	13.0	15.8
Japan	1.8	1.5	2.2	3.0	2.4

Source: CEPG (1979).

later stages of the merger wave (see the discussions in the individual country chapters and in the sources cited under Table 1-8). Studies for the United Kingdom and West Germany on a disaggregated level confirm that mergers have played a dominant role in the observed changes in market concentration in these two countries (Hannah and Kay 1977; Müller 1976). Unfortunately there are no comparable studies for other European countries.

CONCENTRATION AND COMPETITION: AN INTERNATIONAL PERSPECTIVE

It will be generally accepted that increased concentration (measured in terms of concentration ratios and the like) does not necessarily imply a decline in the effectiveness or vigor of competition. This has been particularly true in relation to the world economy during the last two decades. We have seen above that there has been a rise in the level of aggregate or market concentration in most industrial countries, especially during the 1960s; this was most likely also associated with a rise in aggregate concentration for the world economy as a whole—for example, the proportion of the world market economies' industrial assets accounted for by the 200 largest multinationals. Nevertheless, there are good reasons, as well as evidence, to suggest that in this period there has been more rather than less competition in the world economy than before. The main cause for this is the massive liberalization and expansion of world trade in industrial products that has occurred during the last two decades. As Table 1-9 shows, since 1961 there has been a sharp increase in import penetration ratios in all the industrial countries. Between 1961 and 1978, the ratio of manufactured imports to GNP has tripled in the United Kingdom and the United States and increased by two and a half times in the EEC countries and by approximately 50 percent in Japan.

Tables 1-10 and 1-11 report on the results of a recent comprehensive OECD study (Hill 1979) of profitability in advanced capitalist economies

Table 1–10.   Gross Rates of Return in Manufacturing in Advanced Capitalist Economies, 1955–1975 (percent)

	Canada	United States	Japan	West Germany	Italy	Sweden	United Kingdom
1955	19.3	24.1	19.9	24.0	12.8	12.7	13.6
1960	15.3	21.7	32.0	21.9	12.0	12.9	13.7
1961	14.9	20.9	32.9	20.5	11.9	12.0	12.1
1962	16.0	22.4	29.2	18.3	11.0	11.3	11.1
1963	16.4	23.4	28.9	17.1	9.7	10.1	11.6
1964	17.0	24.7	29.2	18.4	8.4	11.2	12.1
1965	15.4	27.1	26.0	19.0	9.1	11.6	11.8
1966	14.6	27.5	26.6	17.0	10.2	10.5	10.6
1967	13.5	24.5	29.6	16.9	10.2	10.4	10.4
1968	14.6	24.6	31.7	19.3	10.3	10.8	10.4
1969	14.4	21.9	31.4	18.8	10.5	11.5	10.1
1970	12.5	18.0	30.9	17.1	10.2	13.2	8.8
1971	12.8	18.6	27.6	15.4	8.8	10.3	8.6
1972	13.8	20.4	25.1	13.9	9.0	9.9	8.6
1973	15.3	20.7	22.4	13.6		12.1	7.4
1974	15.5	18.1	18.0	13.4		14.7	5.6
1975	13.5	19.4	18.2	11.7		11.4	4.5

Source: Hill (1979).

Note: Gross (i.e., before depreciation) operating surplus is measured as a percentage of gross capital stock, both based on national accounting data and both measured at current prices. For full details, see Hill (1979).

over the period 1955–1975 (for an earlier study of the subject, see OECD 1977b). Abstracting from the cyclical fluctuations, the tables suggest that there has been a long-run fall in both gross and net rates of return[15] in most industrial countries, especially since about the middle 1960s. This impression is confirmed by Table 1–12, which shows that there has indeed been a trend decline in profitability—whether measured in terms of rates of return or of the share of profits in value added in manufacturing—in almost all the leading countries.[16] Although a variety of factors could have contributed to this long-run decline in profitability, the latter must also reflect the increased intensity of international competition. There is, however, evidence that this increased international competition is of an oligopolistic variety in which large multinational companies compete, usually in non-price terms, (see, for example, Parry 1973). This is also indicated by the fact that despite the deep post-1973 recession in the world economy, there has been no tendency for industrial prices to fall.

Finally we note that in contrast to the 1960s, in recent years a number of European governments (e.g., the West German, the United Kingdom, the French) have become very concerned about the problems of mergers and rising industrial concentration. Despite the evidence of falling profits and

Table 1–11. Net Rates of Return in Manufacturing in Advanced Capitalist Economies, 1955–1975 (per cent)

	Canada	United States	Japan	West Germany	Italy	Sweden	United Kingdom
1955	25.3	34.3	20.9	31.1	14.5	13.9	19.6
1960	18.2	30.3	35.0	25.7	14.7	14.2	18.1
1961	17.7	29.0	33.8	23.4	14.3	12.8	15.2
1962	19.6	32.0	28.9	20.0	12.7	11.8	13.4
1963	20.3	34.2	28.2	18.2	10.3	9.9	14.1
1964	21.2	36.6	27.6	19.8	8.3	11.7	15.0
1965	18.5	40.9	23.9	20.4	9.7	12.2	14.4
1966	17.0	40.8	24.9	17.5	11.7	10.6	12.5
1967	15.3	34.4	28.8	17.5	11.6	10.3	12.2
1968	17.0	34.2	31.5	21.3	11.8	10.9	12.2
1969	16.8	29.2	30.6	20.7	12.2	12.2	11.6
1970	13.8	22.0	28.1	18.2	11.5	14.6	9.6
1971	14.3	23.4	23.5	15.6	9.4	10.3	9.3
1972	16.0	26.9	20.2	13.4	9.9	9.8	9.3
1973	18.6	27.6	15.7	12.9		13.3	7.6
1974	18.7	22.2	13.1	12.7		16.9	4.8
1975	15.5	25.4	13.9	10.0		11.7	2.9

Source: Hill (1979).
Note: Net operating surplus as a percentage of net capital stock; both series based on national accounting data and both measured at current prices. See Hill (1979) for full details.

increased intensity of international trade, this concern does appear to have arisen in part from fears of welfare losses due to increased monopoly power.[17] Two other factors, however, seem to be more important reasons of concern in the present situation facing the European governments as well as the antitrust authorities in the United States. First, they are most anxious about inflation, and it is believed that the rate of inflation might be reduced by a tougher competition policy. Second, in view of the high levels of concentration that already exist, there is a concern with the political (and to some extent the employment) implications of any further increases in concentration. These issues will be analyzed in Chapter 11, which discusses the appropriate policies toward mergers.

SUMMARY OF THE CHAPTER AND THE PLAN OF THE BOOK

Most industrial capitalist countries have experienced a vast merger wave during the last two decades and particularly in the 1960s. In many of these countries, this merger wave has been at least as big, if not

Table 1–12.   Profit Shares and Rates of Return in Manufacturing in Advanced Capitalist Economies: Trend Percentage Rates of Change, 1958–1976[a]

	Manufacturing			
	Profit share P/Y (%)		Rate of Return P/K (%)	
Country	Gross	Net	Gross	Net
Canada	−0.4	−0.8	−1.1	−1.4
United States	−0.1	−0.3	−0.4	−0.7
Japan[b]	−0.9	−1.7	−1.8	−3.9
Australia[b]	−0.5	−0.9	—	—
Denmark[b]	−1.5	—	—	—
Germany	−2.3	−4.2	−3.1	−4.6
Italy[c]	−2.0	−2.5	−1.7	−2.0
Netherlands	−1.1	−1.1	—	—
Sweden	−0.1	−0.4	−0.6	−0.9
United Kingdom	−3.4	−6.2	−5.4	−8.5

Source: Hill (1979).

[a] These figures show the trend percentage changes from year to year in the share or rate of return, not the number of percentage points by which the share or rate of return changes—for example, a fall from 20 percent to 19 percent represents a decline of 5 percent (i.e., 1/20 × 100) in the table, not 1 percent.

[b] The trends for these countries cover the period 1958–1975.

[c] The trend for Italy covers the period 1955–1972.

bigger, than ever experienced before. It has been argued here that in Western Europe, increased international trade and capital movements and government policies were important factors contributing to the simultaneous occurrence of the merger wave in the various countries. On the other hand, it is suggested that in the United States, institutional factors related to the managerial control of large corporations and the availability and practice of the new acquisition device of a tender-offer, among other influences, were more important. Mergers have also been responsible for the large increase in concentration in manufacturing industry,[18] which has occurred during this period in most countries. However, we have argued that despite increased concentration, competition in the world economy is more intense than before.

The following chapters examine the causes and effects of mergers within each individual country. Chapter 2 provides the common analytical framework and describes the statistical tests that are carried out for each country. Chapters 3 through 9 report on the studies for Belgium, the Federal Republic of Germany, France, the Netherlands, Sweden, the United Kingdom, and the United States. Although these chapters have a common frame of reference, it is intended that each country report should also be complete in itself by providing a broad overview of the main features of the merger movement in that country. The implications of the results of these studies for the theory of the firm are discussed in Chapter 10. Finally, Chapter 11 takes up again some of the themes of the present chapter and discusses issues of public policy toward mergers in Europe and the United States in the light of the empirical results.

NOTES

1. The 2000 or so "large" manufacturing corporations in the United States account for about 85 percent of all corporate manufacturing assets. A "large" company is one with assets of $10 million or more.
2. For the sources of the statistics cited in this and the previous paragraph, see: for the United Kingdom, Singh (1971, 1975) and Hughes (1976); for the United States, Scherer (1970), Blair (1972), and FTC (1969); for Sweden, Rydén (1972); for the Netherlands, de Jong (1976); for West Germany, Hughes (1976); and for France, Jenny and Weber (Chapter 5, this volume).
3. See, for example, the discussion of data sources in the individual country chapters. See also Prais (1976).
4. Where merger value series exist, similar conclusions appear to follow, but the data are even more hazardous to use because of the well-known problems of price-level variations and asset valuation. (Cf. Hannah 1976a.)
5. A company A is deemed to have "taken over" a company B if it acquires more than 50 percent of B's shares; however, if A and B combine to form a new legal entity, C, it is regarded as a merger. The distinction between these two forms of amalgamation is entirely a legal one with little economic significance. In fact, statistics show that of the 80 percent or so of the company deaths due to takeovers and mergers, about 75 percent were caused by takeovers and 5 percent by mergers.
6. "Merging to Survive," *Fortune*, February, 1967, pp. 74–79, cited in Scherer (1970).
7. Jenny and Weber, see Chapter 5. For a useful general survey of tax effects and concentration in Europe in the 1960s, see van Hoorn (1971).
8. For instance ITT's switch to an acquisition-based domestic growth policy in the United States in the mid-1960s was directly based upon factors such as these. See Sampson (1973:69ff); and United States Senate (1969, vol. 3:258ff).
9. For the degree of management control in the United Kingdom and United States firms, see the recent comprehensive survey in Scott (1979), which also contains some evidence for European economies other than the United Kingdom.
10. There is some evidence discussed later that suggests that the performance of the conglomerate mergers has not been very good; however, neither has it been particularly bad.
11. The understatement would be greater for the United States than for the United Kingdom firms, since the former are larger and are therefore more likely to invest abroad. Size is known to be an important determinant of foreign investment (Horst 1972).
12. It is important to note that these results relate to manufacturing only. When the whole nonfinancial sector is considered, asset concentration remained at around 41 percent for the top 200 from 1958 to 1967 and declined to 39.5 percent by 1975 (FTC 1979).
13. A "proof" would require information on the initial distribution of plant sizes operated by the large firms, industrial distribution of large firms, and so forth.

14. This is likely to be true despite the qualifications discussed earlier and whether aggregate concentration is measured in terms of output or assets.

15. These are the so-called "entity" (as opposed to the "equity") rates of return and are based on national accounting data. The "gross rate of return" measures gross (i.e., before depreciation) operating surplus as a percentage of gross capital stock, both measured at current prices; similarly, the "net rate of return" indicates net operating surplus (i.e., after depreciation) as a percentage of net capital stock. For the conceptual and statistical difficulties involved in the estimation of the rates of return and of the profits shares in value added, see Hill (1979).

16. Although all the figures in Table 1–12 have a negative sign, those for Japan and the United States are found to be very sensitive to the period chosen for the analysis. There may not, therefore, be a long-term decline in profitability in these two countries.

17. This paradox finds its most acute expression in the case of the United Kingdom, a country for which it will be singularly difficult to argue that there has been a decline in competition, notwithstanding the very substantial increase in industrial concentration in the economy. Many sectors of the United Kingdom manufacturing industry are suffering heavily from the impact of foreign competition. Indeed, the trend increase in the rate of growth of manufactured imports and the increase in international competition are major causes of the long-term industrial disequilibrium in that country (see, Singh 1977a,b, 1979; Blackaby 1979). Nor could it be argued that strange antitrust policies are required to curb monopoly profits being earned by large companies (see, Hughes 1978; Hughes and Singh 1978).

18. The reader is reminded that the empirical analysis in this book is largely concerned with manufacturing industry; the conclusions do not necessarily apply to other sectors of the economy.

Chapter 2

Hypotheses about Mergers

Alan Hughes, Dennis C. Mueller, and Ajit Singh

All merger studies for the individual countries in this book report three kinds of results: (1) how the merging firms differ from the ones that do not merge, (2) certain tests of hypotheses concerning determinants of mergers, and (3) those concerning the effects of mergers. The results are based on empirical investigations carried out at a microeconomic level within each country and refer to mergers that took place during the merger wave of the 1960s. This chapter discusses the economic rationale and motivation for the specific hypotheses and issues that have been examined in the empirical studies.

CHARACTERISTICS OF MERGING AND NONMERGING FIRMS

There are three reasons for comparing the premerger characteristics of the various groups of merging and nonmerging firms: acquiring

The authors of this chapter take joint responsibility for its contents. Hughes and Singh were primarily responsible for drafting the sections on merging firms' characteristics and mergers' welfare and policy implications, and Mueller for the middle two sections on mergers' determinants and effects. The last section on tests reflects the joint work of all the international project members.

and nonacquiring, acquiring and acquired, acquired and nonacquired. First, such comparisons bear directly on a range of issues that are important from the point of view of both economic theory and policy. A major question of current theoretical interest is the nature of the selection mechanism generated by the normal workings of competitive markets and its implications for the behavior of economic agents (Hahn 1973; Winter 1971). As far as markets in the real world are concerned, the phenomenon of takeovers and mergers assumes crucial significance in this context with respect to the operation of large management-controlled firms that are characterized by the divorce of ownership from control (Manne 1965; Singh 1971, 1975). Such firms typically operate in imperfect product markets and seldom go bankrupt; their main cause of death is usually takeover. In the absence of perfect or highly competitive product markets, takeovers provide the main, if not the only, market mechanism through which the managers of the large oligopolistic corporations could in practice be effectively disciplined (for a full discussion of these issues, see Singh 1971). It is, therefore, important to know which kinds of firms are taken over and which kinds are not.

Neoclassical economists hypothesize that the selection process represented by the takeover mechanism selects the "efficient"—that is, the profit-maximizing—firms and punishes nonmaximizers (see, for example, Meade 1968). On the other hand, managerial theorists such as Galbraith (1967), Marris (1968), and Mueller (1969) have argued that because of diverse imperfections of the stock market, the takeover mechanism is more likely to favor the survival of large firms or those that pursue fast growth, rather than those that are efficient in the neoclassical sense. A comparison of the characteristics of living (non-taken-over) and dead (taken over) firms should produce direct evidence on this issue. At the simplest level, it will show, for instance, to what extent (if any) the takeover mechanism does select the "efficient" firms for survival and "punish" the inefficient ones by forcing their disappearance through acquisition. Similarly, a comparison of the "acquiring" firms with the firms they acquired will give some indication of whether the more efficient tend to take over the less efficient.

The second reason why an analysis of the comparative characteristics of the merging and nonmerging firms is of interest arises from the consideration that mergers in the various countries took place in rather different economic and institutional environments. Therefore, these characteristics could also be systematically different among countries. It was seen in Chapter 1 that because of antitrust laws, the United States has relatively few horizontal mergers compared with other countries. Similarly, it is reasonable to hypothesize that other characteristics of merging firms (e.g., their profitability, growth, size) may also be different in different economic environments. In this context, it is of special interest to see in what way the features of merging firms differ between countries (e.g., the United

States and United Kingdom) in which market forces and particularly the stock market play a major role and countries (e.g., West Germany and France) in which banks or the government have been more important in the merger process.

Third, a knowledge of the profile of the various groups of merging and nonmerging firms is necessary for a fuller understanding of the subsequent results of the empirical analyses with respect to the determinants and effects of mergers.

THE DETERMINANTS OF MERGERS

A major group of hypotheses about mergers existing in the literature can be conveniently divided into two broad categories: determinants and effects. Although the predicted effects of mergers will obviously have a relationship to the hypothesized determinants of mergers, this division will be useful both for conceptualizing the basic theories and, more importantly, for analyzing the results.

The hypotheses concerning the determinants of mergers can be further divided into several categories (see, for example Steiner 1975: 30–31). We shall employ the following three categories in our discussion here: "Real" changes in demand or cost conditions, speculative motives for mergers, and managerial motives.

"Real" Changes

The most frequently hypothesized causes of mergers are to bring about an increase in profits by either increasing the market power of the firm or reducing its costs or both. Market power may be increased by a merger, either by affecting the elasticity of demand for the firm's products or by raising barriers to entry. The latter will allow firms to earn higher profits either by raising their limit price (changing their effective elasticity of demand) or by allowing them to earn profits at their present price for a longer period of time. Mergers can increase a firm's market power in several ways, depending upon the type of merger involved.

The simplest case is undoubtedly the horizontal merger. A merger between two firms in the same industry that increases the acquiring firm's market share may allow it to engage more effectively in tacit or explicit collusion with other firms in the industry and thereby to charge a higher price. Horizontal mergers can also increase barriers to entry if they are coupled with cost reductions. An existing or potential entrant may be deterred from competing with a larger firm in an industry if it knows that the firm's costs are lower and, thus, that the firm would be better able to engage in a competitive price war than the potential competitor itself.

Vertical integrations can have similar potential effects. A firm with substantial market power in one market can, through backward integration, provide a captive outlet for the products of a firm one step back in the production chain, thereby increasing the effective market power of the purchased firm. Such a vertical linkage can make competition more difficult for those firms operating in the supply market. A vertically integrated firm can also constitute a threat to potential entry by requiring that to compete effectively, any potential entrant enter all markets in which the firm operates. Such entry obviously requires both more capital and managerial talent and therefore may be more difficult to achieve.

Conglomerate mergers have also been deemed to have potential anticompetitive effects. These are usually referred to under the heading of reciprocity. Reciprocity is a form of two-way linkage between firms of the same type as exists in a one-way direction under vertical integration. Two firms that are each potential purchasers of one another's products may, upon merger, provide captive markets for one another's products, thereby increasing the market power of each. Actual and potential entrants into either market may be at a competitive disadvantage due to the captive nature of the demand for each firm's products.

Each form of merger can also be a cause of cost reductions. When plant or multiplant economies of scale in production exist, a horizontal merger can be the source of cost reductions for firms of less than minimum efficient size. Vertical integrations can also reduce production costs when production processes require closely integrated steps in the production chain or by reducing the transportation costs between steps in the production chain or by reducing the uncertainties involving successive stages of production, thereby increasing firm efficiency. All three forms of mergers can be sources of reduction in various overhead costs of the firm. Research and development departments, marketing expenditures, legal assistance departments, finance, and so on may be subject to minimum efficient scale characteristics that make a large firm—be it integrated within a market, vertically across markets, or heterogeneously across markets—more efficient. (For a detailed discussion of the possible plant and multiplant economies of scale, see Scherer, et al., [1975].) In addition to these, increasing size and/or diversification can make various organizational changes more efficient. Of particular note here is the potential for shifting from a U-form to an M-form organizational structure as size and diversification increase (Williamson 1970). Organizational changes of this type bring about both potential managerial efficiencies and savings in capital costs. This is potentially particularly true of the M-form organizational structure, in which central management teams are seen as playing essentially the role of the capital market in allocating capital efficiently among the various separate divisions of the corporate organization.

Independent of the form of organization structure a firm takes, however, size and diversification may make a firm better able to raise capital in the market and thereby bring about a real reduction in its costs. Related to this is the potential reduction in risks that diversification can bring about. A reduction in risks both can reduce the firm's effective cost of capital and its real costs of undertaking investment and expansion by making planning more efficient and reducing the costs of having to go into the market to raise capital as the firm's profits vary over the cycle. In addition, the potential cost involved in a bankruptcy may also be reduced as the firm's profits are stabilized through increases in size and diversification. Related to this is the argument put forward by Donald Dewey (1961) that mergers are an inexpensive way for a "falling firm" to liquidate its assets. Even when bankruptcy is not in question, mergers may be the most profitable way for a family-controlled firm's management to liquidate its assets in the firm upon retirement. Bengt Rydén (1972) has found this to be an important cause of mergers in Sweden.

Particularly in recent years, possible tax advantages from mergers have been emphasized as a cause of merger activity.[1] Obviously the potential for reaping these savings through mergers will differ from country to country, depending on the tax code. The capacity to realize these economies may also differ from company to company. It should be noted in this context that while these economies are "real" with respect to the firms involved, if the economies are only a savings in taxes, these savings will not be "real" with respect to the economy at large.

Speculative Motives

Various arguments have been put forward that mergers are in part or perhaps entirely motivated by speculative or expectational motives. One variant on this type of hypothesis is Michael Gort's (1969) economic disturbance theory of mergers. Since Gort's hypothesis is one of the more recent contributions to this literature, and since several writers have argued that the theory is supported by the evidence, it will pay to examine Gort's argument in somewhat more detail.

It seems reasonable to assume that at any given time there will be differences in individual expectations about the future profit stream of a firm and thus about the present value of a firm's stock. This difference of opinion about the value of a firm's stock can be depicted by means of a frequency distribution as in Figure 2-1. Stockholder differences in opinion will differ because of different quantities of information the stockholders hold, different evaluations of this information, and different degrees of optimism and pessimism about the firm's future. As a first approximation, it seems reasonable to assume that a distribution of expectations would

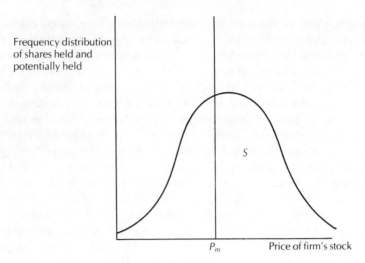

Figure 2–1. Nonuniform stockholder expectations about a firm.

take the form of a single peaked frequency distribution as depicted in Figure 2–1. At any given time there are a given number of shares of the firm's stock outstanding, and the market price of the firm, say P_m, will be that price at which the area under the frequency distribution to the right of P_m is equal to the number of shares of the firm's stock outstanding. When the frequency distribution of stockholder expectations is of the type depicted in Figure 2–1, it is unlikely that mergers will take place due to the changes in expectations of the present and potential holders of a company's stock. Changes in expectations to the right and left of P_m that leave the number of stockholders to the right of P_m unchanged leave the market price of the firm's stock unchanged. A full shift of the distribution to the left or to the right will lower or raise the firm's stock price accordingly.

Changes in expectations of this type should not lead to mergers, however, but simply to changes in the equilibrium price of the firm's stock and to the distributions of holdings among stockholders. An increase in the general expectations about the firm's future profitability may lead some individuals who previously placed a value on the firm's stock of less than P_m to value it as more than P_m and to begin purchasing the firm's stock. Stockholders who held the firm's stock but were on the margin of selling it (i.e., had expectations that placed a value on the firm's stock of at or slightly to the right of P_m) will sell the stock if their expectations have not changed. Thus, in an orderly market one expects changes in stock holdings to take place among those on the "margins" of buying and selling the firm's stock and not to lead to the large block exchanges that are necessary to bring about a merger. The more tightly the distribution of expectations is distributed around the current market price of the firm's stock, the more

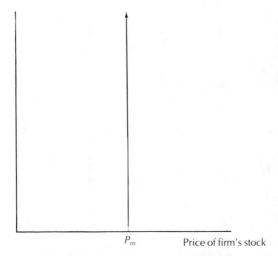

Figure 2–2. Uniform stockholders expectations about a firm.

rapidly holdings of the firm's stock will change hands in response to a change in expectations and the resulting change in the market price of the firm's stock. When shares of stock change hands rapidly in response to changes in expectations, the market price of the firm's stock will adjust quickly to reflect these changes in expectations, and the opportunities for large blocks of the firm's stock to change hands will be limited.

Since it is these changes in large blocks of stock that are necessary to bring about a merger to reequilibrate a disequilibrium in the market for the firm's stock, we can expect mergers to be less frequent the more homogeneous the stockholder expectations are with regard to the firm's future profitability. The most extreme assumption about the homogeneity of expectations about a firm's future is to assume that all actual or potential holders of a firm's stock hold identical expectations about the value of its stock. The frequency distribution of expectations in this case is a single spike at the current market value of the firm's stock, as depicted in Figure 2–2. It is this kind of assumption about expectations that underlies the capital-asset-pricing model, which has been used extensively to study both the behavior of the stock market and, in particular, the behavior of the stock market with respect to mergers. When expectations are of this type, all stockholders are either actual or potential holders of the firm's stock at any given time. That is, either a stockholder includes shares of the firm's stock in his portfolio or is indifferent between including shares of this firm's stock and some other constellation of shares in his portfolio (i.e., all stockholders have an efficient portfolio which can or does include this firm's stock). Any change in expectations, under the assumption of completely homogeneous expectations across all stockholders, results in immediate

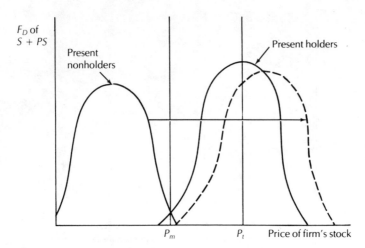

Figure 2–3. Optimistic shift in expectations by nonshareholders.

change in the market price of the firm, and an instantaneous adjustment in all portfolio holdings of the firm's stock. Thus, mergers on the basis of expectational criteria are essentially ruled out by assumption when one deals with the capital-asset-pricing model.[2]

Mergers can be explained via differences in expectations, if one begins by assuming that there are significant differences in expectations between the holders of a firm's stock and those nonholders of the firm's stock who might be induced to purchase it. Figure 2–3 (adapted from Steiner 1975, p.36), depicts two frequency distributions of expectations about the firm's present value based upon its likely future earnings. The distribution to the right represents the expectations of the present holders of the firm's stock, the distribution to the left, those of the present nonholders. Once again, the area under the distribution of expectations of the holders must equal the number of shares of stock outstanding. The small tails of the two distributions that fall on opposite sides of the equilibrium price line P_m represent holdings and nonholdings of those individuals whose expectations about the firm's present value differ from the actual market price of the firm by less than the transactions costs of buying or selling the firm's stock. The existence of two different distributions of expectations about the firm's future can be rationalized by assuming that the individuals who currently hold the firm's stock have access to different information than those individuals who do not hold the stock, or by assuming that they evaluate the information they hold differently, or simply by assuming that they are much more optimistic about the firm's future on the basis of the information they hold than nonholders of the firm's stock.

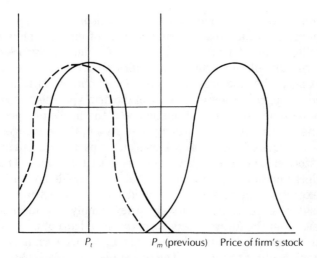

P_t P_m (previous)   Price of firm's stock

Figure 2.4. Pessimistic shift in expectations by nonshareholders.

Some such assumption about stockholder expectations is implicit in Gort's economic disturbance theory of mergers. Given the two distributions of preferences as depicted in Figure 2–3, mergers might take place in a period of rapid upheaval in stockmarket prices through the rapid shift of one of the distributions of expectations. For example, suppose that stockmarket prices are rapidly rising and that a large group of nonholders of the firm's stock simultaneously has a rapid increase in expectations about the future profits of the firm taking the form of a rapid rightward shift of their expectations' function from its present postion to the dotted line position in Figure 2–3. Were this to take place, then a significant number of nonshareholders would have expected values for the firm's stock that are not only above the present market value of the firm, but are above the price that will have to be offered to current holders, P_t, for their shares and take over the entire company.

Similarly, in a rapid decline of stockmarket values, the present holders of the firm's stock could experience a rapid and simultaneous decline in the expected worth of the company's stock, shifting their frequency distribution of expectations far to the left. If the nonholder's expectations did not shift as rapidly or as far, a situation similar to that depicted in Figure 2–4 might result in which the new (dotted line) frequency distribution of expectations of present holders is to the left of that of present nonholders and the firm can be taken over at a price P_t, which is less than the previous market price of the firm, but more than the firm's equilibrium market price would be if all present holders attempted to sell their shares in the market.

Thus, under Gort's economic disturbance theory of mergers, one can expect mergers to take place during periods of either rapidly rising or rapidly falling market prices. In a period of rising stockmarket prices, mergers will take place whenever outsiders gather information about the firm's prospects that the present holders do not obtain, if this information leads them to upgrade their evaluation of the firm's prospects significantly or if they become far more optimistic about the firm's prospects on the basis of the information they already hold. Again, these changes must be coupled with a lack of change of optimism on the part of present holders. In a falling stock market the reverse process must take place. The present stockholders must gather information that outsiders do not have, leading them to expect a rapid or even more rapid decline in the firm's stock price than outsiders expect. Alternatively, they simply become much more pessimistic about the future prospects of the firm than outsiders are, again leading them to sell the firm. In either case, we have an asymmetry of expectations leading to merger: Outsiders become relatively more optimistic, insiders relatively more pessimistic.

An additional asymmetry is introduced when it is noted that mergers are not consummated by individuals "in the market" but by firms, and thus it is the expectations of the managers of the acquiring firms that are decisive. Thus, for mergers to take place as a result of a divergence of expectations between buyers and sellers, the buyers (managers of the acquiring firm) must be more optimistic about the acquired firm's future than (1) its own managers, (2) its stockholders, and (3) the stockholders of the acquiring firm itself.

By the above interpretation, increases in merger activity should be associated with both rapid upswings and downswings in stockmarket prices. It is well known, however, that merger activity tends to increase with rapid upswings in stockmarket prices, but usually is curtailed very rapidly when stockmarket prices fall. This is somewhat surprising, in the context of the economic disturbance theory of mergers, because collapses in bull markets tend usually to be more precipitous than the preceding increases, and thus one would expect greater discrepancies in expectations during market downturns than during the preceding upswings. This alone would lead one to expect, on the basis of the economic disturbance theory, that peaks in merger activity would occur during the collapses in stockmarket prices that follow great bull markets. Since the contrary is generally the case, one has what seems to be a significant contradiction to the economic disturbance theory of mergers.[3] In testing the economic disturbance theory, therefore, we shall not focus upon aggregate swings in stockmarket and merger activity but will look at the individual firm movements in stock prices to see whether the disturbance theory can find support at this more microlevel.

The economic disturbance theory of mergers seems somewhat difficult to reconcile with the hypothesis that firms are operated in the interest of their stockholders, at least to the extent that it is the stockholders' interests, as they see them, that are involved. For if the holder of stock in a potential acquiring firm has an increased evaluation of the shares of stock of another firm, one would assume that he or she would simply go out and purchase them. The same is true in reverse for a holder of a firm's stock who became pessimistic and wanted to sell it. For companies whose stock is widely held, therefore, we would expect changes in expectations on the part of stockholders to lead to buying and selling of their shares. For these activities to take place in mass blocks, one would assume that the companies would either have to be tightly held by the stockholders, so that changes in the expectations of a few persons can lead to exchange of large blocks of stock, or that it is the expectations of the inside and outside managers that govern these transactions. This latter assumption can be rationalized in terms of stockholder welfare if one assumes that the managers maximize stockholder welfare as they, the managers, see it and perhaps do so in ways in which the present stockholders do not agree. Alternatively, one can simply assume that it is the managers' own interests and expectations that govern the decision and not those of the stockholders.

The large capital gains that accompany bull markets can lead to windfall gains to speculators, and to the extent that these gains can be brought about through merger, they may themselves constitute a separate incentive for merger. The promoters' profits of individuals who arranged mergers during the first two great merger waves in the United States were often argued to be major factors in explaining many mergers in these periods.[4]

Promoters' profits may also be a factor in modern merger activity, although outside promoters do not seem to be as predominant as they once were. It is possible, however, that some of the firms, which engage in heavy merger activity during bull markets, are managed by individuals who are essentially playing the same role as outside promoters played in earlier days. Thus, these inside managers might obtain large financial gains via the promoters' profits generated through merger activities, even though there were no economic gains generated from the mergers. This could take place, for example, through the speculation on the part of managers of both the acquiring and acquired firms in the stock of the acquired firm before the merger is announced. Since most mergers take place through the payment of a large premium to the stockholders of the acquired firm, any individuals who purchased on a high margin the stock in these firms prior to the mergers' announcement would stand to make large gains. Considerations such as these raise a possibility of a conflict of interest between inside managers and outside stockholders regarding merger activity.[5]

Managerial Motives

The possibility that mergers may be motivated in part by managerial efforts to make personal gains from the mergers that are not shared by both sets of stockholders leads directly into the broader set of hypotheses falling under the heading of "managerial theories of the firm." The most relevant here for explaining merger activity are the managerial models of Baumol (1967) and Marris (1964), which argue that managers pursue sales or growth maximization. Mergers are an obvious and quick way to expand a firm's size, and managers who are willing to sacrifice some profits and present value of firm's stock to achieve sales or asset growth may be willing to undertake mergers that cannot be explained on other grounds (Mueller 1969; Singh 1971). We shall not try to test these managerial theories directly. Instead, they will be left as a residual of sorts from the real change hypotheses discussed above. If we find that mergers tend not to be profitable, then an explanation of merger activity based on the profitable pursuit of market power or cost savings seems somewhat untenable. Even here, however, it is difficult to distinguish between the managerial theories and the real profit gain theories. For it can always be argued that the managers expected to obtain an increase in market power or reduction in costs that would have improved profits, but failed to do so.

Even more difficult is the distinction between the managerial theories and hypotheses of speculative motives or differences in expectations. Promoters' profits and inside managerial gains are obviously very closely related to other potential managerial motives. But even the expectational hypothesis may be hard to differentiate. Gort himself has found that mergers are, on the average, unprofitable from the point of view of the stockholders of the acquiring companies (Gort and Hogarty 1970). Gort chooses to explain this result, however, not by assuming a conflict of interest between managers and stockholders of acquiring firms, but by arguing that the managers of acquiring firms are risk takers who are willing to bet against the unfavorable odds of success that the Gort-Hogarty results imply on the chance of coming up with one of the few highly successful mergers that Gort and Hogarty find. Since the managers of acquiring firms are betting with other people's money—represented by the value of their company's stock—it is hard to differentiate this motive ex post from one that would simply assume that the managers are pursuing their own objectives at the expense of the stockholders' welfare. Rather than trying to devise tests beforehand to separate among these competing hypotheses, we shall simply look at what the results are and try to eliminate those hypotheses that are clearly inconsistent with the results and then focus on those that remain.

EFFECTS OF MERGERS

It is easiest to discuss the possible effects of mergers in terms of the three broad categories of mergers—horizontal, vertical, and conglomerate.

Horizontal Mergers

Conceptually, we can distinguish between two possible consequences of a horizontal merger: its impact on the market power (price elasticity of demand) of the acquiring firm and its impact on its costs (Williamson 1968). We shall interpret any increase in entry barriers stemming from the merger as affecting the firm's limit price and thus its effective elasticity of demand. These two consequences can in turn be divided into income changes for the factor owners and welfare gains and losses to customers stemming from price and quality changes. To see the possible effects more clearly, consider the following simple examples.

First, assume that a merger takes place that affects neither costs nor market power. The simplest way to depict such a merger is to assume firm demand schedules that are at every price isoelastic and identical cost curves. Two such firms are depicted in Figure 2–5 with demand schedules

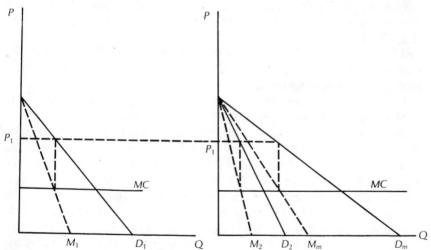

Figure 2–5. Horizontal merger leaving market power and efficiency unchanged.

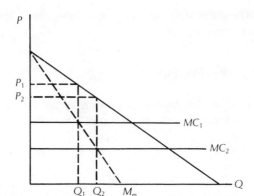

Figure 2–6. Horizontal merger improving efficiency.

D_1 and D_2. Profit maximizing price remains unchanged at P_1. Following the merger, output of the merged firm is the sum of the outputs of the two premerging firms; profits are the sum of profits for the two merging firms; profits as a return on capital or a percent of sales are unchanged.[6]

Next, consider a merger that produces an increase in efficiency without changing market power. Such a merger can be depicted by assuming the same two firms merge as above and that the new, postmerger demand schedule is again the horizontal sum of the two individual demand schedules and is therefore isoelastic to them at every price. If costs did not change, we would have the results of Figure 2–5. Assume, however, that costs fall to MC_2, as in Figure 2–6. Profit-maximizing price now falls to P_2, and output expands to Q_2. Profits in toto and as a percent of sales and capital increase, assuming that the capital-labor ratio remains unchanged. Note that in general such an increase in profit rates should induce entry and drive down price, unless entry is somehow blockaded. This could be the case if the cost decline was the result of some economy of scale requiring a large percent of the total market.[7]

Last, consider a merger that increases market power and leaves costs unchanged. A merger can be said to result in an unambiguous increase in market power if it makes the demand schedule of the new firm more inelastic at every price than the demand schedules of the two merging firms. Assume the same two firms merge as in Figures 2–6 and the right-hand side of Figure 2–5, but that the new demand schedule is a parallel shift of firm one's demand schedule, as depicted in Figure 2–7. The horizontal distance between the two demand schedules is drawn equal to the output of firm 2 at the initial price P—that is, if the firms left the price unchanged, the output of the new firm would be the same as the sum of the outputs of the two merging firms. The fall in the firm's elasticity of demand, however, raises the profit-maximizing price to P_2. Thus, the

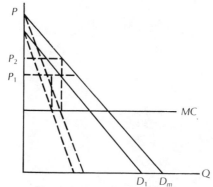

Figure 2–7. Horizontal merger increasing market power.

newly merged firm should have a higher price, smaller output, and higher profits as a percent of both sales and capital.

Table 2–1 summarizes these predictions of the change in the key variables for the three types of mergers. Note that the type of merger cannot be distinguished by examining either the change in profits or the profit rate. Both market power and efficiency increases should increase these variables. The type of merger can be distinguished by looking at the change in product price, real output, or productivity. These variables are in general difficult to obtain. For this reason, it will probably be useful to take advantage of the fact that a profit-maximizing firm always operates in the elastic portion of its demand schedule. This condition ensures that sales will increase for a merger, which only improves efficiency, and decrease for a merger, which only increases market power. We thus have an unambiguous test of the type of merger undertaken. If both market power—that is, demand inelasticity—and efficiency increase at the same time, then the test determines the net impact of these two effects.

The last column of Table 2–1 presents the predictions for the change in labor force. For a merger, which improves economic efficiency, no prediction can be made. The impact on the number of laborers employed will depend upon the extent to which the efficiency increase came about through reductions in the labor force and the extent to which output is expanded by the resulting fall in product price. For a market-power-increasing merger, employment should fall.

Note that the table provides no possibility for profits to decline as a result of a merger. It is difficult to see how a merger could result in a decrease in market power. Thus, profits should decline following a merger only if costs rise. Such mergers might take place if (1) managers miscalculate the effects of the merger on costs or, possibly, demand; (2) the merger is motivated by considerations other than profit maximization; or

Table 2–1. New Values of Selected Variables

Effect of Merger	P_m	Q_m	S_m	π_m	$\left(\frac{\pi}{K}\right)_m$	L_m
No change in market power or efficiency	$= P_1(= P_2)$	$= (Q_1 + Q_2)$	$= (S_1 + S_2)$	$= (\pi_1 + \pi_2)$	$= \left(\frac{\pi}{K}\right)_1 = \left(\frac{\pi}{K}\right)_2$	$= (L_1 = L_2)$
Market power unchanged, efficiency improved	$< P_1(= P_2)$	$> (Q_1 + Q_2)$	$> (S_1 + S_2)$	$> (\pi_1 + \pi_2)$	$> \left(\frac{\pi}{K}\right)_1$	Unknown
Market power increased, efficiency unchanged	$> P_1(= P_2)$	$< (Q_1 + Q_2)$	$< (S_1 + S_2)$	$> (\pi_1 + \pi_2)$	$> \left(\frac{\pi}{K}\right)_1$	$< (L_1 + L_2)$

m = value for newly created firm.
$1, 2$ = two premerger firms.
P = price.
Q = output.
S = sales.
L = labor.
π = profit.
K = capital stock.

Table 2–2. **Change in Selected Variables as a Result of a Horizontal Merger and Appropriate Conclusions**

$\Delta \frac{\pi}{K}$	ΔS	Δr	ΔL	Conclusion
+	+	+		Improvement in efficiency; consumers and owners (managers) benefit
+	−	+		Increase in market power; owners benefit, consumers lose
−	−	−		Consumers and owners both worse off; managers erred or pursued other goals
−	?	+		Temporary decline in profits due to adjustment costs; owners will benefit in long run
			−	Workers probably worse off due to loss in wages

(3) the cost increase is temporary (adjustment costs) and the long-run increase in profits will more than offset it. The latter possibility is particularly troublesome for the present studies, since we are in general limited to a few years of observations following a merger. We shall attempt to compensate for this limitation, however, by calculating the rate of return on holding a share of the acquiring firm's stock before and after the merger. A merger, which in the long run increases the return on capital of the acquiring company, should at the time of its consummation result in a rise in the price of the acquiring firm's shares and thus an increase in the returns earned by common shareholders. Thus, if it is foreseen that the decline in profits for an otherwise profitable merger is temporary, then in a perfect stockmarket, this knowledge should be reflected in a rise in the return on the firm's common shares, even though the profits of the firm may fall immediately following the merger. The validity of such a test, however, depends crucially on how perfect the stockmarket pricing process actually is.

The above considerations suggest the following set of tests for the impact of a horizontal merger. Measure the sales, the total labor force, the return on capital, and the return on a share of the acquiring firm's stock before the merger. Compare each variable in the postmerger period with the predicted value for the same variable if the two firms had not merged (see below). Draw the conclusions as indicated in Table 2–2.

It should be noted that a merger might result in a net increase in market power (row 2) and still be deemed socially desirable, if it produced a sufficiently large decrease in costs, as well as the increase in market power, so that the income gains of the owners outweighed the consumer surplus triangle loss of the consumers (Williamson 1968). To test for such possibilities we would need estimates of the elasticity of demand for each merging firm, estimates that we do not have. Instead, therefore, we have tested to discover those mergers resulting in one net effect or the other.

Vertical Acquisitions

The above logic can be extended to consider vertical integrations though the tests cannot be applied directly. When a large firm acquires one of its suppliers, the sales of the latter disappear. If the merger has no impact on either the costs or the market power of the acquiring firm, the price of its final product should not change nor, therefore, should its final output or sales. Profits will increase to equal the sum of the profits of the two companies; the return on capital will equal a weighted average of their two returns. If the merger improves the acquiring firm's efficiency it should lower price and expand sales. Thus, the same predictions can be made, thinking of sales now as just the sales of the acquiring firm, as in row 1 of Table 2–2. A vertical integration, which increases the acquiring firm's market power, should result in higher prices, higher profits, and lower sales (the same prediction as in row 2). The predictions of rows 3 and 4 follow in the same way.

When a large firm acquires one of its buyers, its sales expand by the amount of sales of the acquired firm and contract by the amount of purchases by the acquired firm of the acquiring firm's final product. If this latter number were known, a prediction of sales in the absence of market power and economy of scale effects could again be made, and one could proceed using Table 2–2 with predicted sales appropriately defined. In the absence of such a number, one can only test to see if the owners and/or workers benefited from such an integration. Note that if one assumes that the value added to worker ratio remains unchanged, one can test for an economies of scale effect by seeing if the number of workers increased or not.

Conglomerate Mergers

A merger between two firms in unrelated markets, which affects neither their market power nor their efficiency, should leave each firm's price, quantity, sales, profits, and so forth unchanged. Sales of the newly formed company will be the sum of the sales of the two merging firms, its profits will be the sum of their profits, and so on. Mergers that improve the efficiency of the companies will lead to lower costs; lower profit-maximizing prices; and sales for the combined company that sum to more than those for the two merging firms, assuming again that the firms' maximized profits and price in the elastic portions of their demand schedules. Mergers that increase market power should lead to higher prices and an increase in sales that is less than the combined sales of the two merging companies. Thus, the same tests as were applied to horizontal mergers should be applicable to conglomerates. All of the tests described under horizontal mergers will thus also be applied to conglomerates with the same predictions made.

Given the unrelated nature of the products brought together in a conglomerate merger, it is often more difficult to see how either cost efficiencies or market power increases come about from such mergers. Reductions in overhead costs have been argued with respect to conglomerates, however, and to the extent that these occur, they should be reflected in overall reductions in the firm's cost margins and expansions in sales and output. Case study evidence of conglomerates suggests that these cost efficiencies and market power increases have not been forthcoming, however (FTC 1972).

Hypotheses concerning the potential reductions in risks through diversification that mergers can bring about seem most, if not solely, relevant for conglomerate mergers. Since most of the risks a firm faces are cyclic or industry related, horizontal and vertical mergers should not adequately protect the firms from such risks. The "quiet life" a monopolist might reap is better treated as an aspect of market power accumulation. When risk is reduced, no change in price or costs need come about, and none of the above tests may indicate an increase in efficiency. Yet the merger may be socially beneficial by improving the efficiency of the capital market. (Note that such a merger should lower the cost of capital of the firm, and thus its long-run marginal costs, and allow price reductions and expansion to follow.) The above tests for sales and profit changes should still be applicable.

The bulk of the literature on the effects of conglomerate mergers on risk employs the capital-asset-pricing model (Lintner 1971). Using this model, the expected return on a security can be expressed as

$$E(R_i) - R_f = \alpha_i + \beta_i (E(R_m) - R_f)$$

where $E(R_i) \equiv$ expected return on security i,
$R_f \equiv$ risk free rate of return,
$E(R_m) \equiv$ expected return on the market portfolio,
$\alpha =$ intercept, expected to be zero,
$\beta_i =$ slope of characteristic line.

There are two measures of risk one might consider relevant, the variance in the return on i, and β_i. The latter captures the extent to which the return on i varies directly with the market return. The higher the β_i, the less is to be gained in terms of diversifying market risk by purchasing this stock, and the higher its $E(R_i)$ must be. A variety of performance measures can be devised from the above model (Weston, Smith, and Shrieves 1972; Jensen 1972). These measures are not all independent, however, and one can conveniently focus on two that deal with either the variance in return on i (σ_i), or β_i:

$$\text{Sharpe's measure} \quad \frac{E(R_i) - R_f}{\sigma_i}$$

$$\text{Treynor's measure} \quad \frac{E(R_i) - R_f}{\beta_i}$$

An increase in either measure as a result of a merger represents an increase in the rate of return per unit of risk and thus an improvement in the performance of the firm.

EFFECTS OF MERGERS: WELFARE AND POLICY IMPLICATIONS

As noted in Chapter 1, the governments in a number of industrial countries are currently searching for appropriate policies toward mergers, and an important purpose of the merger studies in this book is to assist in this task. Unfortunately, the lack of comparable data across countries has restricted our study to the effects of mergers on only a small number of variables—firm profitability, size, growth, share prices, and gearing (leverage). In assessing the implications for government policy of the effects that may be observed, it is therefore essential to examine further the implicit welfare model of the preceding section and to underline some of its limitations.

This model represents the traditional approach to the assessment of the social efficiency of mergers and to the discussion of competition policy. It is firmly based upon the analysis of the Paretian properties of competitive equilibrium. Social efficiency is attained by maximization of the following welfare function:

$$W = (TR + S) - (TC - R)$$

where TR = total revenue, S = consumers surplus, TC = total costs, and R = intramarginal rents.

Under the usual assumptions, with competitive equilibrium prices, $TR + S$ is assumed to represent social benefits and $TC - R$, social costs. The approach thus involves a partial equilibrium trade-off of the operating and transaction cost gains from merger against any allocative efficiency losses that may arise from higher monopolistic prices (Harberger 1971; Williamson

1968, 1977). Within the terms of the model, the effects of mergers on variables such as size and profitability translate directly into social welfare measures and can therefore provide a significant and useful guide to social policy.

There are a number of well-known theoretical and practical difficulties in the application of this approach to merger policy, however, These include the Lipsey-Lancaster issues of second best, the problems of external economies and diseconomies, the difficulties of appraising alternative methods of obtaining the scale gains associated with merger, and the problems that arise from the neglect of income distribution consequences and the political considerations surrounding antitrust enforcement.[8] There are, however, more fundamental problems, which arise from the static equilibrium nature of the approach itself, to which we should like to draw special attention. (We follow Hughes and Singh (1978) in the following analysis.) The model assumes the economy to be in full employment equilibrium; this makes strict application of its results questionable in the real world situations of disequilibrium and unemployment.

At the simplest level, suppose a merger between two firms increases monopoly power but does not lead to economies of scale and to a reduction in costs per unit of output (rather, total output is reduced due to monopoly pricing). Let us, however, assume that the merger generates an extra million pounds (£1 million) of exports (or displaces imports of similar value). Under the assumption of the orthodox equilibrium model, this would be an unambiguous case of monopoly welfare loss (as indicated in row 3 or Table 2–2). Such a judgement would nevertheless be invalid in a disequilibrium economy, which is characterized by unemployed resources and a balance of payments constraint. In such an economy, the social value of an extra £1 million of exports is likely to be greater than its market value (i.e., an extra £1 million of exports would lead to an increase in demand and output of more than one million due to the relaxation of the balance of payments constraint). Equally, in similar circumstances, a merger that produced cost savings in excess of any adverse monopoly power effects might still be socially inefficient if it worsened the trade balance—through, for instance, a change in the international composition of inputs or outputs.

The above considerations are of much more general relevance, and from the policy point of view extremely important, in the present situation of the world economy. Most of the economies studied in this book are experiencing long-term trend increases in unemployment (by postwar standards) and what is popularly known as "deindustrialization." (For an analysis of "deindustrialization" in the advanced countries and its significance, see Singh 1979.) To illustrate with an extreme example, the United Kingdom economy does not only suffer from short-term disequilibrium of the kind mentioned in the last paragraph; its current position is also characterized by long-term "structural disequilibrium" (in the sense discussed in Singh 1977a). The manufacturing sector, which is of crucial significance for the United Kingdom's position in the world economy, is increasingly unable to generate sufficient net exports to ensure current account balance for the economy at full employment at a reasonable exchange rate.[9] This is so despite the fact that during the last fifteen years, mainly due to currency depreciations, costs and prices have moved in the United Kingdom's favor relative to those in competitor countries. The United Kingdom economy is thus forced to operate below its productive potential, which incidentally makes the competitive position worse than before. Some, but by no means all, of the other countries included in this study, which are heavily trade dependent, are similarly constrained (though none as acutely as the United Kingdom) by their balance of payments. In the case of the United Kingdom, a large body of research indicates that trade imbalances arise from long-term structural weaknesses on the "supply" side (as opposed, for example, to peculiarities in the pattern of the United Kingdom demand (Stout 1979).

To deal with problems of this kind, governments in a number of advanced countries have adopted active industrial policies to promote structural change, product innovation, technical progress, and so forth so that their industries could compete more effectively in the world economy. In countries such as Belgium, this has involved planning agreements between the largest companies and the government to achieve specified goals (in terms of exports, etc.) in return for government assistance. The United Kingdom under the last Labour government similarly had an active supply side policy—the so-called industrial strategy—that emphasized cooperation between workers, managers and government, under the aegis of the Sector Working Parties (SWPs). The SWPs attempted to identify the main problems of modernization and efficiency in the key sectors of industry and to devise suitable programs (including interfirm cooperation) to deal with them.

The essential point of the preceding discussion in the present context is that policy toward mergers cannot be properly considered in isolation from the government's overall industrial policy and objectives (Hughes 1978). Where governments intervene in the markets to a large degree and pursue an active industrial policy (which is often the case in many of the advanced countries other than the United States), the production cost and selling price data of the individual merging firms may be not just an inadequate, but a misleading guide to an appraisal of their social efficiency. Thus, merger-induced increases in firm size, in addition to the consequences mentioned in Table 2–2, may also have important threshold effects and enable successful exporting and innovative activity to occur.[10] Mergers may also lead to rapid plant rationalization in response to industrial change and can have similar effects to certain kinds of interfirm cooperation agreements in reducing uncertainty and promoting higher levels of investment and of product and process innovation than might otherwise be the case (Richardson 1961). Effects of this kind may substantially improve nonprice as well as price competitiveness of the country in the world economy, and some would doubtless be reflected in the accounts of the individual firms concerned. There may, however, be beneficial effects external to the firms themselves or that confer no relative advantage and that arise from mergers. Thus the creation of concentrated market structures as a result of merger may lead to more efficient investment expansion paths for all the remaining firms (Hjalmarsson 1977) or lead to effective government economic assistance (Stoneman 1978) and the possibility of improved indicative planning. In interpreting the results of the microeconomic empirical studies in this book for government policy, the importance of these factors should not be ignored.

DATA AND METHODOLOGY

To examine the various issues and hypotheses outlined above, data were gathered on an individual firm basis in each of the seven countries. The objective was to gather data on firms undertaking mergers during the period 1962–1972. In some cases, however, it was not possible to gather data on mergers for all years.

To compare the premerger characteristics of the merging and nonmerging firms, we sought to gather data for the five years preceding a merger for both the acquiring and the acquired firms. These data would then be compared with data for the same years for the corresponding groups of nonacquired and nonacquiring firms.

Similarly, to test the hypotheses of the determinants of mergers, the premerger characteristics of the merged firms would be compared with data for the same years for a control group composed of either a matched pair of nonmerging firms or, in some cases, with industry averages. Thus, for example, to see whether economies of scale is a plausible explanation of merger activity with respect to horizontal mergers, we tested the average size of a pair of merging firms in an industry at the time of a merger against either the average size of a pair of randomly selected nonmerging firms from the same industry or simply against the average size of a firm in the industry. Similar tests were conducted with respect to the other hypotheses about determinants (see detailed notes below).

To test the various hypotheses about the effects of mergers, we sought to gather data on a pair of merging firms for five years before the merger and for five years after. Once again, it was not possible in all cases to have five years of data before and after each merger, and we had to settle for what data were available. Each hypothesis concerning the effects of mergers was then tested, using again a paired matched sample or industry average technique. Thus, the profitability of a merged firm in the five years following a merger relative to the profitability of the two merging firms in the five years preceding a merger is compared to the relative profitability of a matched sample of nonmerging firms over the same two five-year periods or to industry profitability trends over the same time interval.

Each of the hypotheses is tested on data gathered within the respective countries. Thus, all comparisons are made within a country, and problems of differing definitions of variables across countries are alleviated. Differences in definitions of profits, assets, or similar variables may differ across countries, but they should not affect significantly the comparisons of changes in these variables within any given country. Nevertheless, the countries do differ in the conventions used to define profits, assets, and some of the other variables, and this does create some problems. For example, a great deal of flexibility seems to exist in West Germany and some of the other continental European countries in the discretion that firms have in arranging their accounting data to yield different levels of profit for the same year's data. This means that the ability of firms to show higher profits, let us say, following a merger, due not to the merger's effects, but to accounting variations, will differ across countries. There was, however, little that we could do to rectify this situation. The data that we have were difficult enough to come by as it is and are essentially all that are available in the respective countries.

SPECIFIC TESTS

Background

Control Groups. The basic methodology underlying the statistical tests was to compare the firms merging within a country to those that did not merge in terms of various operating or financial characteristics before the merger took place or to compare the changes in these characteristics following a merger with changes in the same variables during the corresponding time period for nonmerging firms. Merging firms were defined simply as any firms that merged during the 1962–1972 period for which data on both the acquiring and acquired firm were available, excluding essentially financial institutions (e.g., banks, insurance companies) and regulated or government-controlled firms (e.g., utilities, transportation companies). The sectors included differ somewhat from country to country, and the individual country reports should be checked. The requirement that data on both the acquiring and the acquired firms be available limited the samples of merging firms to those listed on the national stock exchanges, so that both of the merging firms are typically of reasonably large size.

The goal was to define the control group as firms that had not merged over the ten-year period of the study. The merger waves in each country were of such magnitude, however, that very few companies engaged in no merger activity at all. A nonmerging firm was thus defined as one that had undertaken only a few acquisitions of small, unlisted firms.

Even under this more relaxed definition of a nonmerging firm, it was not possible in each country to define the control group to include firms that had not merged over the entire ten-year period. In some cases, therefore, the samples of nonmerging firms were made up of firms that had not engaged in merger activity (other than perhaps a few acquisitions of unlisted firms) during the period corresponding to that used in the tests of its paired, merging firm. Thus, for example, a steel firm that had not merged during the period 1960–1964 might be included in the control group of nonmerging firms as the counterpart to a steel firm undertaking a merger in 1965 for purposes of comparing the premerger characteristics of merging and nonmerging firms, even though the nonmerging steel firm might have undertaken a merger in 1968.

Growth Rates. A number of tests require the projection of the growth of a characteristic of the firm (e.g., sales) in the absence of a merger. What we have done in these cases is assume that the sales of the acquiring firm (S_A) and of the acquired firm (S_B) would have grown at the same rate as those of their respective industries. Thus, if IS_t^A is the industry sales in year t of the industry of which firm A is a member and $IS^B t$ the industry sales of the industry of which B is a member, then the projected sales in year $(t + i)$ of the firm formed by combining A and B in year t is

$$S_{t+i}^C = S_t^A \ \frac{IS_{t+i}^A}{IS_t^A} + S_t^B \ \frac{IS_{t+i}^B}{IS_t^B}$$

Rate of Return on Stock. The rate of return in any year from holding a stock throughout the year is the divided payment in that year D_1 plus the capital gain from holding the stock the entire year $(P_1 - P_0)$ divided by the stock's price at the beginning of the year (P_0)

$$r = \frac{D_1 + (P_1 - P_0)}{P_0}$$

If stocks are held more than one year, however, dividends and capital gains cannot be weighted equally. A dollar of dividends earned in period $(t + 1)$, on a stock sold at the end of some later period is more valuable than a dollar of capital gains earned in (t + 1), because a dollar of dividends earned in (t + 1) can be reinvested and earn interest, while a dollar of capital gains earned in (t + 1) is obtained only when the stock is sold. Thus, in calculating rates of return on stocks held for longer than one period, we adjust the dividend payments earned to allow for their reinvestment. To do this, we employ estimates of the rate of return earned on the "market portfolio" in each country (a diversified portfolio of corporate stocks). Calling this return r_M, the return from holding a given stock five years is

$$r = \frac{D_1(1 + r_M)^4 + D_2(1 + r_M)^3 + D_3(1 + r_M)^2 + D_4(1 + r_M) + D_5 + P_5 - P_0}{P_0}$$

This formula adjusted for the number of years of data is used in computing rates of return on corporate stock.

Other Definitions. The variables used in the study are standard accounting variables and are not defined here. Peculiarities in these variables as they exist in the various countries are noted in the respective country reports. Throughout the study the acquiring firm is referred to as firm A; the firm it buys as firm B; and the combination of A and B existing after the merger as firm C.

Characteristics of Merging and Nonmerging Firms

The premerger characteristics of the merging and nonmerging firms are compared in terms of the following variables: size, profitability, profits variability, growth, leverage, price-earnings ratio, and stockholder return. The comparisons are made on an interfirm cross-section basis, and the groups compared are (1) the acquiring and the acquired; (2) the acquired and the nonacquired; (3) the acquiring and the nonacquiring. The variables are based on accounting and stockmarket data; the precise accounting definitions are given in the respective country chapters.

The choice of these variables was largely dictated by the availability of data across countries rather than strictly by the nature of the issues raised concerning the takeover selection mechanism. Nevertheless, at a somewhat crude level, they do bear directly on some of the hypotheses discussed there. The neoclassical hypothesis can be put in terms of the market selecting firms for survival on the basis of their past performance (approximated here by the variables profitability and growth) or their future prospects (indicated by the price-earnings ratio). Galbraith's conjecture that the takeover selection process favors the large firms and Marris's that it selects growing firms can be examined in terms of the size and growth characteristics of the various groups of merging and nonmerging firms.

(For a fuller discussion of these and other variables in relation to questions of market selection processes and market discipline, see Singh 1971.)

The statistical analysis compares the respective group means for each of the variables and tests for the statistical significance of the observed difference. Although this is a straightforward exercise, there are some general points that are important in interpreting the results. First, it is necessary to keep in mind the fundamental distinction between "statistical" significance and "economic" significance. This is a simple point, but one that is often overlooked in applied economic analysis. Statistical "significance" is concerned only with the question of whether or not an observed difference between sample means could have arisen by "chance"—that is, merely through sampling variation. However, if the sample sizes are large enough, even the smallest observed difference between sample means (e.g., a 0.001 percent difference between the mean profitability of taken-over and surviving firms) could be highly significant statistically. Yet such a result may have little economic significance.

Second, there are good reasons, both economic and statistical, for thinking that unless such analysis is done on an individual industry basis or by means of an appropriate sample design that explicitly recognizes the aggregation problem, there is a danger of aggregation bias in the results. This is because both the incidence of takeovers and the motivation and environment for takeovers are known to differ greatly between industries; there are also large interindustry differences in the characteristics of firms. (For a discussion of the aggregation problems in interfirm analysis of this type, see Singh 1971; and Singh and Whittington 1975.) Therefore, whenever possible, the statistical analyses were conducted both on an individual industry basis and in an appropriate way for all industries together. In countries where sufficient data were not available, the investigators have attempted to deal with the question of aggregation bias in other ways and have suitably qualified their results where necessary.

Third, in relation to the economic issues of the stockmarket selection process, it should be noted that the statistical analysis conducted here has been of a limited kind and can only be regarded as a preliminary step to a fuller examination of these major questions. Specifically, the analysis has been done only on a univariate basis. Because of the intercorrelation between variables, it is not possible to obtain an accurate profile of firms "selected" by the market for survival (and hence of the nature of the selection mechanisms) without a multivariate analysis. Further, the univariate investigations that have been carried out have also been of a limited variety. The analysis has been confined to examining the differences between the average characteristics of various groups of firms; more refined analyses of the degrees of overlap between the groups with respect to these characteristics would be required for rigorous tests of the various hypotheses concerning the selection mechanism. Some studies of this kind are available for the individual countries (notably the United Kingdom); but they could not be attempted here on a uniform basis for all countries. Nevertheless, the results of even the limited investigations are of considerable interest, especially when comparisons are made between countries.

Tests of Determinants

Size Comparisons. If economies of scale are an important factor determining merger activity, there should be some tendency for smaller firms to merge more often than larger ones, unless all of the firms in the industry are below minimum efficient size. To test this hypothesis for horizontal mergers, we compare the average size of merging firms within an industry with the average size of nonmerging firms within the same industry. Our sample of merging firms includes all of the acquiring (A) and acquired (B) firms engaged in horizontal mergers. The control group samples of nonmerging firms were formed by picking at random two nonmerging firms from the same industry as a pair of merging firms in the merging firm sample. Given these two samples of equal numbers of firms, we then compared both the arithmetic mean of their sizes based on the various size characteristics (listed in the appendix to this chapter) and the geometric means of their sizes. The geometric means were calculated because it was assumed that most of the size variables would be positively skewed (i.e., approximate the lognormal distribution) and thus that the geometric mean would be more appropriate.

A finding that the average size of merging firms is less than the average size of nonmerging firms in the same industries cannot unambiguously be interpreted as support for the economies of scale hypothesis. It could be that smaller firms are more likely to merge because they are attempting to increase their market shares relative to the larger firms. This goal might be pursued to make bargaining for shares in collusive agreements or other monopoly-power-related profits easier to obtain. Thus, a finding that merging firms are on average smaller than other firms in the same industry is a necessary but not sufficient condition for support of the economies of scale hypothesis. In contrast, however, a finding that firms that merge are on the average larger than nonmerging firms in the same industries would seem to be clearly inconsistent with the economies of scale explanation of mergers and to require the rejection of this hypothesis and thus implicitly would support a merger for a monopoly motive.

Risk. Horizontal mergers are less likely to be explained by risk-spreading motives, than are either, probably, vertical integration mergers or, certainly, conglomerate mergers. Thus, the various hypotheses about risk-spreading motives for merging will be tested both for the entire samples of merging firms and for the subsamples of conglomerate mergers whenever the latter are large enough to allow a division of the sample into two parts.

Variance in profits. Our first test of risk-spreading characteristics will simply be to see whether firms that merge have greater variations in profit levels than firms that do not merge. To standardize for size differences among firms, we shall work with the coefficient of variation rather than the raw variance in profits. For the pairs of merging firms, we shall form for each pair the ratio of the largest of the coefficients of variation in profits to the smallest of the two coefficients of variations in profits where these have been calculated for the five years preceding the year of merger. The control groups will be formed in the usual way with randomly selected nonmerging firms from both the acquired and acquiring firm industries. The largest of the two coefficients of variation is placed in the numerator, the smaller of the two in the denominator to form a statistic for the control group. The data for the control group firms are from the same five-year period as used for the paired, merging firms. The test statistic for the control group firms is again the ratio of the largest of the two coefficients of variation to the smallest. The mean of these ratios is then formed for the sample of merging firms and for the sample of nonmerging firms. A standard *t*-test is used to compare the means of these two samples. In addition to running this test for the pairs of merging firms, the test will be run for the sample of acquiring firms and their matched sample of nonmerging firms and for the sample of acquired firms and the matched sample of nonacquired firms.

Leverage. There are various hypotheses about differences in leverage ratios among firms that may lead to differences in risk (see, e.g., Baumol and Malkiel 1967). These hypotheses can be transformed into hypotheses concerning the determinants of mergers, if one assumes that the differences in risks attributable to differences in leverage ratios can be a cause for merger activity. Here the hypothesis would have to be that the firms with in some sense either relatively high leverage ratios or relatively low leverage ratios will be more likely to engage in merger activity than firms with "normal" leverage ratios. The problem is to define tests to determine what relatively high or low leverage ratios are.

The first and most direct test of differences in leverage ratios causing mergers is to take the absolute value of the difference between the leverage ratios for two merging firms in the year of the merger (with the leverage ratio defined as long-term debt divided by the sum of long-term debt and stockholder equity) and to compare that to the absolute value of the differences between the leverage ratios for paired nonmerging firms. Absolute values are used because it does not seem on a priori grounds that it would matter whether the acquiring or acquired firm had the largest of the two leverage ratios. If avoiding leverage-created risks is an important determinant of mergers, then highly levered firms should seek out firms with low leverage as merger partners and vice versa. The statistical test to be applied here will again be to compute the mean absolute value of the differences in leverage ratios for the merging and nonmerging samples of firms and to perform a t-test on the differences between the two means of these samples.

Similar tests can be run looking at either the acquiring firms only or the acquired firms. We thus test to see whether the variance in leverage ratios for acquiring firms was greater than the variance in leverage ratios for a matched sample of nonmerging firms. Firms for the latter sample were again selected from the same industries as the acquiring firms and, wherever possible, were matched by size as well. We then compared the variances of the two samples to see whether there was a statistically greater variance in the leverage ratios among the acquiring firms than among nonmerging firms. The same test was repeated for a sample of acquired firms and a sample of nonacquired firms.

Last, a rather simple hypothesis about leverage and risk can be examined by testing whether the acquiring or the acquired firms have consistently higher (lower) leverage ratios than the corresponding groups of nonmerging firms. These tests were carried out as a part of the analysis of the premerger characteristics of the merging and nonmerging firms.

Economic Disturbance Hypotheses. There are a number of possible tests of the economic disturbance theory of mergers. We shall undertake two. The economic disturbance theory argues that mergers are more likely when stock market values are rapidly changing than when they are not. Extending this hypothesis to the microlevel, it would seem to suggest that acquisitions of firms whose stock prices are more rapidly changing will be more likely than acquisitions of firms whose stock prices are not rapidly changing. To test this hypothesis, we compute the ratio of the highest price earnings ratio (P/E) for an acquired firm in the year preceding its acquisition to the lowest price earnings ratio for this firm in this year. This becomes one observation in the sample of acquired firms. We form the same ratio of high to low price earnings ratios for a matched, nonacquired firm in the same year. This is one observation in the control group sample. We compute the mean values of these ratios for the two samples of acquired and matched nonacquired firms and compare these sample means using a *t*-test. Since the economic disturbance theory is not specific as to what period of time is appropriate preceding a merger, we test the disturbance theory using not only the ratios of high to low P/Es for the year preceding the merger but also those for the two years preceding the merger and for the three years preceding the merger.

An alternative interpretation of the economic disturbance theory is to argue that in periods of rapid stock market fluctuation "bargains" will appear and that these bargains will be gobbled up by other firms. Bargains should appear in the form of low prices relative to expected earnings. To test this hypothesis, we compute the mean of the high and low P/Es for the acquired firms in the year preceding a merger. The mean between the high and low P/Es for the matched nonacquired firms is then computed, and the sample means for the mean high lows for acquired and nonacquired firms are compared using a *t*-test. This test is again repeated not only for the year preceding the merger, but for the two years preceding the merger and for the three years preceding the merger. If the economic disturbance theory is correct, acquired firms should have lower mean P/Es than non-acquired firms.

Tests of Effects

Profitability. Regardless of whether mergers are motivated to achieve market power or economies of scale or other efficiency gains, they should, if the managers of acquiring firms are seeking to maximize profits, result in an increase in the profit rate of the newly formed firm over what the weighted average of the profit rates of the two combining firms would have been had they not merged. This hypothesis is tested in three ways. First, we form the weighted average of the profit rates of firms *A* and *B* over the five-year period preceding a merger. This weighted average is then subtracted from the average profit rate of the newly formed company (*C*) over the five-year period following the merger. This is one observation in the sample of merging firms. Two matched, nonmerging firms are then chosen, and the weighted average of their profit rates over the five-year period preceding the merger is subtracted from the weighted average of their profits over the five-year period following the merger. This is one observation for the control group of nonmerging firms. The mean of the differences in post- and preprofit rates for the sample of merging firms is then compared, by using a *t*-test, with the mean difference in weighted average of post- and premerger profit rates for the sample of nonmerging firms. This test is run for profits on stockholder equity, profits on total assets, and profits on total sales. Wherever possible, we have used both before and after tax profits in running these tests.

As an alternative to the matched sample for our control group, we projected the profit growth of a typical firm in an industry as described at the beginning of this subsection. Namely, we form the ratio of the profit rates for all firms in an industry over the five-year period following a merger to the ratio of the profit rates for all firms in an industry over the five-year period preceding a merger. These ratios were then used to project the profit levels of the acquired and acquiring firms in the absence of a merger. The weighted average of these projected profit rates was then one observation in the control group. The sample mean of these projected profit rates for the control group was then compared to the sample mean profit rates for the merged firms using a t-test. Again, these tests were run using both before and after tax profits where possible and forming profit rates on stockholder equity, total assets, and sales.

As the third test, we simply compared the change in the average profit rates of the merged firms in the five years following a merger with the change in the respective industry averages, again using both definitions of profits in the three profit ratios.

Size. Assuming that the mergers have on an average been profitable, some indication of whether they were profitable because of monopoly power increases, or efficiency gains, can be obtained on the basis of the above discussion by looking at the changes in size of the firm following the merger. As argued above, we would expect the firm to become somewhat smaller in sales or some other indicator of size— as, for example, assets— if the merger was one that increased market power; somewhat larger if it increased economies of scale and other efficiency indicators.

The first variant of a change in size test is to compute a weighted average of the growth rates in the size variables for the two merging firms over the five-year period preceding the merger. This is then subtracted from the growth in the size variable for the newly formed company following the merger. This becomes one observation in the merging firm sample. A matched observation in the nonmerging firm sample is formed from a pair of nonmerging firms matched by industry, size, and time period to the two merging firms. The weighted average of the growth rates of these firms before and after the merger is taken, and the first difference of these weighted averages constitutes one observation in the nonmerging firm sample. The mean first differences in growth rates for the sample of merging and nonmerging firms are then compared by means of a t-test. The same test is then run comparing the ratios of the after and before merger growth rates, instead of the first differences. The test is also run using the leverage ratios before and after the merger.

As a still additional variant of this test, the growth in sales of the two merging firms after the merger are projected using the growth in industry sales as described in the introductory remarks to this section. The weighted average of the projected growth rates of the two merging firms in the five years after the merger then becomes one observation in the nonmerging firm control group sample. The sample of merging firm growth rates is formed by using the actual growth rate in sales of the merging firms in the five-year periods following the merger. The mean values of these growth rates are then again compared using the t-test. The tests are run on sales, total assets, assets net of depreciation on plant and equipment, employment, and leverage ratio. The same tests are also run using as the control group the growth rates in the various variables for the matched industry.

Stockholder Performance. To test whether the stockholders of the acquiring firm benefited from the merger, we must compute the rate of return on holding a share of the acquiring firm's stock before and after the merger. To test for an improvement in performance as measured by the return on stockholder equity, we chose to use as the before merger period the five years before the merger took place and to experiment with different postmerger periods for rates of return calculations. Since some of the gains from the merger may be anticipated slightly before or at the time the merger is announced, one of our "post"-merger periods is the year of the merger itself. We also calculated the rates of return on acquiring firm shares for the period of the merger plus the following year, the period of the merger plus the following two years, and the period of the merger plus the following three years.

Our first test of the profitability of the merger from the point of view of the stockholders was to form the difference in the rate of return on a share of the acquiring firm's stock in the postmerger period (defined in the four ways described above) and the premerger period. The control group sample was again drawn from nonmerging firms in the same industry and for the same periods of time. The difference in the rate of return for a nonmerging firm for the post- and premerger period was then formed to constitute one observation in the control group sample. The test for an improvement in performance of the acquiring firm was then to compare the mean change in rate of return on acquiring firms' stock to the mean rate of change for the same periods for the sample of nonacquiring firms using a t-test. As before, we compared the rates of return for the acquiring firms with observations on rates of return for all firms in the acquiring firms' industries for the comparable time periods. Our third test of performance along these lines, was again to project the rate of return performance of the acquiring firm, applying the industry trend rates to the premerger rates of return of the acquiring firm. These projected rates of return for the four different postmerger time periods constituted observations for the control group samples. The mean values of these projected rates of return were then compared with the mean values of their actual rates of return using a t-test.

To take into account the changes in risks that a merger may bring about, we computed the Sharpe measure of performance for the acquiring firm in the five-year premerger period, and the various postmerger periods as defined above. The change of performance as measured for one firm by this measure between the two periods then became one observation in the merger sample. We again chose a matched nonacquiring firm and computed the before and after merger Sharpe measures for this firm for the same time periods. This became an observation in our nonmerging sample. We then compared by means of a t-test the mean change in the Sharpe measure of performance for the acquiring firms to the mean change in performance for the nonacquiring firms. The same tests were repeated in the same way using the Treynor measure of performance. This completed our empirical tests of performance. The following appendix briefly states the esentials of each test for convenient future reference. The subsequent seven chapters use the same numbering when presenting the results for each test.

APPENDIX: LIST OF SPECIFIC TESTS

This appendix lists for easy reference the tests for determinants and effects of mergers described in Chapter 2. For each country, the results of these tests are preceded by analyses of the comparative characteristics of merging and nonmerging firms. A standard format is used in these comparisons. The groups compared are as follows:

AG   The sample of acquiring firms;
AD   The sample of acquired firms;
MAG   The sample of matched nonacquiring firms, matched by size and industry of the acquiring firm;
MAD   The sample of matched nonacquired firms, matched by size and industry of the acquired firm;
C   A control group sample of firms that neither made acquisitions nor were acquired during the study's time period.

The groups are compared in every case in terms of the mean values of the variables given below.

1. Size—measured usually by (a) sales, (b) the book value of the total assets of the firm, (c) the book value of the "net assets" (i.e., total assets—depreciation). The size of the acquired firm at the last

accounting date before takeover would then be compared with the size of the acquiring or the matched nonacquired firm at the corresponding date (i.e., the same accounting year). For reasons indicated earlier in the chapter, the analysis is done in terms of log size as well as size.

2. Profitability—measured in terms of (a) the rate of profit on equity, (b) the rate of profit on the firm's total net assets, (c) the ratio of profits to sales. The indicators are averaged over five years preceding the merger.

3. Variation in Profits—measured by the coefficient of variation of profits over the five years preceding the merger.

4. Growth—measured by the rate of growth of the size (i.e., sales or net assets) of the firm over the five years preceding the merger.

5. Leverage—measured by the ratio (debt/debt + equity) and averaged over the five years preceding the merger.

For each variable, the tables in the subsequent chapters report its mean value in group I ($\bar{X}_1$), the number of firms in the group (N_1, the mean values in group II ($\bar{X}_2$), and the number of firms in group II (N_2); the statistic ($\bar{X}_1 - \bar{X}_2)/S^{11}$ where S is an estimate of the assumed common standard deviation in the two populations (for the purposes of the t-test) is sometimes given, as is the statistical significance of the observed difference in group means. Where appropriate, the results of a nonparametric test (the binomial probability test) are also reported.

Finally, it should be noted that the premerger characteristics of the various groups of firms are also compared in terms of (1) the price-earnings ratio, measured over one, two, and three years respectively preceding the merger; and (2) the return on stockholder equity measured over one or more years preceding the merger. The results of these tests are reported in the sections on the determinants and effects of mergers.

Determinants and Effects

The tests for determinants and effects of mergers are given below. Subsequent chapters will present their results using the same numbering followed in this appendix. Except for tests 2.3 and 2.5, which deal with differences in variances and employ an F-test, all comparisons are between sample means using a standard t-test.

Tests for Determinants

Size Comparisons

1.1 Sales. The sum of the sales for the two merging firms in year t constitutes one observation for the merging sample. The sum of the sales for the two matched control group firms is one observation for the control group samples. The test compares the geometric means of the two samples.

1.2 Total assets. The same as 1.1 with total assets replacing sales.

1.3 Net of depreciation plant and equipment. The same as 1.1 with net plant and equipment replacing sales.

Risk Comparisons

2.1 Variation in profits. The coefficients of variation in profits for the two merging firms and the two control group firms are formed using data on profits for the five years preceding the merger. The ratio of the largest to the smallest of these is formed for the two merging firms. The same is done for the two control group firms. The means of these two samples are compared. Mean coefficients of variation in profits for acquiring and acquired firms were also compared with the means for the control groups.

2.2 Leverage (gearing) ratio. Leverage rates (debt/debt + equity) are formed for the two merging and control group firms. The mean absolute values of the differences in leverage ratios are then compared.

2.3 The variance in leverage ratios for acquiring firms is compared with that of the control group firms.

2.4 The mean leverage ratio for acquiring firms is tested against that for the control group.

2.5 The same as test 2.3 using acquired firms and their control group.

2.6 The same as test 2.4 using acquired firms and their control group.

Gort's Disturbance Theory

3.1 Change in price earnings ratio. The ratio of the highest to lowest P/Es for the acquired firm in the year preceding the merger is one observation for the merging sample. The analogous ratio is formed for the control group. The two sample means are compared.

3.2 The same ratios are formed for the two years preceding a merger for the merging and control group firms. The sample means are compared.

3.3 The same as 3.2 using data on the three years preceding the merger.

The Bargain Theory

4.1 The level of the price-earnings ratio. The mean of the high and low P/Es of the acquired firm in the year before the merger is one observation in the merger sample. The analogous mean constitutes one observation for the control group.

4.2 The same as 4.1 except averaged over the two years preceding the merger.

4.3 The same as 4.1 except averaged over the three years preceding the merger.

Tests for Effects

Profitability
5.1 Rate of profit on equity. The weighted average of the profit-to-equity ratios over the five years preceding the merger for the two merging firms is subtracted from the profit-to-equity ratio of the merged firm over the five years following the merger to form one observation for the merging sample. The analogous variable is formed for the control group pair, using weighted averages both before and after the merger. The two sample means are compared.

5.2 The same as 5.1 using profits on total assets.

5.3 The same as 5.1 using profits on sales.

6.1 Rate of profit on equity—industry comparisons. The weighted average of profits on equity for the two merging firms over the five years preceding the merger is divided into the profits-to-equity ratio for the merged firm over the five years after the merger to form one observation for the merger sample. The ratio of the average profit-equity ratio for all firms in the industry after the merger to average profits-equity before the merger is one observation in the control group. The two sample means are compared. (*Note*: When both firms are not in the same industry a weighted average of industry profit-equity ratios is used, with the equity values for the acquired and acquiring firms serving as weights.)

6.2 The same as 6.1 using profits on total assets.

6.3 The same as 6.1 using profits on sales.

7.1 Profits-equity—predicted performance tests. The ratio of post-merger year to premerger year profit to equity ratios is formed for the industry as in test 6.1. This ratio is then multiplied by the weighted average of the profit-to-equity ratios of the two merging firms over the five years preceding the merger to form an observation for the predicted profit-equity rate for the merged firm after the merger. This is then compared with its actual profit rate.

7.2 The same as 7.1 using profits on total assets.

7.3 The same as 7.1 using profit to sales.

Changes in Size and Leverage
8. Sales.

8.1a The difference between the growth in sales for the merged firm over the five years following the merger and the weighted average growth in sales for the two merging firms over the five years preceding the merger is one observation for the merger sample. The difference between the weighted average growth in sales for the two control group firms over the five year period after the merger and the five years before the merger is one observation for the control group. The mean differences between the two samples are compared.

8.1b   The same as 8.1a using ratios instead of differences.

8.2a,b   The same as 8.1a,b using total assets.

8.3a,b   The same as 8.1a,b using net of depreciation plant and equipment.

8.4a,b   The same as 8.1a,b using leverage.

8.5a,b   The same as 8.1a,b using employment.

9. Comparison with industry growth.

9.1 Sales. The mean growth rates of merging firms over the five postmerger years are compared with the mean growth rates of their respective industries.

9.2–9.5 These tests follow 9.1 using, respectively, total assets, net of depreciation plant and equipment, leverage, and employment.

10. Comparison with predicted performances.

10.1 Sales. The growth in sales for a merged firm over the five years following a merger is predicted from its premerger sales and the growth rates of the industry or industries of the two merging firms using the formula described in Chapter 2. The mean value of this predicted growth rate is compared with the mean value of the merging firms' actual growth rates.

10.2–10.5 These tests follow 10.1 using, respectively, total assets, net of depreciation plant and equipment, leverage, and employment.

Change in Return on Stockholder Equity

11.1 Comparison with Control Group. An observation for the merger sample is the difference between the return on a share of the acquiring firm's stock in year of the merger, t, and the average return on one of its shares over the five preceding years. An observation for the control group is defined analogously using a firm matched by size and industry to the acquiring firm. The means of the two samples are compared.

11.2 The same as 11.1 with the postmerger period defined as the year of the merger and the first year following it $(t, t + 1)$.

11.3 The same as 11.1 defining the postmerger period as $(t, t + 1, t + 2)$.

11.4 The same as 11.1 defining the postmerger period as $(t, t + 1, t + 2, t + 3)$.

12.1–12.4 Comparison with industry. Observations for the acquiring firms are formed as in test 11. For a control group observation, the average return on a share of stock for all firms in the acquiring firm's industry is used. The differences in means for these two samples are compared over the analogous time periods as in tests 11.1–11.4.

13.1–13.4 Comparisons with predicted performance. The observations for the acquiring firms are formed as in tests 11 and 12. The control group observations are formed by predicting the acquiring firm's return on a share of equity in the postmerger period from its premerger returns and the change in returns earned on the average share in the industry, as in the formula given in Chapter 2. The tests are run for the same periods as in tests 11 and 12.

Risk Adjusted Performance Tests

14.1 Sharp's measure. Sharp's measure of risk-adjusted rate of return is computed for the five years preceding the merger and the year of the merger. The difference between the two values becomes one observation for the merger sample. An observation for a control group firm matched by size and industry is defined analogously. The sample means are compared.

14.2–14.4 Analogous to 14.1 using respectively $(t, t + 1)$, $(t, t + 1, t + 2)$, and $(t, t + 1, t + 2, t + 3)$ as the postmerger time periods.

15.1–15.4 Treynor's measure. These tests are identical to those described under test 14, but with Treynor's measure, as described in Chapter 2, replacing Sharp's.

NOTES

1. For a brief survey of the potential tax advantages from mergers in the United States context and further references to the relevant literature, see Steiner (1975: 75–95).
2. John Lintner (1971:109,n.22) argues that the market price of the stock depends on the long and short holdings of all stockholders who hold a firm's stock. A reassessment of the firm's stock by some stockholders resulting in a change in stock price would, by Lintner's argument, lead to a change in the holdings of all other stockholders. Thus, the notion of a marginal stockholder is "mythical." While this is one view of the world, I do not see that it is the only reasonable view. The above arguments assume that a small change in a stock's price leads some stockholders to change their holdings (those on the "margin" of buying or selling) but leaves other holdings unchanged.
3. Gort argues that mergers are more likely in upswings in stock market activity than in downturns: "when security prices are low relative to their mean value over a period of years, managers and long-term investors will tend to consider the shares of their firm undervalued. The stockholders of firms that are potential acquirers, on the other hand, can be expected to resist acquisition prices that are far above those at which the individual investor can purchase securities in the open market on his personal account. Consequently, valuation discrepancies of the type needed for acquisitions to occur will be far more frequent in periods of high than in periods of low security prices" (1969:628). Thus, he assumes that stockholders and managers base their current valuations of their company's stock on the recent past, but nonholders do not. During an upswing stockholders will tend to undervalue the earnings' growth of their company—that is, they will tend to be bearish relative to nonholders. During a downswing they are again looking backward and tend to be bullish relative to nonholders. This asymmetry seems implausible unless one assumes

that managers of acquiring firms are somehow more prone to taking risks than other managers or than stockholders. This may in fact be a behaviorally realistic assumption, but it then begins to transform Gort's thesis into a variant on one of the managerial theories of the firm, since it is the wealth of their stockholders that managers are risking when they acquire other firms. The interpretation in the text assumes that an over- (under-) valuation of a company's stock at any given time is as likely for stockholders and managers, as a group, as it is for nonholders.

4. This point is discussed in detail by Markham (1955), who also surveys the relevant literature.

5. Evidence that this has occurred in the United States is reviewed in Mueller (1977).

6. Obviously, assumptions of constant marginal cost and economies of scale are not perfectly consistent. The constant marginal cost assumption is graphically convenient. The fall in costs can be most easily thought of as coming about via a shift to a larger and more efficient plant that has constant marginal costs over the relevant ranges of plant output.

7. Of course, the demand schedule for a single firm is drawn under a ceteris paribus assumption that is violated if the merger is between two firms in the same industry. But if the firms are relatively small this will not affect the discussion significantly. Here one might want to think of firms being in a Hotelling-like spatial competition along a linear market. If two firms some distance apart merge, horizontal summation of their demand schedules does not change the elasticity of the combined schedule. If two adjacent firms merge, interdependence is affected; the new demand schedule is more inelastic.

8. Many of these difficulties are explicitly recognized by Williamson in his seminal paper on this issue (Williamson 1968). They are developed further in a number of other contributions (Berry 1969; Crew and Rowley 1971; Davis and Whinston 1967; Posner 1969, 1975; Rowley and Peacock 1975; Rowley 1973).

9. This statement raises a number of interrelated issues and is based on a large literature that now exists for the United Kingdom economy. See further Singh (1977a) and the contributions in Blackaby (1979).

10. In many advanced countries (e.g., France and West Germany) exports are typically done by very large firms, and mergers may therefore lead to increased exports through the creation of bigger firms.

11. This statistic gives some additional information; it can be regarded as a rough indicator of the degree of overlap between the two groups. More precisely, when the variable is normally distributed and has equal variance in the two populations and when the two populations are of equal size, there is a simple relationship (tabulated in Cochran 1964) between $(\bar{X}_1 - \bar{X}_2)/S$ and the probability of misclassification. The latter refers to the probability of classifying a firm to one or the other of the two groups on the basis of the observed value of the variable and an appropriate decision rule that minimizes the probability of misclassification.

Chapter 3

Belgium, 1962–1974

Anne-Marie Kumps and Robert Wtterwulghe

GENERAL BACKGROUND

Trends and Merger Statistics

Mergers are one means for obtaining external growth. In Belgium one must distinguish between two forms of merger: a "merger" in the strict sense, in which two companies are joined to form a new legal entity with both of the merging companies disappearing as separate legal entities, and an absorption of one company by another in which only the former disappears. The difference between the two forms of merger is more legal than economic, however. We have thus analyzed both mergers sensu stricto and absorptions as "mergers," as this term is usually used by economists. It should be noted that for tax purposes, most "mergers" in Belgium actually occur in the legal form of an absorption.

We have excluded from this study two other forms of external growth that may have similar economic effects to mergers, but are quite different from a legal point of view. One is the direct transfer of a controlling interest from one party to another, and the other is a takeover bid. Takeover bids are under the control of the Banking Commission in the same way as new public issues; the direct transfer in

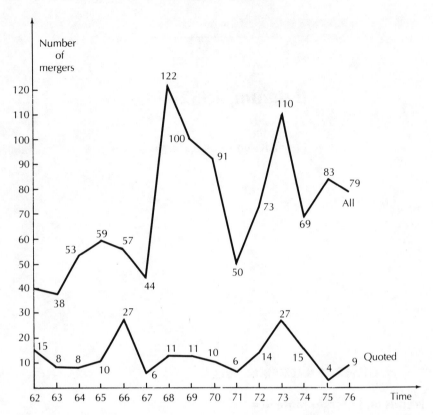

Figure 3–1. Number of mergers in Belgium, 1962–1976. (*Source:* DAFSA 1957–1976.)

fact allows the transaction to avoid falling under any specific institutional rules. It appears as a simple contract for the sale of shares and requires only a stockbroker or banker as intermediary. This freedom from surveillance explains why direct stock transfers are often used to transfer participation in control. Since no systematic data gathering for stock transfers of this type occurs, we are not able to include them in our study of merger activity. Figure 3–1 shows the evolution of mergers and absorptions of corporations that took place in Belgium during the period 1962–1976. It also includes the number of transactions involving at least one quoted company.

Some tendency toward a rise in merger activity appears over the considered time span. Two separate periods can be distinguished. Between 1962 and 1967 the annual amount of mergers varies little; from 1968 and 1976 the average annual level is higher and the variation much stronger. One also notices two peaks—1968 and 1973 with, respectively, 122 and 110 mergers—while in 1971 the level drops to 50. It is interesting to notice that the peaks have been observed during years marked by political events such as the troubles of May 1968 and the 1973 monetary crisis born from the dollar devaluation and the petroleum shortage. If one pushes further, one observes that the majority of mergers made during the year 1973 took place during the third quarter of that year and coincide precisely, therefore, with the marked rise in petroleum costs.

Not considering the years 1966 and 1973, the movement of mergers concerning at least one quoted company appears more stable and less oriented toward a rise than the movement relative to the whole of corporations.

Table 3–1 presents the evolution over time of the number of mergers, the gross national product at market price, and the stock exchange index. Figure 3–2 shows the evolution of these three variables. Note that, aside from the period running from 1969 to 1970, movements in the number of mergers and the stock exchange quotation indexes are similar. These indexes also show some concordance with changes in the level of GNP.

INSTITUTIONAL BACKGROUND

The analysis of an economic phenomenon like mergers cannot neglect the institutional aspect. So, we shall examine briefly the legal context in which this movement of mergers has developed in Belgium.

The Merger and the Protection of Shareholders and Creditors

In Belgium, mergers are not covered under company law. They are thus subject to the general principles of company law and are usually defined as "an agreement by which one or more companies bring, in an exchange of shares, the whole of their properties, either to another already existing company, or to a newly organized company which absorbs them."[1] As a contract, a merger requires the agreement of both companies.

In the case of an absorption, the operation is analyzed from the point of view of the acquiring company as an increase in capital by contribution in kind and for the acquired company as a liquidation. Doctrine and jurisprudence agree that these two decisions have to be taken by an extraordinary general meeting of shareholders governed according to the rules and necessary conditions for the modification of the bylaws. Moreover, the extraordinary general meeting of the acquiring company must have a report presented by an external auditor specially nominated by the board of directors.[2] In the case of a merger, the legal prescriptions are those relating to the creation of a new company and to the liquidation of the two former companies.

Table 3–1. Mergers, GNP, and Stock Prices, 1962–1976

	Number of Mergers				Rate of Variation of the Number of Mergers (percent)	GNP (market price) Basis 1963 = 100		Stock exchange index Basis 1963 = 100	
	1 quoted	2 quoted	Others	Total		Index	Rate of Variation (percent)	Index	Rate of Variation (percent)
1962	6	9	26	41	−7.4	95.5	+4.7	100.00	
1963	5	4	29	38	+39.0	100.0	+6.9	100.04	−1.0
1964	6	2	45	53	+11.0	106.9	+3.5	99.04	−14.0
1965	6	4	49	59	−3.5	110.6	+2.8	85.125	−4.0
1966	8	19	31	58	−23.0	113.7	+3.6	81.91	+7.0
1967	2	4	38	44	+177.0	117.6	+5.1	87.81	+8.0
1968	8	3	111	122	−22.0	123.6	+6.5	95.57	−5.0
1969	6	5	89	100	−9.0	132.6	+6.5	90.62	+9.5
1970	4	6	81	91	−45.0	140.5	+4.0	99.32	+13.0
1971	5	1	44	50	+46.0	145.7	+5.7	112.24	+19.0
1972	3	11	59	73	+50.0	154.5	+6.3	133.29	−20.0
1973	14	13	89	110	−37.0	164.2	+4.1	106.58	−1.5
1974	13	2	54	69	+20.0	170.9	−1.8	104.88	−5.0
1975	4	0	79	83	−5.0	167.8		99.93	
1976	4	5	70	79					

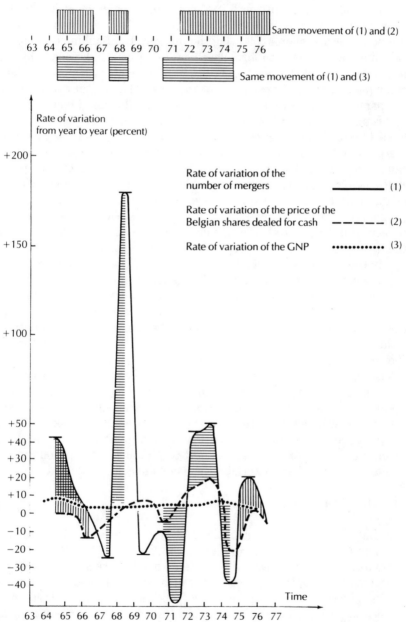

Figure 3–2. Cyclic variations in merger activity, common share prices, and GNP.

Aside from these legal requirements, it has become customary for merging companies, which call on public savings, to obtain first the advice of the Banking Commission.[3] The interested parties must in any case submit themselves to this audit procedure, once they request quotation for the newly issued shares following the merger. The Banking Commission has thus had occasion to formulate various recommendations, which fill to a certain extent the lacunae of the law on commercial companies. These recommendations are aimed at giving the shareholders of the two concerned companies the same types of information.[4] The Banking Commission has also reminded the companies that the law states that merging firms are to have identical social objectives. Until January 6, 1958, conglomerate mergers and some vertical mergers were impossible to consummate because they implied a change in the social objectives of the companies concerned. Such mergers were possible only with the unanimous consent of the shareholders. Since that date, following a change in the law on commercial companies, merging companies must submit special dispositions introducing a proceeding similar to the one concerning the change in the bylaws but characterized by stricter requirements.[5]

For the creditors of the acquired companies, the general principles of the law concerning bonds apply. The merger cannot interfere with their interests. It is, in fact, for them a *res inter allios acta*, and it is dependent upon the liquidator of the acquired company to take the necessary measures for payment of the debts. The creditors can take action against the acquiring company[6] and are in position to exercise the existing rights of the acquired company.

The legal system governing mergers has not been subjected to appreciable changes during the period studied. No rule has intervened to change the information constraints or the conditions for effectuating these transactions. By comparison with direct transfers of control, or takeover bids, mergers require decisions by an extraordinary general meeting of shareholders and in this respect are subject to additional information requirements that make their materialization more difficult.[7]

The Merger and The Worker

The Belgian law of September 20, 1948, established the Workers/Management Council. Since the royal decree of October 16, 1958, this council is compulsory for companies with more than 150 workers. This law was conceived as a crucial step toward democratization of the economy. It had as its objective the creation of a political body to facilitate communication between workers and management. The exchange of information through the Enterprise Council was to have provided workers a forum for bettering their situation in the company, but as yet this has not been practically achieved. Also adopted in 1973 was a new detailed rule that gives the Enterprise Council the right to certain forms of information.[8] The objective is to assure the workers a better inside view of the company. This information is much more detailed and thorough than the information available to the holders of the capital, who are legally considered owners of the company.

Besides the basic information, yearly and periodic, that is stipulated by this rule, the Enterprise Council has access to relevant information when new and important circumstances for the company appear.[9] In a merger, the Enterprise Councils of both companies have to be informed.

This requirement is legally limited to specified types of information from the company management and is obligatory whatever form the external growth takes. Since the obligation is limited to the provision of information, one cannot conclude that this legal requirement has influenced the movement of mergers in Belgium. Nevertheless, the requirement has led to informal negotiations with the trade unions whose purpose it is to ensure guarantees of employment and to obtain rights after the merger.[10] In addition, Belgian social legislation can have an indirect but important impact on the results of a merger. The social laws protect the right of employment. Consequently, worker dismissals as part of a reorganization and rationalization of the enterprise are often possible only at high cost.

The Control of Mergers by the State

The state's control of mergers can be considered in terms of the legal constraints imposed on the merging companies and the state's tax treatment of merging firms. Until now, the Belgian authorities have not considered it useful to require that mergers between Belgian companies submit to preliminary control by public authorities—with one exception. Mergers between banks are submitted to the Banking Commission for preliminary authorization.

The government has nevertheless required notification of acquisitions by individuals or corporations of national companies with assets of over one hundred million francs. This obligation to provide information, which, however, is not punishable, exists whatever the legal form utilized. In theory, it does not result in the prohibition of any mergers. Only one type of external growth, acquisition by public offer, is submitted to the discretional authorization of the Ministry of Finance when launched by a company from a country that is not a member of the EEC.[11] Thus, mergers have not been subject to specific governmental restrictions. A recently proposed law on competition policy, however, does aim to submit mergers to a preliminary control by the public authorities.

In contrast, the fiscal aspects of mergers have held the legislature's interest. Following the fiscal common law, a merger implies sharing of the companies' capital. In practice, the companies concerned are thus submitting to a special assessment established on the difference between the amounts distributed in cash, shares, or any other form and the fully paid capital still to be reimbursed.

The legislature has intervened to favor mergers by providing a neutral fiscal system. The first law was enacted, on temporary basis, in November 1953. It was refined in 1955. New legislation was taken in 1959 in the same direction. These rules have since been modified, notably in 1964, 1971, and 1973, but without changing either the general philosophy of the original act or the economic consequences for the companies. Under these rules, mergers can be realized in exemption of income tax duties. In a parallel way, the acquiring company is granted the benefit of the continuation of the amortization policy made by the acquired company. However, the acquiring company is not allowed to deduct from its taxable income a loss shown by the acquired company. To better insure fiscal neutrality, since 1964 the acquiring companies benefit from the rights of the acquired companies in matters of nontaxation of the deposits on the increased values or of the distribution of previously taxed reserve funds to the limit that these components can be found in their assets. The shareholders of acquired and merged companies benefit by the same fiscal neutrality. The "increased values" they experience are considered as not realized.[12]

Mergers are also subject to indirect taxation, for they imply, as we have seen, a contribution in kind. For this reason, they should be submitted to the common law on shareholder contributions. Since 1965, the contributions realized via merger are submitted to a duty reduced by one-half, insofar as the contributions are realized on behalf of an acquiring company having its real management office on the territory of a member of the EEC.[13]

GENERAL CHARACTERISTICS
OF MERGING FIRMS

This section compares the characteristics of acquiring and acquired firms with those of companies that were not participants to a merger. Our analysis concerns all the acquisitions of 100 percent of the assets or stocks of another company during the period 1962–1974. Since we shall study some characteristics over a five-year period before merger, our control firms are those that were not involved in a merger during the period 1957–1974.

Our sample of acquiring, acquired, and control firms consists only of quoted companies of the manufacturing and retail sectors. We consequently excluded banks, insurance companies, electricity trusts, holding companies, transports, coal mining, and miscellaneous industries.

The group of acquiring firms includes all the quoted companies that undertook a merger (forty), the group of acquired firms includes all the quoted companies that were taken over during the period (thirty-five), and the control group includes all the firms that neither acquired nor were acquired themselves (eighty). We also have seven firms that were acquiring and acquired later on. Thus our sample includes one hundred and sixty-two firms. For this section we did not work with "matched" samples of acquiring and acquired firms.

Variables Used

The comparison of the characteristics of the acquired, acquiring, and other firms are made in terms of the following main variables—size, profitability, profits variability, leverage, and growth. These variables are approximated by a number of different indicators, based on the accounting data of the individual firms. Size is measured as the "book" value of net and total assets. Profitability is measured by posttax profits on equity and total assets and gross trading profit on equity and total assets. Profit variability is measured by the coefficient of variation of the firm's profits. The indicators of profit mentioned above are used for this test. Leverage is expressed in four ways: long-term liabilities as a percentage of total equity; short-term liabilities as a percentage of total assets; total debts as a percentage of total assets; and long-term liabilities as a percentage of short-term liabilities. Growth of size, profitability, and leverage are also calculated, utilizing for profitability and leverage the four indicators mentioned above.

Time Period Used

The characteristics of the various groups of firms are compared on inter-firm cross-sections. For profitability, variability of profits, leverage, and growth, the value of each indicator is averaged over the five accounting years before acquisition for the acquiring and acquired firms and over a comparable period for the control groups. Size and leverage are measured by the book value of the firm's net or total assets at the last accounting year before merger. We also calculated leverage for the year before the merger.

Comparison of Acquired and Acquiring Firms

Table 3–2 illustrates a selection of results comparing the characteristics of the group of acquiring with those of acquired firms. The results pertain to all industries together and may therefore be subject to an aggregation bias. There are indeed important interindustry differences in the characteristics of firms, and the objectives for mergers could differ between industries. Nevertheless, our sample was too small to conduct an analysis on an individual industry basis.

Table 3–2. Comparison of the Characteristics of Acquiring and Acquired Firms

Variable	Company Type		Number of Observations		Mean Value		t^a	Statistical Significance (percent)
	1	2	n_1	n_2	$\bar{x}_1$	$\bar{x}_2$		
Size ($t - 1$)								
Equity	AG	AD	68	39	3,584,910,964	923,312,771	0.002	<1
Total assets	AG	AD	68	39	5,094,461,087	1,309,869,710	0.001	<1
Profitability ($t - 1, t - 5$)								
Net profit/equity	AG	AD	67	39	0.044	0.052	0.431	No
Trading profit/equity	AG	AD	67	39	0.195	0.161	0.370	No
Net profit/total assets	AG	AD	67	39	0.030	0.036	0.335	No
Trading profit/total assets	AG	AD	67	39	0.120	0.105	0.401	No
Coefficient of variation ($t - 1, t - 5$)								
Net profit/equity	AG	AD	59	36	0.008	0.370	0.120	No
Trading profit/equity	AG	AD	59	36	0.244	0.262	0.978	No
Net profit/total assets	AG	AD	59	36	0.193	0.344	0.487	No
Trading profit/total assets	AG	AD	59	36	0.840	0.261	0.186	No
Leverage ($t - 1, t - 5$)								
Long-term debt/equity	AG	AD	59	36	0.212	0.182	0.316	No
Total debt/total assets	AG	AD	59	36	0.438	0.363	0.071	7
Long-term debt/short-term debt	AG	AD	59	36	0.782	0.925	0.406	No
Short-term debt/total assets	AG	AD	59	36	0.290	0.221	0.059	6
Leverage ($t - 1$)								
Long-term debt/equity	AG	AD	68	39	0.239	0.173	0.031	3
Total debt/total assets	AG	AD	68	39	0.456	0.366	0.028	3
Long-term debt/short-term debt	AG	AD	68	39	0.842	0.747	0.565	No
Short-term debt/total assets	AG	AD	68	39	0.293	0.240	0.157	No

Table 3–2. *(continued)*

Variable	Company Type		Number of Observations		Mean Value		t^a	Statistical Significance (percent)
	1	2	n_1	n_2	$\bar{x}_1$	$\bar{x}_2$		
Growth ($t - 1, t - 5$)								
Total assets	AG	AD	59	36	0.129	0.064	0.048	5
Net profit/equity	AG	AD	59	36	0.032	0.086	0.641	No
Trading profit/equity	AG	AD	59	36	0.025	0.093	0.351	No
Net profit/total assets	AG	AD	59	36	0.031	0.061	0.770	No
Trading profit/total assets	AG	AD	59	36	0.039	0.059	0.766	No
Long-term debt/equity	AG	AD	59	36	0.100	0.084	0.835	No
Total debt/total assets	AG	AD	59	36	0.040	0.074	0.381	No
Long-term debt/short-term debt	AG	AD	59	36	0.177	0.016	0.061	6
Short-term debts/total assets	AG	AD	59	36	0.030	0.096	0.077	8

[a]To test the various hypotheses about the determinants and the effects of the mergers in Belgium, we have used a subroutine that does not show the classical value of t as a result. But the subroutine directly provides the total value of the areas of the student distribution from the lower and upper tails to the computed (but not shown) t. Thus, the result of the t-test computed by the subroutine is a rate that is the probability of error if H_0 is rejected, assuming H_0 is true. This rate is compared with the level $\alpha = 10$ percent that we have chosen as the significance level.

Concerning the size variable, it appears from Table 3–2 that the mean differences between acquiring and acquired firms are statistically significant (at the 1 percent level). In terms of equity and total assets, acquiring companies are several times larger than acquired companies. Indeed, the average size of acquiring firms (in millions of Belgian francs) is 3,584.9 in terms of equity and 5,094.5 in terms of total assets, while the mean of the acquired firms is only 932.3 in terms of equity and 1,310.0 in terms of total assets.

The leverage figures show that the ratios of total debts to total assets and short-term liabilities to total assets are larger for the acquiring group. The difference is significant at the 7 and 6 percent levels, respectively. Total debt represents 0.438 of total assets in the acquiring group while the ratio is 0.363 in the acquired group. Acquiring firms seem more levered as measured by short-term debt than acquired firms. This difference is, however, not significant for the year before merger. During this later period, the ratio of long-term liabilities on total equity is larger in the acquiring group, 0.239, versus 0.173 in the acquired group.

With respect to growth, the rate of growth in total assets is larger for the acquiring firms than for the firms they acquired. The differences between the rates of growth of long-term to short-term debts, and short-term liabilities to total assets are also significant. Acquiring firms seem to accrue long-term liabilities, while acquired firms accrue short-term debts. These results confirm that there is no significant difference between acquiring and acquired firms in the year before merger in terms of short-term debt on total assets. The figures of Table 3–2 show that there is no difference between the profitability of acquiring and acquired firms. This fact seems to prove that there is no favorable financial leverage in the acquiring group. Except in terms of trading profit on total assets, the profitability of the acquiring group is more stable than that of the acquired group. The difference between the coefficients of variation is not significant, however.

Comparison of Acquiring and Nonacquiring Companies

Table 3–3 gives the differences between the characteristics of the acquiring companies and the control group of all nonacquiring and non-acquired firms. Indeed, each indicator of an acquiring company is compared with the mean of the indicators for all companies of the same sector for a similar period. Table 3–3 shows that acquiring companies are larger than the control firms and that they have a much faster growth rate of total assets. The results are significant at the 0 and 5 percent level, respectively.

Concerning profitability, it appears with respect to the four tests that acquiring companies are significantly less profitable than the control group

—3.8 versus 7.1 percent in terms of net profit on equity and 2.6 versus 3.8 percent in terms of net profit on total assets. In relation to the profit variability, there is only a significant difference in terms of net profit to equity. The acquiring firms appear much more stable than the other group—0.008 versus 0.402. This phenomenon confirms that the acquiring firms, while not very profitable, are nevertheless firms whose profits are relatively stable.

With respect to leverage, there are no significant differences between the two groups, except for the year before the merger, where the proportion of long-term liabilities to equity is significantly higher for the acquiring group—0.234 versus 0.196. Concerning the rate of growth of profitability or leverage, there is no difference.

Comparison of Acquired and Control Firms

Table 3–4 shows the differences between the acquired and the control group firms. There exist no significant differences between the two groups in either size or growth in size.

With respect to profitability, acquired firms are on average less profitable than the control firms. The result is, however, significant only for trading profits. On the other hand, the growth rate of profitability is higher for the acquired group, and the difference is again significant for trading profits. This result can be partially attributable to the formula used— profitability $(t - 1)$ − profitability $(t - 5)$/profitability $(t - 1/4)$. Indeed, in the year before acquisition, the balance sheets of the acquired firms are often redressed. With respect to leverage, acquired firms appear significantly less levered in terms of total debt to total assets and short-term liabilities. Again, these two indicators of leverage grow at a faster rate for the acquired group—7 and 9 percent against 0.9 and 0.7 percent for the control group.

The statistically significant differences between acquired, acquiring, and other companies can be summarized as follows:

Size: acquiring > acquired = others;
Profitability: others > acquired = acquiring;
Total debt/total assets: acquiring > acquired < others;
Short-term debt/total assets: acquiring > acquired < others;
Growth of total assets: acquiring > acquired = others.

In conclusion, it appears that the acquiring firms are significantly bigger in terms of total and net assets than the firms they acquire. Furthermore, there exists no difference in size between the acquired and control companies. Concerning profitability, we see that acquiring and acquired

Table 3-3. Comparison of the Characteristics of Acquiring and Control Firms

Variable	Company Type		Number of Observations		Mean Value		t^a	Statistical Significance (percent)
	1	2	n_1	n_2^a	$\bar{x}_1$	$\bar{x}_2$		
Size (t − 1)								
Equity	AG	C	59	59	2,534,213,349	578,105,348	0.002	<1
Total assets	AG	C	59	59	3,556,449,578	842,403,280	0.002	<1
Profitability (t − 1, t − 5)								
Net profit/equity	AG	C	59	58^b	0.038	0.071	0.001	<1
Trading profit/equity	AG	C	59	58	0.197	0.261	0.081	8
Net profit/total assets	AG	C	59	58	0.026	0.038	0.037	4
Trading profit/total assets	AG	C	59	58	0.119	0.165	0.009	<1
Coefficient of variation (t − 1, t − 5)								
Net profit/equity	AG	C	59	58	0.008	0.402	0.085	8
Trading profit/equity	AG	C	59	58	0.244	0.155	0.589	No
Net profit/total assets	AG	C	59	58	0.193	0.795	0.112	No
Trading profit/total assets	AG	C	59	58	0.840^c	0.094	0.261	No
Leverage (t − 1, t − 5)								
Long-term debt/equity	AG	C	59	58	0.212	0.182	0.241	No
Total debt/total assets	AG	C	59	58	0.438	0.462	0.419	No
Long-term debt/short-term debt	AG	C	59	58	0.782	0.763	0.881	No
Short-term debt/total assets	AG	C	59	58	0.290	0.327	0.234	No
Leverage (t − 1)								
Long-term debt/equity	AG	C	60	60	0.234	0.196	0.071	7
Total debt/total assets	AG	C	60	60	0.460	0.474	0.685	No
Long-term debt/short-term debt	AG	C	60	60	0.841	0.663	0.159	No
Short-term debt/total assets	AG	C	60	60	0.300	0.357	0.162	No

Table 3–3. *(continued)*

Variable	Company Type		Number of Observations		Mean Value		t^a	Statistical Significance (percent)
	1	2	n_1	n_2^a	$\bar{x}_1$	$\bar{x}_2$		
Growth $(t − 1, t − 5)$	AG	C	59	58	0.129	0.070	0.056	6
Total assets	AG	C	59	58	0.032	−0.010	0.589	No
Net profit/equity	AG	C	59	58	0.025	−0.008	0.327	No
Trading profit/equity	AG	C	59	58	0.031	−0.001	0.658	No
Net profit/total assets	AG	C	59	58	0.039	−0.010	0.129	No
Trading profit/total assets	AG	C	59	58	0.100	0.047	0.279	No
Long-term debt/equity	AG	C	59	58	0.040	0.015	0.144	No
Total debt/total assets	AG	C	59	58	0.177	0.035	0.091	9
Long-term debt/short-term debt	AG	C	59	58	0.030	0.009	0.218	No
Short-term debts/total assets	AG	C	59	58				

[a] Each characteristic of acquiring firms was compared to the mean of the same characteristic of all control firms of the same sector for the same period.

[b] For one acquiring firm (5311), we had no data for the control firms, so $n_1 = 59$ and $n_2 = 58$.

[c] If we eliminate two firms (1722 and 2212), we obtain $\mu_1 = 0.230$.

Table 3–4. Comparison of the Characteristics of Acquired and Control Firms

Variable	Company Type 1	Company Type 2	Number of Observations n_1	Number of Observations n_2	Mean Value $\bar{x}_1$	Mean Value $\bar{x}_2$	t	Statistical Significance (percent)
Size ($t - 1$)								
Equity	AD	C	36	36	990,413,703	857,814,795	0.636	No
Total assets	AD	C	36	36	1,385,997,287	1,175,538,983	0.655	No
Profitability ($t - 1, t - 5$)								
Net profit/equity	AD	C	36	36	0.055	0.072	0.132	No
Trading profit/equity	AD	C	36	36	0.171	0.224	0.068	7
Net profit/total assets	AD	C	36	36	0.037	0.042	0.514	No
Trading profit/total assets	AD	C	36	36	0.111	0.145	0.056	6
Coefficient of variation ($t - 1, t - 5$)								
Net profit/equity	AD	C	36	36	0.370	0.530	0.161	No
Trading profit/equity	AD	C	36	36	0.262	0.253	0.867	No
Net profit/total assets	AD	C	36	36	0.344	0.777	0.301	No
Trading profit/total assets	AD	C	36	36	0.261	0.257	0.947	No
Leverage ($t - 1, t - 5$)								
Long-term debt/equity	AD	C	36	36	0.182	0.206	0.344	No
Total debt/total assets	AD	C	36	36	0.363	0.437	0.035	3
Long-term debt/short-term debt	AD	C	36	36	0.925	1.007	0.665	No
Short-term debt/total assets	AD	C	36	36	0.221	0.284	0.050	5
Leverage ($t - 1$)								
Long-term debt/equity	AD	C	36	36	0.187	0.208	0.424	No
Total debt/total assets	AD	C	36	36	0.382	0.445	0.071	7
Long-term debt/short-term debt	AD	C	36	36	0.809	0.740	0.680	No
Short-term debt/total assets	AD	C	36	36	0.246	0.290	0.178	No

Table 3–4. *(continued)*

Variable	Company Type		Number of Observations		Mean Value		t	Statistical Significance (percent)
	1	2	n_1	n_2^a	$\bar{x}_1$	$\bar{x}_2$		
Growth ($t - 1, t - 5$)								
Total assets	AD	C	36	36	0.064	0.076	0.398	No
Net profit/equity	AD	C	36	36	0.086	-0.041	0.258	No
Trading profit/equity	AD	C	36	36	0.093	-0.066	0.028	3
Net profit/total assets	AD	C	36	36	0.061	-0.063	0.201	No
Trading profit/total assets	AD	C	36	36	0.059	-0.067	0.054	5
Long-term debt/equity	AD	C	36	36	0.084	0.027	0.350	No
Total debt/total assets	AD	C	36	36	0.074	0.009	0.041	4
Long-term debt/short-term debt	AD	C	36	36	0.016	-0.027	0.216	No
Short-term debts/total assets	AD	C	36	36	0.096	0.007	0.011	1

firms are less profitable than comparable nonmerging firms. The growth rate of assets is faster for the acquiring group than for the acquired and control samples. This observation is more consistent with a search for size objective than with profit maximization.

One concludes that the companies that do not participate in any merger during the studied period have an average profitability higher than the ones that do participate, either as acquiring or as acquired, in the merger process. This comparison goes against the neoclassical theory, where the optimal allocation of resources would imply the takeover of the least effective companies (i.e., the least profitable) by the managers of the best performing firms. Here the acquiring companies appear to be no better managed than the companies they acquire. With respect to the ratio of debt to total assets, it appears that the acquiring firms are more levered than the firms they acquire, which are in turn less levered than the control firms.

REPORT OF BASIC FINDINGS

The preceding section has compared the characteristics of the acquiring, acquired, and control quoted firms. This section examines the determinants and effects of mergers between quoted companies during the period 1962–1974. The selected firms have been grouped into industries on a two-digit level of aggregation, namely:

- Plantation and breeding (farming and livestock),
- Construction,
- Food and drink industries,
- Textile industries,
- Paper products,
- Chemical industries,
- Mineral oil refining,
- Pottery and glass,
- Iron and steel,
- Metal products,
- Gas and electricity,
- Retail sector.

Seeing that we have no control firms in three sectors—plantation and breeding, mineral oil refining, and pottery and glass—we excluded from our analysis the mergers undertaken in those sectors. (namely, Federated Malay Rubber Company [0801]; Plantations de Telok–Dalam [0802]; and Petrofina–Petrocom [2901–2902]. A complete list of the thirty-five studied mergers is available from the authors.) In total we have twenty acquiring firms from which eighteen were pure acquiring and two were acquiring but were then acquired later (Henelgaz [4901]; Cie Belge pour l'exploitation du gaz et de l'électricité du Borinage [4904]); thirty-five acquired firms in which four were acquiring before being acquired (Metallurgie d'Espérance Longdoz [3305]; Cie des Metaux d'Overpelt Lommel et Corphalie [3316]; Cie Belge pour l'exploitation du gaz et de l'électricité en Elandra Occidentale [4904]); and seventy-eight control firms.

Data

We encountered many difficulties gathering the data needed to test the several hypotheses on the determinants and effects of mergers presented in Chapter 2. We do not possess in Belgium a standardized accounting plan, so we had to render the balance sheets of the firms homogeneous. A description of the data is available separately from the authors. It is important to note that for Belgium it was impossible to find data concerning sales, employment, and profits before taxes for all the firms during the studied period. Thus, we were not able to compute all the tests. And as we did not possess data concerning the market return of all securities, we have eliminated Formula 14, the Sharpe and Treynor measures.

Interpretation of the Results
of the Specific Tests

The results of the statistical tests are presented in detail in Table 3–5 and numbered in the same order as in the other chapters.

Determinants. *Size comparisons.* We have approached the problem of the respective size of merging and control firms, both in terms of total assets and net of depreciation plant and equipment in two ways. First, we have compared the average size of acquiring plus acquired firms to the average size of two matched (paired) control firms selected at random in the same sector, for the year before the merger.

Second, we have compared the average size of acquiring and acquired firms to the average size of all the control firms of the concerned sector. When a firm undertook several operations during a year, we have considered it as one merger. This fact explains why we have twenty-six mergers in the sample.[14] Analysis of the table shows that all the results are significant. The average size of a merging firm is 7386 million in total assets while that of a control firm is 906 million and that of a matched pair of nonmerging firms is 1788 million. Therefore, it seems reasonable to reject

Table 3–5. Results of the Statistical Tests

Formula Version Test	Variable	Company Type		Number of Observations		Mean Value		t^a	Statistical Significance (percent)
		1	2	n_1	n_2	$\bar{x}_1$	$\bar{x}_2$		
	Determinants								
	Size comparisons								
1.1	Data not available								
1.2	Total assets, arithmetic mean $t-1$	AGAD	MAGAD	26	26	7,385,618,560	1,788,277,941	0.023	2
Extra test	Total assets, arithmetic mean $t-1$	AGAD	C	26	26	7,385,618,560	906,515,512	0.009	1
1.3	Net of depreciation plant and equipment, arithmetic mean $t-1$	AGAD	MAGAD	26	26	4,247,352,188	1,151,982,567	0.056	6
Extra test	Net of depreciation plant and equipment, arithmetic mean $t-1$	AGAD	C	26	26	4,247,352,188	573,239,773	0.024	2
	Risk comparisons								
2.1a	Ratio of coefficients of variation of profits								
	Net income/equity	AGAD	MAGAD	35	26	7.112	7.685	0.876	No
	Trading profits/equity	AGAD	MAGAD	35	26	3.257	4.773	0.232	No
	Net income/total assets	AGAD	MAGAD	35	26	5.003	8.634	0.082	8
	Trading profits/total assets	AGAD	MAGAD	35	26	3.544	5.372	0.159	No
2.1b	Coefficient of variation of profits, mean								
	Net income/equity	AG	C	26	26	0.135	0.453	0.323	No
	Trading profits/equity	AG	C	26	26	0.294	0.177	0.058	6
	Net income/total assets	AG	C	26	26	0.514	0.775	0.656	No
	Trading profits/total assets	AG	C	26	26	0.295	0.180	0.059	6

Table 3–5. *(continued)*

Formula Version Test	Variable	Company Type		Number of Observations		Mean Value		t^a	Statistical Significance (percent)
		1	2	n_1	n_2	$\bar{x}_1$	$\bar{x}_2$		
	Net income/equity	AD	C	35	35	0.417	0.542	0.236	No
	Trading profits/equity	AD	C	35	35	0.265	0.258	0.901	No
	Net income/total assets	AD	C	35	35	0.397	0.799	0.346	No
	Trading profits/total assets	AD	C	35	35	0.250	0.263	0.810	No
	Net income/equity	AG	AD	26	35	0.135	0.417	0.379	No
	Trading profits/equity	AG	AD	26	35	0.294	0.265	0.660	No
	Net income/total assets	AG	AD	26	35	0.514	0.397	0.504	No
	Trading profit/total assets	AG	AD	26	35	0.295	0.250	0.491	No
2.2	Leverage ratios, difference ($t-1, t-5$)	AGAD	MAGAD	35	35	0.208	0.248	0.574	No
2.3	Leverage ratios, variance ($t-1$)	AG	C	26	26	0.022	0.003	F0.000	<1
2.4	Leverage ratios, mean ($t-1$)	AG	C	35	35	0.233	0.198	0.271	No
2.5	Leverage ratios, variance ($t-1$)	AD	C	35	35	0.021	0.003	F0.000	<1
2.6	Leverage ratios, mean ($t-1$)	AD	C	35	35	0.184	0.212	0.311	No
Extra test	Leverage ratios, mean ($t-1$)	AG	MAG	26	26	0.233	0.238	0.914	No
Extra test	Leverage ratios, mean ($t-1$)	AD	MAD	35	35	0.184	0.149	0.395	No
3.1	Gort's disturbance theory P/E ratio ($t-1$) ratio high to low	AD	C	35	35	1.328	1.405	0.088	9
3.2	P/E ratio ($t-1, T-2$) ratio high to low	AD	C	35	35	1.299	1.368	0.070	7
3.3	P/E ratio ($t-1, t-2, t-3$) ratio high to low	AD	C	35	35	1.306	1.371	0.057	6

Table 3–5. (continued)

Formula Version Test	Variable	Company Type 1	Company Type 2	Number of Observations n_1	n_2	Mean Value $\bar{x}_1$	$\bar{x}_2$	t^a	Statistical Significance (percent)
	Bargain theory								
4.1	P/E ratio ($t - 1$) mean value	AD	C	34	34	10.354	2.858	0.247	No
4.2	P/E ratio ($t - 1$, $t - 2$) mean value	AD	C	34	34	31.351	9.077	0.075	7
4.3	P/E ratio ($t - 1$, $t - 2$, $t - 3$) mean value	AD	C	33	33	29.369	11.607	0.085	8
	Effects								
	Profitability								
5.1	Net income/equity 5 years after the merger minus 5 years before	AGAD	MAGAD	21	21	−0.004	−0.019	0.114	No
5.2	Net income/total assets 5 years after the merger minus 5 years before	AGAD	MAGAD	21	21	−0.004	−0.016	0.027	3
5.3	Data not available								
6.1	Net income/equity 5 years before merger divided by 5 years after	AGAD	C	21	19	0.769	0.571	0.454	No
6.2	Net income/total assets 5 years before the merger divided by 5 years after	AGAD	C	21	19	0.836	0.787	0.897	No
6.3	Data not available								
7.1	Net income/equity ($t + 5$)	AGAD actual	AGAD predicted	19	19	0.040	0.029	0.394	No
	Net income/total assets ($t + 5$)	AGAD actual	AGAD predicted	19	19	0.026	0.023	0.806	No
7.2	Data not available								

Table 3–5. *(continued)*

Formula Version Test	Variable	Company Type		Number of Observations		Mean Value		t^a	Statistical Significance (percent)
		1	2	n_1	n_2	$\bar{x}_1$	$\bar{x}_2$		
8.1	Changes size leverage Data not available								
8.2a	Total assets; growth rate 5 years after minus 5 years before	AGAD	MAGAD	21	21	0.014	0.007	0.854	No
8.2b	Total assets; ratio of growth rates 5 years after to 5 years before	AGAD	MAGAD	21	21	2.394	1.424	0.213	No
8.3a	Net of depreciation plant and equipment; growth rates difference	AGAD	MAGAD	21	21	0.022	0.006	0.750	No
8.3b	Net of depreciation plant and equipment; ratio of the growth rates	AGAD	MAGAD	21	21	2.397	4.801	0.287	No
8.4a	Leverage growth rates difference	AGAD	MAGAD	21	21	-0.042	0.025	0.128	No
8.4b	Leverage ratio of the growth rates	AGAD	MAGAD	21	21	1.901	2.672	0.345	No
8.5	Data not available								
9.1	Data not available								
9.2	Total assets; growth rate 5 years after the merger	AGAD	C	20	20	0.116	0.315	0.436	No
9.3	Net of depreciation plant; growth rate 5 years after the merger	AGAD	C	20	20	0.124	0.070	0.306	No
9.4	Leverage growth rate 5 years after the merger	AGAD	C	21	21	-0.002	-0.026	0.277	No
9.5	Data not available								

Table 3–5. *(continued)*

Formula Version Test	Variable	Company Type		Number of Observations		Mean Value		t^a	Statistical Significance (percent)
		1	2	n_1	n_2	$\bar{x}_1$	$\bar{x}_2$		
10.1	Data not available								
10.2	Total assets ($t + 5$)	AGAD actual	AGAD predicted	17	17	9,357,182,625	8,910,531,472	0.929	No
	Total assets ($t + 5$)	AGAD actual	AGAD predicted	20	20	11,710,933,320	13,275,088,250	0.804	No
10.3	Net of depreciation plant and equipment ($t + 5$)	AGAD actual	AGAD predicted	17	17	5,893,173,897	5,796,841,039	0.978	No
	Net of depreciation plant and equipment ($t + 5$)	AGAD actual	AGAD predicted	20	20	6,885,375,499	7,633,087,157	0.845	No
10.4	Leverage ($t + 5$)	AGAD actual	AGAD predicted	17	17	0.270	0.338	0.225	No
	Leverage ($t + 5$)	AGAD actual	AGAD predicted	20	20	0.279	0.327	0.347	No
10.5	Data not available								
	Changes, stockholder performance								
11.1	Return (t, $t − 5$, $t − 1$)	AG	MAG	26	26	−0.029	0.018	0.077	8
11.2	Return (t, $t + 1$, $t − 5$, $t − 1$)	AG	MAG	26	26	−0.053	−0.021	0.378	No
11.3	Return (t, $t + 1$, $t + 2$, $t − 5$, $t − 1$)	AG	MAG	26	26	−0.041	−0.007	0.308	No
11.4	Return (t, $t + 1$, $t + 2$, $t + 3$, $t − 5$, $t − 1$)	AG	MAG	23	23	−0.033	0.028	0.162	No
12.1	Return (t, $t − 5$, $t − 1$)	AG	C	26	26	−0.029	−0.019	0.699	No
12.2	Return (t, $t + 1$, $t − 5$, $t − 1$)	AG	C	26	26	−0.053	−0.026	0.405	No
12.3	Return (t, $t + 1$, $t + 2$, $t − 5$, $t − 1$)	AG	C	26	26	−0.041	−0.008	0.283	No

Table 3–5. *(continued)*

Formula Version Test	Variable	Company Type		Number of Observations		Mean Value		t^a	Statistical Significance (percent)
		1	2	n_1	n_2	$\bar{x}_1$	$\bar{x}_2$		
13.1	Return (t)	AG actual	AG predicted	25	25	0.046	−0.037	0.035	3
	Return (t)	AG actual	AG predicted	26	26	0.045	0.001	0.420	No
13.2	Return (t, t + 1)	AG actual	AG predicted	25	25	0.021	−0.047	0.255	No
	Return (t, t + 1)	AG actual	AG predicted	26	26	0.020	0.068	0.713	No
13.3	Return (t, t + 1, t + 2)	AG actual	AG predicted	25	25	0.032	−0.085	0.142	No
	Return (t, t + 1, t + 2)	AG actual	AG predicted	26	26	0.033	0.587	0.420	No
	Risk-adjusted performance tests								
14	Data not available								
15	Data not available								

[a]To test the various hypotheses about the determinants and the effects of the mergers in Belgium, we have used a subroutine that does not show the classical value of t as a result. But the subroutine directly provides the total value of the areas of the student distribution from the lower and upper tails to the computed (but not shown) t. Thus, the result of the t-test computed by the subroutine is a rate that is the probability of error if H_0 is rejected, assuming H_0 is true. This rate is compared with the level $\alpha = 10$ percent that we have chosen as the significance level.

the hypothesis that, in Belgium, mergers are to obtain economies of scale; merging companies are larger in average size than two randomly selected firms, as well as larger than the average of all nonmerging companies. To the contrary, it seems more likely that mergers are motivated to achieve market and extramarket power. Nevertheless, since this conclusion is based on comparisons on the Belgian national market alone, it has to be tempered. A comparison at the EEC level could show that the size of merging firms is similar to that of other European firms in the same sector.

Risk Comparisons. The second test (2.1a) computes, for a five-year period before merger, the ratio of the coefficients of variation in profits of acquiring and acquired firms and compares it to that of two firms chosen at random in the same sector, the largest coefficient of variation being always put in the numerator. If one firm undertook several acquisitions in the same year, we only took into consideration one observation for the control group, so we have thirty-five pairs of acquiring-acquired firms and twenty-six pairs of control firms. The coefficient of variation is analyzed in different ways. First, net profit and trading profit are reported each time to equity. Then this coefficient is calculated using net profits and trading profits to total assets. Analysis of Table 3–5 shows that the mean of the ratio of coefficients of variation of merging firms is systematically below the mean of the ratio of the coefficients of variation of control firms. However, only the coefficient concerning net profits to total assets is statistically significant and of such magnitude as to be of economic interest —5 for the merging firms and 8.63 for the control pairs. The merging firms seem to have more stable net profit. This result should be compared to the results stated in the preceding section, which seem to demonstrate that acquiring and acquired firms are less profitable than control firms. These firms seem to follow a policy of profit stabilization instead of one of maximization of profit. We shall see that this analysis has to be further refined by taking into account the difference between net and trading profit.

Formula 2.1b compares the mean of the coefficients of variation of profits in the various groups of companies —acquiring toward control, acquired toward control, and acquiring toward acquired firms. Table 3–5 shows that most of the results are not statistically significant. When comparing the coefficients of variation of trading profits to equity and of trading profits to total assets, we see that on the average, the coefficient of variation of acquiring firms is higher than that of control firms—respectively, 0.294 against 0.177 for trading profits to equity, and 0.295 against 0.180 for trading profits to total assets. When net profits are used, the opposite result appears, although the tests are not significant. These differences probably stem from the definitions of net and trading profits. Trading profits vary directly with the commercial activities of the company, while net profits also reflect the company's self-financing, capital depreciation, and profit distribution policies. The results seem to suggest that acquiring companies adjust their self-financing and depreciation policies more systematically to stabilize their net profits, perhaps because they must rely on these funds to pursue their external growth objectives.

Two tests were made using leverage. The first covers five years before the merger and compares the differences in absolute values between leverage ratios of acquiring and acquired companies with those of randomly selected control group firms. The second test compares the mean and variance of the leverage ratios for the acquiring and acquired firms in the year before the merger with those of their respective sectors. The first test's results are insignificant. An examination of the different sample variances indicates that both acquiring (0.022) and acquired (0.021) firms have significantly greater variability in their leverage policies than the control group firms (0.003).

Gort's disturbance theory. According to the economic disturbance theory developed by Gort, an increased dispersion of evaluations of a company's value should result in some potential buyers placing a higher value on the firm than its market value, thus precipitating a merger. Acquired firms should be characterized by greater dispersions in market values by this theory. Formula 3 tries to test this hypothesis for mergers in Belgium. Ratios between the higher and lower quotations are compared for acquired and control firms during various periods. Each time, we notice that the average ratio between the highest and lowest quotations is significantly lower for acquired companies—respectively, 1.328 against 1.405 for one year before merger, 1.299 against 1.368 for two years before, and 1.306 against 1.371 for three years before merger.

Control firms exhibit a larger gap between the highest and the lowest quotations than the acquired companies. This contradicts Gort's hypothesis. On this basis, one cannot conclude that the merger movement in Belgium could be explained by economic disturbances that alter the expectations of individuals and thereby lead to changes in ownership.

Bargain theory. Another explanation sometimes used to explain mergers is that there is an underevaluation of the acquired firms. Distortions inside the company should, for example, explain a bad estimate by the stock market. For instance, a weak management leading to bad business performance, a difference in objectives between those in control of the company and shareholders, or even deficient information by the market could result in "bargains." These distortions could appear as an underevaluation of quotations, especially in price-earnings ratios lower than for other companies.

To test this hypothesis, formula 4 compares average price-earnings ratios, based on a simple average between the highest and lowest in a year, for acquired companies and for control group firms. This analysis is for three periods, one, two, and three years before the merger. It proves each time that the average of price-earnings ratios is higher for acquired companies. Nevertheless, results are statistically significant only for the period covering two and three years before merger. Here also it seems that the hypothesis is not confirmed. In fact, acquired companies are distinguished by a very clearly higher price-earnings ratio on average than the control sample—thirty-one against nine and twenty-nine against eleven for two and three years before merger. This implies that the market estimate would be higher for acquired companies and that these companies would not be underestimated on the market.[15]

Effects of mergers. *Profitability.* To test for the impact of mergers on company profitability, the weighted[16] averages of the profit rates of the merging firms over the five years preceding the merger are subtracted from the average profitability of the newly formed company over the five years following the merger and compared with the analogous variable formed for a pair of control group firms. Table 3–5 shows that the results based on net profit to equity and net profit to total assets are better for merging firms than for control group companies. Both sets of companies performed less well in the postmerger period than in the premerger period due to a conjunctural decline in the economy, but the merging firms experienced a smaller decline in profitability in the postmerger period than the control group companies (−0.004 and −0.004 for the merging firms against −0.019 and −0.016 for the control groups companies). The difference in profit rates was statistically significant for net profits to total assets, but not for net profits to equity.

Formula 6 compares the ratio of post- to premerger profit rates for the merging companies to the same ratios computed over all control group firms. The results resemble those of test 5. The merging companies do better than the control group averages, but the differences are statistically insignificant.

Formula 7 compares the average profitability of merging firms over a five-year period after merger with the predicted value of profitability assuming the two firms had not merged. To compute the latter, one multiplies the weighted average profitability before merger by the ratio of postmerger to premerger profitability of the control group firms as calculated in Formula 6. As shown in Table 3–5, the results of Formula 7 are not statistically significant. Nevertheless, they are in the same direction as the previously obtained ones, showing better performances for merging firms than for control firms. In terms of net income to equity, actual profitability is 0.04 while predicted profitability is 0.029. Concerning net income to total assets, actual profitability is 0.026 while predicted profitability is 0.023.

Thus, in all tests the merging firms performed better than the control group companies in that their profit rates declined by less in the post-merger period than those of the control group firms. For only one test (5.2) was the difference between sample means statistically significant, however.

Growth comparisons. Formula 8 compares the ratios of the weighted averages of the growth rates of the merging firms before and after the merger with the analogous ratios formed for the control group companies with respect to total assets, net of depreciation plant and equipment, and leverage. For each measure the merging firms have a higher mean growth rate than the nonmerging companies, but the differences in sample means are all statistically insignificant.

Formula 9 compares the growth rates of the merging firms over five years after the mergers with those of their respective industries. Once again, the merging firms exhibit faster growth, but the differences between the samples remain insignificant.

Formula 10 compares the realized values of total assets, net of depreciation plant and equipment, and leverage with the projected values obtained by multiplying the premerger figures for the merging companies by the growth rates of their respective industries. The results again indicate faster growth for the merging firms, but once again the differences in sample means fail to pass conventional statistical level cutoffs.

Change in return on a common share. The aim of Formula 11 is to compare the return on a share of an acquiring firm's stock with that of a randomly selected control group company matched by industry.[17] The comparisons are made for the differences in rates of return between the five years before a merger and holding periods after the merger of one, two, three, and four years, respectively. On the average, the returns on a share of the acquiring firm's stock are lower after the merger than before ——0.029, −0.053, −0.041, and −0.033, respectively, for one, two, three, and four years after the merger. This finding is not systematically true of the matched control group companies, which also exhibited more stable differences in returns. For only one comparison, the year following the merger, was the difference in the means between the two samples statistically significant (8 percent), however. The returns earned in this year may be influenced by "digestion" and dilution problems.

In Formula 12, the comparison is between the acquiring firms and all of the concerned control group companies. As for the preceding formula, the results are each time worse for the merging firms than for the control group companies, but the differences here are never significant.

In Formula 13, achieved rates of return are compared with predicted returns based on industry trends. These results are produced for samples of twenty-six and twenty-five, the latter formed by dropping an observation for textiles that appeared to bias the results. In all instances the results favor the nonmerging firms, but in only one comparison, the year after the merger for the twenty-five observation sample, are the results significant (3 percent). We conclude that there is no evidence that stockholders of acquiring firms are made better off by the mergers.

CONCLUSIONS

When we survey the several aspects analyzed, we reach the following conclusions:

1. Mergers are undertaken by firms characterized by big size and a size growth policy. Nothing permits us to confirm the classical hypothesis according to which merger would be a process to better the allocation of invested assets. The acquiring firms are not more profitable, and the mergers did not modify this situation. Indeed, the tests did not permit us to infer an improvement in profitability.

2. Nevertheless, the acquiring firms exhibited both before and after the mergers more stable profits—defined in terms of net profit but not in terms of trading profits. This fact leads us to conclude that acquiring firms through their size and growth policies are able to stabilize their total profit by "financial" gains due to the realization of assets and accounting devices.

3. In addition, we estimate that the search for big size can be explained not only by search for market power but also by search for "extra"-market power.

4. The acquiring firms seem disposed to carrying greater debt than the other firms. Again, these findings have to be related to the size of the acquiring firms. Big size facilitates negotiations with financial intermediaries, the more so as the several firms are linked through their asset holdings. In fact, more than half of the acquiring firms are linked through their Belgian holdings. Belgium is a very export-oriented small market. The search for "extra"-market power seems much more plausible here than in some larger countries. Belgium has been defined as the model of a "concerted economy." The economic and social decisions are in fact the result of negotiation between organized groups—public authorities, trade

unions, and representatives of the large corporations. Firms of big size are involved on several levels of the concerted economy. They are thus able effectively to exercise influence on public decisions concerning economic and social problems.

NOTES

1. A. Raucq, société anonyme, Répertoire notarial (Bruxelles: Larcier, 1972), T. XII, p. 303.
2. Art. 34 des Lois coordonnées sur les sociétés commerciales.
3. Commission Bancaire, Rapport 1966, p. 139 and following; Rapport 1972/73 p. 142 and following.
4. Commission Bancaire, Rapport 1972/1973, p. 143. R. Wtterwulghe, *La Commission Bancaire, une experience originale de magistrature économique. Actes du Colloque sur la Magistrature économique Bruxelles, Bruylant, Leuven* (Paris: Oyez, 1976).
5. Article 70 bis des Lois coordonnées sur les sociétés commerciales.
6. Article 1166 du Code Civil.
7. For a comparison, see R. Wtterwulghe and A.M. Kumps, *Fondements Structurels de l'Entreprise* (Paris: Cujas, 1977), p. 131, ff.
8. Arrêté royal du Novembre 27, 1973.
9. Ibid., art. 4 to 14, 15 to 23, 24 to 26, respectively.
10. See Wtterwulghe and Kumps, pp. 285–88.
11. Art. 108 du Code de commerce.
12. Article 38 du Code des impôts sur les revenus.
13. Until 1965, mergers were submitted to the same taxation as other contributions to companies—namely, 1.60 percent. From 1965 to 1972, this taxation was 1.25 percent for mergers. The same principle stays in application after 1972 but the taxation on contributions being reduced to 2 percent, the taxation of contributions of mergers stays reduced to one-half—that is, 1 percent. Since 1976, the taxation on contributions is reduced to 1 percent and the one on merger to 0.50 percent.
14. Intermills (2601) undertook three acquisitions in 1965; Intercom (4906) undertook seven acquisitions in 1966; U.C.E. Linaluc (4912) two acquisitions in 1966. So we have thirty-five operations less nine operations, for a total of twenty-six operations.
15. For Formula 4, when earnings were zero we eliminated the firm.
16. Assets in the year before the merger were used as weights.
17. But not matched by size, since our control group population was not large enough to allow for matching by both size and industry.

Chapter 4

Federal Republic of Germany, 1962–1974

J. R. Cable, J. P. R. Palfrey, and J. W. Runge

GENERAL BACKGROUND

The Merger Mechanism

In Germany very few legal mergers occur in which the partners are
formally integrated and one or both loses its separate identity. But for
every legal merger in the 1970s there have been seven or eight economic
mergers in which the effective control of one company passes to another
via the acquisition of a significant ownership interest (see the following
section). The controlling interest may sometimes be built up in stages.
Even where it reaches 100 percent, a legal merger does not invariably
follow: rather, the two firms otherwise continue to operate as separate
legal entities. In comparison with the United Kingdom and the United

Work on the German study was made possible by a research grant from the Anglo-German
Foundation for the Study of Industrial Society, whose support we gratefully acknowledge.
The authors also gratefully acknowledge the assistance of Gerald Nelson and Winfried
Seeringer in compiling a merger list and in data collection. We are indebted to Professor Otto
Poensgen for the provision of additional data and to Annerose Engelhardt, Rolf Hochreiter,
Joachim Schwalbach, and officials of the Federal Cartel Office for their assistance with the
sections dealing with institutional background, policy, and the record of merger activity.
Responsibility for the views expressed and the conclusions reached remains with the authors.

States, merger activity takes place further from the center of public attention, and takeover raids are rare.

The main reasons why German merger activity should take this form are to be found in two features of the institutional framework. One is the relatively low dependence of German companies on the equity market for finance. The other is the nature of German competition policy in practice toward cartels and interfirm cooperation.

The principal types of private sector German company are the *Aktiengesellschaften* (AG) and the *Gesellschaften mit beschränkter Haftung* (GmbH), both of which enjoy limited liability status; the *Kommanditgesellschaften* (KG), which have unlimited liability but enjoy certain tax and borrowing advantages (amended in 1977); and the mixed form GmbH and Co KG, in which the party with full liability takes on the legal persona of GmbH, thus effectively avoiding unlimited liability. AG companies are on average much the largest, with assets of DM 23 million in 1969, as against DM 0.5 million for the GmbH type, although the latter do include some large concerns, among them the subsidiaries of multinational companies such as Unilever and Philips. But GmbH companies predominate numerically, totaling 168,423 in 1977, compared with only 2,149 AG companies. Moreover, while the number of GmbH companies has increased more than two and a half times over the last decade, the number of AGs has declined by about 7 percent.[1]

GmbH companies are subject to only minimal information disclosure requirements, but only AGs can seek stock market quotations. The development of their relative numbers over the last ten years suggests that in the German context the former advantage is much preferred to the latter. The relative unimportance of having direct access to the stock market is confirmed by the fact that less than a quarter of AG companeis are actually quoted (469 out of 2177 in 1976). Moreover, the importance of the stock market as a direct source of funds seems to be not only small but declining. Thus, the number of quoted companies has fallen by around a quarter since the mid-1960s and the ratio of equity to total capital in quoted companies from around 30 to nearer 25 percent.

The relative unimportance of the stock market is balanced by the fact that German banks play a much more active role than their United Kingdom and United States counterparts both in providing finance for industry and in the direction of corporate affairs. It is to be expected that the influence of the banks extends to merger activity.

The main features of German competition policy are outlined in a later section. For the present we simply note that the coordination of activities following economic mergers in Germany would almost certainly contravene the antitrust laws of the United States and competition policy in the United Kingdom.

The Incidence of Mergers 1958–1977

Official merger statistics are compiled by the Federal Cartel Office (B Kart A) and the Federal Statistics Office (SB). The former records mergers notified under section 23 of the 1957 Act against Restraint of Competition (GWB). For this purpose a merger is where a 25 percent, 50 percent, and/or majority of voting capital is acquired and where a market share of at least 20 percent is reached or exceeded. The SB series dates from 1951 but includes only legal mergers. During the period 1970–1976 these represented less than 12 percent of mergers notified under section 23 of the GWB.

Although the B Kart A series is imprecise as to when effective control has changed hands, it is the only authoritative index of merger activity for West Germany. Table 4–1 and Figure 4–1 show the number of mergers in each year from 1958 to 1977 both overall and for the industrial sector. Both the overall and the industrial series suggest exponential growth. However, the numbers must be interpreted with caution. In particular, the pre- and post-1973 statistics are not strictly comparable. Prior to 1973, the B Kart A itself had to identify when notifiable mergers had occurred and request information. As a result the pre-1973 statistics are incomplete, and the proportion of all section 23 mergers they include may have varied. In the view of B Kart A officials, there was a significant increase in B Kart A reporting activity after 1967, when serious discussions on introducing merger controls began. From 1974 (when merger control was first introduced) the onus to report merger activity was shifted to the companies, so that except for illegal nondisclosure, the series is complete.

Nevertheless, it is clear that there has been a very significant rise in merger activity over the twenty-year period. Although the absolute level of merger activity in the early years is probably much understated, the statistics show a fourfold increase between 1957 and 1968. There followed a distinct merger wave between 1969 and 1971. The wave is seen more clearly when we consider annual deviations from the trend increase in the number of mergers (Figure 4–2).[2] Although the dimensions of this wave may have been exaggerated by increased reporting activity on the part of the B Kart A, its existence cannot be due to this alone, for increased reporting would explain only the initial increase and not the subsequent fall in the number of mergers. Moreover, the surge in merger activity in Germany was more or less contemporaneous with merger booms in the United States, Britain, and elsewhere, which is suggestive of common underlying causal factors prompting mergers rather than of vagaries in statistical reporting. After a comparative lull in merger activity for two years, further explosive growth occurred after 1973, which, paradoxically, was the year in which legal control was enacted. By 1977 the total number

Table 4–1. Entry, Exit, and Mergers in the Federal Republic of Germany, 1958–1977

Year	Corporations AGs (including KGs aA) plus GmbH		Incorporations (plus Reorganizations)		Exits		Exits from Liquidations and Bankruptcy		Reported Mergers According to Sec. 23, GWB		Year
	Number (Dec. 31)	Capital (billion DM)	Number	Capital (billion DM)	Number	Capital (billion DM)	Number	Capital	Total	Industrial	
1958	35,931	36,499	2,695	670	1,907	1,011	703	38	15	14	1958
1959									15	14	1959
1960	37,762	43,955	3,460	770	2,388	1,968	716	42	22	21	1960
1961	41,173	50,903	3,545	675	1,410	479	821	112	26	24	1961
1962									38	33	1962
1963	49,394	61,093	4,646	684	1,597	551	1,027	83	29	23	1963
1964	52,816	65,612	5,321	619	1,881	608	1,158	96	36	25	1964
1965	56,580	72,369	5,800	770	2,030	604	1,266	112	50	46	1965
1966	60,444	77,917	6,199	816	2,3	655	1,491	202	43	38	1966
1967	64,734	82,735	6,970	900	2,660	701	1,595	173	65	50	1967
1968									65	58	1968
1969	76,018	94,180	9,220	1,203	2,886	1,211	1,486	141	168	117	1969
1970	82,450	99,526	10,428	3,025	3,998	5,839	1,710	326	305	222	1970
1971	90,778	108,660	12,582	1,947	4,374	2,734	1,934	215	220	141	1971
1972	102,961	117,017	17,038	2,645	4,957	3,828	2,085	248	269	158	1972
1973	114,323	126,051	16,507	2,182	5,811	3,449	2,507	317	243	145	1973
1974	124,466	135,654	15,589	1,720	6,244	1,783	3,149	430	318	185	1974
1975	135,571	145,457	18,066	1,755	7,763	2,661	3,178	599	448	244	1975
1976	149,410	152,588	20,758	1,525	7,789	2,593	3,242	485	453	229	1976
1977	170,612	162,857							554	267	1977

Source: Statistiches Jahrbuch, Federal Statistics Office, Wiesbaden, annual volumes.

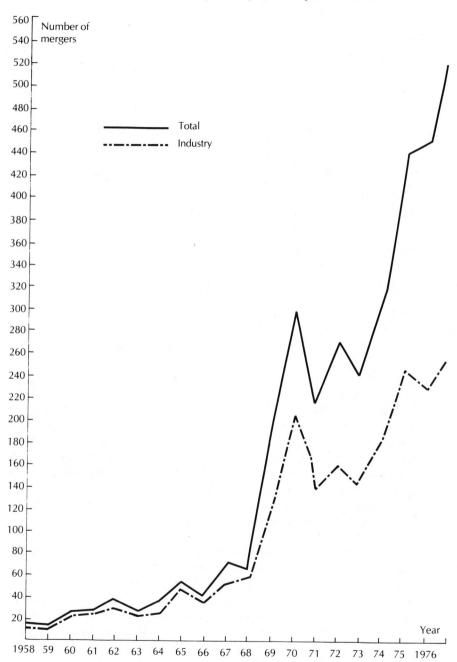

Figure 4–1. Number of mergers in the Federal Republic of Germany, 1958–1976.

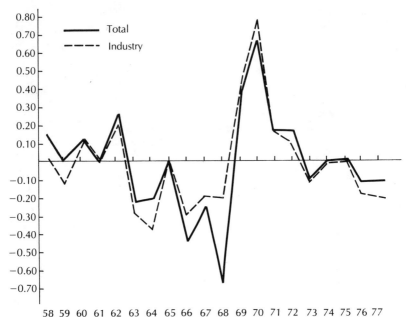

Figure 4–2. Deviations from merger series trend.

of mergers had reached almost twice the previous 1970 peak, and in this case we know that the post-1973 figures are reliable.

However, this somewhat overstates the growth of merger activity in some ways, since there has been a relative increase in the number of small mergers because of the presence of a size threshold in the 1973 merger law. In view of this, some would no doubt argue that the economic significance of the most recent merger wave is exaggerated. Without question a series recording the value of assets or turnover involved, if available, would be informative, but it is by no means certain that such a series will be superior in capturing the impact of mergers on competition, since the combination of smaller firms in smaller markets can have just as serious effects as between large firms in large markets. That is, whether a simple merger count of an assets series best captures the impact of mergers depends not just on the absolute size of the merging firms, but on size relative to the market. Moreover, by the systematic acquisition of small firms in series, a market leader can achieve much the same effect as by a single large acquisition.[3] The whole question of how the disappearance of firms of different size affects competition in practice remains largely unresearched, especially in Germany.

Whether the present German merger rate can go on increasing, either in line with the past trend or on some lower growth path, is open to speculation. Assuming that the motive to merge persists, this is a matter of whether there are binding constraints in the system that frustrate merger desires. In particular, an upper bound on the rate of merger could be set either when the capacity of the system to undertake the process is reached (as the available time of management and of legal and financial intermediaries becomes fully committed) or when the stock of potentially acquirable firms is depleted. In fact, neither constraint seems likely to become binding—at least not in the near future. Despite the extraordinary increase in the 1970s, the level of merger activity reached in Germany is not disproportionate by international standards. In Britain, for example, over 43 percent of quoted companies were taken over between 1957 and 1969, at a peak rate of one per working day in 1968, and this, of course, takes no account of mergers affecting the more numerous unquoted company sector (Kuehn 1975). Moreover, to put the level of merger activity into national perspective, mergers in the section 23 GWB sense amounted to only approximately 13 percent of the number of voluntary and involuntary liquidations over the period 1970–1976 (Table 4–2). At the same time, the astonishing increase in the rate of formation of new companies (Table 4–1, column 3) suggests an expanding rather than declining supply of potentially acquirable new firms.[4] In 1976 there were over forty-five times as many births of new companies as there were section 23 type mergers. Thus, it seems that there is little to stop the merger rate increasing as long as the motive to merge is sustained.

Merger Intensity and the Level of Economic Activity

Analysis of the relationship between the rate of merger activity and the state of the German economy must be tentative due to the shortcomings in merger statistics. Such analysis is useful, however, not merely because of what it reveals about the connection between mergers and the movement of the economy, but also because if any systematic relationship emerges, the merger statistics themselves take on more credibility.

The explosive growth shown in the merger series is of course not matched in other series such as GDP, gross fixed investment, and the share price index. To facilitate comparison, we therefore compare annual deviations from trend in all cases.[5] This procedure should in any case help to bring out any cyclical patterns in the data more clearly.

The annual deviations from trend in mergers, compared with GDP, investment, and share prices, are plotted in Figures 4–3 through 4–5. A quite definite association is apparent in all cases, and in particular the boom at the end of the 1960s is quite evident in each of the series. Closer inspection, however, suggests a change in the relationship between

Table 4–2. Reported Mergers According to Section 23, GWB, by Industry[a]

Branch Number	Product group	1958–1977	1958–1968	1969–1972	1973–1977
11	Bergbauliche Erzeugnisse	56	11	27	18
205	Mineralölerzeugnisse	173	6	14	153
220	Stein und Erden	101	10	23	68
23	Eisen und Stahl	176	8	44	124
232/6	NE-Metalle und -Metallhalbzeug	95	15	34	46
	Giessereierzeugnisse	6	1	0	5
238	Erzeugnisse der Ziehereien und Kaltwalzwerke	11	1	7	3
24	Stahlbauerzeugnisse	49	4	18	27
242	Maschinenbauerzeugnisse	199	33	81	85
244, 8	Landfahrzeuge	103	35	34	34
246	Wasserfahrzeuge	2	1	0	1
244, 8	Luftfahrzeuge	21	4	13	4
250	Elektrotechnische Erzeugnisse	232	52	88	92
252/4	Feinmechanische und optische Erzeugnisse, Uhren	23	12	4	7
256	Eisen-, Blech- und Metallwaren	49	17	17	15
258	Musikinstrumente, Spielwaren, Turn- und Sportgeräte, bearbeitete Edelsteine	9	2	2	5
200	Chemische Erzeugnisse	310	55	112	143
2425/25071	Buromaschinen; EDV	11	—	—	11
224	Feinkeramische Erzeugnisse	28	10	4	14
227	Glas und Glaswaren	44	12	8	24
260/1	Schnittholz, Sperrholz und sonstiges bearbeitetes Holz	1	1	0	0
260/1	Holzwaren	2	0	1	1
26	Holzschliff, Zellstoff, Papier und Pappe	47	8	10	29
4/5/8	Papier- und Pappewaren	18	8	1	9
	Druckereierzeugnisse, Lichtpaus- und verwandte Waren	8	1	6	1
210	Kunststofferzeugnisse	18	5	10	3
215	Gummi- und Asbestwaren	28	9	7	12
270	Leder	0	0	0	0
271/2	Lederwaren und Schuhe	4	1	2	1
275	Textilien	33	7	11	15
276	Bekleidung	4	1	3	0
R28/9	Ernährungsindustrie	139	14	40	85
R28/9	Tabakwaren	42	8	15	19
3	Bauwirtschaft	18	0	2	16
	Total	2,054	346	638	1,070

Source: Tätigkeitberichte des Bundeskartellamtes.
[a] bis 1971 nach dem überwiegand betroffenen Wirtschaftsbereich
ab 1972 nach dem erwerbenden Wirtschaftsbereich
ab 1972 Branche Büromaschinen EDV ausgewiesen

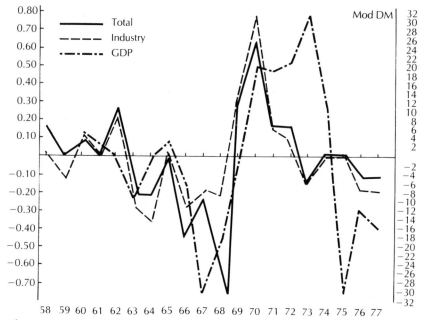

Figure 4–3. Deviations from trend: mergers and GNP. (*Sources:* Mergers—Reports of the B Kart A; GDP—Statistisches Jahrbuch, Kart A.)

mergers and the other indicators occurring in 1970–1971. Up to that point mergers move more or less in step with GDP and investment and seem to lag share prices by one period. Thereafter it is mergers that lead, giving rise to a suggestion of contrary motion in the last three to four years. Thus, in particular, the 1970 peak level of mergers was not sustained or increased through the boom years up to 1973, when both GDP and investment remained high in relation to trend. Rather, as we have seen, the merger rate first fell back and then remained steady for two years, before resuming its rapid post-1973 rise.

The change in the phasing of the relationship also occurs in the case of share prices, but to a less marked degree. Overall, it is to movements in the share price index that merger activity seems to correspond most closely. This is in line with the evidence for the United States and United Kingdom (see in particular Nelson 1959; and Hannah 1974b). It is, however, slightly surprising at first sight, since as we have seen, the stock market in Germany plays a comparatively minor role in merger activity. What this could suggest is that even in the United States and Britain the link between share prices and merger activity arises less because of the direct part played by share prices in merger deals than because the underlying sentiment that accompanies bull markets is also that which favors mergers.

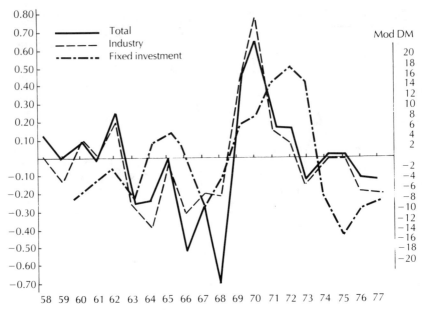

Figure 4–4. Deviations from trend: mergers and investment. (*Source:* Mergers—Reports of the B Kart A; investment—Statistisches Jahrbuch.)

Coming at precisely the point from which the merger rate began to accelerate, the shift in the relationship between mergers and economic indicators may be important for policy purposes, and further investigation is clearly warranted. One hypothesis to be tested would be that the earlier, relatively low level merger activity was that of an economy at a stage of development in which the need for structural change was perceived as modest, so that the volume of mergers quietly followed the level of general activity. The later phase, on this view, might then be seen as one where the need for more thoroughgoing structural adjustment was needed. The fact that merger activity was rising especially sharply as the economy went into the mid-1970s recession might be taken as preliminary support for this view, and as we shall see later in the chapter, the recent pattern of vertical and diversifying mergers shows at least superficial signs of structural response in industries particularly affected by adverse economic conditions. However, an alternative hypothesis would be that whereas in the 1960s priorities of national recovery and development were still uppermost in mergers, as in other aspects of economic life, the 1970s merger wave

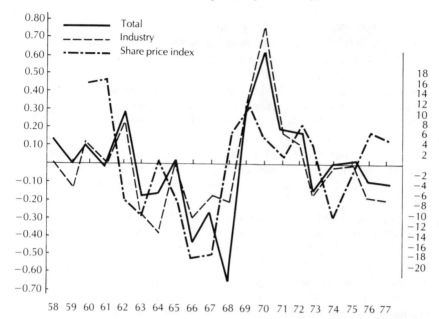

Figure 4–5. Deviations from trend: mergers and share prices. (*Source: Mergers—Reports of the B Kart A; share prices—Statistisches Jahrbuch.*)

represents a kind of corporate "affluence effect," as with rising incomes generally, management began to pursue non-cost-minimizing, non-efficiency-oriented types of objectives associated with corporate growth.

The Industrial Composition of Merger Activity

Analysis of German merger activity by industry is also impeded by an inconsistency in the statistical series. Up to 1971 mergers were classified by principal product, taking the effect of the merger into account, whereas from 1972 the classification was by reference to the acquiring firm only. Once again, however, it is possible to draw some inferences from the data, despite their limitations.

Over the twenty year period 1958–1977 there has been an increase in the proportion of mergers taking place outside the industrial sector. This tendency is apparent both before and after the 1972 change in the basis of the statistics. The ratio of industrial to total mergers in the periods 1958–1968, 1969–1972, and 1973–1977 was 85.6, 66.3, and 53.1 percent, respectively. For the period 1958–1977 as a whole, industrial mergers averaged 60.7 percent, but in the final year the proportion was as low as 48.1 percent. However, this tendency is exaggerated in the statistics, due to the introduction in 1972 of the category "multisector firms" (*Mehrere-wirtschaftsbereiche*), which is included in the nonindustrial sector. This was designed to accommodate mergers where the acquiring firm was widely diversified and would of course include, and might even consist primarily of, firms heavily diversified among industrial as well as non-industrial sectors. The number of mergers in this category rose rapidly to seventy-eight in 1975 (17.4 percent of the total in that year) and then stabilized at roughly this level. If these mergers are deleted from the analysis, we then find that the ratio of industrial to (the adjusted) total mergers in the periods 1958–1968, 1969–1972 and 1973–1977 becomes 85.6, 67.2, and 63.1 percent, respectively—a much less significant decrease.

Within the industrial sector, mergers have been heavily concentrated in a small number of industries. Thus between 1958 and 1977, approximately 45 percent were accounted for by only four industries and nearly 80 percent by ten (Table 4–3). Moreover, the identity of the most merger-intensive industries has changed very little. In descending order of merger incidence, the top six industries for the period as a whole are chemical products, electrical engineering, machine tools, iron and steel, mineral oil products, and food processing. With one exception, all appeared in the top six in both the merger wave of 1969–1972 and the period of rapid merger growth from 1973–1977 (Table 4–3). The exception is mineral oil products, which ranked only thirteenth during the merger wave but rose to top place in the league table for 1973–1977.

Three sectors dominated nonindustrial merger activity, the multisector firm category apart. Again in descending order of merger incidence, these were credit institutions, commerce and commercial services, and public utilities (Table 4–4).

In both the industrial and nonindustrial sectors, the majority of mergers were horizontal—that is, between firms in the same industrial category. Nonhorizontal mergers occurred primarily within rather than across the broad industrial versus nonindustrial groupings—(69.6 percent of industrial mergers were within their own sector, of which 47.6 percent were horizontal; 81.9 percent of nonindustrial mergers were in their own sector, of which 57.3 percent were horizontal). However, the detailed statistics, especially for later years, reveal some tendency for credit institutions to make acquisitions in the construction, food processing, and, to a lesser extent, the textile industries. Similarly, in the industrial sector, the mineral oil product industry shows an outstanding tendency toward forward vertical integration into commercial activities, with 100 out of 165 mergers in this industry over the period 1970–1977 being of this type. To a much lesser extent, the iron and steel industry was also involved in this kind of activity, followed at some distance by vehicles, electrical goods,

Table 4–3. Mergers from Industrial Sectors

Industry	1969–1972			1973–1977			1958–1977		
	Rank	Number of mergers	Percent of total	Rank	Number of mergers	Percent of total	Rank	Number of mergers	Percent of total
Chemical products	1	112	17.6	2	143	13.4	1	310	15.1
Electrical engineering	2	88	13.8	4	92	8.6	2	232	11.3
Machine tools	3	81	12.7	5=	85	7.9	3	199	9.7
Iron and steel	4	44	6.9	3	124	11.6	4	176	8.6
Mineral oil products	(13)	(14)	(2.2)	1	153	14.3	5	176	8.6
Food processing	5	40	6.3	5=	85	7.9	6	139	6.7
Nonferrous metals and semifinished metals	6	34	5.3	(8)	(46)	(4.3)	(9)	(95)	(4.6)
Total	—	638	100.0	—	1070	100.0	—	2054	100.0
Combined share:									
Top four industries	—	325	50.9	—	512	47.9	—	917	44.6
Top six industries	—	399	62.5	—	682	63.7	—	1232	60.0
Top ten industries	—	501	78.5	—	859	80.3	—	1587	77.3

Source: Derived from Table 4–2.

Table 4–4. Mergers from Nonindustrial Sectors

Branch Number	Product group	1958–1977	1958–1968	1969–1972	1973–1977
4	Handel u. Handelshilfsgewerbe				
	Handwerk	179	11	19	149
	Genossenschaften	0	0	0	0
	Kulturelle Leistungen	59	3	11	45
	Filmwirtschaft	6	4	0	2
R70/1	Sonstige Dienstleistungen	17	1	1	15
0	Land- und Forstwirtschaft, Garten- und Weinbau, Fischerei und Jagd	13	5	7	1
5	Verkehrswirtschaft	55	12	11	32
60	Kreditinstitute	438	5	199	234
61	Versicherungen	63	1	19	43
	Versorgungswirtschaft	166	16	44	106
	Mehrere Wirtschaftsbereiche	332	—	13	319
	Total	1,328	58	324	946

and chemicals. While a thoroughgoing analysis of the industrial pattern of merger activity is beyond the scope of the present study, these diversifying tendencies are clearly comprehensible in the light of the effects on different industries of adverse economic conditions in the 1970s.

Merger Activity by Type of Merger

Detailed statistics on the incidence of vertical, conglomerate, and horizontal mergers are available only since 1970. They are summarized in Table 4–5. Horizontal mergers remain the largest single category overall and, as we have seen, in both the industrial and the nonindustrial sectors. However, the proportion of all mergers that are horizontal has declined from three-quarters or more to two-thirds or less during the 1970s.

The proportion of conglomerate mergers between firms with neither horizontal nor vertical links premerger shows an initial decline from 1970–1971 levels but has since tended to oscillate. The lack of any significant relative increase in the incidence of conglomerate mergers is at first sight surprising in view of the sharp increase after 1972 of mergers initiated by multisector firms that we saw in the last section, for it might be presumed that these mergers would be predominantly of the conglomerate type. However, to reconcile the evidence we must infer otherwise: though the acquiring firms were already conglomerates, in many cases the acquired firms stood in some horizontal or vertical relationship to one or other of the acquiring firm's activities before the merger.

The number of vertical mergers increased more than fivefold between

Table 4–5. Horizontal, Vertical, and Conglomerate Mergers, 1970–1977

	Horizontal		Vertical		Conglomerate		
	Number	(Percent)	Number	(Percent)	Number	(Percent)	Total
1970	217	(74.6)	27	(9.3)	47	(16.2)	291
1971	167	(76.3)	19	(8.7)	33	(15.1)	219
1972	218	(81.6)	21	(7.9)	28	(10.5)	267
1973	196	(81.0)	19	(7.9)	28	(11.6)	242
1974	235	(73.9)	50	(15.7)	33	(10.4)	318
1975	336	(75.0)	53	(11.8)	59	(13.2)	448
1976	283	(62.5)	113	(24.9)	57	(12.6)	453
1977	367	(66.2)	122	(22.0)	65	(11.7)	554
1970–1977	2,091	(72.3)	424	(15.2)	350	(12.5)	2,793

Source: Report on the activities of the Federal Cartel Office.

1970 and 1977 in absolute terms and more than doubled relative to mergers as a whole. These increases came mainly in two large steps in 1974 and 1976. In the previous section we saw that the industrial pattern of vertical-integrating mergers between the industrial and nonindustrial sectors was rather suggestive of a defensive response to adverse circumstances. It is therefore not surprising that the main increases in vertical mergers should be seen to occur in the wake of the oil crisis in 1973 and the deepest year of recession, 1975.

The Development of Competition Policy in the Federal Republic

The first departure in modern times from a laissez-faire competition policy in Germany was a 1923 decree dealing with cartels. While technically forbidding abuses in this area, the decree remained largely ineffective. After the Second World War, a 1947 Allied ordinance prohibited cartels and monopolization (subject to various escape clauses) and became the forerunner of the 1957 Act against Restraint of Competition (GWB). This act, amended in 1966, 1973, and 1976, forms the basis of current policy and established the Federal Cartel Office (B Kart A), the body responsible for implementing the legislation. Later, an independent Monopolies Commission (MK) was established under the 1973 amendment, primarily to keep the operation of the policy under review.

The main targets of the legislation are cartels (restrictive agreements) and cartellike arrangements; the abuse of market-dominant positions held by firms; and, since 1973, mergers. In 1973 resale price maintenance was also prohibited (with minor exceptions), although recommended prices are still allowed. Separate legislation was enacted in 1977, primarily to protect the weaker side in a transaction against market power and to ensure a reasonable balance of interests.

In the cartel area, the legislation disallows all contracts or agreements between firms "insofar as they are likely to influence, by restraining competition, production or market conditions with respect to trade in goods or commercial services." There are, however, a fairly large number of exceptions, falling into two main categories. The first includes agreements relating to service arrangements, rebates, rationalization, standardization, specialization, and external trade. These must be reported to the B Kart A and can continue in force (usually for no more than three years) if, within three months, the B Kart A raises no objection. The second group, including agreements about patents, samples, industrial secrets, and others, is closely regulated and requires specific exemption from the B Kart A. Details of exempted agreements are kept in the Cartel Register. Price fixing and the enforcement of sales conditions by suppliers are forbidden, except for the sale of books and magazines.

Holding a market-dominant position is not illegal per se, but abuse of such a position (as defined by legislation) is prohibited. The 1973 amendment introduced a number of specific criteria for determining where market dominance exists, relating to both market structure and the conduct of enterprises. Market dominance is presumed if one firm controls a third of the market (unless its turnover is less than DM 250 million); if three firms control 50 percent; or if five firms control two-thirds. Financial resources and cartelization may also be considered in determining the existence of market dominance, and since 1973, barriers to entry have also been a permitted criterion, though in practice only barriers related to financial resources have tended to be considered. "Abuse" is not defined by the act. This is left open to the interpretation of the B Kart A, in the light of the overall purpose of the act on the one hand to maintain freedom of competition while on the other hand to promote the development of individual enterprises.

Proposals to bring mergers within the scope of the legislation failed in 1947 and 1957, and merger control took effect only from January 1, 1974. Under the present legislation a merger is defined as the purchase either of a firm's assets or of 25, 50 percent, and/or a majority of the voting shares. From 1973 a two-tier notification system has been in force. Where two (or more) parties have a turnover of at least DM 1000 million, advance clearance from the B Kart A is required. Notification without advance clearance is required where the merger would result in a market share of 20 percent or more; where one party has a 20 percent share in another market; or where the merger partners together employ 10,000 people or have annual turnover of at least DM 500 million, unless one has less than DM 50 million turnover. When a merger is proposed, the B Kart A is required to establish whether a market-dominant position is created or strengthened and is empowered to prohibit the merger unless satisfied by the parties that competition will nonetheless be promoted in the relevant markets.

The provisions of the legislation apply mainly to manufacturing industry and mining. Certain areas are explicitly excluded from its scope. These include banking, insurance, transport authorities, energy, and public utilities. The 1976 amendment brought newspaper mergers within the scope of the act.

As the principal enforcement agency, the B Kart A has rather wide investigative powers, with authority to search premises, seize relevant documents, and hear evidence from witnesses. It also makes decisions, operating as a quasi-court, and imposes fines for infringements. The principal remedy available to the B Kart A is to make prohibitions, whether of cartel arrangements, the abuse of market dominance, or mergers. (Private individuals can also initiate civil proceedings for damages.) However, certain positive measures to encourage competition via countervailing power have recently been introduced. Thus the 1973 amendment authorized measures to facilitate cooperation between small and medium-sized businesses, and a working group to consult with firms on this issue was set up by the B Kart A in 1976. There are no powers to break up companies. Appeals against B Kart A decisions lie to the courts, and in the case of mergers there is an additional right of appeal to the economics minister, on grounds of advantages to the economy in general or an overriding interest to the public.

The Monopolies Commission is an independent, five-member advisory body. It is required to evaluate the prevailing degree of economic concentration and its foreseeable development in the light of economic policy, in particular competition policy. In this connection it is required to indicate any amendment to the provisions of the 1957 act that it considers necessary. The second of two very lengthy MK biannual reports was published toward the end of 1978. The commission may also be called on for specific advice (*Sondergutachten*) in the case of merger appeals to the economics minister.

Competition Policy Impact and Current Development

Existing German competition law appears strict. It is firmly embedded in and backed by law, and its coverage is potentially wide. By comparison with the United Kingdom and most other countries, the investigative powers of the B Kart A are very great. Responsibility for investigation, decisionmaking, and imposing penalties is all concentrated on a single body, the B Kart A, and this arguably reduces delays and avoids any dissipation of the power of the legislation, as compared with the situation in other countries where responsibility is divided.

Yet there are signs that the legislation has not had the impact that might have been expected. On the cartel side there are many exemptions, as we have seen. Moreover, the 1957 GWB apparently did not stimulate German merger activity in the late 1950s and early 1960s in the way that, for example, the 1956 Restrictive Practices Act is widely believed to have done in Britain, with mergers substituting for the interfirm agreements that had been abandoned. In this connection, the predominance of *partial* mergers may be significant. It is hard to believe these do not lead to the effective coordination of activity between separate legal entities of an essentially cartel-like nature. If constraints on such behavior were strong, there would be a preference for 100 percent takeovers, to "internalize" this coordination and put it beyond reach of GWB. But we do not observe this. Thus, either partially merged firms do not coordinate their activities; or they do, with little interference from the cartel laws. Of the two, the latter seems more likely. Thus, in this sense observed behavior suggests that effective control over cartel-like behavior is not strong. The paradox of strictly enforced legal controls alongside apparently weak effective control most likely arises from the difference between the legal and the economic meanings of what is a cartel.

So far as monopoly and merger control is concerned, the problematical aspect of the legislation is to clarify what constitutes market dominance and to define its abuse. The legislation has proved quite ineffective to deal with oligopoly or "complex monopoly" situations. For although abuse of collective market dominance is prohibited, the courts have ruled that there must be no competition within the group. Yet in practice it is often with the more pervasive, oligopolistic market dominance that competition policy has to deal. As is widely recognized, such dominance can have serious anticompetitive effects even when not all forms of competition are absent. More generally, a recent B Kart A suggestion to abandon the whole concept of market dominance in order to make merger control effective reflects adversely on its use elsewhere in competition policy.

Although merger control is relatively recent, it is already evident that the size thresholds for exemption in the 1973 rules are too high. Nearly half of the total number of mergers since the controls were introduced have escaped. Of these, 90 percent fall under the *Anschlussklausel* (connecting clause) under section 24(8) GWB, where one, usually the acquired, firm has less than DM 50 million turnover. As a reference point, the £5 million gross assets criterion available in United Kingdom merger control translates into a maximum combined turnover of only DM 35–40 million for the merging firms together.[6]

Tighter merger controls featured prominently in government proposals for a fourth amendment to the basic competition law, submitted to the Bundesrat in May 1978, which covered many aspects of the law. Both recommendations concerning mergers implemented recommendations made by the MK in its first, 1976 report.[7] The first would have reduced the size threshold below which a merger cannot be prohibited or reversed from DM 50 million to as little as DM 2 million where the acquirer has DM 1 billion turnover. Thus, in both the MK report and the government proposals, it was recognized that giant mergers (*Elfantenhochzeiten*) are not the only threat to competition.

The second proposal to amend merger controls was to introduce additional criteria for establishing market dominance in merger cases. In its 1976 report, the MK considered the 1973 criteria adequate for horizontal merger cases, for which they were designed, but insufficient for vertical and conglomerate mergers. The proposed additional criteria would presume market dominance where there was a combination of several market-dominant positions; market dominance with greater absolute firm size; creation of mammoth enterprises with over DM 10 billion turnover; or a threat to intermediate-sized markets by large firms.

The proposals met with opposition in the Bundesrat and at the time of writing are being revised. Meanwhile, in response to the MK report, the B Kart A had in 1977 suggested an alternative reform. This would entirely separate merger control from the question of market dominance, while introducing a single criterion on the American pattern of a "deterioration in competitive conditions" that it was felt would be quicker and easier to demonstrate. In its second, 1978, report the MK was divided, with two members expressing a preference for the B Kart A suggestion and three adhering to the original MK line and supporting the government proposals. There was, however, unanimity that some tightening of merger law is required. Precisely what form this will eventually take has yet to be seen.

EMPIRICAL TESTS FOR ALTERNATIVE MERGER CAUSES AND EFFECTS

Data Base

A satisfactory list of mergers taking place in the study period 1964–1974 was available to us neither from the publications of the Federal Statistical Office (SB), which deals only with legal mergers,[8] nor the Cartel Office (B Kart A), which began publishing merger lists only in 1973. The sample of merging firms therefore had to be compiled from press notices and reference works on the ownership of firms.[9] One hundred thirty-four cases of economic mergers, defined as the acquisition of a 50 percent interest or more in another firm, were identified in this way. Exclusion of non-AG companies,[10] for which data problems were insuperable, reduced this number to around one hundred. Further problems of data availability with the AG firms resulted in a final sample of fifty-five merger cases, equivalent to 3.1 percent of all section 23 GWB mergers during the period 1964–1974.

The time profile of the merger sample corresponds reasonably well to that of merger activity as a whole. Although cases in the sample represented 5.8 percent of all section 23 GWB mergers between 1964 and 1968 and only 2.6 percent from 1969–1974, it will be remembered that there was some systematic underreporting in the GWB series in the earlier period. In absolute terms, only fifteen of the cases in the sample occurred before 1969 as against forty during the later, more merger-intensive, years.

The industrial distribution of the merger sample also reflects that for all mergers fairly accurately. If anything, the most merger-intensive industries (chemical products together with mineral oil products, electrical engineering, machine tools, and iron and steel) are slightly overrepresented in the sample, with just over 55 percent of merger cases (classified according to the industrial activity of the acquiring firms)[11] compared with 45 percent of all mergers between 1950 and 1977 and 50 percent 1969–1972.

The sample contains a mixture of merger cases occurring before and after the qualitative change in merger activity around 1970–1971. Our sample contains approximately two-thirds "old-style" and one-third "new style" mergers.

To carry out the statistical tests reported in subsequent sections, annual series for the following variables were extracted for each firm from published sources:

1. Net of depreciation plant and equipment (*Sachanlagen*)
2. Total assets (*Bilanzsumme*)
3. Equity capital (*Eigenkapital*)
4. Retained earnings (*Rücklagen, gesetzlich und frei*)
5. Total revenue (*Umsatzerlöse*)
6. Before tax profit (*Jahresüberschuss*)
7. Manual and nonmanual employment (*Zahl der Arbeiter und Angestellten*)

For our control group on nonmerging firms and the accompanying data we are indebted to Professor O. Poensgen at the University of the Saarland in Saarbrücken. The control group consists of fifty-seven randomly chosen firms. Wherever possible the pairing of merging firms with their respective control firms was by reference to both size and industry. A merging firm that engaged in more than one merger is paired with the same control firm in each case. Nevertheless, because the merging firms (acquiring and acquired) outnumber those in the control group, it was sometimes necessary to use the same control firm for more than one merging firm. Such repeated use of certain control firms will in general not impart systematic bias provided that the firms used repeatedly are drawn randomly from the control group as a whole or (given that the statistical tests mostly involve comparing group means and variances) that the repeated firms have the same mean and variance as the control group itself. In our case the selection of firms from the control group is not necessarily random, but there is reason to suppose the "bias" included may correct for an existing bias in the original control group itself in that this underrepresents large firms. Thus, the control group with repeats may actually be preferable to the original control group.[12]

Characteristics of Merging and Nonmerging Firms

Before proceeding to the empirical tests of merger causes and effects, it may be helpful to review in general terms the premerger characteristics of the merging and nonmerging companies. Table 4–6 presents comparisons of group means for acquiring, acquired, and control firms in terms of five variables.

The most striking difference to appear is that the acquiring firms were several times larger than both the firms they acquired and those of the two control groups. There is also some suggestion that the acquiring firms had been growing faster than the acquired ones, for although the average growth rates are not significantly different at the normal confidence limits, positive differences were repeatedly found in eight out of the nine industries. Acquired companies, on the other hand, had been growing at little more than half the rate of their nonmerging counterparts. This large difference is statistically significant and is repeated in eight of the nine individual industries.

Differences in profit performance among the groups were small and generally insignificant. Acquiring firms on average slightly outperformed acquired firms, but were themselves outperformed by the nonacquiring group, though the differences were not statistically significant nor was there a systematic pattern of differences across individual industries. The acquired firms performed least well of all groups and significantly less well than their control group at the 10 percent confidence level. Stability of profit was significantly greater among acquiring than acquired firms, both across the sample as a whole and in all but one industry. The acquiring firms' profits were also less volatile than those of the nonacquiring control group, the (negative) difference being significant at 7 percent for the whole sample and consistently negative in eight of nine industries. Finally, there were essentially no significant and systematic differences in the degree of

Table 4–6. Premerger Characteristics of Merging and Nonmerging Firms

	Arithmetic Means		Differ-ence $\bar{X}_1 - \bar{X}_2$	Number of Observa-tions	t	Industries	
	$\bar{X}_1$	$\bar{X}_2$				Difference +ve	Total
Acquiring (AG) versus Acquired (AD)							
I Size (assets)	1776.6	202.8	157.4	50	5.85***	9***	9
II Growth	9.3	7.0	2.3	47	1.6	8**	9
III Profitability (profits/							
assets)	0.04	0.03	0.01	47	1.4	7	9
IV Variability of profit	2.2	3.1	−0.97	45	−2.1**	1**	9
V Leverage	0.63	0.63	−0.00	43	−0.06	3	8
Acquiring (AG) versus Matched Nonacquiring (MAG)							
I Size (assets)	1820.1	73.9	1746.2	51	6.72***	9***	9
II Growth	9.5	8.1	1.5	46	1.19	4	9
III Profitability (profits/							
assets)	0.04	0.05	−0.01	49	−1.36	3	9
IV Variability of profit	2.2	3.5	−1.3	48	−1.85*	1**	9
V Leverage	0.62	0.56	−0.07	45	2.75**	4	9
Acquired (AD) versus Matched Nonacquired (MAD)							
I Size (assets)	192.7	77.5	121.9	54	1.80*	5	9
II Growth	6.5	12.0	−5.5	47	−2.59**	1**	9
III Profitability (profits/							
assets)	0.03	0.04	−0.01	48	−1.75*	3	8
IV Variability of profit	3.1	2.9	0.2	41	0.47	4	9
V Leverage	0.63	0.64	−0.01	45	−0.29	3	8

*** denotes significant at 1 percent or better.
** denotes significant at 5 percent or better.
* denotes significant at 10 percent or better.

leverage with one exception—namely, a significant positive difference between acquiring firms and their control group. However, even here the result was not stable across industries.

Thus, the general picture that emerges is of acquisitions of smaller by extremely large firms with average to good profitability and growth records, significantly more stable profits than the other groups, and higher leverage ratios than nonacquiring companies (though not than the other groups). The acquired companies, though much smaller than their acquirers, were somewhat larger than nonmerging firms and were possibly less profitable and certainly much slower growing than nonacquired companies: Further interpretation of these observed differences is reserved for the two following sections, in which the results of the statistical tests of alternative merger causes and effects are reported.

Statistical Tests on the Determinants of Mergers

Test 1 Size Comparisons. The comparisons of geometric mean sizes of pairs of merging firms and their nonmerging equivalents across all industries in the German sample shows that the merging firms are significantly larger than the control firms, by a factor of between 3.6 and 5.4 depending on the size measure chosen (Table 4–7). Moreover, the tendency for merging firms to be large is found consistently in each industry taken separately as well as for the sample as a whole. While it may be that some individual mergers were undertaken for scale economies reasons, the evidence is inconsistent with the hypothesis that pursuit of scale economies is the general or overriding motive. On the other hand, the evidence is not inconsistent with a pursuit of a market power hypothesis, for in this case the larger the firms involved in a merger, the greater the impact on market share.

Test 2.1 Variation in Profits. Table 4–8 reports the results of the empirical tests for differences in the (premerger) variability in profits for merging and nonmerging firms for the German sample. It should be remembered when interpreting them that the sample included mainly horizontal mergers, so that any evidence of risk motives is likely to be weak. The comparisons show that acquiring firms have significantly less variability of profit than their nonmerging counterparts, both across all industries and in eight of nine individual industries. They were also significantly less risky than the firms they acquired across the sample as a whole and in all nine separate industries. However, acquired firms exhibited a degree of fluctuation in profit that was almost identical with that of the matched, nonacquired firms. Not surprisingly in view of these results, the (geometric mean) comparison between pairs of merging and nonmerging firms shows the merging pairs to have the more stable profits, though the differences are now not statistically significant. What we are observing here could well be not attributable to risk motives, but merely a side effect of the difference in size between merging (especially acquiring) and nonmerging firms, given that size and variability are quite likely to be inversely related, as in some previous studies (e.g. Samuels and Smyth 1968). A simple correlation between firm size (assets) and variability of profit for all (merging and nonmerging) firms in our sample in fact yielded a very small negative coefficient, insignificant at the 5 percent level.

It can, however, be argued that the above test, which looks at only the overall variability of a firm's profits, may fail to detect risk motives that are actually present. This is because if a firm is seeking to reduce its riskiness by merger, or to buy a firm that seems cheap to it given that firm's risk profile in relation to firms on average, the best firm to acquire will not necessarily be one with high or low variability of profit, but one in which fluctuations in profit run counter to those in the acquiring firm. As an additional test, we therefore investigated the relative covariance of profits between merging and nonmerging firms. Here, we would interpret a

Table 4–7. Determinants: Size Comparisons in Merger Year

					All industries				
	Company Type		Merger	Number of companies		Mean values		AGAD/	
Variable	1	2	Type	1	2	1	2	MAGMAD	t
Geometric means of									
1. Sales	AGAD	MAGMAD	All	48	48	272,218	59,928	4.54	7.08*
2. Assets	AGAD	MAGMAD	All	52	52	229,027	42,066	5.44	7.66*
3. Plant and equipment	AGAD	MAGMAD	All	50	50	54,335	15,099	3.60	5.03*

* Significant at 1 percent or better.

significantly smaller positive or larger negative covariance of profit among merging than nonmerging firms as evidence of the presence of risk motives.

Since our data series were on an annual basis, only a small number of observations could be used in calculating the relevant covariance.[13] The results, bearing in mind this limitation, showed an identical degree of covariance of profit in merging and matched nonmerging pairs of firms, to three decimal places.

Tests 2.2–2.6 Leverage (Gearing) Ratio. In the analysis of German mergers the leverage ratio (LEV) was derived from the following variables:

$$LEV = \frac{\text{Total Capital} - (\text{Equity} + \text{Reserves})}{\text{Total Capital}}$$

Taken together, the results of tests 2.2–2.6 are not consistent with the

Table 4–8. Determinants: Comparison of Coefficients of Variation of Profit Three to Five Years before Merger

	Company Type		Merger	Number of Companies		Mean Values	
Variable	1	2	Type	1	2	1	2
Coefficient of variation of profit							
1. Arithmetic mean	AG	MAG	All	43	43	0.293	0.961
1. (a) Arithmetic mean	AG	AD	All	40	40	0.287	0.827
2. Arithmetic mean	AD	MAD	All	35	35	0.764	0.728
3. Geometric mean	AGAD	MAGMAD	All	30	30	2.639	3.788

** Significant at 5 percent or better.

Number of Industries			$\dfrac{t}{\sqrt{N}}$	Binomial Significance Level (percent)
Difference positive	Total	Proportion positive		
8	8	1.000	1.02	0.78
9	9	1.000	1.06	0.39
8	8	1.000	0.71	0.78

presence of leverage-created, risk-reducing motives for merger. The two tests comparing variances 2.3 and 2.5 are wholly insignificant. Some support for the risk motive hypothesis is suggested in test 2.4, which shows that acquiring firms were significantly more highly geared than their control group partners across the sample as a whole. However, this result may be due to the presence of some dominating extreme values, since in five of nine industries the reverse was true. Moreover the situation seems to be more that the matched acquiring firms had "abnormally" low leverage ratios than that the acquiring firms were abnormally high. Thus the mean for the MAG firms is the lowest of all groups, and in fact the acquiring firms took over firms (AD) with slightly higher leverage ratios than themselves, which in turn were identical with those for the matching nonacquireds. Had reduction in leverage been the motive for merger, the AG firms should have been seeking partners from among their matching nonmerging group or firms similar to them (assuming this were possible). In any event they

Difference (ratio)	t	Difference Positive	Total	Proportion Positive	$\dfrac{t}{\sqrt{N}}$	Binomial Significance Level
−0.668	−2.30**	1	9	0.111	−0.351	3.91
−0.540	−3.16**	0	9	0.000	−0.500	0.39
0.036	0.17	4	9	0.444	0.029	100.00
0.697	−1.41	3	9	0.333	−0.258	50.78

Table 4-9. Comparison of Leverage Ratios, Premerger Year

Variable	Company Type 1	Company Type 2	Merger Type	Number of Companies 1	Number of Companies 2	Mean Values 1	Mean Values 2
Leverage ratios							
2.2 Absolute differences (arithmetic means)	AGAD	MAGMAD	All	39	39	0.118	0.153
2.3 Variances	AG	MAG	All	49	49	0.016	0.015
2.4 Arithmetic means	AG	MAG	All	49	49	0.625	0.574
2.5 Variances	AG	MAD	All	42	42	0.018	0.014
2.6 Arithmetic means	AD	MAD	All	42	42	0.654	0.654

**Significant at 5 percent or better.

should not have been acquiring firms with higher leverage ratios than themselves. And if average increase were intended, we should have observed higher than normal leverage among the acquired firms.

The result for the absolute values test 2.2, which indicates a negative absolute difference in leverage ratios between merging firms and nonmerging pairs of firms, just fails to achieve significance at the 10 percent level and is consistent with the ranking of the various groups in terms of mean leverage ratios.[14]

Statistical Tests of Merger Effects

Tests 5-7 Post- versus Premerger Rates of Return on Assets, Equity, and Sales. At the conventional confidence levels, none of the differences in profit performance, measured in three different ways, between merging firms and the various counterfactuals are statistically significant (Table 4-10). However, in all nine comparisons the sign of the difference is positive; the merging firms did better. Their relative superiority is least marked in comparison with matched nonmerging firms, followed by the comparison with projected performance. In relation to industry performance, merging firms avoided the decline in industry profits experienced by firms as a whole, though bearing in mind the tendency for merging firms to be relatively large, this could have little to do with merger per se but rather be due to large firms doing better than the industry average over the relevant periods. Nevertheless, bearing in mind the effect of small sample size on the *t*-test and the possibility of downward bias in postmerger profitability of merging firms due to adjustment costs, it seems reasonable to conclude that the results give some, if slight, suggestion of increased profit rates due to merger. Certainly, although not significant within the normal limits, the results are more suggestive of an increase in rates of return after a merger than of a decrease.

Difference (ratio)	t	Difference Positive	Total	Proportion Positive	$\dfrac{t}{\sqrt{N}}$	Binomial Significance Level
−0.035	−1.654**	2	9	0.22	−0.265	17.97
	F = 1.069	3	6	0.50		100.00
0.056	2.193**	4	9	0.44	0.313	100.00
	F = 1.206	4	6	0.67		68.75
−0.0004	−0.01	4	9	0.44	−0.003	100.00

To attempt to determine whether the slight increase in profitability arose from market power or efficiency effects we turn to a comparison of post- with premerger firm size. The comparison is again in terms of geometric means, for the same reasons as apply to the earlier test 1.

Tests 5B–7B Post- versus Premerger Size Levels (geometric means). The main problem in comparing post- and premerger size levels lies in the choice of size variable. Ideally we should use a measure of real or physical output. But this is neither directly available, nor can it be derived from sales revenue in the absence of data on prices at firm level. The problem is therefore to choose from the available alternatives the best proxy measure for real output.

Observed changes in sales revenue will of course reflect changes in real output, but also include price effects. These are positive in the market power case and negative in a pure efficiency case. Hence, if sales revenue is used to proxy real output changes, the expected changes are both biased toward zero. A total assets measure is less likely to be affected by the price effects of merger. However, its relationship to real output will change if the merger leads to changes either in the utilization rate of the firm's capital or in technology involving more or less capital-intensive techniques, either of which could happen as a result of efficiency changes. An increase in the utilization rate would result in an understatement of the true output change (i.e., impart negative bias), while a change to more capital-intensive methods leads to positive bias. A total assets measure is also prone to (upward) revaluation of assets following merger, which also introduces positive bias. Similar problems arise in the case of equity and plant and equipment measures. Thus, there is no completely satisfactory solution, though the sign of the likely biases is to some extent predictable.

Results of the post- versus premerger size level tests are reported in Table 4–11 for all available measures. Again, none of the differences are

Table 4–10. Post- versus Premerger Profitability (tests 5 through 7)[a]

| | Comparison With | | | | | | | | | | |
| | Matched nonmerging firms (test 5) | | | | Industry performance (test 6) | | | | Projected performance (test 7) | | | |
Profit Rate Variable	Merging firms AGAD	Nonmerging firms MAGMAD	Difference	t	Merging firms AGAD	Industry	Difference	t	Merging firms AGAD	Projected performance	Difference	t
Return on assets	−0.003	−0.006	0.003	0.18	0.005	−0.013	0.017	1.10	0.043	0.036	0.007	0.65
Return on equity	0.063	0.028	0.035	0.35	0.132	−0.016	0.148	1.12	0.297	0.230	0.066	0.68
Return on sales	0.025	−0.002	0.027	0.79	0.020	−0.010	0.030	1.16	0.040	0.036	0.004	0.55

[a] Rates of return are three- (minimum) to five-year averages.

Table 4–11. Post- versus Premerger Size Levels (tests 5B through 7B); geometric means

| | Matched nonmerging firms (test 5B) | | | | Comparison With | | | | | | | |
| | | | | | Industry performance (test 6B) | | | | Projected performance (test 7B) | | | |
Size Variable	Merging firms AGAD	Nonmerging firms MAGMAD	Difference	t	Merging firms AGAD	Industry	Difference	t	Merging firms AGAD (millions)	Projected performance	Difference	t
Assets	1.84	1.66	1.11	1.83*	1.76	1.65	1.07	1.58	2.21	2.07	0.24	0.24
Plant	1.15	1.63	0.71	−1.29								
Equity	1.39	1.36	1.02	0.35	1.33	1.26	1.06	0.88	0.33	0.31	1.06	0.20
Sales	1.54	1.59	0.97	−0.37	1.54	1.61	0.95	−0.71	2.56	2.69	0.95	−0.15

* Significant at 10 percent or better.

Table 4–12.   Post- versus Premerger Growth Rates (tests 8–10)

Growth in Size Variable	Arithmetic means				Geometric means			
	AGAD	MAGMAD	Differ-ence	t	AGAD	MAGMAD	Ratio	t
Assets	2.535	0.743	1.792	0.54	1.120	0.921	1.217	0.49
Plant and equipment	6.738	5.130	1.608	0.24	1.130	2.173	0.520	−0.88
Equity	1.545	−3.552	5.097	0.845	0.213	0.659	0.323	−0.67
Sales	1.165	2.911	−1.746	−0.39	1.007	1.362	0.739	−0.827

Comparison With Matched nonmerging firms (Tests 8, 8A)

* Significant at 10 percent or better.

significant at the normal (5 percent) level. But in contrast to the profitability tests, we here observe a mixed sign pattern. If randomly distributed among the various tests and size measures, this would be consistent with the hypothesis of no significant differences either way. However, all the differences in terms of assets (and equity) are positive (and significant at around 7 percent in the AGAD/MAGMAD comparison), whereas for sales revenue they are consistently negative. Bearing in mind that there are more sources of positive than of negative bias on the assets measure, whereas the tendency will be for the sales revenue changes to be pulled toward zero, there are some grounds for suspecting a tendency for output to fall. But clearly the results of tests 5B–7B will support only the most tentative of conclusions.

Tests 8–10 Post- versus Premerger Growth Rates of Plant and Equipment, Assets, Equity, and Sales.   The statistical tests on merger effects are taken a further step in tests 8–10, where we consider postmerger changes in the growth rates (i.e., first differences) of four size variables— assets, plant and equipment, equity, and sales. Once again, the three counterfactuals used in tests 5–7 are employed.

As in the previous tests, the measured differences between the actual performance of merging firms and that which could have been expected are statistically insignificant in all cases save one (Table 4–12). The exception is the markedly less great fall in the growth rate of sales as between merging firms and their relevant industries (test 9), which is significant at just over 6 percent. Taking the tests as a whole, we again observe a mixed sign pattern. Nine of the fourteen differences are negative, including all three in the comparison against projected performance (test 10). However, in contrast with the size level tests, the sign pattern is not consistent across tests for any given size variable, and the results seem to be rather sensitive to sample size, which varies across tests. In general tests 8–10

Industry Performance (Test 9)				Projected performance (Test 10)			
Arithmetic means				Arithmetic means			
AGAD	Industry	Differ-ence	t	AGAD	Projected performance	Differ-ence	t
1.207	2.513	−1.307	−0.67	10.045	19.932	−9.877	−1.45
0.201	2.950	−2.799	−0.63	6.553	10.034	−3.480	−0.53
−0.801	−6.037	5.237	1.960*	11.425	21.701	−10.276	−1.09

increase rather than reduce the tentativeness of any conclusions that can be drawn about postmerger changes in size (output). The ambiguity of test outcomes is, of course, to be expected if, as is not unlikely, the sample contains individual instances in which both market power and efficiency effects predominate.

CONCLUSIONS

In common with almost all developed market economies, West Germany experienced a merger wave at the end of the 1960s. Although the available statistics underestimate the true number of mergers in the preceding period, a distinct surge in the level of merger activity can be discerned from 1969 to 1971. However, unlike most other countries, Germany has also seen a continuing rapid growth of mergers throughout the 1970s. While the quality of the statistical record vitiates firm conclusions, it seems that the major reorganization of corporate ownership and control through mergers that occurred in the 1950s and 1960s in other countries, notably the United Kingdom and United States, may now be taking place in Germany a decade or so later.

As in most other European countries, but unlike the United States, German mergers have tended to be horizontal, though vertical mergers have increased recently. There has been an increase in the proportion of mergers taking place outside the industrial area, but throughout the last two decades, mergers have been highly concentrated in a few merger-intensive industries, notably chemical products (together with mineral oil products), electrical engineering, machine tools, and iron and steel. As another influential source (the MK) has observed, most merger-intensive industries are among those in which seller concentration has increased most sharply over the period.

From a community viewpoint, the central question is whether the structural adaptation that mergers brings about works generally for the social good or ill. In this regard, the results of our statistical tests for alternative merger causes and effects do not suggest significant gains. The fact that the merging firms are very much larger than nonmerging firms appears to rule out the pursuit of scale economies as the overriding motive of this elimination, and the alternative, monopolization, explanation gains indirect support. Nor does it appear from the results that the German mergers can be interpreted as a strategy calculated to improve the risk-bearing capacity of the productive system. As far as postmerger performance is concerned, one could observe no statistically significant changes due to merger in the relevant performance variables. Strictly speaking, this implies that while mergers do not demonstrably do great harm, neither do they appear to do positive good. When, however, we look at the overall pattern of results, observing the numbers and distribution of positive and negative signs, the suggestion is less one of exploited efficiency improvements and output gains and more indicative of increased market power.

It must be remembered, however, that the merger sample is biased toward larger mergers, where it could be argued that the scope for scale economy gains may be untypically low. Also, as we see in analyzing the relationship between merger incidence and the level of economic activity, a qualitative shift in merger activity may have taken place around 1970–1971. If so—and pending further analysis the suggestion must remain purely speculative—the merger sample analyzed would likely contain about two-thirds "old style" to one-third "new style" mergers. Whether, if such a qualitative shift did occur, the change was for better or worse must remain a matter for future enquiry. Only two slight indications of positive social purpose in mergers seem discernible throughout the whole of the analysis we have undertaken. One is that the most merger-intensive industries (chemicals, together with mineral oil products; electrical engineering; machine tools; and iron and steel) could all be described as areas that have been unusually subject to technological disturbance and/or substantial demand shifts. As such, they are areas in which the need for structural adaptation to changed conditions might be thought both unusually great and socially desirable. Second, it was observed that the increases in vertical mergers might perhaps be interpreted as logical reactions to adverse conditions following the 1973 oil crisis and 1975 recession.

Unless more than compensated for by economic efficiency gains—and perhaps even then—the social and political consequences of increased economic power through mergers will probably be thought of as outcomes to be avoided. Taking all the evidence from our study together, there appears to be very little that could be put forward against an outright merger ban or some similarly strong policy based on this premise. The existing German policy toward mergers is very far from being a strong one in at least two respects. First, as has been stressed elsewhere, a very large part of merger activity falls outside the scope of the controls because of the laxly drawn escape clauses. Second, the widespread occurrence of partial rather than full legal mergers argues that, unless the majority of mergers are mere portfolio investment exercises with no attempt to coordinate firms' behavior, which seems unlikely, the effective constraints on inter-firm coordination via the cartel laws must be weak. While some tightening of the legal provisions in the first area is in prospect, there is no indication of a parallel move in the second. Finally, there is a good case that can be made for policy change in the adjacent area of company information dis-closure. As is widely recognized and as our experience in carrying out this study confirms, it is extraordinarily difficult to obtain the information necessary to evaluate the performance of German companies, whether involved in mergers or not. Measures to increase the public accountability of firms, especially GmbH companies, would serve many social purposes, as well as permitting a more definitive assessment of the origins and social purposes of mergers.

NOTES

1. Statistisches Jahrbuch, Federal Statistics Office, Wiesbaden.
2. The values plotted in Figure 4–2 are annual residuals from the regressions: $N_T = 2.3644e^{0.202t}$ $(r = 0.9763)$ for all mergers, and $N_I = 2.4150e^{0.1684t}$ $(r = 0.9653)$ for industrial mergers.
3. Two striking examples of large firms making acquisitions in series are Veba and Rheinisch-Westfälisches Elektrizitätswerk AG, with forty-seven and forty-five acquisitions respectively over four years. See Kantzenbach (1978).
4. Although it is likely that a significant proportion of the new GmbH companies represents subsidiaries of AG companies that find it attractive to expand in this way for reasons of information disclosure and tax advantage. Such companies would not generally be available for takeover.
5. Trends were fitted as follows:
   Mergers: see preceding sections;
   GDP: $Y = 400.0693 + 23.5547t$, $r = 0.9904$;
   Investment: $Y = 94,393,92 + 3599,25t$, $r = 0.8714$;
   Share index: $Y = 89.0588 + 0.5201t$, $r = 0.2278$.
   Similar conclusions to those drawn below emerge if linear trends are fitted to the subperiods 1958–1968 and 1968–1977.
6. The calculation assumes that turnover is roughly double the value of assets. This figure is based on a sample of over eighty large United Kingdom companies and is probably an overestimate for equivalent, more capital-intensive German firms. £1 = DM 3.7.
7. Monopolkommission: Hauptgutachten I, "Mehr Weltbewerb ist möglich," Nomos Verlagsgesellschaft (Baden-Baden, 1976).
8. Legal mergers, with formal integration and one or both partners losing their separate identity, represent a small minority of all mergers in Germany. For every legal merger in

the 1970s there have been around seven or eight economic mergers, in which the effective control of one company passes to another via the acquisition of a significant ownership interest.

9. *Handbuch der Aktiengesellschaften* (HdA) Hoppenstedt, annual series; and *Wer gehört zu Wem?* Commerzbank, annual series.

10. *Aktiengesellschaften* include the largest German companies, of which there were 2149 in 1977. Only AG companies may seek stock market quotations. Disclosure requirements are minimal for the much more numerous (168,000) GmbH (*Gesellschaften mit beschräubter Haftung*) company type.

11. In the absence of official classification numbers, merging firms were allocated to industries by reference to their principal activities as listed.

12. For the merging n-firm group X we seek a true matching group Z, also with n numbers. In fact we have only Y with $m < n$ firms. For the repeated use of certain members of group Y to be legitimate requires (a) $\bar{Y}$, $\sigma_Y^2 = \bar{Z}$, σ_Z^2 for any variable used in the comparisons and (b) the repeated firms Y_1 are drawn randomly from Y, or $\bar{Y}_1 = \bar{Y}$, $\sigma_{Y_1}^2 = \sigma_Y^2$. In fact, inspection of firm size in the data suggests $\bar{Y} < \bar{Z}$ but $\bar{Y}_1 > \bar{Y}$. Hence, means and variances for the control group with repeats may be closer to $\bar{Z}$, σ_Z^2 than are $\bar{Y}$, σ_Y^2 themselves.

13. In each case we used the maximum number of observations available, going outside the maximum five-year premerger period used in other tests.

14. Thus we have AG (0.63) $>$ MAG (0.57) and AD (0.65) = MAD (0.65) but |AG − AD| (0.02) < |MAG − MAD| (0.08).

Chapter 5

France, 1962–1972

Frédéric Jenny and André-Paul Weber

There are no official statistics in France on merger activity, and the market shares of the largest firms in each industry are not systematically computed by the National Institute of Statistics (France's equivalent of the American Bureau of Census). It is therefore somewhat difficult to get an accurate picture of the evolution of industrial concentration. However, there is no doubt that the political circles and the business community were in favor of increased concentration during most of the 1960s. From this point of view *The American Challenge* of J. J. Servan-Schreiber reflects perfectly the conventional wisdom of that decade. The views of the French elite were at best simplistic and based on three observations: First, the American firms were, on average, larger than the French firms; second, the American firms had, on average, lower unit costs than French firms; third, the American firms were, on average, more innovative than French firms. There was no doubt in the minds of government officials or of business leaders that those three facts were linked by causal relationship and that if the American firms were more innovative and more competitive than French firms, it was because they were larger. The conclusion of such reasoning was that if French industry wanted to meet the challenge of increasingly stiff international competition and if France wanted to remain economically independent, the average size of industrial firms had to be increased and French industries had to become more concentrated.

Given the extent of these proconcentration feelings, it is not surprising to find that the number of mergers seems to have increased dramatically during the 1960s and that the administration not only did not discourage this merger wave but facilitated its occurrence and initiated mergers in those industries in which public firms were among the leaders. There is also some evidence that market concentration increased over that period.

Before tackling the question of the determinants and effects of mergers, we will devote three sections to an overview of the recent structural changes in the French industrial sector. The first section will briefly present what we know about the pattern of merger activity during the 1950–1976 period. In the second section we will summarize the industrial policy of the French government during the 1960s. Finally, we will present some evidence on the trend in concentration at the industry level between 1961 and 1969. Most of the data that we use for the first and the third sections comes from an earlier study that we conducted for the French Planning Commission in 1972 (Jenny and Weber 1974). Whenever possible the statistics have been updated to cover the 1972–1976 period.

THE MERGER MOVEMENT, 1950–1976

As we mentioned at the beginning of this chapter, there are no official statistics on merger activity in France, and not all firms are required to publicize their mergers. There is thus no way to have an exhaustive view of merger activity. However, by using various sources of information we were able to follow the merger activity of a sample of 1690 firms over a twenty-five year period. This sample includes all the firms that were listed on the stock market in 1969 plus a number of firms that were not listed on the stock market that same year but were subject to a 1966 law that requires that large firms disclose a variety of information about their activities, their financial status, and their plans for mergers if they have any.

Our analysis will tell us something about the merger activity of those 1690 firms. However, one should keep in mind that this analysis will give us a biased view of merger activity over the period 1950–1975 for at least three reasons. The first is that the definition of mergers that we had to use is fairly large. It includes not only cases in which one firm was acquired by another but also cases in which only part of a firm was acquired or cases in which the acquiring firm owned a majority of the stock of the acquired firm before the merger. Second, the firms in the sample are large, and we have no way of knowing the merger activity of small unlisted firms. The third and potentially more serious source of bias comes from the fact that the firms in the sample were alive in 1969. This is due to the fact that because of poor sources of information, it was impossible to trace the pre-1969 history of large or listed firms that had disappeared either through merger or through bankruptcy. Thus, if a listed firm was acquired before 1969 by

Table 5–1. Distribution of Merger Activity, 1950–1976

Sector	Firms	Acquiring Firms Number	Percent	Nonacquiring Firms Number	Percent	Mergers Number	Percent
Activity outside metropolitan France	56	20	1.89	36	5.66	54	1.44
Energy	27	17	1.61	10	1.57	52	1.39
Manufacturing	749	513	48.62	236	37.16	1912	51.28
Transportation and communication	72	36	3.41	36	5.66	104	2.78
Commerce	200	131	12.41	60	10.86	525	14.08
Services	506	307	29.09	199	31.33	1028	27.57
Undefined	80	31	2.93	49	7.71	53	1.42
Total	1690	1055	99.90	635	99.90	3728	99.90

another listed firm—say in 1965—but had acquired prior to that date a series of firms, those mergers do not appear in our statistics. This will result in an underestimation of the merger activity of large or listed firms for the period 1950–1969. To the extent that we have complete records for the 1969–1976 period, we were able to take into account all the mergers that the 1690 firms conducted after 1969. While there is no doubt that our analysis of merger activity is seriously impaired by the imperfection of the data source, we feel justified in presenting it for two reasons. First, it is, as far as we know, the only long-run analysis of merger activity in France. Second, as we shall see, some of the results would seem to be unaffected by the third bias we mentioned.

The distribution by industrial sectors of all the firms in the sample as well as the distribution of acquiring firms and of mergers is given in Table 5–1.

As we can see from Table 5–1, the 1055 acquiring firms initiated 3728 mergers during the 1950–1976 period. At such a high level of aggregation, the average propensity to merge for the acquiring firms seems to be roughly the same whatever sector they are in. However, an examination of merger activity at the two-digit level (the French two-digit level is intermediary between the two- and three-digit levels of the U. S. Standard Industrial Classification) shows that there are striking differences between industries belonging to the same sector. Thus in the industrial sector, the average number of mergers per acquiring firm is high for industries such as glass manufacturing (7.6), heavy electrical equipment (6.2), metal production (7.28), and fat (7.0), but low for slow-growing traditional industries that have a relatively stable technology such as furniture making (2.1), leather works (2.5), and paper and cardboard (2.8). Table 5–2 gives the distribution of acquiring firms at the two-digit industry level as well as the number of mergers they initiated.

Another interesting feature of the merger activity is the distribution

Table 5–2. Merger Activity of a Sample of 1690 Firms, 1950–1977; Distribution of Firms and Mergers across Two-digit Industries

Industry	Number of Acquiring Firms (1)	Number of Nonacquiring Firms (2)	Number of Mergers (3)	Total Number of Firms (4 = 1 + 2)
Main activity outside France	17	36	29	53
Agriculture	3	—	25	3
Electricity	1	2	1	3
Gas	—	1	—	1
Water, urban heating	4	5	7	9
Petroleum	12	2	44	14
Iron extraction	3	—	7	3
Extraction of nonferrous metallic minerals	1	1	1	2
Cut stones and stone products	9	8	27	17
Miscellaneous minerals	3	3	5	6
Blast furnaces and steel mills	7	7	22	14
Non ferrous metals	7	3	51	10
Metallurgy	6	3	29	9
Primary transformation of metals	9	4	30	13
Foundries	32	15	76	47
Machinery {	25	13	58	38
	8	2	22	10
Miscellaneous metallic products {	11	5	30	16
	4	1	12	5
Shipbuilding	7	2	13	9
Motor vehicles and car bodies	18	11	93	29
Aircraft	4	2	8	6
Electric and electronic equipment	31	13	192	44
Watches, precision instruments	16	2	30	18
Glass and glassware	6	3	46	9
Ceramic	7	3	25	10
Building materials	19	11	66	30
Construction {	20	9	51	29
	25	8	105	33
Chemicals and allied products {	43	9	169	52
	20	4	65	24
Rubber and asbestos	4	5	11	9
Fat	7	2	45	9
Flour and other grain mill products	8	4	31	12
Bakery products	4	1	8	5
Sugar and confectionery products	39	20	174	59
Dairy products	10	4	43	14
Canned products	8	2	19	10
Miscellaneous food and kindred products	5	2	81	7

Table 5–2. (Continued)

Industry	Number of Acquiring Firms (1)	Number of Nonacquiring Firms (2)	Number of Mergers (3)	Total Number of Firms (4 = 1 + 2)
Refrigeration	6	—	13	6
Weaving and knitting mills	26	16	74	42
Miscellaneous textile industries	4	2	20	6
Clothing	4	2	7	6
Fur products	1	1	1	2
Leather goods	4	2	10	6
Shoes	1	—	2	1
Lumber and wood furnitures	7	4	15	11
Paper and allied products	19	12	54	31
Printing and publishing	7	10	54	17
Jewelries	—	1	—	1
Toys, games	1	1	1	2
Office supplies	2	2	4	4
Other miscellaneous fabricated products	2	—	7	2
Plastic products	3	1	5	4
Road carriers	10	5	23	15
Rail carriers	5	16	12	21
River carriers	3	2	12	5
Sea carriers	10	9	37	19
Air carriers	1	—	9	1
Auxiliaries of carriers	7	4	11	11
Food stores {	43	16	158	59
	6	2	24	8
Nonspecialized commerce	15	12	67	27
Commerce of raw materials {	20	17	117	37
	3	—	5	3
Commerce of textile products	10	1	43	11
Miscellaneous commerce	1	3	6	4
Hotels	13	10	32	23
Recycling	2	—	7	2
Auxiliaries of commerce {	8	3	16	11
	10	5	50	15
Real estate	34	28	71	62
Banks, holdings	226	133	866	359
Insurance companies	39	28	81	67
Managing agents	2	—	3	2
Cinemas	2	—	3	2
Other entertainments	3	5	3	8
Other services	1	5	1	6
Undetermined[a]	31	49	53	80
Total	1055	635	3728	1690

[a] For lack of data.

Table 5–3.   Mergers by Sector

Economic Sector	1950	1951	1952	1953	1954	1955	1956	1957	1958	1959	1960
Activity outside metropolitan France	—	—	2	1	1	—	2	—	—	—	1
Energy	1	1	—	—	6	—	7	—	7	—	5
Industry	22	13	26	39	18	46	56	29	39	56	67
Transportation	1	—	—	4	3	3	6	—	1	7	—
Commerce	1	2	2	13	9	6	5	9	7	12	26
Services	4	13	18	17	14	19	14	13	12	41	42
Undefined	—	—	1	1	—	5	2	—	1	1	1
Total	29	29	49	75	51	79	92	51	67	117	142

over time of mergers. Table 5–3 shows the number of mergers each year and for each sector of the economy. The table shows that there has been an overall increase in the number of mergers over time until 1973. More specifically, we can distinguish five periods. The overall level of merger activity was quite low between 1963 and 1957, with an average annual number of mergers of sixty-nine. A first increase in merger activity followed the creation of the European Economic Community (1959–1964) and the average annual number of mergers for those five years rose to 165. In 1965 and 1967, as we shall see below, merger laws giving a favorable tax treatment to merging firms were enacted, and they seem to have had an impact on merger activity since the average annual number of mergers reached a peak of 233 for the four following years (1967–1970). The level of merger activity remained quite high until the end of 1973 with an average of 180 mergers per year during 1971–1973. Finally, it seems that merger activity declined significantly during 1974–1976 since the average number of mergers for those years was only 124. The merger movement in the industrial sector closely parallels the overall merger movement.

As we pointed out, our analysis could be biased because we could not take into account the mergers initiated by firms that were acquired before 1969. Thus, up to that year there might be a systematic underevaluation of the number of mergers. Our finding that the number of mergers increased at the beginning of the 1960s and again after the merger laws were enacted could be due to this bias if the firms that were acquired during the 1960s were large listed or unlisted firms that had been heavy acquirers in the 1950s. Although we cannot rule out such a possibility with certainty, our impression is that unless the characteristics of the acquired firms changed drastically around 1969 (and we have no reason to believe that they did), our results are unlikely to be due only to faulty statistics. Indeed, after 1969, acquired firms tended to be small, and they had a lower propensity to merge in the past than acquiring firms.

A third feature of merger activity during 1950–1976 is explored in Table 5–4, which gives for each sector the frequency with which acquiring firms merged. As can be seen, a small number of firms were very heavy ac-

1961	1962	1963	1964	1965	1966	1967	1968	1969	1970	1971	1972	1973	1974	1975	1976	Total
—	—	—	1	1	—	4	5	16	9	5	1	2	—	3	—	54
2	2	2	1	4	—	—	5	2	2	—	—	—	4	—	1	52
87	116	116	96	97	120	112	111	136	107	98	83	71	58	47	46	1912
3	4	9	3	3	6	—	12	11	9	6	—	4	3	2	4	104
19	19	30	9	32	10	49	29	20	25	39	31	59	22	27	13	525
56	27	71	53	36	58	70	58	78	54	30	66	44	38	44	38	1028
—	1	—	5	—	2	1	1	—	6	1	2	—	5	12	5	53
167	169	228	168	173	196	236	221	263	212	179	183	180	130	135	107	3728

quirers during the period. Thus, thirty-three firms merged more than fifteen times during the twenty-five-year period, and they are responsible for one-fifth of the total acquisitions (763 out of 3728). Similarly, 226 firms (roughly one-fifth of all acquiring firms and 13 percent of all the firms in the sample) merged at least five times between 1950 and 1976, and they initiated 60 percent of all mergers (2176 out of 3728). At the other end of the distribution, approximately 60 percent of the acquiring firms merged only once or twice. It is worth noting that in our analysis of the determinants and effects of mergers we will have to eliminate—in most cases—the mergers initiated by frequent acquirers because the effects of these mergers tend to become inextricably entangled. However, it is possible that the motivations and the performances of the frequent acquirers are different from those of firms that merged only occasionally.

A last characteristic of the merger activity that was noted in our 1974 study is worth mentioning. We studied the subsample of mergers over the period 1970–1972 from the point of view of the respective size of the merging firms and from the point of view of the economic nature of the mergers (vertical, horizontal, conglomerate). In many instances we had to go back to the annual reports to the shareholders to decide whether a merger was vertical or conglomerate, and it is possible that in some cases we misjudged the true nature of the merger. From the point of view of size we distinguished three cases: mergers between firms of comparable sizes (type I); mergers in which the size of the acquired firm was less than 70 percent of the acquiring firm size (type II); mergers in which the acquiring firm acquired only part of another firm (type III). The results of the analysis are given in Table 5–5.

The table shows that in 75 percent of all cases the acquiring firm was larger than the acquired firm by at least 30 percent. The table also shows that about half the mergers were horizontal during the 1970–1972 period.

Although our description of the merger movement is somewhat sketchy due to the difficulty of gathering data, it appears that the 1960s were characterized by a merger wave that was not limited to the manufacturing sector. This merger wave seems to have peaked at the end of the decade.

Table 5–4. Numbers of Mergers and Acquiring Firms

Economic Sector	Number of Mergers over the Period															Total Number of Acquiring firms	Total Number of mergers
	1	2	3	4	5	6	7	8	9	10	11	12	13	14	15 or more		
Activity outside metropolitan France	12	5	—	—	2	—	—	—	—	—	—	—	—	—	1	20	54
Energy	10	2	1	1	—	—	1	1	—	—	—	—	—	—	1	17	52
Manufacturing	168	106	83	46	26	11	15	17	7	3	5	5	3	1	17	513	1912
Transportation	13	7	7	2	2	1	2	—	2	—	—	—	—	—	—	36	104
Commerce	53	19	13	8	11	8	7	2	—	2	1	1	1	—	5	131	525
Services	123	71	28	21	17	11	7	4	6	3	1	1	—	5	9	307	1028
Undefined	19	8	2	1	—	—	—	1	—	—	—	—	—	—	—	31	53
Total	398	218	134	79	58	31	32	25	15	8	7	7	4	6	33	1055	3728

Table 5-5. A Categorization of Merger Activity

Economic Sector	Total Number of Mergers	Type I	Type II	Type III	Horizontal	Vertical	Conglomerate
Activity outside metropolitan France	15	3	12	—	7	4	4
Energy	2	—	2	—	2	—	—
Manufacturing	288	30	266	32	139	75	74
Transportation	15	1	11	3	10	2	3
Commerce	95	15	54	26	49	27	19
Services	150	10	122	18	66	29	55
Undefined	9	4	2	3	?	?	?
Total	574	63	429[a]	82	273	137	155

[a]Over the 1970–1972 period, 149 mergers were ones in which the acquiring firm held more than 50 percent of the shares of the acquired firm at the time of the merger. These were all Type II mergers.

1960s is the importance of mergers in the financial sector. A number of those mergers occurred between holding corporations that had subsidiaries in the manufacturing sector. It is therefore possible that some of those mergers were prompted by industrial considerations and that they resulted in some kind of integration or of increased cooperation among manufacturing firms. Unfortunately, we were not able to assess the extent of this phenomenon.

THE GOVERNMENT POLICY OF THE 1960s

Having reviewed the evidence on the merger movement, we will now briefly summarize the government industrial and competition policies of the 1960s. As we mentioned in the introduction, the government favored increased concentration during most of the 1960s. This is not to say that it completely ignored the problems created by anticompetitive practices in concentrated markets. As a matter of fact, a competition law primarily designed to fight cartel agreements was enacted in 1956. The law was revised in 1963, and its scope extended to include monopolistic practices by individual firms. But as we have argued elsewhere (Jenny and Weber 1975), very limited means and very little importance were given to the Commission Technique des Ententes et des Positions Dominantes (the administrative body in charge of overseeing application of the law). What is more, the penalties for firms entering competitive agreements or monopolizing markets were so light that the deterrent effect of the competition law was practically nil.

Rather than actively promoting competition among firms, the government tried to increase the size of French firms and to induce them to is more, the penalties for firms entering competitive agreements or monopolizing markets were so light that the deterrent effect of the competition law was practically nil.

Rather than actively promoting competition among firms, the government tried to increase the size of French firms and to induce them to specialize production in the hope that this would improve the efficiency of the French economy. The government thus directly engineered numerous mergers and cartellike agreements betwen leaders of key industries and indirectly facilitated mergers between firms of all sizes through the 1965 and 1967 merger laws.

The heavy hand of the government was clearly visible in the public sector of the economy. Thus, for example, in 1965 two large oil companies (Régie autonome des Pétroles and Bureau de Recherche des Pétroles) were merged to give birth to ERAP (Entreprise de Recherche et d'Activité Pétroliere). In 1966, two of the leading nationalized banks (Banque Nationale pour le Commerce et l'Industrie and Comptoir National d'Escompte de Paris) merged, and they became the Banque National de Paris (BNP). In 1966, major reorganizations in the chemical industry led to the merger of large public firms. Numerous structural changes also occurred in the automobile industry under the sponsorship of the government as well as in aircraft manufacturing, although in those industries the government relied more often on specialization agreements among the firms involved than on outright mergers. Finally, it is worth noting that at the beginning of the 1970s, important mergers occurred between public insurance companies.

But the government was also able to influence merger activity between private firms directly whenever the public sector was one of the major customers of those firms or whenever they needed public subsidies to survive. Thus, for example, in 1966 the steel producers were bailed out of a severe financial crisis through government subsidies on the condition that they would modernize their equipment and concentrate. A similar condition was imposed on shipbuilders, who are also heavily subsidized. In industries such as electrical equipment, telecommunication, and railroad car repairing, the fact that the public sector was a major customer led to mergers and increased concentration.

The government tried to induce mergers between private firms in a more general way through the enactment of the 1965 and 1967 merger laws. These laws reduce the tax on issuing shares when the issue of new shares is the by-product of a merger. What is even more important for the merging firms, the 1965 and 1967 laws decrease substantially the tax rate on capital gains when those capital gains accrue from a merger. Although originally the merger laws were supposed to be in effect only until 1969, they have been reenacted on a yearly basis since then.

THE EVOLUTION OF THE CONCENTRATION OF INDUSTRIES

Given the efforts of the government to increase the average size of firms during the 1960s and given the intense merger activity of the large firms during that decade, one may wonder what happened to the structure of industries. This is not an easy question to answer in France given the paucity of data on industrial structure. However, while we were doing our study for the planning commission, the Ministry of France computed for us the concentration ratios (i.e., the shares of the four largest firms in the total sales of the industry) for all the two-digit manufacturing industries between 1961 and 1969 at the two-digit level and between 1963 and 1969 at the three-digit level. Although the shortcomings of such an indicator for measuring concentration are well known and although the period under consideration is rather short, this was the sole data source that we could use to try to analyze the trends of concentration in the manufacturing sector. We shall briefly summarize the results of the analysis.

Altogether it seems that concentration increased slightly during the 1960s. Table 5–6 shows that both the average concentration ratio in the manufacturing sector and the weighted average concentration ratio (with the total sales of each industry used as weights) increased by about two points over the period. The table also shows that most of this increase occurred between 1965 and 1969.

Although there seems to be an upward trend in concentration ratios during the 1960s, the differences between the mean concentration at the beginning of the period and at the end are not statistically significant at the 5 percent level either at the two-digit or at the three-digit level.

When one looks at the variation in the concentration ratios of each three-digit manufacturing industry, it appears that between 1963 and 1969 C_4 has increased in 140 industries, decreased in 88 industries, and remained constant in ten cases. Some of the industries have experienced rather large increases in C_4. Thus among the 140 industries for which ΔC_4 was positive, it was larger than 8 in 41 cases, larger than 5 in 66 cases, and larger than 4 in 77 cases. Similarly, some of the industries for which ΔC_4 was negative experienced a rather large decline in their concentration.

The fact that some industries experienced an increase in concentration whereas some others moved toward a more competitive structure prompted us to try to analyze the relationship between ΔC_4 at the industry level and various potential determinants of concentration trends (Jenny and Weber 1978). More specifically, using a multiple regression analysis, we tried to relate ΔC_4 to the original level of concentration of the industry, to the importance of barriers to entry (economies of scale, absolute capital cost requirement, differentiation), and to the growth rate of the industry.

Table 5–6. Changes in Average Concentration Ratios in Manufacturing

	1961	1963	1965	1967	1969
Three-digit level (238 manufacturing industries)					
Average C_4		42.28			45.08
Weighted average C_4		34.26			35.88
Two-digit level (48 manufacturing industries)					
Average C_4	25.75	26.21	25.98	26.70	27.88
Weighted average C_4	20.08	20.21	19.42	20.73	22.11

Source: Data supplied by the Ministry of Finance.

The results show that there is a negative and statistically significant (at the 5 percent level) relationship between ΔC_4 and the level of concentration at the beginning of the period and a positive and significant relationship between the change in concentration and the level of certain barriers to entry (economies of scale and absolute capital cost requirement). It thus seems that in some concentrated industries either leading firms misjudged the height of barriers to entry (if they were trying to maximize their profits in the long run) or they chose to maximize their profits in the short run, thereby facilitating entry. (For further discussion of these results see, Jenny and Weber 1978.)

It is somewhat difficult to link in a rigorous way the loose ends that we have accumulated in our brief survey. 1965 appears to be a pivotal year in three ways. First, the government enacted the first merger law, which gave an incentive for firms to merge in 1965; second, it seems that a merger wave started in 1965; third, the level of concentration, on an industry basis, increased faster after 1965 than it did before. Although we do not have sufficient data to substantiate the claim that there is a causal relationship between these three facts, economic reasoning leads us to believe that they are connected. As we shall see, the statistical analysis of the determinants and effects of mergers, to which we now turn, gives us some circumstantial evidence that there is a direct link between the 1965 merger law and increased merger activity. It also enables us to assess the extent to which mergers lead to better economic performance for the merging firms.

STATISTICAL ANALYSIS OF THE DETERMINANTS AND EFFECTS OF MERGERS

To carry out a statistical analysis along the lines defined in Chapter 2, we first had to identify those mergers for which we could gather the relevant data over at least a four-year period for the acquired firm. Numerous problems arose during our search.

All the firms listed on the French Stock Exchange and contemplating a merger must file an application with the "Commission des Operations de Bourse" (COB, the French equivalent of the American SEC). This standardized application must, in principle, include the balance sheets of the acquiring and acquired firms for the five years preceding the merger as well as various information crucial to our analysis. The COB thus provided the main data base for our investigation. However, as we found out, the applications were often incomplete, particularly as far as the acquired firm was concerned. As a consequence, a number of mergers that took place during the period 1962–1972 had to be dropped from our sample.

A second problem arose because some acquiring firms had engaged in multiple mergers either during the same year or in successive years. In those cases in which the acquiring firm had merged with several firms during the same year or over a two-year period, all the mergers were lumped together, and the variables for the acquiring firm were recorded for the four (or five) years preceding the first merger and the four (or five) years following the last merger. Multiple mergers over a period longer than two years were a more serious problem as it was generally impossible to weed out the influence of each merger and difficult to gather the relevant variables for the premerger and postmerger periods. Those cases were then dropped from the analysis.

A third problem was that in some cases it turned out to be impossible to find a suitable set of matching firms for the acquiring or the acquired firm. Several criteria were used in the matching process. Matching firms had to be in the same three-digit industry (although this requirement was relaxed in a few cases in which the two-digit industry was narrowly defined from the standpoint of the market); they had to be in the same size class as the merging firms; and they had to have a sales-asset ratio similar to that of the merging firms. The first criterion ensured that the matched firms had the same main line of business; the second criterion was used to avoid systematic differences in the performance of matched firms due to their sizes (on the difference in performance due to size in France, see Jenny and Weber 1976); the third criterion avoided the problem of matching firms with widely different levels of diversification or of vertical integration. When a suitable set of matching firms was not found for the acquiring or the acquired firm, the merger was dropped from the sample.

A fourth problem came from the fact that many large manufacturing companies are subsidiaries of holding corporations. Thus a number of important mergers initiated by holding corporations during the period under consideration might have been prompted by industrial considerations. However, these mergers could not be included in our sample because of accounting difficulties. Indeed, holding corporations are not required to provide the accounts of their subsidiaries or even to give a detailed list of their holdings.

A fifth, and last, problem arose because a majority of the mergers initiated by firms listed on the stock market involved the acquisition of unlisted firms. To have as large a number of observations as possible, we decided to keep in the sample those mergers between listed acquiring firms and unlisted acquired firms whenever we could find a suitable listed matched firm for the acquired firm. In other words, we eliminated only those cases for which the unlisted acquired firm was so small that no listed firm in the same three-digit industry could be used as a control firm or those cases in which the unlisted acquired firm and the potential listed control firms had widely divergent asset-sales ratios.

Since one would expect significant differences in the capital structure of listed and unlisted firms, the tests on leverage were run on the subsample of mergers for which the acquired firms were listed as well as on the total sample of mergers. The tests involving the use of price-earning ratios were

Table 5–7. Distribution of Acquiring and Acquired Firms Across Two-digit Industries (sample used in the analysis of the determinants and effects of mergers)

Industry	Acquiring Firms	Acquired Firms	Year of the Merger
Cut stone and stone product	2	3	1970, 1971
Nonferrous metal	1	1	1972
Aircraft construction	1	1	1971
Electric and electronic equipment	3	7	1969, 1970, 1971
Watches, precision instruments	1	1	1971
Building materials	1	1	1967
Construction	2	3	1970, 1973
Chemicals and allied products	3	3	1968, 1970
Rubber and asbestos	2	2	1967, 1972
Flour and other grain mill products	1	1	1970
Sugar and confectionery	5	9	1965, 1969, 1970
Miscellaneous textile industries	1	2	1967
Leather goods	1	3	1970
Lumber and wood furniture	1	1	1969
Paper and allied products	3	6	1968, 1970
Printing and publishing	2	2	1970, 1972
Road carriers	1	1	1970
River carriers	1	2	1968
Sea carriers	1	1	1968
Auxiliaries of carriers	1	1	1970
Food stores	9	11	1967, 1969, 1970, 1973
Total	43	62	

run exclusively for the subsample of mergers for which the acquired firms were listed.

Our final sample includes sixty-two horizontal mergers for which the acquiring firm held less than 50 percent of the shares of the acquired firm prior to the merger. In twenty-five cases the acquired firm was listed on the stock market. Five nonhorizontal mergers could have been included in the sample. They were excluded, however, because their number was insufficient to justify specific tests on vertical or conglomerate mergers and because their inclusion in the sample might have obscured the analysis of the determinants and effects of horizontal mergers (see Table 5–7).

Finally, one should note that we were not able to secure all the variables required for the statistical analysis for each and every merger included in the analysis. Each test is therefore carried out on the subsample for which we had the relevant information (employment was never available).

Before presenting the results of the tests on the determinants and effects of mergers, we shall briefly compare the characteristics of the four sets of firms (acquiring, acquired, nonacquiring and nonacquired).

COMPARISON OF THE VARIOUS SETS OF FIRMS

The comparisons between the various sets of firms were made on the basis of five main indicators—size, profitability, variability of profits, debt-asset ratio, and growth. For each one of the last four indicators, three types of tests were performed—acquiring firms versus acquired firms, acquiring firms versus matched nonacquiring firms, and acquired firms versus matched nonacquired firms. In the case of the first indicator, however, for obvious reasons pertaining to the matching process, the acquiring and acquired firms were not compared to their matched sample but to the rest of the industry. The rest of the industry is defined in those cases as all the firms listed on the stock market (in the same three-digit industry) that were neither acquiring nor acquired during the period under investigation. For the size comparisons three variables were used—total sales, total assets, and net assets. The size referred to is the size of the firms the year before the merger (i.e., the last year for which the acquired firm reported sales and assets figures). The test on the variability of profits is done by comparing the coefficients of variation of profits (before tax) for the four sets of firms. For the profitability comparisons we used the average after tax profit rates on sales, assets, and equity capital for the four years preceding the merger. The profit figure is net of interest payment and depreciation. The variable chosen for the leverage test is the average debt-asset ratio for the four years preceding the merger. Finally,

Table 5–8. Comparisons of the Characteristics of Acquiring and Acquired Firms

	Number of Obser- vations	Mean Value		Mean Differ- ence	t	Significant at the 5% Level
		AG	AD			
I. Size						
Log sales (all cases)	62	5.01	4.42	0.59	10.29	Yes
Log sales (listed acquired firms)	25	4.91	4.03	0.88	2.93	Yes
Log assets	59	5.10	4.36	0.73	5.99	Yes
Log net assets	62	4.93	4.32	0.60	10.91	Yes
II. Profit Variability						
Coefficient of varia- tion of after tax profits	39	0.33	0.56	−0.23	−1.72	No
III. Profitability						
Profitability–sales	62	2.04	1.14	0.90	1.60	No
Profitability–net assets	61	2.53	1.79	0.73	1.82	No
Profitability–equity capital	60	6.03	3.40	2.63	1.78	No
IV. Leverage						
Debt–assets (all cases	56	0.54	0.54	0.00	−0.08	No
Debt–assets (listed acquired firms)	25	0.54	0.55	−0.01	−0.28	No
V. Growth						
Total assets	32	11.82	11.08	0.74	0.28	No
Sales	56	12.47	11.73	0.73	0.32	No

average annual growth rates of total assets and total sales are used in the growth comparison. Tables 5–8 through 5–10 summarize the results of the analysis.

Table 5–8 shows that acquiring firms, on the average, are larger and more profitable than acquired firms; they also have more stable earnings. However, in a statistical sense only the size comparison is significant at the 5 percent level. Given that some horizontal mergers between very large manufacturing firms were initiated by their parent holding companies and had therefore to be left out of our sample, it is possible that the significant difference in size between the merging firms is due to a biased sampling of the population of all horizontal mergers in manufacturing. However, there is no reason to believe that our sample is biased as far as the population of direct horizontal mergers is concerned (i.e., those mergers that did not involve holding corporations). The difference in profitability between acquiring and acquired firms fails to pass the 5 percent level of significance, but one should note that the absolute value of the mean differences are

Table 5–9. Comparisons of the Characteristics of Acquiring and Nonacquiring Firms

	Number of Obser- vations	Mean Value		Mean Differ- ence	t	Significant at the 5% Level
		AG	Rest of industry			
I. Size						
Log sales (all cases)	62	5.01	4.68	0.33	5.87	Yes
Log sales (listed acquired firms)	25	4.91	4.14	0.77	2.57	Yes
Log assets	59	5.10	4.78	0.31	5.84	Yes
Log net assets	62	4.93	4.57	0.35	5.54	Yes

	Number of Obser- vations	Mean Value		Mean Differ- ence	t	Significant at the 5% Level
		AG	MAG			
II. Profit Variability						
Coefficient of varia- tion of profits after tax	39	0.34	0.38	−0.04	−0.51	No
III. Profitability						
Profitability–sales	62	2.04	1.26	0.77	1.43	No
Profitability–net assets	61	2.53	1.87	0.65	1.35	No
Profitability–equity capital	60	6.03	4.03	2.00	1.62	No
IV. Leverage						
Debt–assets (all cases)	56	0.54	0.51	0.02	0.90	No
Debt–assets (listed acquired firms)	25	0.55	0.54	0.007	0.23	No
V. Growth						
Total assets	58	11.77	10.80	0.97	0.48	No
Sales	56	12.47	10.40	2.07	0.99	No

quite important and that the *t* ratios are significant at the 10 percent level. The same remark holds true for the difference between the coefficients of variation.[1] On the contrary, there does not seem to be any significant difference either statistically or economically between the acquiring and the acquired firms as far as the debt-asset ratio or the rate of growth are concerned.

If we now turn to the comparison of acquiring firms and nonacquiring firms, Table 5–9 shows that acquiring firms are, on the average, significantly larger than other firms in their industry. They also appear to be somewhat more profitable than their matched nonacquiring firms, although the evidence there is quite weak from a statistical point of view. Finally, the profit variability, the leverage ratio, and the growth rate of the

Table 5–10. Comparisons of the Characteristics of Acquired and Nonacquired Firms

	Number of Obser-vations	Mean Value		Mean Differ-ence	t	Significant at the 5% Level
		AD	Rest of industry			
I. Size						
Log sales (all cases)	62	4.42	4.68	−0.25	−4.04	Yes
Log sales (listed acquired firms)	25	4.03	4.14	−0.11	−0.417	No
Log assets	59	4.36	4.78	−0.41	−3.31	Yes
Log net assets	62	4.32	4.57	−0.25	−3.59	Yes

	Number of Obser-vations	Mean Value		Mean Differ-ence	t	Significant at the 5% Level
		AD	MAD			
II. Profit Variability						
Coefficient of varia-tion of profits after tax	35	0.59	0.48	0.10	0.51	No
III. Profitability						
Profitability–sales	62	1.14	2.39	−1.25	−1.43	No
Profitability–net assets	61	1.79	2.53	−0.73	−1.28	No
Profitability–equity capital	60	3.40	5.74	−2.34	−1.60	No
IV. Leverage						
Debt–assets (all cases)	56	0.54	0.45	0.08	2.73	Yes
Debt–assets (listed acquired firms)	25	0.54	0.46	0.07	1.94	No
V. Growth						
Total assets	32	11.08	9.14	1.95	0.88	No
Sales	56	11.73	9.97	1.76	0.80	No

acquiring firms do not seem to be different from those of the matched nonacquiring firms. The size comparison between the acquiring firms and the geometric mean of the firms in their industry that were neither acquiring nor acquired during the 1950–1975 period indicates that the acquiring firms were in general among the largest in their industry. The absolute value of the mean difference between the profitability of the two samples of acquiring and nonacquiring firms is smaller than the mean difference in the absolute value of profitability between acquiring and acquired firms and is less significant statistically. Finally, although the acquiring firms seem to have a somewhat lower variability of profits and a slightly higher debt-asset ratio and growth rate than their matched firms, the absolute value of the mean differences are small, and their level of significance is low.

Table 5–10 gives the results of the comparison between acquired and nonacquired firms. The acquired firms are significantly smaller (at the 5 percent level) than the other firms in their industry, and they have a significantly higher debt-asset ratio than their matched firms. They also appear to be less profitable than firms in the control group, although the difference is not significant at the 5 percent level.

We can summarize our analysis of the characteristics of the various sets of firms as follows:

Size: Acquiring > Rest of the Industry > Acquired;

Profitability: Matched Acquired > Acquiring ≥ Matched Acquiring > Acquired;

Profit Variability: Acquired ≥ Matched Acquired > Matched Acquiring ≥ Acquiring;

Leverage: Acquired ≥ Acquiring ≥ Matched Acquiring > Matched Acquired;

Growth: Acquiring ≥ Acquired ≥ Matched Acquiring ≥ Matched Acquired.

Altogether it appears that firms with a low average profitability and a high debt-asset ratio have a higher probability of being acquired than the others. However, if comparative efficiency was the main factor explaining which firms merge and which ones are absorbed by mergers, we would expect to find the acquired firms to be larger and the acquiring firms to be smaller than their industry average. Indeed there seems to be in France an overall negative relationship between size and profitability at the firm level (see Jenny and Weber 1976).[2] The finding that acquiring firms are larger and acquired firms smaller than their industry average then leads us to believe that the discipline provided by the merger mechanism does not apply equally to firms of all sizes. More specifically, large inefficient firms appear to have a better chance to survive than small inefficient firms, and small efficient firms are either less prone to acquire other firms or they are prevented from doing so.

DETERMINANTS OF MERGERS

Size Tests

Given the specific way in which the nonacquiring and nonacquired samples were constructed, the size tests were made by comparing the logarithm of the geometric mean of the merging firms with the logarithm of the geometric mean of all the firms in the industry that were neither acquired nor acquiring during the period under investigation. The results are given in Table 5–11.

Table 5–11. Determinants: Size (test 1)

Variable	Number of Mergers	Mean Value		Mean Difference	t	Significant at the 5 Percent Level
		AGAD	Rest of industry			
Log sales	62	4.71	4.68	0.03	0.75	No
Log assets	59	4.73	4.78	−0.05	−0.82	No
Log net assets	62	4.62	4.57	0.05	0.84	No

As we saw in the previous section, acquiring firms are on the average larger than firms that did not merge and the latter are significantly larger than firms that were acquired. Thus it is perhaps no surprise that the average size of merging firms is not statistically (or economically) different from the average size of nonmerging firms.

There does not seem to be a tendency for smaller firms to merge more often than larger ones, and therefore the desire to reach minimum efficient scale does not seem to qualify as the primary common motive of firms that merge unless one assumes that the largest firms in each industry have a suboptimal scale (a heroic assumption). If acquiring firms do not seek to overcome—through mergers—a handicap due to suboptimal scale, it is still conceivable that the acquired firms are poor performers because of their small size. However, as our comparison of the various sets of firms has shown, the firms in the nonacquired group are both small and highly profitable compared to the other firms. This would therefore seem to indicate that, on average, the disadvantages of costs incurred by the small firms in our sample are not such that they condemn those firms to disappear either through mergers or through bankruptcy.[3] These considerations reinforce our conclusion that the economies of scale motive is not decisive in explaining merger activity. It is then possible that large firms acquire small firms to increase their market shares, and hence their monopoly profits, or to enhance their bargaining position in collusive agreements.

Risk Spreading

A priori it does not seem that horizontal mergers can be explained by risk-spreading considerations. Indeed, firms belonging to the same three-digit industry are likely to be subject to the same business fluctuations. However, one should note that the firms are assigned to a three-digit industry on the basis of their single most important line of activity even if this activity represents but a minor part of the firm's total operations. Thus it is still possible that within an industry, risky undiversified firms may want to merge with less risky (and presumably more diversified) firms.

Table 5–12. Determinants: Risk (test 2)

Variable	Number of Mergers	Mean Value		Mean Difference	t	Significant at the 5 Percent Level
		AGAD	MAGAD			
High-low ratio of variation coefficient	31	3.59	5.62	−2.02	−1.53	No
Difference in leverage: absolute value (all cases)	56	0.16	0.20	−0.04	−1.66	No
Difference in leverage: absolute value (listed acquired firms)	25	0.12	0.19	−0.07	−2.00	No
		AG	MAG	F-test		
Variance of leverage	56	0.025	0.040	0.61		No
		AD	MAD			
Variance of leverage	56	0.042	0.047	0.61		No

Also, even if we assume that all the firms belonging to the same three-digit industry have the same level of diversification, some may have a higher leverage ratio than others and face a higher financial risk. We therefore ran tests on the ratio of variation coefficients and on the leverage ratios. The results of these tests are shown in Table 5–12.

As expected, the results of the tests do not support the risk-spreading hypothesis. Indeed, the first test indicates that firms that merge have a smaller ratio of high-low variation coefficients than firms that do not merge. The second test shows that the absolute value of the difference in leverage ratios is smaller for merging firms than for nonmerging firms, and thus it does not seem that the firms that merge do so because one has an extremely high leverage ratio and the other an extremely small leverage ratio. As the third test shows, this results holds even if we limit our analysis to the sample of mergers for which the acquired firm was listed on the stock exchange. The fourth and fifth tests, finally, show that there were no significant differences in the variances of the leverage ratios of the acquiring firms and of their matched firms or in those of the acquired firms and of their matched firms. Thus, risk spreading can be ruled out as a common motive of the merging firms.

However, as we saw when we compared the four sets of firms, the acquired firms have significantly higher leverage ratios than the nonacquired firms. We also saw that the leverage ratios of the acquired (small) firms were on the average similar to those of the acquiring (large) firms. If one assumes that the variance of earnings is larger for a small firm than for a large firm, it may well be that within an industry the optimal leverage ratio is lower for a small firm than for a large firm and that small firms with a leverage ratio comparable to that of large firms face a higher financial risk than the large firms or than the small firms with a low leverage ratio. In

Table 5–13. Determinants: Bargain Theory (test 4)

Variable	Number of Mergers	Mean Value		Mean Difference	t	Significant at the 5 Percent Level
		AD	MAD			
PE ratio ($t - 1$) (mean value)	20	36.01	36.73	−0.72	−0.66	No
PE ratio ($t - 1$), ($t - 2$) (mean value)	20	32.32	36.40	−4.08	−0.44	No
PE ratio ($t - 1$), ($t - 2$), ($t - 3$) (mean value)	20	32.87	35.94	−3.07	−0.35	No

such a case, for the small firm, reducing its debt-asset ratio or merging into a larger firm—even if this larger firm has the same leverage ratio—would be two alternative ways to reduce risk. Thus, we cannot exclude the possibility that risk spreading is a factor inducing highly geared small firms to merge.

Economic Disturbances

Due to the difficulty of gathering the appropriate data for the acquired firms, we had to limit our analysis to the bargain interpretation of the disturbance motive theory. More specifically, we had to restrict our tests to the comparison of the mean price–earning ratios of the acquired firms and of the matched nonacquired firms and to a limited number of observations. The results of the tests are given in Table 5–13. The results indicate that if the acquired firms have, on the average, lower price–earning ratios than nonacquired firms, the mean difference in the price–earning ratios between the two sets of firms is very small and statistically insignificant. Thus, there is no support for the bargain version of the economic disturbance theory.

EFFECTS OF MERGERS

Profitability

Three sets of tests were carried out to try to assess the impact of mergers on profitability. First, we compared the difference between the average premerger and postmerger rates of profit for the merging firms and for the nonmerging firms; next, we compared the ratios of the postmerger to the premerger average rates of profit for the merging firms and for the industry; finally, we compared the postmerger average profit rates of the merging firms with their predicted value. The average profit rates are computed after taxes over a period of four years before and after the merger. The results are given in Tables 5–14, 5–15, and 5–16.

Table 5–14. Effects: Difference In Profitability (test 5)

Variable	Number of Observations	Mean Value		Mean Difference	t	Significant at the 5 Percent Level
		AGAD	MAGAD			
Profits − equity (difference)	40	−0.0201	−0.0018	−0.0184	−0.79	No
Profits − assets (difference)	40	−0.0050	−0.0026	−0.0024	−0.41	No
Profits − sales (difference)	40	−0.0082	−0.0022	−0.0060	−0.82	No

Table 5–15. Effects: Profitability, Comparison with Industry (test 6)

Variable	Number of Observations	Mean Value		Mean Difference	t	Significant at the 5 Percent Level
		AGAD	Industry			
Rate of profit on equity (after/before)	23	0.022	0.681	−0.657	−1.072	No
Rate of profit on sales (after/before)	23	0.2572	0.6226	−0.365	−0.659	No
Rate of profit on net assets (after/before)	18	0.2507	0.5584	−0.307	−0.576	No

Table 5–16. Effects: Profitability, Comparison with Predicted Performance (test 7)

Variable	Number of Observations	Mean Value		Mean Difference	t	Significant at the 5 Percent Level
		Actual	Predicted			
Rate of profit on equity	23	0.0219	0.0504	−0.028	−1.276	No
Rate of profit on sales	23	0.0106	0.0261	−0.0155	−1.270	No

There is no support for the hypothesis that mergers in our sample have resulted in an increase in the profit rate for the merging firms over what the weighted average of the profit rates of the two combining firms would have been had they not merged. Rather it appears that for the four years following the merger, the profit rates of the firms that merged were on the average lower than they would have been otherwise, although the differences are not significant at the 5 percent level. Specifically, Table 5–4 shows that the profit rates declined between the premerger and the postmerger period both in the sample of merging firms and in the sample of nonmerging firms but that the decline was more important for the merging firms. Table 5–15 shows that the profit rate of merging firms also declined more than the average profit rate of their industry. Finally, Table 5–16 shows that actual performance of the merging firms was on the average lower than the predicted rate when this predicted rate was computed on the basis of premerger profit rate and of industry trend.

It is possible that these results are due to the comparatively short period of time (four years after the merger) under consideration. Indeed, the advantages, for the acquiring firms, accruing from the merger either through increased monopoly power or through scale economies (if they exist) might be offset immediately after the acquisition by the costs incurred in absorbing the acquired firm and in reorganization. Thus we cannot exclude the hypothesis that in the long run (say ten years after the merger), the profit rates of the acquiring firms are significantly higher than the profit rates of the matched nonmerging firms or than those of the industry. The fact that most mergers occurred during the 1965–1972 period makes it impossible to test such a hypothesis at this time. In any case, our analysis of the characteristics of the merging firms leads us to believe that if, in the long run, merging firms prove to have higher profit rates than their matched nonmerging firms or than their industry, it is more likely that this will be due to increased market power rather than to increased efficiency.

Changes in Size and Leverage

Additional tests were run to see whether merging enhances the ability of firms to grow internally. Specifically, the average growth rates of the acquiring firms after the merger were compared to the weighted average growth rates of the sample of nonacquiring firms and of the industry. The variables used were total sales, total assets, net assets, and debt-assets. The average annual growth rates for the four-year period following the merger were computed for the first three variables. In the case of the debt-asset ratio, data limitations compelled us to use a three-year period. The results of these tests are reported in Tables 5–17 through 5–20.

All the t-tests are insignificant at the 5 percent level, and the mean differences are very small from an economic point of view. We cannot reject the hypothesis that the acquiring firms do not grow faster (internally) after their mergers than they would have grown had they not merged. Thus there is no reason to believe that the opportunities of internal growth are different for acquiring firms than they are for firms that do not merge. This of course does not rule out completely the managerial motive for mergers, since the acquisition itself leads to an increase in the growth rate of the acquiring firm in the year of the merger, but it would at least lend credence to the idea that if managers are growth maximizers, they see mergers as a way to achieve a durable faster growth rate. These observations must, however, be accepted with caution since the post-merger period was relatively short.

Table 5–17.   Effects: Difference in Growth Rates (test 8a)

	Number of Observations	Mean Value AGAD	Mean Value MAGAD	Mean Difference	t	Significant at the 5% Level
Sales	43	0.0357	0.0496	−0.014	−0.68	No
Total assets	27	0.0412	0.0329	0.0082	0.45	No
Net assets	29	0.0299	0.0777	−0.047	−1.30	No
Debt–assets					−0.07	No

Table 5–18.   Effects: Ratio of Growth Rates (test 8b)

	Number of Observations	Mean Value AGAD	Mean Value MAGAD	Mean Difference	t	Significant at the 5% Level
Sales	43	0.563	1.0747	−0.5116	−0.41	No
Total assets	27	1.572	1.4297	0.1423	0.40	No
Net assets					−0.81	No
Debt–assets					−0.82	No

Table 5–19.   Effects: Comparison with Industry Growth Rates (test 9)

	Number of Observations	Mean Value AGAD	Mean Value Industry	Mean Difference	t	Significant at the 5% Level
Sales	27	0.1156	0.1080	0.0075	0.27	No
Net assets	21	0.1182	0.1272	−0.009	−0.69	No
Debt–assets	20	1.99	1.87	0.12	−0.20	No

Table 5–20.   Effects: Comparison with Predicted Performances (test 10)

Variable	Number of Observations	Mean Value Realized	Mean Value Predicted	Mean Difference	t	Significant at the 5 Percent Level
Sales	26	327.47	345.34	−17.87	−0.67	No
Net assets	21	278.32	294.38	−16.06	−0.95	No
Debt/assets	20	0.631	0.624	0.007	0.13	No

Change in Return on Stockholder Equity

To complete our analysis of the effects we ran a series of tests to see whether the shareholders benefited from the mergers. We thus compared the differences between the post- and premerger rates of return on a share of common stock for the acquiring firms and for the matched nonacquiring firms. The 1965 legislation on mergers, as we saw, allows acquiring firms to reevaluate parts of the assets that they acquire and enables them to make various tax deductions. One would then expect, ceteris paribus, an increase in the rate of return on the shares of the acquiring firms immediately after the merger. The difference between the rate of return of the year of the merger and the average premerger rate of return should therefore be larger for acquiring firms than for the matched nonacquiring firms.

The expectations of shareholders on the long-run profitability of the merger also affect the evolution of the rate of return on the acquiring firm's shares. If shareholders anticipate long-run gains from the merger, ceteris paribus, the price of the shares of the acquiring firm will be bid up in the year of the merger or in the years immediately following it, and the rate of return on the firm's share will increase even more than if the tax deduction effect is the only one at work. Conversely, if the shareholders expect the merger to be a failure, the price of the shares will decline, and this effect may well offset the tendency of the rate of return to increase due to the tax break.

In our analysis the premerger rate was in all cases the average rate for the five years preceding the merger. The year of the merger (t) was always the first year of the postmerger period. The results of the analysis are given in Table 5–21.

The tests suggest that the shareholders benefit from the mergers since the difference in the rate of return between the postmerger and the premerger period is significantly larger for acquiring firms than for the matched nonacquiring firms when the postmerger period is the year of the merger. The mean difference between the variables tends to decline when a longer postmerger period is taken into consideration. This could merely reflect the fact that after the price of the acquiring firm's shares has been adjusted to take into account the tax gains and the new expectations about long-run profit rates, the rate of return on the shares of the acquiring firm and the rate of return on the shares of the matched nonacquiring firm should not be different. However, the last test reveals that in year $t + 3$, the rate of return on the acquiring firms' shares is lower than the rate of return on the shares of the matched nonacquiring firms although the difference fails to be significant statistically at the 5 percent level.[4] The same observation holds for year $t + 4$ when the rate of returns of both sets of firms are computed for that year.

Altogether one is left with the impression that the shareholders definitely benefit from the tax break in the year of the merger and that it is possible that they expect long-run profits from the merger at that time. There is, however, some indication that two years after the merger the shareholders either revise downward their positive expectations (if they had any in the first place) about the outcome of the merger or simply begin

Table 5–21.   Effects: Change in Return on Stockholder Equity (test 11)

Variable	Number of Observations	Mean Value		Mean Difference	t	Significant at the 5 Percent Level
		AG	MAG			
Difference in average rate of return (post-merger period, year t)	43	14.93	3.37	11.55	3.69	Yes
Difference in average rates of return (post-merger period, year t, t + 1)	43	8.84	0.22	8.62	1.99	No
Difference in average rates of return (post-merger period, year t, t + 1, t + 2)	43	9.38	3.58	5.80	1.29	No
Difference in average rates of return (post-merger period, year t, t + 1, t + 2, t + 3)	43	8.62	6.53	2.09	0.27	No

to expect the acquiring firms to perform worse than the matched nonac-quiring firms. These declining expectations continue or deepen as further time elapses.

Risk-adjusted Performance Test

Mergers would seem to lead to a reduction in risk only to the extent that they bring together firms that are in different industries since most of the risks a firm faces are cyclical or industry related. Horizontal mergers could conceivably lead to a reduction in risk only to the extent that firms that are classified in the same industry are in fact largely diversified and diversified in different industries. Our analysis of the characteristics of the various sets of firms does not warrant such an assumption, and therefore we did not carry out the tests on the Sharpe and Treynor measures.

CONCLUSION

The results of the statistical analysis we carried out are only tentative due to various methodological problems mentioned in Chapter 2 and to the difficulties associated with the data collection. However, they enable us to make a few comments on the industrial policy followed by the French government during the decade 1965–1975.

As we saw in the first section, laws were passed in 1965 and 1967 to facilitate mergers among firms. The following five years were character-ized by a high level of merger activity, and the importance of the assets transferred through mergers increased dramatically during this period

(Jenny and Weber 1972:32). It thus seems likely that the merger wave was at least partly due to the 1965–1967 laws and that the slight increase in overall market concentration observed at the end of the 1960s was partly the result of this merger wave.

The premerger policy of the 1960s was the consequence of three explicit assumptions on the part of government officials. First, facilitating mergers would help relatively small firms to overcome their cost disadvantage by enabling them to increase rapidly their size and their efficiency; second, even for the largest firms in each industry there were efficiency gains to be obtained through mergers (or, in other words, the average cost curves never slope upward); third, the higher concentration brought about by mergers would not result in misallocation of resources due to an increase in monopoly or oligopoly power because of the international competition. Those three hypotheses explain why the 1965 law on mergers applied to all mergers whatever their nature and the industries in which they occurred.

We have already shown, in an earlier study (Jenny and Weber 1976), that there is a positive (and statistically significant at the 5 percent level) relationship in France between the level of market concentration (measured by the four-firm concentration ratio) and industry profitability. We have also shown, in the same study, that there is an overall negative relationship between firm size and profitability and that the largest firms are not, generally speaking, more efficient than average size firms. We thus had reasons to believe that the last two assumptions of the French government were not supported by empirical evidence and that an all-out policy in favor of increased concentration presented the danger of facilitating mergers initiated by large firms and leading to increased inefficiencies and/or misallocation of resources due to monopoly power. The study of the determinants and effects of horizontal mergers sheds some light on the mergers that have indeed taken place and on the private and social gains accruing from them.

Our analysis shows that the economies of scale motive was not predominant for the firms involved in horizontal mergers. It seems more likely that the acquiring firms tried to capture capital gains by taking advantage of the tax cut provided for by the merger laws and of the higher unit cost of capital for small firms than for large firms.[5] The exploitation of the differential in the unit cost of capital for large and small firms could explain in particular why larger than average firms tended to acquire smaller than average firms. The acquired firms were firms with a high variability of profits and a higher than optimal debt-asset ratio for their size. The combination of these two characteristics led to high fixed capital costs and low profitability. It is thus possible that merging is an alternative to bankruptcy for some of the small acquired firms. The shareholders of the merging firms benefited from the merger, as evidenced by the increased rate of return on shares of the acquiring firms the year of the merger. This increase in the rate of return of shares reflected the capital gains aforementioned and, possibly, an expected improvement in the performances of the firms. However, there does not seem to be any support for the idea that the profit or growth performances of the acquiring firms in the short-run postmerger period are different from what they would have been in the absence of a merger or from what they are for the industry average. Thus, mergers do not seem to increase the efficiency of acquiring firms in the short run. As we pointed out, it is not possible to assess the long-run impact of mergers because the merger wave is too recent. The only (and tiny) piece of evidence on the long-run effects of mergers is that shareholders tend to revise their expectations downward a couple of years after the merger. This indicates either that they were overoptimistic when the merger took place or that they now expect the performances of the merging firms to be worse than they would have been in the absence of a merger.

The analysis thus suggests that the only potential social gain from the merger mechanism comes from economies of scale in raising capital and that for some small firms with a nonoptimal capital structure, merging might be a socially less wasteful way to disappear than going bankrupt. But since we have no reasons to believe that economies of scale in raising capital suddenly increased in the mid-1960s, it seems that the 1965 and 1967 merger laws resulted in mergers that were not prompted by the capital market considerations aforementioned and did not lead to increased efficiency for the merging firms. To be sure, it also appears that, overall, the monopoly power of the acquiring firms was not significantly increased by the mergers they entered into, and some may argue that the case against the merger laws of 1965–1967 is not clear cut. However, even if one assumes that market structures and efficiency are not altered by mergers, it is hard to find any economic justification for the redistribution of income from the taxpayer to the shareholders of the merging firms via the tax cut provided for in the merger legislation. What is more, it is clear that in the long run, a succession of mergers in an industry can eventually lead to a level of concentration such that collusive behavior can develop, even if each merger in itself did not result in an obvious increase in the monopoly power of the merging firms.

The French administration has finally acknowledged that not all mergers are good and that some of them can definitely lead to a misallocation of resources. A new merger law was passed in 1977, and in the future, the government will be able to oppose mergers among firms having a substantial combined market share whenever it thinks that the potential social costs of the proposed mergers outweigh the potential social benefits. (The government can prevent horizontal mergers if the combined share of the merging firms is larger than 40 percent of the market.) From an economist's point of view, this seems to be a step in the right direction. However, the 1965 and 1967 merger laws are still on the books, and one can only hope that they will be repealed soon since they do not seem to have any socially redeeming value.

NOTES

1. However the difference in the profit variability between acquiring and acquired firms might be due to the fact that the acquiring firms are large whereas the acquired firms are small. Indeed, the coefficient of variation is negatively correlated to size.
2. This negative relationship between size and profitability shows up in the analysis we have conducted. The firms in the sample of nonacquiring and the sample of nonacquired were chosen on the basis of their industry classification, size, and asset-sales ratio. It appears that the (small) nonacquired firms are on the average more profitable than the (large) nonacquiring firms. The difference is statistically significant at the 5 percent level.
3. This statement holds true only if one can assume that the activities of the firms that are compared to each other in the same three-digit industries are homogeneous.
4. The mean rate of return for the acquiring firms in year $t + 3$ is equal to 6.32, and the mean rate of return for the control group is equal to 15.38. The t value equals -1.20.
5. On the capital gains due to the ability of large firms to refinance the assets of small firms at lower costs even with perfect capital markets, see J. Lintner (1971). On an empirical evaluation of the cost of capital differential between small firms and large firms in the United States, see "Economies of Scale at Plant and Multi-Plant Levels: Detailed Evidence," unpublished complement to F. M. Scherer et al. (1975).

Chapter 6

The Netherlands, 1962–1973

Henk Peer

CONCENTRATION IN DUTCH INDUSTRY

The 1960s witnessed a wave of merger activity in every Western industrial country. As can be expected for the small and open economy of the Netherlands this wave touched upon the structure of Dutch industry as well.

In 1971 Janssen attempted to quantify concentration and the shifts within industrial patterns in the Netherlands. More specifically, he raised the question as to what extent concentration changed the industrial patterns. Thus, the objects of the study were growth of enterprises and their plants and the changes in concentration ratios. He used the Lorenz curve as a measure of relative concentration (de Jong 1972: Ch 2). This measure takes both the percentage share of enterprises and the percentage share of employees in enterprises of different sizes into consideration. Only concentration in manufacturing, with the exception of the construction and milk and dairy product industries, was measured. Basically, he tested whether the structure of the manufacturing industry took the shape of a regular-shaped pyramid with some large enterprises on the top, more enterprises on the medium level, and many on the bottom level or was altogether different (i.e., an upside-down pyramid, referred to by Berle and Means and by Galbraith, or a pyramid kinked inward on the medium level,

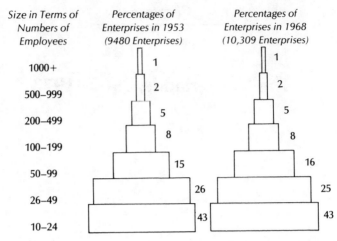

Figure 6–1. Structure of Dutch industry: enterprise concentration. *Source:* Janssen (1971: 20.)

referred to by Perlmutter). He concluded that the structure was a regular-shaped pyramid expanding at all levels at nearly the same rate. This is shown for 1953 and 1968 in Figure 6–1. The only change that took place in these fifteen years was a 1 percent shift of the enterprises from the size 25–49 class to the size 50–99 class.

Examining the percentage distribution of the number of employees over the different size classes, the picture is somewhat different. This is indicated in Figure 6–2. The distribution of employment over the different size classes reveals the shape of an upside-down pyramid. The most important change that took place between 1963 and 1968 in this respect was an employment increase of 8 percent in the largest class. There was an employment decrease of 1 percent to 2 percent in all other classes.

The conclusion that the distribution of enterprises over size classes is rather stable over time, while a large part of employment is concentrated in a small number of large enterprises, is justified. The other portion of employment is rather evenly distributed over a large number of small- and medium-sized enterprises.

A comparison with two other industrial nations (Table 6–1) shows that the structure of the manufacturing industry in the Netherlands is not different from those in the United States and West Germany.

Until 1980 Janssen predicts increased concentration. However, he expects that the industrial structure will still have the regular pyramid

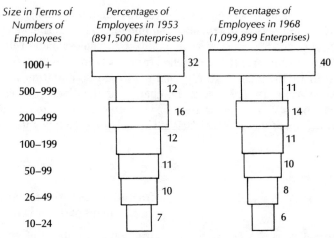

Size in Terms of Numbers of Employees	Percentages of Employees in 1953 (891,500 Enterprises)	Percentages of Employees in 1968 (1,099,899 Enterprises)
1000+	32	40
500–999	12	11
200–499	16	14
100–199	12	11
50–99	11	10
26–49	10	8
10–24	7	6

Figure 6–2. Structure of Dutch industry: employee concentration. *Source:* Janssen (1971: 21.)

shape, expanding in depth and height. During the period 1963–1973, one can conclude unambiguously that this merger wave led to more concentration in Dutch industry. Many concentration measures are available (see de Jong 1972) in the industrial organization literature. One of the more appropriate measures is the entropy measure of concentration or the Theil coefficient. It is a fairly unambiguous measure that varies with the inequality of the size distribution and with the number of enterprises. Moreover the measure reflects an increase or decrease in the level of concentration with increasing (decreasing) merger activity. In a recent study by P. Janus (1975) from the Dutch Central Statistical Office this

Table 6–1. International Comparison of the Structure of Manufacturing Industries

	1953–1954		1967–1968	
	Percent Enterprises in Manufacturing	Percent Employed in Manufacturing	Percent Enterprises in Manufacturing	Percent Employed in Manufacturing
United States	22	78	21	79
West Germany	21.5	70.5	21	79
Netherlands	23	77	21	79

Source: Janssen (1971: 25).

Theil coefficient was computed for the total manufacturing sector (excluding 37, manufacture of transport equipment; 38–39, other manufacturing industries; 51–52, construction; and 61–62, wholesale and retail trade) of the Dutch economy. It has declined from 13.17 in 1950 to 12.51 in 1963 and to 11.65 in 1971. The latter period shows an acceleration in the rate of concentration. In Table 6–2 the change of the Theil coefficient for different industries is computed for the two periods involved. For the computation of the Theil coefficients in each year the following formula was used:

$$H(x) = \sum_{g=1}^{g} x_g^{2}\log\frac{1}{x_g} + \sum_{g=1}^{g} x_g^{2}\log\frac{x_i^{2}}{x_g} \log\frac{x_g}{x_i}$$

x_i $(i = 1, 2, \ldots, N)$ fraction of the ith enterprise in total employment of the industry.

x_g $(g = 1, 2, \ldots, G) = \sum_{i \in s_g} x_i$ fraction of group s_g of enterprises in total employment of the industry

An increase in concentration has taken place in all but one industry in the period 1963–1971. Only the petroleum refineries show some deconcentration, but a declining deconcentration when compared with the period 1950–1963. The manufacture of wearing apparel and shoes, beverages and tobacco, and the food manufacturing industries increased concentration very much in the period 1963–1971 as compared to the printing, publishing, and allied industries; paper and paper products; chemicals and rubber products; and metal products and machinery. Between these two groups of industries one finds a group with moderate concentration increases in the period 1963–1971 such as electrical equipment, textiles, leather, and wood products.

Concentration changes can be decomposed into two components—the change in the number of enterprises and the change in their relative sizes. This might need some explanation. If there is a complete equal size distribution of all N enterprises in an industry, then $x_i = 1/N$ for all i. The measure of entropy is in this case minimal and equal to $H(x) = \sum_{i=1}^{N} x_i^{2}\log 1/x_i = {}^2\log N$. With the relative concentration $(\bar{H})$ one can measure to which extent the actual concentration approaches this minimum: $\bar{H}_t = H_t(x)/\log N_t$, $(t = 1963, 1971)$. Concentration, as a ratio between the actual value of the Theil coefficient in 1963 and 1971, can thus be expressed as the product of the ratio of relative concentrations and the ratio of the number of enterprises:

$$\frac{H_{1963}(x)}{H_{1971}(x)} = \frac{\bar{H}_{1963}}{\bar{H}_{1971}} \cdot \frac{\log N_{1963}}{\log N_{1971}}$$

In Figure 6–3 one can find this decomposition of concentration between

Table 6–2.   Change in Entropy Measure in Dutch Industry

		Δ*H Change in Entropy Measure*	
		1950–1963	*1963–1971*
20–21	a. Food-manufacturing industries	−0.78	−0.67
	b. Manufacture of beverages and tobacco	−0.67	−0.77
22	Textile industry	−0.27	−0.52
23	Manufacture of wearing apparel and shoes	−1.00	−0.86
24	Leather industry	−0.68	−0.53
25	a. Manufacture of wood	−0.42	−0.54
	b. Manufacture of furniture	−1.31	−0.64
26	Manufacture of paper and paper products	−0.09	−0.38
27	Printing, publishing, and allied industries	−0.18	−0.04
28	Petroleum refineries	+0.79	+0.42
29–31	a. Manufacture of chemicals	−0.18	−0.46
	b. Manufacture of rubber products	+0.32	−0.40
32	Manufacture of earthenware, glass, lime, and stoneware	+0.16	−0.47
33	Basic metal industries	—	—
34–35	Manufacture of metal products and machinery	+0.15	−0.40
36	Manufacture of electrical equipment	+0.52	−0.49
37	Manufacture of transport equipment	—	—
38–39	Other manufacturing industries	—	—
51–52	Construction	—	—
61–62	Wholesale and retail trade	—	—

Source: Janus 1975: 33, Table 1.

1963 and 1971. Dots above the $H_{1963}/H_{1971} = 1$ hyperbola imply increasing concentration. This upper area is divided into three parts. To the left of the log $N_{1963}/\log N_{1971} = 1$ vertical line the number of enterprises and concentration have increased, while relative concentration decreased; under the $\bar{H}_{1963}/H_{1971} = 1$ horizontal line in this upper area the number of enterprises decreased, while both concentration and relative concentration increased. In the rectangular area that is left in the upper area, the number of enterprises goes down and concentration increases while relative concentration declines. The cluster of dots in the figure clearly shows that concentration has increased and that this increase has mainly been caused by a decline in the number of enterprises. In the meantime relative concentration has decreased slightly as well. We already concluded from Table 6–2 that the food manufacturing, beverages, and tobacco increased in concentration, whereas the petroleum refineries clearly decreased in concentration in the period 1963–1971. From Figure 6–3 we can get an idea of which of the two factors played the dominant role. In the petroleum industry one finds deconcentration with only a slight increase in the number of enterprises, so that the increase in relative concentration gave the

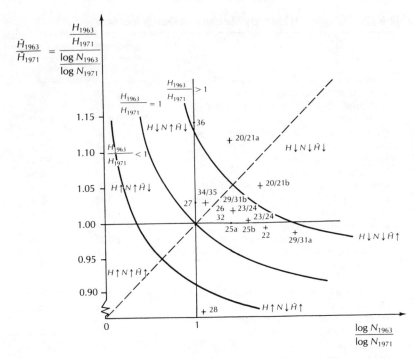

Figure 6–3. Concentration changes in the Netherlands, 1963–1971. (*Source:* Janus 1975:22.)

biggest contribution to the deconcentration of this industry. Comparing the food manufacturing industry with the manufacture of beverages and tobacco we see a higher contribution of the change in the relative concentration than in the change in the number of enterprises. In the electrical equipment industry concentration increased very much with no change in the number of enterprises, so it is the decline in relative concentration that mostly accounts for this change.

The difference between the minimal concentration and the actual concentration of an industry is called the redundancy: $R_t = {}^2\log N_t - H_t(x)$, $t = (1963, 1971)$. Subtracting R_{1963} from R_{1971} and rearranging gives the changes in the entropy measure:

$$H_{1963} - H_{1971} = [\log N_{1963} - \log N_{1971}] + [R_{1971} - R_{1963}]$$

The first bracketed term is the contribution of the change in the number of enterprises, while the second bracketed term indicates the contribution of the change in size distribution. In Figure 6–4 the contribution of the

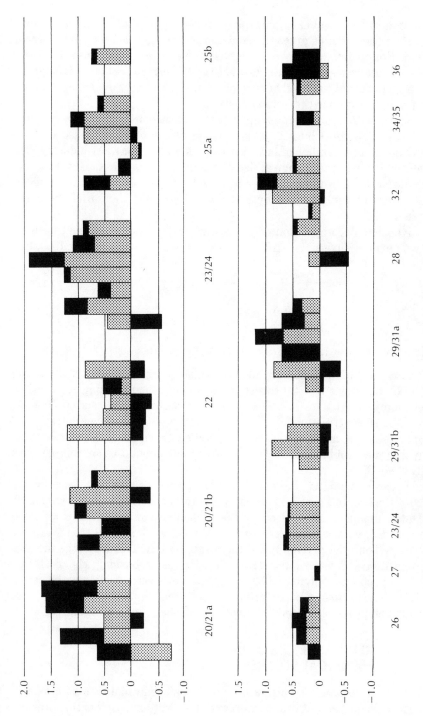

Figure 6–4. Sources of concentration change by industry. (*Source:* Janus 1975:23.)

change in the number of enterprises is lightly shaded, whereas the dark part of the columns gives the contribution of the change in size distribution. For each industry we distinguish one or several columns referring to the subindustries (three digits) that can be formed within each industry. Since this is not the level of analysis of our own study, we do not comment on concentration in these subindustries.

The picture that emerges supports the conclusions that have been drawn before. The contribution to the change of the entropy measure of the change in the number of enterprises is dominant for most industry. The contribution of the change in size distribution is much less, except for food manufacturing and electrical equipment. In petroleum one finds deconcentration mainly caused by a change in size distribution of the enterprises.

Another decomposition of the change in the Theil coefficient between two periods is possible—$\Delta H = H_{1963} - H_{1971}$—in which for $t = 1963, 1971$

$$H_t = \sum_{g=1}^{G} x_g{}^2 \log \frac{1}{x_g} + \sum_{g=1}^{G} x_g \sum_{k=2}^{\kappa} x_k{}^2 \log \frac{1}{x_k}$$

$$+ \sum_{g=1}^{G} x_g \sum_{k=1}^{\kappa} x_k \sum \frac{x_j}{x_k}{}^2 \log \frac{x_k}{x_j}$$

in which x_k $(k = 1, 2, \ldots, \kappa) \equiv \sum_{j \in sk}$: fraction of subindustry s_k in industry s_g.

A change in the first term after the equality sign is the contribution from the G industries to total concentration of the manufacturing sector of the economy. A change in the second term between 1963 and 1971 is the weighted contribution of the k subindustries to total concentration. A change in the last term is the weighted contribution of the concentration within the k subindustries. The results of this computation are reproduced in Table 6–3.

It can immediately be seen that in the period 1963 to 1971 the industries 20–24 accounted for 88.5 percent of the total concentration increase in the Dutch manufacturing sector of the economy. The manufacture of wood, furniture, rubber products, earthenware, glass, lime, and stoneware contributed only 9.1 percent, while the rest (2.5 percent) is due to the changing importance of various industries. Printing and publishing, chemicals, and metal products contributed 90 percent to the deconcentration in the period. The manufacture of paper products, electrical equipment, and the petroleum refineries accounted for 9.9 percent of the deconcentration.

REVIEW OF THE MAIN
EMPIRICAL STUDIES

Two possible empirical approaches are available to ascertain the determinants and effects of mergers. The first approach is the interview

Table 6–3. Decomposition of the Decrease in the Theil Coefficient, 1963–1971

Industry		Contribution to Change in Concentration		Contribution to Change in Deconcentration	
		Absolute	*Percent*	*Absolute*	*Percent*
20–21	Food-manufacturing industries, including beverages and tobacco	0.41	30.7		
22	Textile industry	0.23	17.2		
23	Manufacture of wearing apparel				
24	Shoe and leather industry	0.55	40.6		
25	Manufacture of wood and furniture	0.08	5.9		
29–31	Rubber products	0.00	0.2		
32	Manufacture of earthenware, glass, lime, and stoneware	0.04	3.0		
	Concentration between industries	0.03	2.5		
		1.34	101		
26	Manufacture of paper and paper products			0.00	0.8
27	Printing, publishing, and allied industries			0.12	23.8
28	Petroleum refineries			0.01	2.2
29–31	Manufacture of chemicals and chemical products			0.06	11.9
34–35	Manufacture of metal products and machinery			0.26	54.3
36	Manufacture of electrical equipment			0.03	6.9
		−0.48		0.48	99.0
	$H_{1963} - H_{1971} = 12.51 - 11.65$	0.86			

Source: Janus (1975: 27).

technique. The researcher interviews the management that decides or has decided to merge or to takeover and draws conclusions from the answers received from the interviewed person. The second approach consists of taking a sample of both merged and nonmerging firms and testing whether both samples are possibly drawn from the same population. We have selected this line of approach in our own empirical work. The results of the tests are reported later in the chapter.

Two Dutch studies that adhere to the interview technique will be reviewed in the remaining part of this section. The first is a study by the Stichting Maatschappij en Onderneming (Foundation Society and Enterprise); the second, one by the Centraal Bureau voor Statistiek of the Netherlands (Central Statistical Office of the Netherlands). Finally we

Table 6–4.   Motives for Mergers

Motive	Takeovers (35)	Mergers (20)
A. Improvement of domestic market position	xxxxxxxxxxxxxxxxxxxxxxxx xxxxxxxxxxxxxx	xxxxxxxxxx xxxxxxxx
B. Improvement of market position abroad	xx x x xx	x x xx x
C. Higher rate of growth	xxx xxxxxxxxxxx x xx xxxx xx xxxx	x xxx xx xxxxxxxx
D. Improvement and extension of research	x	x xx xx
E. Strengthening of financial situation		xx xx x xxxxx x x
F. Expansion of the number of products	x xx xx x x xxxxx xxxxxxx	x xxx x x xx x
G. Improvement continuity of employment	xx x	x
H. Labor market reasons	x	
I. Contribution to the restructuring of the industry	x x xx	x
J. Strengthening of the position in advance of a next merger		x x x
K. Protection against a takeover from abroad	x	
L. Difference between stock market value and value of the firm	x x x	
M. Strengthening of position on the factor markets	x x	x
N. Strengthening of the continuity of the firm	x xxx x x	xx x
O. Vertical integration	x x x	x xx

Source: Fusies, een terreinverkenning, Stichting Maatschappij en Onderneming, The Hague, 1970.

report in this section on two other empirical studies, again one from the Stichting Maatschappij en Onderneming and one by the Centraal Bureau voor Statistiek.

The Stichting Maatschappij en Onderneming study was started in 1969 and completed in 1970. The interviews cover the period 1963–1968, which coincides with the first part of the period we are investigating. In this period, 716 mergers between Dutch enterprises took place. A sample of fifty-five enterprises was taken from this set. Interviews of two hours each were held with the management boards of these fifty-five enterprises to gain insight into the motives for mergers, the method of merging, and the effects of mergers.

Since the search for determinants and effects of mergers is the main purpose of this study, only that part that deals with motives and effects will be dealt with in detail. Table 6–4 indicates the results of the study's research on the motives for mergers.

Motives A and B: The table shows that all mergers were undertaken to strengthen the market position—more specifically, the domestic market position. Eighty percent of the mergers within the fifty-five interviewed enterprises were a result of the latter factor. The remaining 20% involved the improvement of the domestic market position and/or the market position abroad. The causes for this can be found in tradition, easy and cheap access to the Dutch market, and the awareness that the relatively small Dutch market is very import prone.

Motive C: In addition to the aim of strengthening market position, the table shows that the achievement of a higher rate of growth ranked second as a motive for mergers. This result does not make clear, however, to what extent an increased rate of growth is really an independent motive. It occurs naturally as a by-product of the above-mentioned merger motive.

Motive D: Improvement or extension of research and development was infrequently mentioned as a merger motive— only six times out of the total fifty-five.

Motive E: It is significant that the strengthening of the financial position or easier access to the capital market played a role only in horizontal mergers. It should be mentioned that nearly all (with the exception of two) of the mergers were undertaken due to acute liquidity problems. Generally, the mergers were a result of those problems expected in the long run. If strengthening of the market position is deleted as a motive for horizontal mergers, the table shows that long-term financial problems were related to the higher rate of growth and the extension of the number of products. One may therefore conclude that the financial bottleneck was a result of the need for capital for activities planned for the future.

Motive F: A more complete and diversified product mix ranks third as a motive, behind competition and growth. If one examines the form in which amalgamation between two enterprises took place, the study shows that 70% of the interviewed mergers were horizontal (i.e., an amalgamation within an industry), 11% were vertical (i.e., an amalgamation between two enterprises in subsequent stages of the production or distribution process), and 13% were conglomerate (i.e., an amalgamation across an industry). One may draw the conclusion that more than half of the horizontal mergers caused only an increase in scale of operation.

Motives G through O: These motives, mentioned by some of the interviewed enterprises, do not play a dominant role in any of the cases. This applies for the motive to cut out weak spots that could threaten the continuity of the firm as well.

To summarize the most important conclusions: Improvement of the domestic market position, increasing the rate of growth, and completion and/or diversification of the product mix were the most important motives for mergers. Horizontal mergers occurred very frequently, followed by conglomerate mergers. Vertical mergers occurred less frequently.

During the period 1971–1973 the Dutch Central Bureau of Statistics investigated the motives for mergers by means of the interview technique. The Bureau gathered information about amalgamations mainly from the press. Although many objections can be raised against this method (see de Jong 1971:159–62), one can assume that not too many amalgamations escaped the records. This is because mergers currently have to be registered in the Netherlands. Since a good summary of the results of this work has recently been reported elsewhere (Jacquemin and de Jong 1976, vol 1:105–108)), we confine ourselves here to the main conclusions that can be derived from the published figures.

The survey distinguishes between acquiring firms, acquired firms, and amalgamated firms. Furthermore, the survey lists (1) main motives for mergers with four possible priorities; (2) motives as a specification of the main motives with three possible priorities; and (3) submotives as a specification of the motives with no possibility of selecting priorities from among them. In the following account, the first figure between brackets refers to 1972; the second, to 1971. The figure preceding the brackets refers to 1973.[1]

For 251 acquiring firms, or 76% (74%, 81%), improvement of the market position was the main motive for merging. The further development and growth of the market was the main motive for merger of 239, or 95% (92%, 98%), of the 251 enterprises. One hundred forty-seven of the 239 firms, or 62% (68%, 71%), mentioned the acquiring of a larger share of the market, and 119 of the 239, or 50% (50%, 40%) mentioned the offering of a greater product mix as a submotive for the development of the market motive.

For 99 firms, or 48% (50%, 38%), financial reasons were mentioned as a motive. For 71, or 34% (35%, 36%), social-psychological reasons were the motive. For 19, or 9% (9%, 21%), market reasons were the motive. Of the 99 firms that mentioned financial reasons as a motive, 50% (56%, 47%) had liquidity problems, 39% (50%, 31%) had equity problems, and 65% (61%, 67%) had profitability problems. Of the 77 firms that mentioned social-psychological reasons as a motive, 38% (36%, 39%) lacked management, 61% (53%, 45%) wanted to force concentrated family wealth out of the company, and 30% (31%, 48%) merged for other personal reasons.

In looking at the acquired firms with market problems, in many cases— 84% (72%, 56%)—there was a sales decrease in the domestic market while for 47% (33%, 60%), there was not enough diversification in the domestic market.

Ninety-three of the 141 amalgamated firms, or 66% (59%, 56%), mentioned the development of the competitive position as the main merger motive. Eighty-five percent (72%, 94%) of these 93 firms endeavored to develop the market. That is, 77% (61%, 80%) tried to extend the share of the market, and 57% (65%, 86%) attempted to broaden the range of products for the market.

We are in full agreement with de Jong's survey (1971a:107) conclusions, which showed that:

1. Acquiring firms were overwhelmingly motivated to take over other firms in order to obtain a larger market share.
2. Acquired firms were mainly motivated by financial and social-psychological factors (no successor, the desire to free the family capital, etc.).
3. Pure mergers appeared to be induced by market considerations.

The Central Bureau of Statistics recently published a follow-up to the investigation of motives leading to mergers in 1971. In this follow-up survey (1971), 192 acquiring firms and 82 amalgamated firms were interviewed. The acquired firms could no longer be interviewed for obvious reasons. The main purpose of the follow-up survey was to determine if the interviewed parties considered the decision made in 1971 to have been successful, partially successful, or not successful at all. The survey found that among the acquiring companies, 76 percent felt the merger had been successful, 16 percent that it had been partially successful, and 8 percent that it had not been successful. Among the amalgamated firms the results were 83 percent successful, 8.5 percent partially successful, and 8.5 percent not successful. (According to the previous motive survey, the improvement of the market position was the dominant motive for both the acquiring firms and the pure mergers.) The percentage of nonsuccessful mergers is about the same for both groups. There is, however, a slight difference in the percentage of successful and partially successful mergers between the two groups. This seems to indicate that in the case of pure mergers one tends to proceed more carefully than in the case of takeovers.

Furthermore, the same (1971) list of motives was shown to the interview participants, who were asked to what extent the motives they mentioned at that time had met their expectations. Table 6–5 shows only the main motive for the 192 acquiring firms and the 82 amalgamated firms concerned.[2] In this table the minus sign indicates results that were worse than expected, the zero sign refers to results that met expectations, and the plus sign indicates results that were clearly better than expected.

As can be expected, the successful (nonsuccessful) acquisitions and pure mergers correlate with the judgments of whether the results of the mergers were positive (negative). One could ask what the reasons were for the disappointing results, especially for the partially successful or non-

Table 6–5. Realization of Expectations (percent)

	–	0	+
Acquiring firms (192)			
Successful (146)	2	71	27
Partially successful (30)	37	50	13
Not successful (16)	75	25	
Amalgamated firms (82)			
Successful (68)	4	61	35
Partially successful (7)	43	14	43
Not successful (7)	71	29	—

Source: Maandstatistiek voor het Financiewezen, March 1975.

successful mergers. Both the acquiring firms and the amalgamated firms frequently mentioned a misjudgment of the other party or integration problems after the merger took place as a cause of the disappointing results.

DATA PROBLEMS AND TEST METHODOLOGY

As with all empirical studies, gathering the data for testing the hypothesis has been a very tedious and time-consuming process in which many arbitrary decisions had to be taken. First of all the set (S_1) of all mergers that took place in the period 1962–1972 had to be formed. Fortunately the Central Bureau for Statistics of the Netherlands had a fairly complete list of all mergers that took place in the Netherlands . However, since this list began only with 1963, we had to drop the year 1962 from the period under investigation. The Central Bureau collects its information mainly from newspapers, such as the *Financiëel Dagblad* and the *Economisch Dagblad*, among others. There was no reason to assume that many mergers were missing from these records from the statistical office. The number of mergers, takeovers, and the like that took place in the period involved is impressive—for 1963, 86; 1964, 84; 1965, 91; 1966, 84; 1967, 128; 1968, 222; 1969, 254; 1970, 171; 1971, 235; 1972, 244—totaling 1599.

However, the Central Bureau for Statistics does not have, and therefore cannot make available, information on balance sheets and profit and loss accounts of the firms involved, so this information had to be gathered from another source—the yearly publications of the enterprises themselves. The Law for the Yearly Accounts in the Netherlands makes yearly publication of balance sheets and profit and loss accounts obligatory for all open incorporated joint stock companies. Observance can be enforced via an appeal at the Enterprise Chamber of the Amsterdam Court of Justice. An archive at the Katholieke Hogeschool Tilburg of the yearly accounts for the open incorporated joint stock companies of the Netherlands (set S_2) contains the balance sheets and profit and loss accounts since 1948 for nearly 400 open incorporated joint stock companies.[3]

However, as all financial analysts know, enterprises try to publish only those figures they really want to publish. Moreover the figures that appear on the balance sheets and profit and loss accounts are very sensitive to the different profit determination and valuation systems that prevail in the Netherlands. A computer model presented at a conference for certified accountants in 1975 in the Netherlands showed the impact on profits of nine different valuation systems. It turned out that variations in profit between zero and almost 100 percent could be caused by choosing an alternative valuation system for determining the figures on the balance sheets. Since enterprises in general do not always publish which kind of valuation system they used or switched to in the yearly publication, it was not possible to adjust these figures for the different valuation systems that obviously have been used.[4] Since no other data were available, we had to work with this set of data. From the intersection ($S_1 \cap S_2$) of the set of all enterprises that were involved in merger activity and the set of enterprises whose stock is traded on the Dutch stock exchange, we took only mergers of enterprises in the manufacturing and retail sectors of the economy.

In deciding in which year a merger actually took place and what kind of merger it was, very pragmatic criteria have been used. Concerning types of mergers, a horizontal merger was defined as a merger between two enterprises that had the same industrial code (two digit) according to the Dutch industrial code (SBI 1970), a code that resembles the SIC code in many respects but allows for some deviations due to special Dutch circumstances.[5] Conglomerate mergers were defined as a merger between two enterprises that did not have the same industrial code. We realize that the latter set automatically includes vertical integration mergers, but since previous studies have shown that the number of vertical integration mergers in the period under consideration was small, we did not try to exclude them from the set of conglomerate mergers. In determining the year in which a merger actually took place, we made use of the fact that obviously the balance sheets and profit and loss accounts of at least one of the enterprises involved in the merger disappear from the data set, since either the two enterprises continue under a new name or the acquired enterprise is integrated into the acquiring firm and loses its name. This means that we defined a merger as having taken place at the time when 100 percent control has occurred, and thus we did not try to experiment with

Table 6–6. Mergers by Sector and Type

Industry	Type	Elements in $S_1 \cap S_2$										Elements in $S_2 - S_1$
		1963	1964	1965	1966	1967	1968	1969	1970	1971	1972	
20–21 Food-manufacturing industries, including beverages and tobacco	H[a]				1							29
	C[a]						1					
22 Textile industry	H											17
	C											
23 Manufacture of wearing apparel other than footwear	H				1			2				8
	C								1			
24 Shoe and leather industry	H											3
	C											
25 Manufacture of wood and furniture	H											9
	C											
26 Manufacture of paper and paper products	H		1									5
	C											
27 Printing, publishing, and allied industries	H											8
	C										1	
28 Petroleum refineries	H											2
	C											
29–31 Manufacture of chemicals and of chemical, rubber, and plastic products	H							2				24
	C							1				
32 Manufacture of earthenware, glass, lime, and stoneware	H											11
	C											
33 Basic metal industries	H											0
	C											
34–35 Manufacture of metal products and machinery	H		2		2	3		1				49
	C				1		1					
36 Manufacture of electrical equipment	H								1			4
	C										1	
37 Manufacture of transport equipment	H				1							12
	C						1	1				
38–39 Other manufacturing industries	H			1			1					1
	C			1			1					
51–52 Construction	H											3
	C											
61–62 Wholesale and retail trade	H					2		2				20
	C	1										

[a] H = horizontal merger; C = conglomerate merger.

defining the precise time at which 50 or 75 percent of the stock had been acquired. This gave us the ultimate sample of horizontal and conglomerate mergers upon which we wanted to test the hypotheses concerning the determinants and effects of mergers in the period 1963–1972.

Next we constructed a control sample for each industry from which we could draw the samples of nonacquiring and nonacquired firms. This set is the difference of the set of enterprises from which we had the balance sheets and profit and loss accounts and the set of all companies involved in mergers for the period under consideration ($S_2 - S_1$) for each industry. As can be seen from Table 6–5, there were not always enough firms in the control group. In those cases we decided to form a combined industry—such as 37 with 38–39.

RESULTS

Determinants

Size. In the first set of tests concerning the determinants of mergers we compared arithmetic and geometric means of measures of size of the sample of horizontal mergers and the sample of nonmerging firms in the same industry. Results are shown in Table 6–7.

In comparing the arithmetic means of the measures of size for horizontal mergers, one can notice that the average sizes of firms engaging in a merger were greater than the average size of the nonmerging control group. However, only for total assets did the *t*-value exceed the 0.05 significance level. The finding that merging firms are on the average larger than nonmerging firms in the same industry seems to be clearly inconsistent with the economies of scale hypothesis of mergers. This hypothesis should therefore be rejected—thus implicitly supporting the monopoly hypothesis of mergers.

The geometric means were calculated because one can assume that the size variables are positively skewed (i.e., approximate the log-normal distribution) and thus the geometric mean would be more appropriate. In

Table 6–7. Size comparisons (test 1)(n = 20)

	Measure of Size		
	Sales	*Total assets*	*Net of depreciation plant and equipment*
Arithmetic mean	1.47	2.20	1.99
Geometric mean	−0.02	0.60	0.33

Entries are *t*-values.

Table 6–8. Risk Comparison, Profits (test 2)

	All mergers, High-Low Coefficient of Variation Ratio	Acquired Firms, Mean Coefficient of Variation	Acquiring Firms, Mean Coefficient of Variation
All mergers (n = 25)	1.03	0.95	−1.20
Conglomerate mergers (n = 10)	0.98	0.80	1.12

comparing the geometric means, the finding is that the average sales of merging firms are smaller than for the nonmerging control group. However, this cannot unambiguously be interpreted as support for the economies of scale hypothesis. It could be that smaller firms are more likely to merge because they are attempting to increase their market share relative to the larger firms in the industry. The geometric means for total assets and net of depreciation plant and equipment present the same picture as in the arithmetic means comparison.

Risk. If one assumes that managers try to reduce risk through a merger or takeover, one could compare whether the merging firms have significantly higher variances in profits than the firms in the nonmerging sample (Table 6–8). Rather than compare raw variances of profits between merging and nonmerging firms, we compared the high-low coefficient of variation ratio in the all mergers and conglomerate mergers tests. The mean coefficient of variation for acquired and acquiring firms was used in the comparison with the nonmerging control group. This procedure was chosen to standardize for size in the control group. The positive *t*-value for the high-low coefficient of variation ratio indicates that on the average, firms in the merging sample were riskier than the firms in the control sample, although the difference was not significant at the 0.05 level. Another test was run for the acquired and acquiring firms separately. The mean coefficient of variation for the acquired firms was greater than the mean coefficient for the nonmerging sample, whereas the mean coefficient of variation for the acquiring firms was smaller than the mean coefficient of variation for the nonmerging control group. This indicates that the less risky acquiring firms took over riskier firms.

However, another adjustment should be made. The all mergers sample includes horizontal mergers as well, but it seems that horizontal mergers should not be explained by a risk-spreading hypothesis. Most of the ups and downs in profits that firms face seem to be industry or cycle related. Conglomerate mergers are perhaps the most reasonable place to look for risk-related motives. Therefore, we ran the same tests for the sample of

Table 6–9. Risk Comparison, Leverage Ratio (test 2)

	All Mergers		Horizontal Mergers		Conglomerate Mergers	
Differences	−0.42		−0.34		−0.03	
	n = 25		n = 17		n = 8	
	Acquiring	*Acquired*	*Acquiring*	*Acquired*	*Acquiring*	*Acquired*
Variance	−1.23	−0.32	−0.52	−0.69	−0.20	−2.25
	n = 34	n = 32	n = 24	n = 22	n = 10	n = 10
Mean	−0.32	0.45	0.05	0.72	0.98	−2.06
	n = 34	n = 32	n = 24	n = 22	n = 10	n = 10

conglomerate mergers. The conglomerate mergers do not present a different picture, if compared with the all mergers high-low coefficient of variation ratio test. This ratio is greater than the mean high-low coefficient of variation for the nonmerging control group. When we broke the sample of conglomerate mergers up into a sample of acquired and acquiring firms, a slightly different picture emerged. Both acquired and acquiring firms had higher mean coefficients of variation than the firms in the nonmerging sample. According to the difference in t-value for the acquired and acquiring firms in the separate conglomerate mergers sample, there is even the indication that the acquiring firms were riskier than the acquired firms.

Instead of using variance in profits as a measure of risk, we could argue that in the real world leverage plays an important role and that highly levered firms are more risky. Several tests are performed, and the results are summarized in Table 6–9.

In the all mergers sample, as well as in the separate horizontal mergers and conglomerate mergers samples, the mean absolute difference in leverage ratio is smaller than in the nonmerging control groups. The difference is not statistically significant, however. This result does not suggest that firms merge to reduce their risk by means of a reduction of their leverage ratios as compared to the average leverage ratio in the nonmerging control group. This inference can be extended if one compares variances in leverage ratio for acquiring and acquired firms for the all mergers, horizontal mergers, and conglomerate mergers samples. The variance in leverage ratios of the conglomerate mergers subgroup differs significantly from the nonmerging control group, supporting the hypothesis that in conglomerate mergers the less risky firms are taken over. For this subgroup the comparison of the mean leverage ratio gave the same result. The mean leverage ratio for the acquired firms is smaller than the mean leverage ratio in the nonmerging control group. The fact that the mean leverage ratio for the acquiring firms in the conglomerate merger sample is greater than the average in the control sample gives further support to this hypothesis.

Table 6–10.   Change in Price-Earnings Ratio (tests 3 and 4)

	Ratio of High-Low Price-Earnings Ratios			Mean Price-Earnings Ratio		
	$t-1$	$t-2$	$t-3$	$t-1$	$t-2$	$t-3$
All mergers ($n = 36$)	1.66	−0.40	−1.00	0.11	−0.20	0.12
Horizontal mergers ($n = 26$)	0.63	−1.20	−1.49	0.79	−0.88	−1.56
Conglomerate mergers ($n = 10$)	0.41	−0.29	−0.05	−0.11	−0.65	−0.46

The conclusion cannot be extended to the subsample of horizontal mergers, as acquiring as well as acquired firms had higher mean leverage ratios than the firms in the control sample. This does not support the hypothesis that reduction of risk was a main motive for horizontal mergers as measured by the leverage ratio.

In summarizing the results on the risk tests we have to conclude that there is not much statistical evidence that reduction of risk as measured by variance in profits or leverage ratios has been a main motive for horizontal or conglomerate mergers. Only the acquiring firms in the sample of conglomerate mergers had a higher mean leverage ratio than the acquired firms. In this case alone, risk reduction might have been a motive for mergers.

The acquired firms in the horizontal mergers and in the conglomerate mergers have both experienced smaller increases in the ratio of high-low price-earnings than the nonacquired firms in the control sample in the two or three years before the merger took place (see Table 6–10). One year before the merger the acquired firms experienced bigger increases in the high-low price-earnings ratio, except for conglomerate mergers. This seems to suggest a specific kind of behavior from the management of the acquiring companies—first, a decision lag of one period before they actually decide to merge and, second, an attitude of waiting until their judgment is confirmed by a higher high-low price-earnings ratio in the year before the merger. There is of course a possibility that the stock price of the acquired firm rises in the year before the merger either because the merger has been announced (although not yet consummated) or because insiders know of the merger and begin buying shares of the to-be-acquired firm. If either of these occur, these two tests are biased in favor of accepting these hypotheses.

The same behavior is implied by comparison of the mean price-earnings ratio of the acquired firms with the mean price-earnings ratio of the nonacquired sample in the two and three year periods before the merger took place. However, in the year before the conglomerate mergers took place the mean price-earnings ratio of the acquired firms was still smaller than in the control group, as opposed to a higher mean price-earnings ratio than the nonacquired firm for the horizontal merger sample. Does this support our intuitive understanding that the management in a conglomerate merger acts more alertly or less cautiously than in horizontal mergers? In the next section on effects we will see if this behavior pays off in terms of return on equity and other variables.

Effects

From Chapter 2 we look for three effects of mergers: (1) no change in market power or efficiency, (2) market power unchanged and efficiency improved, and (3) market power increased and efficiency unchanged. The first effect implies unchanged sales and profit rates. The second effect implies higher sales, and higher profits as a percentage of capital and sales, whereas the third effect implies lower sales and higher profits as a percentage of capital and sales. These tests were performed for both horizontal and conglomerate mergers. The results are reproduced in Tables 6–11 through 6–13.

In Table 6–11 we compare the change of a variable after the merger compared with the change of that variable for the nonmerging control group. In Table 6–12 the rate of change of a variable is compared with the rate of change in the industry to adjust for industry-related changes. In Table 6–13 the predicted postmerger rate of change of a variable is compared with the actual postmerger rate of change of the variable. The predicted postmerger rate of change of a variable is a measure of what the firm would have done if it had not merged.

The results of Table 6–11 do not allow us to give either horizontal or conglomerate mergers a label such as efficiency increased or market power increased, efficiency unchanged. The negative t-values in all entries seems to suggest that market power increased and efficiency decreased for both types of mergers. One wonders if there is another explanation for this feature. One could conjecture that a merger causes integration problems in the years after the merger so that the foreseen monopoly rent increases or efficiency gains do not outweigh the extra costs of reorganizing two units into one enterprise. Of course, this argument applies mainly for horizontal mergers, and as a matter of fact, the decrease in return on capital and of profits as a percentage of sales for the conglomerate merger test are not statistically significant.

The simple change test of Table 6–11 might be misleading, since what

Table 6–11. Comparison with Control Group (tests 5 and 8.1)

| Variable | Sales | Return on | | | Profits as a Percentage of Sales |
		Equity	Total Capital	Total capital after taxes	
All mergers	−3.18	−3.42	−3.30	−3.32	−0.85
	n = 27	n = 31	n = 31	n = 31	n = 31
Horizontal mergers	−2.02	−2.62	−2.27	−2.63	−0.60
	n = 27	n = 22	n = 22	n = 22	n = 22
Conglomerate mergers	−2.09	−1.61	−1.61	−1.54	−1.61
	n = 8	n = 8	n = 8	n = 8	n = 8

Table 6–12. Comparison with Industry (tests 6 and 9.1)

| Variable | Sales | Return on | | | Profits as a Percentage of Sales |
		Equity	Total Capital	Total capital after taxes	
All mergers	−2.50	−0.53	−1.34	−0.35	−0.34
	n = 17	n = 29	n = 29	n = 29	n = 29
Horizontal mergers	−1.95	−0.85	−1.26	−0.98	+0.13
	n = 11	n = 21	n = 21	n = 21	n = 21
Conglomerate mergers	−1.70	+0.37	−0.47	+0.96	−1.25
	n = 6	n = 8	n = 8	n = 8	n = 8

Table 6–13. Comparison with Predicted Performance (tests 7 and 10.1)

| Variable | Sales | Return on | | | Profits as a Percentage of Sales |
		Equity	Total Capital	Total capital after taxes	
All mergers	−0.64	−3.24	−2.59	−2.83	−0.91
	n = 22	n = 19	n = 19	n = 19	n = 19
Horizontal mergers	−0.64	−3.12	−2.43	−2.95	−0.65
	n = 16	n = 12	n = 12	n = 12	n = 12
Conglomerate mergers	−0.16	−1.16	−1.01	−0.58	−0.77
	n = 6	n = 7	n = 7	n = 7	n = 7

has happened to the merging firms might have happened to the industry as a whole due to cyclical fluctuations. Therefore we compared the results of the merging firms with the trend in the industry. The results are reproduced in Table 6–12. Although there is still some evidence that both horizontal and conglomerate mergers have resulted in increased market power, the statistical significance of the differences is less. This applies for the return on capital and for profits as a percentage of sales as well. Profits as a percentage of sales for horizontal mergers improved vis-à-vis the trend in the industry whereas the return on equity and the return on total capital after taxes were higher than the industry trend for the subgroup of conglomerate mergers, although not significant at the 5 percent level.

Finally we predicted the performance of the merging firms for the same variables and compared it with the actual postmerger outcome. The negative *t*-values in all entries of Table 6–13 indicate that there is no reason to assume that merged firms did better than they would have done had they not merged.

The ambiguous picture that emerges with respect to the private effects for the merging firms supports the conclusions of the study by the CBS in which both acquiring firms and the amalgamated firms that were interviewed frequently mentioned a misjudgment of the other party or integration problems after the merger took place as a cause of the disappointing results.

It might also be that these unorthodox results are caused by the methodology we applied in this study. We were limited to a few years of observations following a merger. This is typically a short-run approach. Efficiency gains might materialize only in the long run.

In Table 6–14 the differences of the premerger and postmerger rates of growth of total assets, net of depreciation plant and equipment, and the leverage ratio of the horizontal and conglomerate mergers are compared with the differences for these variables for the nonmerging control group companies. The negative *t*-values for the horizontal and conglomerate mergers in the total assets and the net of depreciation plant and equipment columns imply that the average differences in premerger and postmerger rates of growth have been less than in the nonmerging control group. As far as the change of premerger and postmerger leverage ratio is concerned, the negative values in the last column of the table indicate that this change has been smaller for the merging firms' sample, implying an improvement in the debt-to-equity ratio vis-à-vis the nonmerging control group.

These results do not change significantly when compared with the trend in the industry or with the calculated predicted performance, as can be seen from Tables 6–15 and 6–16. Exceptions are the positive value for the difference in growth rates for conglomerate mergers in Table 6–15 and the positive value for the leverage ratio for the horizontal mergers in Table 6–16. These *t*-values are, however, below the critical level for the number of observations involved. However, one need not conclude that the slowdown in growth of the merging firms rejects the hypothesis that they merged to pursue growth. The merger itself resulted in a large increase in

Table 6–14. Comparison with Control Group (test 8)

Variable	Total Assets	Net of Depreciation Plant and Equipment	Leverage Ratio
All mergers (n = 27)	−2.50	−2.31	−2.22
Horizontal mergers (n = 20)	−0.66	−1.71	−1.25
Conglomerate mergers (n = 7)	−2.13	−1.52	−0.78

Table 6–15. Comparison with Industry Trend (test 9)

Variable	Total Assets	Net of Depreciation Plant and Equipment	Leverage Ratio
All mergers (n = 27)	−1.47	−5.34	−2.81
Horizontal mergers (n = 20)	−1.50	−4.40	−2.53
Conglomerate mergers (n = 7)	+0.01	−3.06	−1.81

Table 6–16. Comparison with Predicted Performance (test 10)

Variable	Total Assets	Net of Depreciation Plant and Equipment	Leverage Ratio
All mergers (n = 22)	−3.97	−2.53	−0.24
Horizontal mergers (n = 16)	−4.06	−2.47	+0.21
Conglomerate mergers (n = 6)	−1.04	−1.11	−1.66

the size of the acquiring firm, and it may be this growth that was pursued. What we can say is that efficiency does not appear to have increased and that if growth was the objective, the large increase in size brought about via the merger was somewhat offset by the subsequent decline in the merging firm's growth rate.

In the last set of tests we try to measure the impact of horizontal and conglomerate mergers on the performance of the acquiring firm from the

Table 6–17. Change of Average Rate of Return on a Share of Common Stock (test 11)

	$t + 1$	$t + 2$	$t + 3$
All mergers	2.03	1.79	0.92
($n = 24$)			
Horizontal mergers	0.71	1.34	1.83
($n = 16$)			
Conglomerate mergers	1.59	1.14	0.96
($n = 8$)			

point of view of stockholders. A direct test can be performed on the return on the stock of the acquiring company before and after the merger. In the postmerger period we experimented with the average rate of return for one, two, and three years after the merger. And again we compared the results with industry trends and the predicted performance of the stocks involved.

In Table 6–17 we see that the average change of the return on stock of the acquiring firm after the merger declines with the length of the postmerger period. If we separate the sample of acquiring firms into subsamples of horizontal and conglomerate acquiring firms an interesting feature can be traced. While the average change of return on a stock gradually improves after the merger for horizontal acquiring firms, the conglomerate acquiring firms show a declining average change of return on a stock in the time periods after the merger. As far as the horizontal mergers are concerned, this might indicate that stockholders do not pay much attention to the short-run decline in return on equity (as we saw before) but expect that in the long run, profits might rise again. This argument does not apply for the conglomerate case. The merged firms continue to exist as separate enterprises and do not have the integration problems that the horizontal mergers have. In the short run their stockholders gain, whereas in the long run these gains seem to level out again.

In the comparison with industry test (Table 6–18), one sees that after three time periods the merged companies gradually do better than the average in the industry as far as the return on stock is concerned. This applies mainly to the horizontal mergers subgroup and not for the subgroup of conglomerate mergers. The comparison with the predicted performance of the acquiring companies (Table 6–19) seems to confirm the results of the first two tests. Horizontal mergers generally do better for their stockholders in the long run than their conglomerate counterparts. The conglomerate acquiring firms do better than the predicted performance only in the period immediately after the merger.

Table 6–18. Comparison with Industry Average Rate of Return Variable (test 12)

	$t + 1$	$t + 2$	$t + 3$
All mergers ($n = 29$)	0.37	0.26	1.17
Horizontal mergers ($n = 20$)	0.75	0.65	2.26
Conglomerate mergers ($n = 9$)	−0.61	−0.71	−1.84

Table 6–19. Predicted Performance of the Average Rate of Return on a Share of Common Stock (test 13)

	$t + 1$	$t + 2$	$t + 3$
All mergers ($n = 24$)	−0.14	−0.68	+0.17
Horizontal mergers ($n = 16$)	−0.86	−0.32	+1.36
Conglomerate mergers ($n = 8$)	+0.45	−1.23	−1.94

The last two tests of this study on the effects of mergers involved a test on the performance of the acquiring firms as measured by the Sharp and Treynor measures. The first measures the gain on the return of the company's stock over the risk-free rate of return per unit of standard deviation, whereas the second measure expresses this gain per unit of volatility. We experimented with different possibilities for defining the postmerger period, including or not including the year of the merger. This was done for the one, two, and three years after the merger. Tables 6–20 and 6–21 give the results. The potential reductions in risk through diversification that mergers can bring about seem to be relevant for conglomerate mergers only. Horizontal or vertical mergers will not protect firms from cyclical or industry-related risks. Examining conglomerate mergers only we see from the bottom lines in Tables 6–20 and 6–21 that a significant improvement in the performance of conglomerate mergers as measured by Sharp's or Treynor's measure cannot be shown. On the contrary, the negative values in the tables seem to indicate that after the merger, losses per unit of standard deviation and per unit of systematic risk have been the rule rather than the exception for all the postmerger periods with which we experimented.

Table 6–20. Sharp's Measure (test 14)

	Year of Merger Included in Postmerger Period				Year of Merger not Included in Postmerger Period		
	t	*t* + 1	*t* + 2	*t* + 3	*t* + 1	*t* + 2	*t* + 3
All mergers (*n* = 24)	0.04	−0.01	−0.09	−0.18	0.67	−0.36	−0.06
Horizontal mergers (*n* = 16)	0.76	0.66	−1.27	−0.32	0.75	−1.12	−0.39
Conglomerate mergers (*n* = 8)	−0.20	−1.47	−2.10	−2.07	−1.77	−2.14	−2.25

Table 6–21. Treynor's Measure (test 15)

	Year of Merger Included in Postmerger Period				Year of Merger not Included in Postmerger Period		
	t	*t* + 1	*t* + 2	*t* + 3	*t* + 1	*t* + 2	*t* + 3
All mergers (*n* = 24)	−1.34	−1.34	−1.35	−1.39	−1.20	−1.27	−1.50
Horizontal mergers (*n* = 16)	−1.38	0.40	−0.03	−0.04	−0.66	0.37	0.03
Conglomerate mergers (*n* = 8)	−0.55	−1.30	−1.00	−3.07	−1.33	−1.35	−2.50

CONCLUSIONS

Mergers can have various effects—effects on industrial or market structures, private effects for the firms and their stockholders, and social effects for consumers. It has been shown for the Netherlands that the merger wave of the 1960s and the early 1970s has unambiguously increased concentration as measured by a declining entropy measure in the manufacturing sector of the economy. Through the impact on the market power of the acquiring firm and the impact on costs, a merger has private effects for firms and for stockholders and social effects for consumers. By using samples of horizontal and conglomerate mergers in the Netherlands over the period 1963–1972 we examined the private and social effects of mergers. The private effects can be measured through the effects on profitability for the firm and through the effects on the rate of return on a company's stock for the stockholders. A merger has a positive social effect if the growth in sales of the newly formed firm exceeds a weighted average growth rate in sales of the merging companies. Another social effect of

Table 6–22. **General Results**

	Rate of Return on on Total Capital	Rate of Return on a Share of Acquiring Firm's Stock	Growth Rate of Sales
All mergers	−2.59	+0.17	−0.64
	n = 19	n = 23	n = 22
Horizontal mergers	−2.43	+1.36	−0.64
	n = 12	n = 15	n = 16
Conglomerate mergers	−1.01	−1.94	−0.16
	n = 7	n = 8	n = 6

mergers—namely, the possible gains or losses in employment—has not been studied due to the unavailability of data. It has been shown elsewhere, however, that there is not much evidence that, on the average, the merger wave has contributed to higher rates of unemployment. The detailed results of our study are presented in the preceding sections. The general results are summarized in Table 6–22 which is based on the tables of the sections on determinants and effects.

In Table 6–22 we have not reproduced the result of the simple change tests or the comparison with industry tests, but the comparison with the predicted performance tests. In this test one compares the private and social effects of the mergers with the predicted situation if a merger had not taken place. Moreover we took as the ultimate effect of the merger its effect on the rate of return on a share of the stock of the acquiring firm three years after the merger. A positive (negative) value in Table 6–22 implies a higher (lower) actual postmerger mean observation for the acquiring company than predicted from the base industry trends. If the horizontal and conglomerate mergers are grouped together, the prediction for the rate of return on total capital is higher than the actual postmerger value, indicating a negative effect of the merger on the profitability of the merging firms. The mean prediction for the rate of return on a share of the acquiring firm's common is less than the mean actual postmerger value for this variable, implying that stockholders benefit from the merger, but that difference is insignificant. The actual growth rate of sales is less than the predicted value, indicating a slight increase in market power of the merging firms, although the statistical significance of this result is also negligible. For the subgroup of horizontal mergers the same picture emerges. There is no evidence of improvement in efficiency and only a slight increase in market power, making the consumers worse off, while the owners benefited from a higher rate of return on a share of the acquiring firm's stock, although the last two t-values are less than the critical value. Finally, the results for the subgroup of conglomerate mergers show no improvement in efficiency. This might not be an important result, due to the unrelated nature of the products of the merging companies. In this case there is also no evidence that the performance of the acquiring firm has made the stockholders better off. There is no significant impact on the position of the consumer in this case as measured by the growth rate of sales.

The results from these tests conform to the overall impression of mergers others have obtained for the Netherlands using survey techniques. Efficiency is not improved by mergers nor are risks reduced. Stockholders are not made better off. The most positive conclusion one reaches is that market power is not significantly increased, consumers are not much worse off. The policy implications of these results are explored in Chapter 11.

NOTES

1. *Maandstatistiek van het Financiewezen*, January 1975 (Centraal Bureau voor Statistiek, The Hague).
2. Ibid., March 1975
3. This archive has been set up and organized by Dr. A. Schoorlemmer for his portfolio analysis study. We are extremely grateful for his permission to use this data source.
4. Inflation will be taken care of automatically in most cases by comparing the nominal results for the merging firm with the nominal results projected on the basis of industry movements.
5. See *Nationale Rekeningen, 1975* (Centraal Bureau voor Statistiek), p.62.

Chapter 7

Large Mergers in Sweden, 1962–1976

Bengt Rydén and Jan-Olof Edberg

GENERAL BACKGROUND—TRENDS
AND MERGER STATISTICS

Sweden, like most other industrialized countries, has during the last decade experienced a wave of corporate mergers in most sectors of its economy. Also as in other countries, this is not a new phenomenon. Although there are no official statistics, it seems evident that there was a first wave of combinations starting in the late 1800s and ending about 1915. (Official registration of mergers began only in 1969.) A second tide came in the 1920s, lasting for some ten years. These merger waves were both characterized by corporate or sectorial crises, often involving a larger number of firms. Several combinations still in existence were born during these years.

The present merger wave has been studied in more detail (Rydén 1972). As can be seen from Figure 7–1, the latest wave began around 1960. Since then, mergers in mining and manufacturing industries have increased steeply, in terms of both the number of acquired firms and the number of employees in these firms, and the trend has been the same outside these sectors. During the period 1946–1976, some 3700 manufacturing companies have been acquired by other manufacturing companies. Partial mergers in the form of acquisitions of operating divisions or

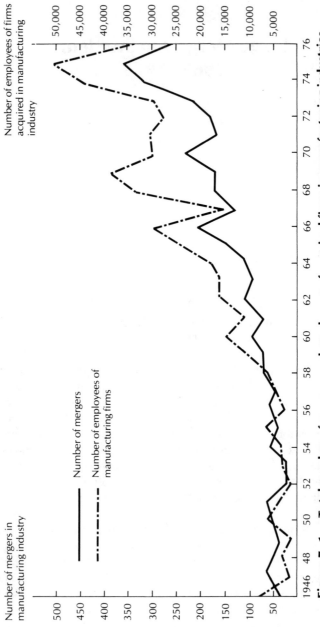

Figure 7-1. Total number of mergers and employees of acquired firms in manufacturing industries.

Table 7–1. Merger Intensity in Thirteen Manufacturing Industries, 1946–1975 (number of employees of firms acquired as a percentage of the total in each industry)

Industry	1946– 1951	1952– 1957	1958– 1963	1964– 1969	1970– 1975	1946– 1975	Total Number of Acquired Firms
Mining	4.3	3.5	3.1	0.9	1.9	13.7	13
Primary metals	2.2	6.5	4.1	6.4	2.9	22.1	27
Fabricated metal products	2.3	1.4	8.2	22.8	27.8	62.5	367
Machinery	1.7	1.4	5.0	8.9	19.6	36.6	389
Electrical machinery	15.6	1.4	5.6	15.1	20.6	58.3	146
Transportation equipment	7.6	0.7	6.8	24.6	27.3	67.0	111
Rubber and chemical products	2.6	2.0	8.6	25.6	27.9	66.7	315
Stone, clay, and glass	1.6	2.0	7.6	24.3	29.7	65.2	215
Timber and wood products	2.5	5.0	2.0	8.7	23.1	41.3	308
Pulp, paper, and paper products	2.6	2.8	8.9	23.6	6.1	44.0	243
Foods and beverages	2.5	3.3	18.2	22.1	51.6	97.7	1025
Textile, clothing, and leather	2.1	1.3	4.8	12.7	25.2	46.1	247
Other manufacturing industries	1.7	0.0	13.7	10.3	44.3	70.0	19
All manufacturing industries	3.1	2.3	7.4	16.6	23.4	52.8	3425

separate product lines are not included in these statistics, nor are foreign firms that have been acquired by Swedish firms and nonmanufacturing firms taken over by manufacturing firms. Nor have we taken account of mergers in the utility sector and building and construction.

According to our data, some 500,000 persons worked for manufacturing firms that were acquired in connection with mergers from 1946 to 1976. This figure should give an appropriate estimate of the total number of persons employed in acquired companies. Those acquired companies not covered by our data are small firms with few employees.[1]

Table 7–1 shows weighted measures of the "merger intensity" in seventeen manufacturing industries, 1946–1975. This period is divided into subperiods of six years each. More than 50 percent of all persons employed in manufacturing industries as an average over the period have been working with companies acquired or merged during the thirty-year period studied. The merger intensity for the period 1964–1975 was more than three times as high as it was for the period 1946–1963. The variation between industries is high. Almost every one of the employees in food-processing industries had been working in companies acquired during the period in question, while the corresponding figure for other manufacturing industries (shipyards), transportation industries, and chemical industries is nearly 70 percent. Mining has the lowest merger intensity, 20 percent.

While since 1946, some 15–20 percent of all manufacturing firms (with five or more employees) were merged by acquisition, the rate is 60 percent for medium-sized firms (200–499) and 50 percent for large firms (500 or more employees). Although there are some indictions that merger activity might have reached a peak during the last few years, the propensity to merge and to make acquisitions still seems to be high, especially among large firms. A number of large mergers have recently taken place—as well as several successfully counteracted merger proposals and takeover bids (e.g., Volvo-Saab Scania and KemaNobel-Swedish Match).

A majority of the merged firms were small or medium-sized family-owned enterprises.The number of companies listed on the Stockholm Stock Exchange is relatively limited, and only in exceptional cases has Sweden experienced raids and takeover battles. The number of listed companies has dwindled by a good third since 1950 (60 out of 150), but there have, of course, been new ones added. During the period 1950–1970, mergers and acquisitions accounted for some 20 percent of the growth of sales of a sample of sixty listed manufacturing firms, and a study of a sample of thirty firms for the period 1970–1975 produces similar results.

A large majority of the mergers have been horizontal (80 percent), leaving only a small part for vertical and conglomerate mergers—some 10 percent each. The conglomerates gained popularity in the late 1960s and early 1970s, but unforeseen difficulties have again made them less popular. The problems of the late 1970s for large sectors of Swedish industry have, again, exerted pressure for defensive horizontal mergers aiming at cutting costs and increasing market power. Some of these "crises mergers" were initiated by the government and resulted in fully or partly government-owned companies (e.g., shipyards, steel, and textiles).

Sweden has a large manufacturing industry in relation to its small domestic market. Exports claim 50 percent of industrial production. This situation generally favors the concentration of production. It is evident that the increasing number of mergers, and especially of large mergers, has pushed this concentration even further and contributed significantly to the fact that a number of important Swedish sectors are now characterized by a monopoly or duopoly (not taking imports into account).

INSTITUTIONAL BACKGROUND

The political and institutional climate has traditionally been favorable to mergers in Sweden. There has been a general understanding among leading politicians and trade unionists of the need for flexibility, change, and restructuring in Swedish industry to keep up with internal and external demands for constantly increasing productivity. It has for many years been generally believed in politically influential circles that large firms are good for the country and that concentration by mergers should be promoted, not prevented. This philosophy has been based on two factors—the competitive international background and the generally accepted goal of full employment and an active labor market policy.

During the postwar period there has been no legislation preventing mergers. The antitrust laws have nothing to say about mergers. There is a widely used option for the government to exempt capital gains of shares from taxation if a proposed merger is deemed to be in the public interest. As a matter of fact, no political or legal authority, nor any union, has had the legal power to prevent a proposed merger. On the contrary, the government has tried to promote mergers in many instances. This climate is important for a general understanding of merger developments in Sweden during the last few decades.

However, a gradual change in this climate is taking place. The non-socialist parties in power since October 1976 are more opposed to mergers than the former, Socialist government, and a proposal of toughened antitrust laws was presented by a government committee in late 1977, including governmental approval of proposed large mergers. A government proposal to that effect was expected in late 1979. Tax exemptions can no longer be taken for granted. The unions, and especially their grassroots members, have gradually become less favorable to the idea of mobility and flexibility and are now often even hostile to it. The employment security act of 1975 makes dismissals much more difficult and costly than earlier, and the codetermination act of 1977 makes merger decisions more complicated and difficult to carry through. A more favorable climate for family-owned firms, as well as new laws and attitudes, indicate a gradual drop from the present merger peak within the next few years.

FINANCIAL BACKGROUND

The characteristics and functioning of the financial markets and the supply of capital available to the corporate sector might be of great importance for the merger climate and hence for the merger rates of a specific country. The data presented here all relate to companies listed on the Stockholm Stock Exchange. Table 7–2 presents some basic data on the Stockholm Stock Exchange.

It should be noted that the issue of new shares is relatively insignificant in relation to the total value of listed shares. The issue of new shares is also

Table 7–2. Some Financial Data on Companies Listed on the Stockholm Stock Exchange

	Number of Companies	Nominal Value of Shares (bill Sw. cr)	Market Value of Shares (bill Sw. cr)	Issues of New Shares as Percent of Total Market Value (bill Sw. cr)	Dividends as Percent of Net Profits	Market Value as Percent of Book Value of Assets
1962	109	6.3	17.6	0.6	—	—
1966	112	9.4	20.0	1.6	57	55 (1967)
1970	106	11.9	24.0	0.2	43	51
1974	105	15.3	33.5	0.6	30	45
1976	98	18.7	43.8	3.0	82	48

Source: Kapitalmarknadsutredningen, SOU (1978:11).

of minor importance for the cash flow of individual companies (Table 7–3). The role of the stock exchange as a supplier of capital is evidently very small in Sweden. The market value of shares related to GNP was 14 percent as of 1976 to compare with 54 percent for the United States, 28 percent for the United Kingdom, 20 percent for the Netherlands, 13 percent for Belgium, 12 percent for West Germany and 9 percent for France.

As Table 7–3 shows, the main capital source is retained profits. The large proportion of investment in equipment and plant is financed by internally generated and retained funds. Dividends normally take 50 percent or less of net profits (Table 7–2).

The profitability, after tax and calculated on adjusted equity as an average of the period 1967–1976 is 5 percent. As Table 7–3 shows, the profitability has dwindled from a high in 1974 to a low point in 1976. In 1977, profits were almost completely wiped out and, in fact, would have been negative were it not for important government subsidies. In 1978, profits improved, but only modestly.

EARLIER MERGER STUDIES

Very few studies on mergers have been published in Sweden. The only theoretical and empirical study using statistical methods, and also the only one in English, is Rydén (1972). There are also a number of smaller case studies, mainly based on interviews and dealing with family-owned firms. Generally speaking, less is known of the effects of mergers than of the determinants, which were studied by Rydén.

Table 7–3. Financial Analysis of Companies Listed on the Stockholm Stock Exchange (billion Swedish crowns and percent)

	1968	1970	1972	1974	1976
Retained profits	4.2 (74)	6.0 (72)	5.8 (65)	14.3 (79)	9.9 (53)
Increase of long-term liabilities	1.4 (24)	2.2 (27)	3.0 (33)	3.5 (19)	7.6 (40)
Issue of new shares	0.1 (2)	0.1 (1)	0.2 (2)	0.4 (2)	1.4 (7)
Total cash flow	5.7 (100)	8.3 (100)	9.0 (100)	18.2 (100)	18.9 (100)
Capital spending, equipment and plants	3.5	6.4	6.2	9.9	13.1
Rate of self-financing (percent)	94	68	85	78	40
Profitability (percent); net profits after tax as percent of adjusted equity	5	5.5	4.2	7.3	2.4
Solvency (percent; equity as percent of total capital)	37.5	34.1	29.8	27.7	25.4

Source: Kapitalmarknadsutredningen, SOU (1978:11).

Although the results of Rydén's study generally had a low statistical significance, they gave no support to the economies of scale hypothesis nor to the "disturbance theory." The monopoly motive seemed to be quite well supported. The study also demonstrated that a majority of the sold firms had poor records of profitability, liquidity, and solvency and that many of them were owned (and run) by people older than the average owner-manager. The main result, however, was that acquisitions and mergers can only be explained by a vast array of different, and sometimes interacting, determinants. This is why statistical means of financial variables of acquirers and acquirees often do not show significant divergences from comparable groups, as will also be demonstrated later in this study.

GENERAL OUTLINE OF PRESENT STUDY

The purpose of the present study is to test, by statistical methods, hypotheses on determinants and economic effects of mergers between large Swedish firms during the period 1962–1976. Only mergers between firms listed on the Stockholm Stock Exchange are analyzed, due to lack of data for a number of important variables of unlisted firms. There are forty such mergers, which comprise only one percent of the total number of acquisitions and mergers registered during the period 1962–1976, but their importance in real terms is much larger. Eighteen percent of the number of employees working in all acquired companies worked for listed firms that were merged.

Table 7–4. Number of Firms of Total Population and Merging Firms

	Total Number of Firms, 1962–1976	Number of Acquired Firms		Number of Acquiring Firms	
		1962–1972	1962–1976	1962–1972	1962–1976
Steel and metals	11	4	4	3	3
Machinery, engineering, transportation equipment	36	9	13	7	8
Construction and building materials	7	2	2	2	2
Timber, pulp, paper, printing	24	4	9	7	9
Food, beverages	7	3	4	1	1
Textile, apparel, leather	4	0	0	0	0
Chemicals	12	3	5	0	1
Utilities	2	1	1	0	0
Wholesale trade	4	0	0	1	1
Retail trade	4	1	2	1	2
Total	111	27	40	22	27

Data on independent variables have been collected for three years before and three years after each merger. The number of mergers studied is forty for the determinants and twenty-seven for the effects, out of a population of one hundred and eleven firms (Table 7–4). The firms included in the population are listed in an Appendix available from the authors upon request. The population includes firms in mining, manufacturing, construction, utilities, wholesale trade, and retail trade.[2] With one exception, companies that were listed after 1972 are excluded. Two firms have been excluded because they were "delisted" for reasons other than merger, and another two have been included in the control group although more than 50 percent of their shares were owned by other listed firms. Three acquiring firms not listed have been added because they made significant acquisitions of listed firms.

Four firms in the population have been both acquiring and acquired. Consequently, the number of companies engaged in mergers between listed firms is sixty-three (forty acquired plus twenty-seven acquiring minus four double counts) out of one hundred and eleven during the fifteen-year period studied.[3] These mergers are rather evenly distributed over the three five-year subperiods—eleven, fourteen, and fifteen. However, three top years can be distinguished—1966, 1969, and 1975. In 1966 and 1975–1976 increased capital gains taxes were expected or introduced, which should explain two of these top years. There has been at least one merger every year since 1962, but the general tendency has been toward more mergers at the end of the period. This patttern is in accordance with the overall Swedish merger trend as depicted in Figure 7–1. Twenty-two of the forty mergers have been horizontal (three-digit industry level), two vertical, six pure conglomerate, and ten nonpure conglomerate (within the same one-digit industry level but with small production or market similarities).

It should be noted that the mergers analyzed, although important, do not cover the total merger activity that the acquiring firms were engaged in during the period studied. The most noticeable omissions are foreign companies taken over, acquisitions of some large or medium-sized firms not listed, and "partial mergers"—that is, the acquisition of subsidiaries, divisions, product lines, and the like. There have of course also been sizeable mergers between firms not listed on the stock exchange.

Important parts of Swedish industry are characterized by firms diversifying into highly different activities. This is especially true for combined steel and forestry industries, sometimes also in combination with chemicals and hydropower. This complicates the classification of certain companies according to industry, with ramifications for the selection of control group data for the classification of mergers in horizontal and conglomerates, and for the relevance of certain analyzed financial variables.

DEFINITION OF DATA AND VARIABLES

A merger is defined as the acquisition by one firm of more than 50 percent of the shares of another firm. The time of a merger is defined as the day (year) when the acquisition takes place (i.e., not when it is announced).

The control group pertinent to a merger consists of all listed firms in the industry of the acquiring company that have not engaged in a merger three years before (determinants analyses) or three years after the merger (effects analyses). In industries with too few firms for a randomized selection of control firms, sectorial aggregates have been used instead of individual control firms. The type of control group used is shown in Appendix B of this chapter.

Since financial data for company groups ("concerns") in Sweden have been published only for a limited number of years, the variables used in this study refer to parent companies. Since the same definitions and the same kinds of data are used for both merged and nonmerged firms, this should not alter accurate discrimination between these two categories (ceteris paribus) except in cases where pairs of merging and nonmerging firms have different organizational setups (centralized-decentralized, M-shaped–U-shaped, etc.).

Swedish tax laws create problems of accurately assessing capital and profit values. Considerable tax depreciation of inventories, machinery, and plants are allowed, and these methods are often used to lower taxable profits. Inventories may be depreciated to 40 percent of their value. Machinery can be written off in five years, plants in fifty years. Important tax deductions are allowed for appropriations to "investment funds" allocated for capital spending later. Since the company tax is about 50 percent, half the value of these funds should be considered part of the equity, and the other half added to debts.

For these reasons, values of capital and profits are often underestimated and should be adjusted for correct assessments. In this study such adjustments have not been possible, with the exception of the investment funds just described. Since the analyses are comparisons of pairs of similar firms with respect to these tax rules and their implementation, the lack of adjustments should not alter the results. Further definitions are as follows:

Total assets: book value of balance sheet total (unadjusted for "over-depreciation" of inventories, plant and machinery);

Equity: book value of equity (capital plus reserves) plus 50 percent of "investment fund";

Debt: book value of long-term liabilities;

Profit (on equity): profit after depreciation, interest, and taxes;

Profit (on sales): profit before depreciation, interest; and taxes (gross profit);

Profit (on total assets): profit after interest revenues but before interest costs and taxes.

REPORT ON BASIC FINDINGS

The data collected and analyzed by nature and time period covered are presented in Appendix A of this chapter, with notations of the number of observations and in which cases the computed differences are statistically significant. As can be seen, the number of observations vary from a minimum of fourteen to a maximum of thirty-nine. Very few of the differences are significant on a 5 percent level, somewhat more on a 10 percent level.

The results of the statistical tests are presented in detail in Appendix B of this chapter. Average values of size, profitability, and other major variables for acquiring, acquired, and control group companies are also shown. Although most of the results are not statistically significant, it might be of interest to discuss the main results of the tests. Provided there is a high standard deviation within the population, a low value of the *t*-statistics may still indicate great differences in the average values of the test variables of merging and control group companies.

Characteristics of Acquiring Firms

The average acquiring firm is significantly larger than the acquired firm and also than the average nonacquiring firm of the same industry. It has been growing faster in size than the acquired firm before the merger but at about the same rate as the nonacquiring firm. Its premerger profit rate is larger than that of the nonacquiring firm and especially than that of the acquired firm. Its leverage ratio was smaller, but growing faster and fluctuating more, than those of both other firms in the years preceding the merger.

Characteristics of Acquired Firms

If the average acquiring firm seems to have been relatively successful before the merger in terms of profits, growth, and the like, the opposite is true for the average acquired firm. It has been growing more slowly and has a poorer profit rate and a higher indebtedness (leverage ratio) than the acquiring firm and, for most variables, also than the average nonacquiring firm of its industry. It is also significantly smaller in sales and assets.

The average price-earnings ratio of the acquired firm is generally higher, and more fluctuating, than that of the nonacquired firm in the three years preceding the merger, especially in the immediately preceding year. This is consistent with its low profits, since the acquired firm's share prices have not decreased at the same rate as its profits. Its profits fluctuate more than both the acquiring and the nonacquiring firms.

Merger Effects

As shown in Chapter Appendix A, the effects of the mergers have been calculated for a three-year period after the merger for various size variables, profits, leverage ratio, rate of return on stock, and risk-adjusted performance (the Sharp and Treynor measures). Comparisons have been made between the performance of the merged firms, on the one side, and for pairs of randomly selected nonmerging firms, industry trends, and predicted values in the absence of merger for the merged firms, on the other side.

The sales growth of the merged firms has been faster after merger than before. This difference is larger for merged than for matched pairs of nonmerged firms. The same is true for total assets, net assets, and employment. The average growth rate after merger is somewhat larger than the comparable industry trend(s)—with the exception of employment, which has grown more slowly than the industry trend.

The rate of profit on equity, assets, and sales of the merged firms was slightly lower after merger than before but a bit higher for the matched pairs of nonmerging firms. The results are equally in disfavor of the merged firms when their profit records after merger are compared with industry trends and with the predicted values in a nonmerger situation. However, of all those comparisons, the only one that produces a statistically significant difference is with the industry trend for profits on equity.

Significant differences have, however, been found for the pre- and postmerger leverage ratio differences of merged and nonmerged firms and also for postmerger differences between merged firms and industry trends. The leverage ratio of the merged firms has increased considerably more than that of nonmerged firms and than the industry trend. The actual ratio is somewhat higher than the predicted.

The overall result of the stockholder performance test is that the immediate effect of the merger on the rate of return on a stock in the acquiring company is more favorable than the effect after a few years. Unrealized expectations seem to have been prevalent. Only for the year of the merger was the average rate of return on a stock higher than for the three-year period before the merger. But this difference was even larger for nonmerging firms. For one, two, and three years after the merger, the return was lower than before merger. Randomly selected nonmerging firms show higher returns from the second year after merger, as do the predictions in case of no merger, while industry average returns are higher only from the third year. None of these results are, however, significant.

The risk-adjusted performance of the merged firms has generally been poorer for every analyzed year following the merger than before. Up to the second postmerger year, it was, however, even less good for the nonmerging firms. From the second year, these showed a better risk-adjusted performance, although still decreasing.

INTERPRETATION OF RESULTS

In this section the results of the statistical tests will be discussed as they relate to the different merger hypotheses previously presented. It should be recalled, however, that most of the differences between merging and control group firms are not statistically significant, which calls for cautious interpretations of the conclusions presented.

Determinants of Mergers

Economies of scale and increased market power. As already reported, the average size of acquiring firms is much larger than that of the acquired, which are also smaller than the nonmerging firms. The average size of the merged firms does not differ very much from that of the nonmerging. It is slightly larger for all variables used, but the difference is insignificant, and the number of observations with a positive difference is generally only slightly higher than that with a negative difference.

Following the hypotheses presented earlier, this finding would seem to be inconsistent with the economies of scale explanation of mergers and to require the rejection both of this and of the market power hypothesis of mergers, since the latter would have required a much larger difference between merging and nonmerging firms than the one found. However, according to assessments of a number of individual Swedish mergers and to preliminary results of case studies as an extension of this study, it seems very probable that both these explanations have been important determinants of a number of mergers in Sweden.

A reason for this divergence might be a number of data problems. In order to get an accurate number of control group firms, it has been necessary to define the industry groups in very broad categories. Thus, some of the comparisons made might be less relevant. Another reason is that in many industries, proper comparisons should not be made within Sweden only, but within a group of countries with which Swedish companies have to compete.

Yet another reason might be the diversity of many of the studied firms. A horizontal merger will in many cases relate to only a part of one of the firms or both. In such cases the sizes measured are automatically exaggerated. Another possible problem is that the variables measured relate to parent companies only, while mergers might have been consummated to reap economic gains from combining subsidiaries of smaller—or larger—size than the parent company.

It might also be argued that because of the methodology used to test these two hypotheses, the difficulty in discriminating between them is not very surprising. If one of the hypotheses is valid for about half of the mergers and the other one for the remaining half, the test results might easily be the ones arrived at.

The conclusion is that although neither the economies of scale nor the monopoly hypotheses are supported by this study, they cannot be rejected. A plausible explanation of a number of horizontal mergers between large Swedish firms is that the companies tried to reach minimum optimum scales, as determined internationally, and in doing so, via merger, also reduced competition between themselves. Good examples of this can be found in the pulp and paper industry, the steel industry, and the automobile industry.

Spreading and reducing risks.   If firms merge to reduce risks, one would expect merging firms to have greater variations in profit levels than nonmerging firms. One would also expect highly indebted (high leverage ratio) firms to acquire low leverage firms to reduce business-cycle-related risks, although the reverse relation (low leverage firms acquiring high leverage firms) does not seem improbable in support of the risk-reducing hypothesis. Evidently, both these cases reduce leverage-related risks for the merged firm.

Contrary to the hypothesis, the merging firms turn out to have significantly lower variation (coefficients of variation) in profit levels than the nonmerging firms. The risk-reducing hypothesis is supported neither by the test of the risk-adjusted performance of the acquiring firms nor by the test of leverage ratios. The difference between the mean values of merging firms' leverage ratios is the same as for the nonmerging firms. The acquired firms are, however, more leveraged than the nonacquired, but evidently not more than what would appear a normal difference between any pair of firms. The fact that both merged firms have a significantly greater variance in leverage ratios than nonmerging firms is difficult to interpret in terms of the hypothesis.

Even if the leverage ratios of the merging firms preceding the merger seem to have little to contribute to explain the mergers, it is evident that the leverage ratios of the merged firms have grown significantly faster than those of nonmerging firms or than they would have done in case of no merger.

Thus, it would seem that Swedish firms have merged not to reduce or spread risks, but to increase their borrowing capacity. This result seems consistent with the fact that the majority of mergers have been horizontal. The conglomerate mergers have been too few to test for this hypothesis separately. But our case studies indicate that risk-spreading might indeed contribute to explain such acquisitions.

Economic disturbances and bargains.   The economic disturbances theory—stating that acquisitions of firms whose stock prices are rapidly changing are more likely than of firms with less fluctuating stocks—is not rejected by our study. Especially during the year preceding the merger, the fluctuation of the acquired firms' stock prices (P/E ratios) was signifi-cantly larger than that for nonacquired firms. The result is consistent even when the test is made for up to three years before the merger.

The bargain theory, however, is not supported. Contrary to the hypothesis, the acquired firms have experienced high stock prices relative to expected earnings, especially during the year immediately preceding the merger. As already suggested, the bargain theory might have more to say about the timing of a merger than about the reasons for it. If so, it would seem more appropriate to use monthly stock price data than annual.

Effects of Mergers

As discussed earlier, the effects of mergers have been analyzed in terms of postmerger changes in profit rates, sales, and stockholder performance. The test results will be interpreted following Table 2–2.

As already reported, the merged firms have experienced a bad profit record following merger, in comparison to the premerger period, when matched with randomly selected nonmerged firms, with industry trends, and with predicted values for the merged firms had they not merged. Neither has the return on a share of the acquiring company developed favorably, by the same comparisons as above, with exceptions for the short period immediately following the merger.

These results do not seem to follow any of the patterns of probable merger effects, based on neoclassical theory. For improved efficiency, with benefits for consumers and owners, positive sizes of the changes of all three variables would be needed. For increased market power, with consumers harmed but owners benefited, a negative sign on the sales change would be expected, with positive signs for the two other variables. Our study has resulted in none of these combinations.

If the decline in profits had been temporary, the long-run increase would probably have been expected and therefore reflected in the share prices. Our study indicates that long-run merger gains might indeed have been expected immediately preceding or following the merger. But these expectations seem to have vanished with time.

As already reported, the risk-adjusted performance of the merged firms has not increased, but rather decreased, after the merger. This result, however, relates to all mergers studied, not only the conglomerate ones.

The direct merger effects on employment have been slightly negative. The postmerger growth of employment has been slower than the industry trend and would have been higher (predicted value) if the firms had not merged.

In summary, our study does not seem to support any of the neoclassical theories of merger motives or merger effects. The private effects on owners and workers seem to have been negative or, at best, neutral. The social effects on consumers, which can only be tentatively assessed, do not seem to have been negative.

The results seem to be more consistent with a managerial merger theory. The growth of the merged firms has increased while profits have decreased after the mergers, which is in accordance with the hypothesis that managers acquire firms to maximize growth and/or size instead of profits. The acquisitions have been expensive judging from their relatively high P/E ratios—that is, their share prices have been higher relative to profits than those of comparable firms. The acquiring firms' higher profit rates and lower leverage ratios indicate low capital costs, which is also consistent with a managerial merger theory. It is also possible that some low leverage firms have wished to increase their indebtedness rapidly— and their size—by merger to reduce the risks of being taken over themselves. Such behavior would also conform with a managerial merger theory.

CONCLUSIONS

The results of our study do not seem to support any of the major theories of merger determinants and effects in a simple and noncontroversial way. The economic disturbance theory is supported, but the formulation of this hypothesis, which has been tested, is doubtful, to say the least. The results render some plausibility to managerial discretionary behavior with respect to acquisitions.

A simplistic summary of our results is that large mergers in Sweden have been harmful, or at best neutral, for stockholders and workers and possibly beneficial for consumers and managements—at least for the short-term effects. We have no possibility to assess the long-term effects, which might of course be generally more favorable. Thus, our study does not provide a sufficient basis for a rejection of the neoclassical merger theories as possible explanations of merger behavior in Sweden. There are many possible reasons for this:

The number of mergers and variable observations analyzed are too small.

The control group is too small for proper random selection of control firms and simultaneously too wide to provide complete comparability for industry and size. In some cases the proper control firm would have to be picked outside Sweden.

It is possible that no, or almost no, company in the population could meet strict control group requirements. Of the approximately fifty nonmerging firms, some have been engaged in other merging activities than those studied here, while others might have been candidates of mergers that, during the period studied, have not been realized.

The data analyzed are too crude or in other ways not good enough to reflect the proper characteristics.

The pre- and postmerger time periods analyzed are too short. Especially for analyzing certain effects of mergers a three-year period is certainly too short.

The hypothesis might not have been correctly or accurately formulated. In several cases the formulations of hypotheses have been influenced by the availability of data, which is a constant problem in studies like this.

Important merger determinants are not covered by the study. One example is the possible expected superiority of growth via mergers compared to internal growth (via "piecemeal" acquisitions) in terms of costs, time, and risks; another is the previously mentioned changes in tax laws on two occasions during the period studied.

The methodology of comparing mean data for merged and nonmerged firms conceals more than it reveals because different merger-relatd firm characteristics with extreme variable values might interact, certainly within the total mass of mergers but possibly also in some individual cases.

Another way of expressing the final point is to submit that merger behavior cannot be explained by one or a few dominating theories alone. This point is especially vital when mergers are studied and merger data are pooled for such a long period as fifteen years, during which period the merger-relevant climate might have changed considerably. It seems very probable that merger patterns observed in Sweden and elsewhere can only be understood with the help of all, or most, theories discussed in this study. It is easy to relate several individual mergers in Sweden during the period studied to each of these theories. The result of our study does not conflict with but rather supports such a contention.

The complexity of merger behavior and the methodological problems confronting statistical tests of merger hypotheses suggest the use of other, supplementary methods for such tests—mainly case studies. These are also important for a better understanding of the merger process, which might be vital for the formulation of hypotheses.

NOTES

1. The figure includes a minor number of double counts of firms that were acquired more than once.
2. Not included are banks, insurance companies, shipping companies, real estate companies, and investment funds and trusts, although such companies are listed on the Stockholm Stock Exchange.
3. If the study had covered the period up to 1978 inclusive, the number of firms would have been sixty-six—forty-three acquired and twenty-eight acquiring.

APPENDIX A: SUMMARY OF DATA COLLECTED, BY NATURE OF VARIABLE (figures denote numbers of observations analyzed)

Variable	AG	AD	AGAD	C	I	P
Time Period						
Sales	39*	39*	39	39*		
Assets	39*	39*	39	39*		
Assets net of depreciation	39*	39*	39	39*		
Time Period						
Sales	22**	22**		22		
Assets	22	22		22		
Assets net of depreciation	22	22		22		
Employment	22	22		22		
Time Period			*t* + 3			
Sales			22			22
Assets			22			22
Assets net of depreciation			22			22
Employment			21			21
Time Period						
Sales			22		22	
Assets			22		22	
Assets net of depreciation			22		22	
Employment			22		22	
Time Period						
Sales			22	22		
Assets			22	22		
Assets net of depreciation			22**	22**		
Employment			22	22		
Profits on equity			25	25		
Profits on assets			26	26		
Profits on sales			26	26		
Time Period						
Profits on equity	26	26		26		
Profits on assets	26	26		26		
Profits on sales	26*	26*		26*		
Time Period						
Profits on equity			26**		26[a]	26
Profits on assets			26		26[a]	26
Profit on sales			26		26[a]	26
Time Period						
Profits variance	34	38*	33**	33–38**		
Time Period			*t*			
Leverage ratio	39	39	38[b]	38[b]–39		

Time period formulas:

$$\frac{(t-1) + (t-2) + (t-3)}{3}$$

$$\frac{(t-1) + (t-2) + (t-3)}{3}$$

$t + 3$

$$\frac{(t+1) + (t+2) + (t+3)}{3}$$

$$\frac{((t+1) + (t+2) + (t+3))}{3} - \frac{((t-1) + (t-2) + (t-3))}{3}$$

$$\frac{(t-1) + (t-2) + (t-3)}{3}$$

$(t+1) + (t+2) + (t-3)$

$(t-1), (t-2), (t-3)$

t

APPENDIX A   (Continued)

Variable	AG	AD	AGAD	C	I	P
Time Period		t				
Leverage ratio variance	39*	39*				
Time Period		$t + 3$				
Leverage ratio			22			22
Time Period		$\dfrac{(t-1) + (t-2) + (t-3)}{3}$				
Leverage ratio	22	22		22		
Time Period		$\dfrac{(t+1) + (t+2) + (t+3)}{3}$				
Leverage ratio			22**		22**	
Time Period	$\dfrac{(t+1) + (t+2) + (t+3)}{3} - \dfrac{(t-1) + (t-2) + (t-3)}{3}$					
Leverage ratio			22*	22*		
Time Period		$t - 1$				
P/E ratio		27		27		
Time Period		$(t-1), (t-2)$				
P/E ratio		27		27		
Time Period		$(t-1), (t-2), (t-3)$				
P/E ratio		24		24		
Time Period		$t - 1$				
P/E ratio high to low		36*		36*		
Time Period		$(t-1), (t-2)$				
P/E ratio high to low		36*		36*		
Time Period		$(t-1), (t-2)$				
P/E ratio high to low		34		34		
Time Period	$t - \dfrac{(t-1) + (t-2) + (t-3)}{3}$					
Rate of return on stock	23			23		
Time Period	$\dfrac{t + (t+1)}{2} - \dfrac{(t-1) + (t-2) + (t-3)}{3}$					
Rate of return on stock	23			23		
Time Period	$\dfrac{t + (t+1) + (t+2)}{3} - \dfrac{(t-1) + (t-2) + (t-3)}{3}$					
Rate of return on stock	23			23		

APPENDIX A   (Continued)

Variable	AG	AD	AGAD	C	I	P
Time Period $\dfrac{t + (t + 1) + (t + 2) + (t + 3)}{4} - \dfrac{(t - 1) + (t - 2) + (t - 3)}{3}$						
Rate of return on stock	23			23		
Time Period t						
Rate of return on stock	22–23				23	22
Time Period $\dfrac{t + (t + 1)}{2}$						
Rate of return on stock	22–23				23	22
Time Period $\dfrac{t + (t + 2) + (t + 2)}{3}$						
Rate of return on stock	22–23				23	22
Time Period $\dfrac{t + (t + 1) + (t + 2) + (t + 3)}{4}$						
Rate of return on stock	22–23				23	22
Time Period $t - \dfrac{(t - 1) + (t - 2) + (t - 3)}{3}$						
Risk-adjusted performance (S)	24			24		
Risk-adjusted performance (T)	14			14		
Time Period $\dfrac{t + (t + 1)}{2} - \dfrac{(t - 1) + (t - 2) + (t - 3)}{3}$						
Risk-adjusted performance (S)	24			24		
Risk-adjusted performance (T)	18			18		
Time Period $\dfrac{t + (t + 1) + (t + 2)}{3} - \dfrac{(t - 1) + (t - 2) + (t - 3)}{3}$						
Risk-adjusted performance (S)	24			24		
Risk-adjusted performance (T)	20			20		
Time Period $\dfrac{t + (t + 1) + (t + 2) + (t + 3)}{4} - \dfrac{(t - 1) + (t - 2) + (t - 3)}{3}$						
Risk-adjusted performance (S)	24			24		
Risk-adjusted performance (T)	18			18		

[a] Annual averages include three years before merger.
[b] Difference between pairs of firms.
AG = acquiring firm
AD = acquired firm
AGAD = merged firms
C = randomly selected control firm
I = industry trend value
P = predicted value based on three-year industry growth

t = year of merger
$t - n$ = number of years before merger
$t + n$ = number of years after merger
n^* = difference between values significant on 10 percent level
n^{**} = difference between values significant on 5 percent level
S = Sharpe's measure
T = Treynor's measure

APPENDIX B: RESULTS OF THE STATISTICAL TESTS

Formula Number	Variable	Company Type		Number of Observations n_T	Mean Values		Difference $\bar{X}_1 - \bar{X}_2$	$t =$ Value	Number of Observations with $X_1 > X_2$ n_p	n_p/n_T	$t =$ Value
		X_1	X_2		$\bar{X}_1$	$\bar{X}_2$					
	Determinants, Size Comparisons										
1.1a	Sales, arithmetic mean three years before	AGAD	MIND	39	624.2	537.5	86.7	1.17	20	0.51	0.16
1.1b	Sales, mean of the natural log three years before	AGAD	MIND	39	6.05	6.06	−0.01	−0.04	20	0.51	0.16
extra test	Sales, arithmetic mean three years before	AG	AD	39	966.7	285.2	681.5	4.54*	33	0.85	4.27*
extra test	Sales, mean of the natural log three years before	AG	AD	39	6.41	5.03	1.38	7.07*	33	0.85	4.27*
extra test	Sales, arithmetic mean three years before	AG	MIND	39	966.7	537.5	429.2	3.28*	26	0.67	2.05*
extra test	Sales, mean of the natural log three years before	AG	MIND	39	6.41	6.06	0.35	2.51*	26	0.67	2.05*
extra test	Sales, arithmetic mean three years before	AD	MIND	39	285.2	524.5	−239.3	−3.54*	4	0.10	−4.90*
extra test	Sales, mean of the natural log three years before	AD	MIND	39	5.03	6.06	−1.03	−6.39*	4	0.10	−4.90*
1.2a	Total assets, arithmetic mean three years before	AGAD	MIND	39	563.6	555.8	7.8	0.05	23	0.59	1.11
1.2b	Total assets, mean of the natural log three years before	AGAD	MIND	39	6.05	6.09	−0.04	−0.41	23	0.59	1.11

APPENDIX B: RESULTS OF THE STATISTICAL TESTS (continued)

Formula Number	Variable	Company Type X₁	Company Type X₂	Number of Observations n_T	Mean Values $\bar{X}_1$	Mean Values $\bar{X}_2$	Difference $\bar{X}_1 - \bar{X}_2$	$t =$ Value	Number of Observations with $X_1 \underset{n_p}{\geq} X_2$	n_p/n_T	$t =$ Value
extra test	Total assets, arithmetic mean three years before	AG	AD	39	890.4	237.7	652.7	5.11*	33	0.85	4.27*
extra test	Total assets, mean of the natural log three years before	AG	AD	39	6.41	4.97	1.44	7.55*	33	0.85	4.27*
extra test	Total assets, arithmetic mean three years before	AG	MIND	39	890.4	555.8	334.6	2.68*	26	0.67	2.05*
extra test	Total assets, mean of the natural log three years before	AG	MIND	39	6.41	6.09	0.32	1.94**	26	0.67	2.05**
extra test	Total assets, arithmetic mean three years before	AD	MIND	39	237.7	555.8	−318.1	−4.29*	6	0.15	−4.27*
extra test	Total assets, mean of the natural log three years before	AD	MIND	39	4.97	6.09	−1.12	−6.05*	6	0.15	−4.27*
1.3a	Net of depreciation, plant and equipment, arithmetic mean three years before	AGAD	MIND	39	286.1	264.8	21.3	0.54	21	0.54	0.47
1.3b	Net of depreciation, plant and equipment, the natural log three years before	AGAD	MIND	39	5.31	5.35	−0.04	−0.25	21	0.54	0.47
extra test	Net of depreciation, plant and equipment, arithmetic mean three years before	AG	AD	39	443.7	130.4	313.7	4.65*	32	0.82	3.95*

APPENDIX B: RESULTS OF THE STATISTICAL TESTS (continued)

Formula Number	Variable	Company Type		Number of Observations n_T	Mean Values		Difference $\bar{x}_1 - \bar{x}_2$	$t =$ Value	Number of Observations with $X_1 \gtrless X_2$ n_p	n_p/n_T	$t =$ Value
		X_1	X_2		$\bar{x}_1$	$\bar{x}_2$					
extra test	Net of depreciation, plant and equipment, the natural log three years before	AG	AD	39	5.66	4.18	1.48	6.82*	32	0.82	3.95*
extra test	Net of depreciation, plant and equipment, arithmetic mean three years before	AG	MIND	39	443.7	264.8	178.9	2.66*	25	0.64	1.74**
extra test	Net of depreciation, plant and equipment, the natural log three years before	AG	MIND	39	5.66	5.35	0.31	1.78**	25	0.64	1.74**
extra test	Net of depreciation, plant and equipment, arithmetic mean three years before	AD	MIND	39	130.4	264.8	−134.4	−3.58*	7	0.18	−3.95*
extra test	Net of depreciation, plant and equipment, the natural log three years after	AD	MIND	39	4.18	5.35	−1.17	−5.56*	7	0.18	−3.95*
2	Risk Motives										
2.1a	Variance in profits, ratio of variation coefficients	AGAD	MAGMAD	33	2.09	2.90	−0.81	−1.72**	10	0.30	−2.23*
2.1b	Variance in profits, variation coefficients	AG	MIND	34	0.32	0.29	0.03	1.13	18	0.53	0.34
2.1c	Variance in profits, variation coefficients	AD	MIND	38	0.42	0.29	0.13	2.25*	21	0.55	0.64

APPENDIX B: RESULTS OF THE STATISTICAL TESTS (continued)

Formula Number	Variable	Company Type X_1	Company Type X_2	Number of Observations n_T	Mean Values $\bar{X}_1$	Mean Values $\bar{X}_2$	Difference $\bar{X}_1 - \bar{X}_2$	$t =$ Value	Number of Observations with $X_1 \gtrless X_2$ $\hat{n}_p$	n_p/n_T	$t =$ Value
2.1d	Variance in profits, variation coefficients	AG	AD	33	0.32	0.42	−0.10	−1.69**	14	0.42	−0.86
2.2	Leverage ratio, absolute differences in mean values	AGAD	MAGMAD	38	0.19	0.18	0.01	0.44	18	0.47	−0.32
2.3	Leverage ratio, variances	AG	MIND	39	0.036	0.006	0.030	$F = 5.72$*	—	—	—
2.4	Leverage ratio, mean values	AG	MIND	39	0.43	0.47	−0.04	−1.42	—	—	—
2.5	Leverage ratio, variances	AD	MIND	39	0.027	0.006	0.021	$F = 4.36$*	—	—	—
2.6	Leverage ratio, mean values	AD	MIND	39	0.49	0.47	0.02	0.76	—	—	—
2.7	Leverage ratio, variances	AG	AD	39	0.036	0.027	0.009	$F = 1.31$	—	—	—
2.8	Leverage ratio, mean values	AG	AD	39	0.43	0.49	−0.06	−1.49	—	—	—
3	*Disturbance Theory*										
3.1	P/E ratio ($t - 1$), ratio high to low	AD	MAD	36	1.50	1.37	0.13	2.29*	22	0.61	1.31
3.2	P/E ratio ($t - 1$), ($t - 2$), ratio high to low	AD	MAD	36	1.42	1.34	0.08	2.95*	22	0.61	1.31
3.3	P/E ratio ($t - 1$), ($t - 2$), ($t - 3$), ratio high to low	AD	MAD	34	1.39	1.35	0.04	1.54	17	0.50	0.00
4	*Bargain Theory*										
4.1	P/E ratio ($t - 1$), mean value	AD	MAD	27	48.08	25.87	22.21	1.11	15	0.56	0.57
4.2	P/E ratio ($t - 1$), ($t - 2$), mean value	AD	MAD	27	40.80	26.11	14.69	1.19	16	0.59	0.94
4.3	P/E ratio ($t - 1$), ($t - 2$), ($t - 3$) mean value	AD	MAD	24	37.02	33.78	3.24	0.21	14	0.58	0.80

APPENDIX B: RESULTS OF THE STATISTICAL TESTS *(continued)*

Formula Number	Variable	Company Type		Number of Observations n_T	Mean Values		Difference $\bar{X}_1 - \bar{X}_2$	$t =$ Value	Number of Observations with $X_1 \geq X_2$ $\hat{n}_p$	n_p/n_T	$t =$ Value
		X_1	X_2		$\bar{X}_1$	$\bar{X}_2$					
5	*Effects, Profitability*										
	Rate of Profit on Equity										
5.1	Three-year period after merger minus three-year period before	AGAD	MAGMAD	25	−0.0095	0.0009	−0.0104	−1.24	10	0.40	−0.98
extra test	Three-year period before merger	AG	AD	26	0.0775	0.0689	0.0086	0.64	16	0.62	1.15
extra test	Three-year period before merger	AG	MAG	26	0.0775	0.0823	−0.0048	−0.38	11	0.42	−0.77
extra test	Three-year period before merger	AD	MAD	26	0.0689	0.0935	−0.0246	−1.07	13	0.50	0.00
5.2	Rate of Profit on Total Assets Three-year period after merger minus three-year period before	AGAD	MAGMAD	26	−0.0050	0.0027	−0.0077	−0.77	11	0.42	−0.77
extra test	Three-year period before merger	AG	AD	26	0.0803	0.0732	0.0071	0.69	18	0.69	1.92**
extra test	Three-year period before merger	AG	MAG	26	0.0803	0.0728	0.0075	0.68	13	0.50	0.00
extra test	Three-year period before merger	AD	MAD	26	0.0732	0.0800	−0.0068	−0.61	12	0.46	−0.38
5.3	Rate of Profit on Sales Three-year period after merger minus three-year period before	AGAD	MAGMAD	26	−0.0016	−0.0001	−0.0015	−0.70	10	0.38	−1.15

APPENDIX B: RESULTS OF THE STATISTICAL TESTS (continued)

Formula Number	Variable	Company Type X_1	X_2	Number of Observations n_T	Mean Values $\bar{X}_1$	$\bar{X}_2$	Difference $\bar{X}_1 - \bar{X}_2$	$t =$ Value	Number of Observations with $X_1 n_p > X_2$	n_p/n_T	$t =$ Value
extra test	Three-year period before merger	AG	AD	26	0.0385	0.0192	0.0193	3.88*	20	0.77	2.69*
extra test	Three-year period before merger	AG	MAG	26	0.0385	0.0316	0.0069	1.08	15	0.58	0.77
extra test	Three-year period before merger	AD	MAD	26	0.0192	0.0278	-0.0086	-2.25*	9	0.35	-1.54
6	*Comparison with Industry*										
6.1	Rate of profit on equity for the new company three-year period after merger compared to the industry average three-year period before and three-year period after merger	AGAD	MIND	26	0.0708	0.0884	-0.0176	-1.77**	6	0.26	-2.69*
6.2	Rate of profit on total assets for the new company three-year period after merger compared to the industry average three-year period before and three-year period after merger	AGAD	MIND	26	0.0729	0.0821	-0.0092	-1.23	9	0.35	-1.54

APPENDIX B: RESULTS OF THE STATISTICAL TESTS (continued)

Formula Number	Variable	Company Type X_1	Company Type X_2	Number of Observations n_T	Mean Values $\bar{X}_1$	Mean Values $\bar{X}_2$	Difference $\bar{X}_1 - \bar{X}_2$	$t =$ Value	Number of Observations with $X_1 > X_2$ n_p	n_p/n_T	$t =$ Value
6.3	Rate of profit on sales for the new company three-year period after merger compared to industry average three-year period before and three-year period after merger	AGAD	MIND	26	0.0319	0.0347	−0.0028	−0.68	11	0.42	−0.77
7	*Comparison with Predicted Performance*										
7.1	Profit on equity	AGAD	PAGAD	26	0.0708	0.0779	−0.0071	−0.28	9	0.35	−1.54
7.2	Profit on sales	AGAD	PAGAD	26	0.0319	0.0324	−0.0005	−0.15	13	0.50	0.00
8	*Change Test*										
8.1	Sales, growth rate three-year period after merger minus three-year period before	AGAD	MAGMAD	22	0.0415	0.0202	0.0213	0.72	11	0.50	0.00
8.1a	Ratio of growth of sales three-year period after merger and three-year period before	AGAD	MAGMAD	22	0.0103	0.0102	0.0001	0.21	11	0.50	0.00
extra test	Growth rate three-year period before merger	AG	AD	22	0.0945	0.0322	0.0623	1.78**	15	0.68	1.67
extra test	Growth rate three-year period before merger	AG	MAG	22	0.0945	0.0992	−0.0047	−0.11	11	0.50	0.00

APPENDIX B: RESULTS OF THE STATISTICAL TESTS (continued)

Formula Number	Variable	Company Type X_1	X_2	Number of Observations n_T	Mean Values $\bar{X}_1$	$\bar{X}_2$	Difference $\bar{X}_1 - \bar{X}_2$	$t =$ Value	Number of Observations with $X_1 \, \hat{n}_p \geq X_2$	n_p/n_T	$t =$ Value
extra test	Growth rate three-year period before merger	AD	MAD	22	0.0322	0.0577	−0.0255	−0.97	6	0.27	−2.08*
8.2	Total assets, growth rate three-year period after merger minus three-year period before	AGAD	MAGMAD	22	0.0266	0.0196	0.0070	0.32	9	0.41	−0.83
8.2a	Ratio of growth of total assets three-year period after merger and three-year period before	AGAD	MAGMAD	22	0.0102	0.0102	0.0000	0.16	9	0.41	−0.83
extra test	Growth rate three-year period before merger	AG	AD	22	0.0914	0.0769	0.0145	1.04	15	0.68	1.67
extra test	Growth rate three-year period before merger	AG	MAG	22	0.0914	0.0768	0.0146	0.55	9	0.41	−0.83
extra test	Growth rate three-year period before merger	AD	MAD	22	0.0769	0.0973	−0.0204	−1.06	9	0.41	−0.83
8.3	Net of depreciation, plant and equipment, growth rate three-year period after merger minus three-year period before	AGAD	MAGMAD	22	0.0516	−0.0229	0.0745	1.98**	14	0.64	1.25
8.3a	Ratio of growth of plant and equipment three-year period after merger and three-year period before	AGAD	MAGMAD	22	0.0104	0.0098	0.0006	1.90**	14	0.64	1.25

APPENDIX B: RESULTS OF THE STATISTICAL TESTS (continued)

Formula Number	Variable	Company Type		Number of Observations n_T	Mean Values		Difference $\bar{X}_1 - \bar{X}_2$	$t =$ Value	Number of Observations with $X_1 \geq X_2$, n_p	n_p/n_T	$t =$ Value
		X_1	X_2		$\bar{X}_1$	$\bar{X}_2$					
extra test	Growth rate three-year period before merger	AG	AD	22	0.0836	0.0559	0.0277	1.05	14	0.64	1.25
extra test	Growth rate three-year period before merger	AG	MAG	22	0.0836	0.0980	−0.0144	−0.41	12	0.55	0.42
extra test	Growth rate three-year period before merger	AD	MAD	22	0.0559	0.0895	−0.0336	−1.09	7	0.32	−1.67
8.4	Leverage ratio, growth rate three-year period after merger minus three-year period before	AGAD	MAGMAD	22	0.0856	−0.0148	0.1004	2.90*	17	0.77	2.50*
8.4a	The ratio of growth of leverage ratio three-year period after merger and three-year period before	AGAD	MAGMAD	22	0.0107	0.0098	0.0009	3.23*	17	0.77	2.50*
extra test	Growth rate three-year period before merger	AG	AD	22	0.0283	0.0188	0.0098	0.42	9	0.41	−0.83
extra test	Growth rate three-year period before merger	AG	MAG	22	0.0283	0.0316	−0.0033	−0.11	10	0.45	−0.42
extra test	Growth rate three-year period before merger	AD	MAD	22	0.0188	0.0334	−0.0146	−0.64	8	0.36	−1.25
8.5	Employment, growth rate three-year period after merger minus three-year period before	AGAD	MAGMAD	22	0.0268	0.0130	0.0138	0.84	11	0.50	0.00

APPENDIX B: RESULTS OF THE STATISTICAL TESTS (continued)

Formula Number	Variable	Company Type X_1	Company Type X_2	Number of Observations n_T	Mean Values $\bar{X}_1$	Mean Values $\bar{X}_2$	Difference $\bar{X}_1 - \bar{X}_2$	$t =$ Value	Number of Observations with $X_1 \gtrsim X_2$ n_p	n_p/n_T	$t =$ Value
8.5a	The ratio of growth in employment three-year period after merger and three-year period before	AGAD	MAGMAD	22	0.0103	0.0101	0.0002	1.10	11	0.50	0.00
extra test	Growth rate three-year period before merger	AG	AD	22	0.0037	−0.0167	0.0204	0.82	9	0.41	−0.83
extra test	Growth rate three-year period before merger	AG	MAG	22	0.0037	0.0072	−0.0035	−0.12	9	0.41	−0.83
extra test	Growth rate three-year period before merger	AD	MAD	22	−0.0167	−0.0031	−0.0136	−0.75	11	0.50	0.00
9	Comparison with Industry Test Merging companies three-year period after merger compared to industry average for the same period										
9.1	Growth of sales	AGAD	MIND	22	0.1299	0.1160	0.0139	0.81	9	0.41	−0.83
9.2	Growth of total assets	AGAD	MIND	22	0.1162	0.1070	0.0092	0.58	11	0.50	0.00
9.3	Growth of plant and equipment	AGAD	MIND	22	0.1181	0.1101	0.0080	0.56	14	0.64	1.25
9.4	Growth of leverage ratio	AGAD	MIND	22	0.0871	0.0453	0.0418	2.03**	15	0.68	1.67
9.5	Growth of employment	AGAD	MIND	22	0.0194	0.0212	−0.0018	−0.12	11	0.50	0.00

APPENDIX B: RESULTS OF THE STATISTICAL TESTS (continued)

Formula Number	Variable	Company Type		Number of Observations n_T	Mean Values		Difference $\bar{x}_1 - \bar{x}_2$	$t =$ Value	Number of Observations with $X_1 \gtrless X_2$	n_p/n_T	$t =$ Value
		X_1	X_2		$\bar{x}_1$	$\bar{x}_2$					
10	*Comparison with Predicted Performance*										
	Three-year period after merger										
10.1	Sales (mill. Sw. cr.)	AGAD	PAGAD	22	1334.3	1288.9	45.4	0.48	9	0.41	-0.83
10.2	Total assets (mill. Sw. cr.)	AGAD	PAGAD	22	1379.3	1382.0	-2.7	-0.04	11	0.50	0.00
10.3	Plant and equipment net of depreciation (mill. Sw. cr.)	AGAD	PAGAD	22	719.9	700.9	19.0	0.33	14	0.64	1.25
10.4	Leverage ratio	AGAD	PAGAD	22	0.4929	0.4517	0.0412	1.51	15	0.68	1.67
10.5	Employment (number of persons)	AGAD	PAGAD	21	11098	11227	-129	-0.25	11	0.52	0.21
11	*Stockholder Performance*										
	Change Test										
	Difference in rates of return from holding a stock in the acquiring company compared to a control group firm										
11.1	Year of merger and three-years before merger	AG	MAG	23	0.0207	0.0609	-0.0402	-0.34	12	0.52	0.20
11.2	One year after merger and three years before merger	AG	MAG	23	-0.0084	-0.0224	0.0140	0.17	9	0.39	-1.02
11.3	Two years after merger and three years before merger	AG	MAG	23	-0.0355	0.0084	-0.0439	-0.70	10	0.43	-0.61
11.4	Three years after merger and three years before merger	AG	MAG	23	-0.0134	0.0155	-0.0289	-0.57	9	0.39	-1.02

APPENDIX B: RESULTS OF THE STATISTICAL TESTS (continued)

Formula Number	Variable	Company Type X_1	X_2	Number of Observations n_T	Mean Values $\bar{X}_1$	$\bar{X}_2$	Difference $\bar{X}_1 - \bar{X}_2$	$t =$ Value	Number of Observations with $X_1 \geq X_2$ n_p	n_p/n_T	$t =$ Value
12	*Comparison with Industry Test*										
12.1	Year of merger compared to three years before merger	AG	MIND	23	0.0207	0.0036	0.0171	0.20	11	0.48	−0.20
12.2	One year after merger compared to three years before merger	AG	MIND	23	−0.0084	−0.0315	0.0231	0.46	9	0.39	−1.02
12.3	Two years after merger compared to three years before merger	AG	MIND	23	−0.0355	−0.0477	0.0122	0.19	11	0.48	−0.20
12.4	Three years after merger compared to three years before merger	AG	MIND	23	−0.0134	0.0084	−0.0218	−0.57	10	0.43	−0.61
13	*Comparison with Predicted Performance*										
13.1	Actual rate of return compared to predicted value the year of the merger	AG	PAG	22	0.1476	0.0646	0.0830	1.08	12	0.52	0.20
13.2	Actual rate of return compared to predicted value one year after merger	AG	PAG	22	0.0612	0.0359	0.0253	0.44	10	0.43	−0.61
13.3	Actual rate of return compared to predicted value two years after merger	AG	PAG	22	0.03-1	0.0738	−0.0397	−0.73	10	0.43	−0.61
13.4	Actual rate of return compared to predicted value three years after merger	AG	PAG	22	0.0582	0.0799	−0.0217	−0.27	10	0.43	−0.61

APPENDIX B: RESULTS OF THE STATISTICAL TESTS (continued)

Formula Number	Variable	Company Type X_1	X_2	Number of Observations n_T	Mean Values $\bar{X}_1$	$\bar{X}_2$	Difference $\bar{X}_1 - \bar{X}_2$	$t =$ Value	Number of Observations with $X_1 \geq X_2$ n_p	n_p/n_T	$t =$ Value
14	*Risk-Adjusted Performance*										
14.1	Difference in Value of Sharpe's measure the year of merger and the pre-merger value	AG	MAG	24	−0.0009	−0.2643	0.2634	0.86	13	0.54	0.40
14.2	Difference in value of Sharpe's measure one year after merger and the pre-merger value	AG	MAG	24	−0.1178	−0.1152	−0.0026	−0.02	9	0.38	−1.20
14.3	Difference in value of Sharpe's measure two years after merger and the pre-merger value	AG	MAG	24	−0.0765	0.0281	−0.1046	−0.40	10	0.42	−0.80
14.4	Difference in value of Sharpe's measure three years after merger and the premerger value	AG	MAG	24	−0.0592	0.0468	−0.1060	−0.89	10	0.42	−0.80
15	*Risk-Adjusted Performance*										
15.1	Difference in value of Treynor's measure the year of merger and the pre-merger value	AG	MAG	14	0.0381	0.0167	0.0214	0.27	10	0.71	1.55

APPENDIX B: RESULTS OF THE STATISTICAL TESTS *(continued)*

Formula Number	Variable	Company Type X_1	X_2	Number of Observations n_T	Mean Values $\bar{X}_1$	$\bar{X}_2$	Difference $\bar{X}_1 - \bar{X}_2$	$t =$ Value	Number of Observations with $X_1 \gtrless X_2$ n_p	n_p/n_T	$t =$ Value
15.2	Difference in value of Treynor's measure one year after merger and the pre-merger value	AG	MAG	18	−0.0200	−0.0408	0.0208	0.85	11	0.61	0.92
15.3	Difference in value of Treynor's measure two years after merger and the premerger value	AG	MAG	20	−0.0124	−0.0051	−0.0073	−0.28	8	0.40	−0.83
15.4	Difference in value of Treynor's measure three years after merger and the premerger value	AG	MAG	18	−0.0101	−0.0130	0.0029	0.14	9	0.50	0.00

AG = acquiring company
AD = acquired company
AGAD = acquiring and acquired companies taken together
MAG = matched acquiring company
MAD = matched acquired company
MAGMAD = matched acquiring and acquired company taken together
MIND = matched industry average
PAG = predicted value for the acquiring company in case of no merger
PAGAD = predicted value for combined acquiring and acquired company in case of no merger
$\bar{X}_1$ = mean value of the tested variable for the merging companies
$\bar{X}_2$ = mean value of the tested variable for the control group companies
** = significant at a 5 percent level
* = significant at a 10 percent level

The Causes and Effects of Takeovers in the United Kingdom: An Empirical Investigation for the Late 1960s at the Microeconomic Level

Andrew Cosh, Alan Hughes, and Ajit Singh

INTRODUCTION

A number of factors distinguish in general terms the nature of merger activity in the United Kingdom from that in other countries. First, although in common with many of the latter, the United Kingdom has experienced an intense and historically unprecedented wave of mergers during the last two decades, the merger wave appears to have started a few years earlier in the United Kingdom than elsewhere. Second, inter-company stock market transactions have played a far more important role in merger activity in the United Kingdom than in other countries, with the possible exception of the United States. This is because, for institutional and historical reasons, the United Kingdom and the United States have the most developed and sophisticated stock markets. In both countries, the number of quoted companies is very much greater than elsewhere. Third, unlike the United States, but more in common with the continental countries, the government in the United Kingdom has followed a benign policy toward mergers, if not positively encouraged them. Thus, there have been few antitrust and other restrictions on the market for corporate control in the United Kingdom. This country therefore provides a unique opportunity to study the nature and efficiency of such a market—(such studies as those by Singh 1971, 1975; and Kuehn 1975).

It is also important to mention a further factor that distinguishes the empirical analysis rather than the institutional framework of merger activity in the United Kingdom. United Kingdom merger statistics, particularly for companies quoted on the stock market, are more reliable and complete than for any of the other industrial countries. The reasons for this are both the statutory requirements of the companies acts and the immense amount of work done by the government departments and the research institutions in the country in producing comparable standardized accounting information on an individual company basis. (These data are described in Singh and Whittington 1968; Singh 1971; Whittington 1971; and Hughes 1977.)

The analysis here concentrates upon the microeconomic aspects of takeovers and considers their impact on the individual company.[1] In particular this chapter analyzes those takeovers that took place in the three years 1967–1969 among those large public companies quoted on the United Kingdom stock exchanges that operated mainly in the United Kingdom and in the manufacturing and distributive industries. An attempt is made however to place these takeovers in a broader historical and institutional perspective so that conclusions based upon their analysis can be more properly assessed.

The chapter is organized as follows: In the following section we consider the definition of takeover used in this study and the institutional forms that takeover has taken in our period of analysis and in earlier takeover movements in the United Kingdom. In the second section we examine those aspects of industrial and competition policy that have formed the immediate backdrop to takeovers in this country in the 1960s. The third section discusses the dimensions of the takeover movement in the United Kingdom in the postwar period and in particular the degree of takeover activity among our population of companies in the years 1967–1969. Section four introduces the approach and terminology adopted in carrying out the specific tests on the determinants and effects of mergers described in Chapter 2. Section five presents a comparison of the premerger characteristics of acquiring, acquired, and other (control group) companies. The results of the tests on the determinants of mergers are given in section six and those of their effects in section seven. The final section draws together our conclusions and suggests possible future directions for research in this field.

DEFINITION OF TAKEOVER

The accounting data for companies quoted on the United Kingdom stock markets—which are the basic source of information for the present study—distinguish between two kinds of merger. First, there are those that involve the acquisition of 50 percent or more of the shares of one company (*A*) by another (*B*). The second category consists of those in which two companies A and B amalgamate to form a new legal entity C. This distinction is purely legal, and the choice between these two forms of merger is affected by financial and administrative considerations rather than by broader economic reasons (Moon 1968; Singh 1971). The most thorough examination of the quoted manufacturing sector in the United Kingdom available so far shows that of the 1599 companies disappearing through merger in the period 1948–1972, only 77 fell in the second category—namely, disappeared through what may be termed amalgamation (Hughes 1977). In this chapter we have excluded amalgamations from the analysis and use the term merger to describe only acquisition or takeover.[2]

There are a number of ways in which acquisition of a controlling share may be affected. The required block of shares in a company may be purchased privately from their owners by a deal between the boards of directors of the companies involved, or a "scheme of arrangement" may be agreed whereby the share capital of one company is canceled and replaced by new shares issued by the other (Davies 1976). Where shares are publicly quoted on the stock exchange they may also be purchased in a piecemeal covert fashion without any prior consultation between the directors or shareholders of the companies involved.

Although such a process is subject to legal restriction requiring disclosure of any significant holdings accumulated,[3] during most of the postwar period the restriction was easy to circumvent by having apparently independent buyers act in concert to accumulate small holdings, all ultimately held on behalf of the would-be acquirer of a controlling interest (Spiegelberg 1973). Nevertheless, such transactions are usually only a preparatory stage to the public announcement of a takeover bid,[4] which appears to be overwhelmingly the most popular method of effecting changes of control on the United Kingdom Stock Exchange. There are no precise figures on acquisition alone available, but of 898 changes of control (including amalgamations) on the stock exchange noted by the City Panel on Takeovers and Mergers in the years 1969–1972, 841 involved the use of the bid technique (Davies 1976).

This prevalence of the bid may be contrasted with its virtual absence from the scene in earlier United Kingdom merger waves at the turn of the century and in the interwar years (Hannah 1947a). In the earlier of these two waves, multifirm amalgamations associated with the flotation of new companies were the predominant form of merger (Macrosty 1907; Payne 1967; Hannah 1974b). In the interwar period, on the other hand, although multifirm combination largely disappeared, most mergers took the form of agreed transactions between boards of directors without resort to open or direct bidding to the shareholders of the companies acquired, even where the companies involved were quoted.

This reflects a number of factors differentiating the postwar and interwar years. In the first place there was a much wider dispersion of share ownership by the 1950s than had existed in the interwar period. In 1936 the average proportion of total votes held by the top twenty shareholders in large quoted companies in the United Kingdom was 30 percent; by 1951 it was 19 percent. At the same time the proportion of shares held by directors declined, as did the number of directors among the largest shareholders, while the number of directors listed as holding no more than their minimum qualifying shares grew (Sargent 1961; Hannah 1976b). Second, the amount and quality of information available to investors grew with the stock market itself and with the increasingly stringent legal requirements relating to the provision of accounting information contained in successive companies acts. These factors tended to reduce the importance of obtaining prior directorial acceptance of takeover proposals, as well as reducing directors' control over information pertaining to their companies. Direct appeals to shareholders became, therefore, more attractive propositions for would-be acquirers.

Third, the economic environment for takeover on the stock exchange in the immediate postwar years was particularly suitable for the development of the bid techniques by astute entrepreneurs (Wright 1962). This was in part due to government exhortation and fiscal discrimination in favor of retained profits (as well as other factors), which depressed share prices because of the associated poor dividend prospects. The result was a discrepancy between market values and the underlying productive value of the assets.[5] Further, many managements with freehold properties in their books from the prewar years had not adjusted their book value in line with general price rises. These companies were excellent targets for astute bidders because of the opportunity afforded once control was gained to sell such properties to institutions looking for safe investments while renting them back for continued use in the business. This situation was particularly notable in retailing where a leaseback arrangement was an attractive proposition, as it realized large surplus cash proceeds for use both for further bids and for internal investment at a time of restrictions on bank lending and control of capital issues by the Capital Issues Committee.

It should be emphasized, however, that although the aggressive takeover bids bred by these factors established the framework for further merger activity in the United Kingdom, they were concentrated in a narrow range of industry and had ceased to be the main force behind it by the late 1950s. The reduction of controls affecting the company sector and the stock market, along with the activities of the bidders themselves, reduced the opportunities for this kind of takeover. The method pioneered by the early tycoons instead became the general weapon of the professional managers who came to dominate merger activity in the United Kingdom after the 1950s in a much wider range of industries (Bull and Vice 1961; Brooks and Smith 1963; Mennel 1962).

However, it is doubtful whether aggressive, free-raiding, takeover bidding can genuinely be said to have survived as a dominant force behind the merger wave. This is especially so if we look not just at the quoted sector but at companies in general, among which it is apparent that the vast majority of mergers are either deals between directors or uncontested bids (Newbould 1970). This is not to deny that very large, very fiercely contested takeover bids have occurred, but in terms of frequency they are a small, though well publicized, proportion of total activity. Just as an "uncontested bid" or an "agreed deal" does not necessarily mean that the merger is a voluntary undertaking by both companies, similarly, the predominant role of the bid technique should not be assumed to show that the merger by agreement practices of the 1920s and 1930s have been entirely replaced by ruthless mergers forced on unwilling victims by aggressive raiders. It is interesting in this respect to note that victim and bidder may come together at the request of the former or because of long-standing mutual interests and contacts between the firms concerned (Newbould 1970).

GOVERNMENT POLICY AND MERGER ACTIVITY

The legislation governing competition policy relating to mergers is mainly contained in Part V of the Fair Trading Act of 1973, which incorporates the provisions in respect of mergers first laid down in the Monopolies and Mergers Act of 1965 (Davies 1976; H.M.G. 1969) and which was in force for the period of our analysis. Broadly speaking, the legislation empowered the secretary of state at the then Department of Prices and Consumer Protection to adopt a pragmatic, case-by-case approach in deciding whether to refer to the Monopolies and Mergers Commission, for investigation, those mergers that met certain qualifying conditions. In particular, those mergers qualified that either would create or intensify a situation in which more than one-quarter of a defined United Kingdom national or regional market was supplied by a single producer[6] or that involved the acquisition of book value of assets of more than £5m. In addition all newspaper mergers over a certain size had to be referred for investigation. Thus in effect the legislation provided for the surveillance of all significant horizontal and large mergers.

Although many mergers met the qualifying conditions of the 1965 legislation, few have been referred for investigation to assess their impact on the "public interest" that the legislation seeks to protect. From 1965 to 1974 it has been estimated that 1038 mergers in the United Kingdom met these conditions, but only 35 were referred to the Monopolies and Mergers Commission (including 6 automatic newspaper references). Of these referrals, only eight were held to be against the public interest, and a further ten were abandoned upon referral (Davies 1976; Gribbin 1974). It is difficult to interpret these figures as suggesting that mergers in the United Kingdom have been subjected to a restrictive competition policy. On the contrary, a number of commentators have concluded that the legislation and its enforcement should be considerably strengthened (Sutherland 1969, 1970; Utton 1974a; Meeks 1977).

In addition to the indirect influence of competition policy, the central authorities have also influenced the level of merger activity by including direct intervention in their industrial policy. In the period of our analysis (1967–1969), the most significant form that direct intervention took was the Industrial Reorganization Corporation (IRC), created by the Labour government in the late 1960s (Young and Lowe 1974). This body, in addition to carrying out investigations of the structure and performance of particular sectors of industry and providing loans and other financing for investment, also acted directly in the financing and promotion of mergers. During its period of active operation between January 1967 and December 1970 (prior to its abolition by the incoming Conservative administration), the IRC was directly involved in a financial, promotional, or advisory capacity in twenty-two mergers of larger quoted companies, involving the acquisition of around £1 billion of net assets by the acquiring companies concerned.[7] These mergers included the largest to occur in the postwar period as a whole, including the acquisition of English Electric and AEI by the GEC, the formation of British Leyland and Rowntree Mackintosh, the acquisition of IPC by Reed, and the formation of Ransome Hoffman Pollard in the roller bearing industry.

It seems fair to conclude that on balance, pragmatism in the practice of competition and industrial policy led to a generally permissive attitude toward merger in the United Kingdom in the postwar period as a whole, including our period of analysis. Privately inspired mergers were rarely referred for investigation, and direct intervention was responsible in part for the many massive mergers that transformed large sectors of manufacturing industry.[8]

THE DIMENSIONS OF MERGER ACTIVITY IN THE UNITED KINGDOM IN THE POSTWAR PERIOD

The United Kingdom has experienced a merger wave of major proportions in the postwar years. As Figure 8–1 illustrates, this wave reached its peak in the late 1960s and early 1970s, when annual expenditure on acquiring controlling interests in companies of all kinds accounted for up to 28 percent of all uses of funds by quoted manufacturing and distributive companies. Until the late 1950s, acquisition expenditure did not rise above 10 percent of total uses; after 1960, it rarely fell below this level. As Figure 8–1 also shows, the pattern of acquisition expenditure over time was roughly similar in both manufacturing and distribution. Within the quoted sector itself, merger activity on this scale has had a

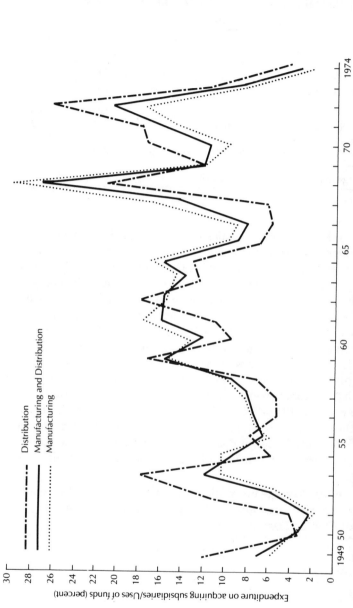

Figure 8–1. Expenditure acquisition of subsidiaries as a percentage of total uses of funds by United Kingdom quoted companies in the manufacturing and distributive industries, 1949–1974. There are changes in the coverage of the underlying population of companies in 1960, 1964, and 1969. For this and other reasons connected with changes in the definitions of expenditure used in the collection and analysis of the data, figures are only roughly comparable over time. (*Sources: Income and Finance of Public Quoted Companies 1949–60 (1962); Business Monitors M3 and M7 (various issues); Statistics on Incomes Prices, Employment and Production (various issues).*)

Table 8–1. Vital Statistics of the Quoted Manufacturing Sector, 1948–1972

		Number	Percent of Row 5
1	Companies in 1948	<u>1919</u>	<u>60.9</u>
2	Continuing companies	598	19.0
3	Births	1233	39.1
4	Deaths	1845	58.5
	(a) of which acquisition and amalgamation	1597	50.7
5	Total number of companies	3152	100.0
6	Double counting (i.e., born and died 1948–1972)	<u>524</u>	<u>16.6</u>
7	Companies in 1972	1307	41.5
8	Percent change in number of companies 1948–1972	−31.9%	

Source: Hughes (1977).

major effect on the numbers of companies remaining in independent existence. An analysis for manufacturing alone shows that merger was the major form of death in the period 1948–1972 and was responsible for the death rate outstripping the birth rate of quoted companies. The net result was the decline of over 30 percent in independent companies that is shown in row 8 of Table 8–1.[9] Row 4a shows that over one-half of all companies existing were subject to merger in this period. Moreover, as the intensity of merger activity increased in the later years of the period, so did the extent to which the large firms were acquired (Singh 1975; Hughes 1976).

Table 8–2 provides some recent estimates of the annual average probability of "dying" through merger for five size quintiles and three subperiods in the years 1948–1972 that confirm this point. In the earlier subperiods the table shows that the largest 20 percent of companies experienced substantially lower death rates by merger than the other 80 percent. In the period 1966–1972, although the largest companies were

Table 8–2. Annual Average Probability of a Company "Dying" Through Merger for Each of Five Size Quintiles in the Years 1949–1972 in the Manufacturing Quoted Company Sector[a]

	Probability of Merger Death		
Size Category	1949–1958	1959–1965	1966–1972
Largest	0.6	2.7	4.1
2	1.5	3.5	5.4
3	1.3	3.8	5.7
4	1.6	4.3	4.5
Smallest	1.7	3.4	4.8
All	1.3	3.6	4.9

Source: Hughes (1977).
[a] It should be noted that this table includes both acquisition and amalgamation deaths.

still somewhat more secure than the rest (with the firms in the top quintile having a 20 percent lower chance of being acquired), their position had deteriorated noticeably.[10] Since 1959, the death rate from merger alone for all groups outstripped previous estimates of the death rate from all causes taken together on the United Kingdom Stock Exchange since the 1880s.[11]

Clearly the causes and economic consequences of activity of this scope and magnitude are of major importance. In this study we focus our attention on the peak merger years of 1967–1969 (see Figure 8–1) and upon those mergers, in those years, that involved the disappearance of larger quoted companies in the manufacturing and distributive industries. Although quoted company mergers are a small proportion of the total number of mergers occurring, they dominate in terms of size and account for the bulk of acquisition expenditure (Hughes 1976).

The number and industrial distribution of the mergers studied here are shown in Table 8–3. There are two points to note about these mergers. First, the companies analyzed constitute the total population takeover deaths in those industries shown in the table where the companies involved were quoted and had net assets of over £500,000, or gross income of over £50,000 in 1964. In all there were 290 takeover deaths involving 233 acquirers. Second, the percentage of takeovers in which both companies involved were classified within the same two-digit industry group, which we term horizontal mergers, was 54 percent within manufacturing industries but below 50 percent in the distributive industries. This implies that in the peak merger years examined in this study horizontal merger was somewhat less predominant than in the merger wave as a whole. Even quite disaggregated studies for the postwar years have suggested that horizontal mergers accounted for 70 percent of the total number of takeovers occurring (Gribbin 1974; Hughes 1976; Newbould 1970). It is apparent, however, that the importance of horizontal takeover has declined as the merger wave has proceeded, and our sample of years represents a culmination of a trend that has seen the proportion of horizontal acquisitions within the United Kingdom quoted manufacturing and distributive sector fall from 68 percent in the period 1950–1956 to 63 percent in the period 1957–1963 to 48 percent in the period 1964–1970 (authors' own estimates based on the DI company accounts data bank).

In view of the almost equal numerical importance of horizontal and other mergers, the following analysis examines the sample as a whole and as two separate categories, horizontal and other.

MICROECONOMIC ANALYSIS OF UNITED KINGDOM TAKEOVERS, 1967–1969

Before presenting the results of the specific tests of the determinants and effects of mergers described in Chapter 2, it will be useful to

Table 8–3. The Number of Companies Acquired, 1967–1969, and Their Industrial Classification by Acquiring and Acquired Company

Industry of Acquired Company	Industry of Acquiring Company																					Acquired Companies	
	21	23	26	31	33	36	37	38	39	41	43	44	46	47	48	49	50	70	81	82	88	Total	of which horizontal
21 Food	6	1	3																	1	1	12	6
23 Drink		10	1																1			12	10
26 Chemicals	1	1	7										1			1	1					12	7
31 Metal manufacturing			4	2	1				1					1								9	2
33 Nonelectrical engineering			3	5	21	3		1	4							2	3	1	2	1	1	47	21
36 Electrical engineering				3	3	14		1										1		1	1	20	14
37 Marine engineering							1															1	1
38 Vehicles					1				1													2	0
39 Other metal				1	2	1		1	2	1			1	1				1				11	2
41 Textiles				1	1	1		1	1	24			1							1		30	24
43 Leather, etc.										1	1											2	1
44 Clothing and footwear										9								1		1		11	0
46 Bricks, etc.													13	1				1				15	13
47 Timber, etc.					1					1			1	2	1		1			2		9	2
48 Paper, etc.										1			1		8	2						10	8
49 Other manufacturing					1	3				1					2	2	4				1	7 (210)ᵇ	2 (113)
50 Construction			1			3								1			4	1		3		13	4
70 Transport, etc.			1					1								1			1	3		4	0
81 Wholesale		1	1	1						2			3				1	2	9	6	3	30	9
82 Retail	2	1	1		2												3		2	6	3	17	6
88 Other services			1															3	3	3	5	16 (80)	5 (24)
Total acquired companies by industry of acquiring company	9	14	23	10	31	27	3	3	10	47	3	0	25	3	10	6	12	10	16	15	13	290	137
Total acquiringᵃ companies	9	10	18	8	30	21	3	3	10	26	3	0	20	3	8	6	11	6	14	13	11	233	

ᵃ Some companies acquired more than one company; therefore they are fewer in number than the acquired companies.
ᵇ Figures in parentheses are column totals up to that point.

compare the characteristics of the acquired, acquiring, and other (control group) firms in the population. Such a comparison, apart from being necessary for a fuller understanding of the subsequent test results, is as explained in Chapter 2 of interest in its own right. It bears directly on a range of economic issues, which are important from the point of view of both economic theory and policy (for a full discussion of these issues, see Singh, 1971, 1975). For example, a major question of current theoretical interest is the nature of the selection mechanism generated by the normal workings of real world markets and its implications for the behavior of economic agents (Hahn 1973, Johnson 1968). (For an account of the various theories concerning the nature of the selection mechanism which is presumed to exist, see Singh 1971; Winter 1971.)

In view of the institutional background to the takeover movement in the United Kingdom described earlier, an examination of these questions is particularly pertinent for this country. For not only has the magnitude of the takeover phenomenon been very significant in the period considered in this study, but, as noted, mergers in the United Kingdom have been less subject to government regulations and restrictions than in countries such as the United States. Furthermore, as we are confining ourselves to mergers of companies quoted on the stock market, and as London possesses one of the most well organized and sophisticated of such markets, it should be possible to observe the kind of selection process produced by the relatively free play of forces in effectively functioning markets.

Variables and Time Periods Used

The comparison of the average characteristics of the acquired, acquiring, and other firms is made in terms of the following variables—size, profitability, profits variability, growth, leverage, price-earnings ratio, and stockholder return.[12] Most of these variables are approximated by a number of different indicators based on the accounting data of individual firms.

Size has been measured in terms of the following indicators: (1) the balance sheet or book value of the net assets of the firm; (2) its total assets; and (3) sales. Net assets are defined as total fixed assets plus current assets net of current liabilities; assets are valued, as is the usual practice in balance sheets, at historic cost net of depreciation. Total assets include both current and fixed assets and are net of depreciation. In relation to sales, it is important to remember that disclosure of these data became obligatory only with the 1967 Companies Act. As a consequence there are many firms, particularly smaller ones, for which such data are not available for the years before 1967.

The profitability performance of companies is indicated by the following variables: (1) profit margin, which is represented by gross trading profits as a percentage of sales; (2) pretax profitability on net assets, where, in line with the definition of net assets given above, pretax profits include investment and other income of the firm and are net of depreciation and any charge for current liabilities (e.g., bank interest), but are taken before the deduction of taxation and long-term interest payments; and (3) posttax profitability on equity assets, where posttax profits comprise retained earnings plus dividends after tax and equity assets represent the book value of assets owned by ordinary shareholders of the firm.

Profits variability is measured by the coefficient of variation of a firm's profits over the last five accounting years. All three indicators of profits —gross trading profits, pretax profits, and posttax profits—are used for this purpose. Growth is measured by two separate indicators—growth of net assets (i.e., the long-term financial capital employed in the firm) and growth of physical assets. Again, two different variables are used to measure leverage: first, a stock measure, which expresses the book value of long-term liabilities plus preference capital as a percentage of the book value of total capital and reserves plus long-term liabilities; and second, a flow measure, which shows the percentage of a firm's posttax income that is allocated to fixed interest and dividend payments. The price-earnings ratio is measured by the ratio of the company's share price to its posttax earnings per share.[13]

The stockholder return for a company is measured by the compound percentage return per annum on holding that company's ordinary shares. The return includes the capital gain and dividend income, including income derived from reinvesting dividend income at a market rate of return.[14] Since considerable work was involved in the collection of data for calculation of the stockholder return, the tests involving this measure were confined to a sample of the group of mergers studied in the other tests.

As noted above, the study examines mergers that occurred in the three years 1967–1969. The analysis for each of these years was carried out separately, but to save space this chapter reports results for all three years together. Most of the variables are measured over the five-year period prior to merger and over three and five years after merger. The price-earnings ratio is measured over the three years prior to merger; however, the size variable is always measured at the last accounting date before takeover.

Definition of the Groups of Firms

The findings reported in the following sections concern the univariate comparisons of the mean values of the above variables for various groups of firms:

1. AG—the group of quoted firms that acquired other quoted firms in the population in the years 1967–1969;[15]
2. AD—the group of companies that were acquired;

3. C—the control group companies, which neither were acquired nor carried out any significant acquisition over the period from five years before the year of merger considered to five years after.

4. MAG—the sample of companies, drawn from the control group, that matched the acquiring companies by industry and, as far as possible, by size of each acquiring company.[16]

5. MAD—the sample of companies, drawn from the control group, that matched the acquired companies by industry and by size for each acquired company.

Further, in every case the analysis was carried out separately for (1) all mergers (A), (2) horizontal mergers (H), and (3) nonhorizontal mergers (NH).[17] With nearly 300 quoted firms in manufacturing and distribution being acquired during the period 1967–1969, there were enough observations for each of the two types of mergers. However, this also unfortunately means a vast array of results including a separate analysis for each industry,[18] of which only a small selection is presented in the tables in the following sections.

COMPARISON OF PREMERGER CHARACTERISTICS OF ACQUIRING, ACQUIRED, AND CONTROL GROUP COMPANIES

The Acquiring and Acquired Companies

Table 8–4 reports results comparing the characteristics of the group of acquiring firms with those of the group of firms they acquired, on a univariate basis. For each main variable results are presented only for a single indicator in each case, since those for the other indicators were broadly similar. However, the table gives figures for each of the two merger types—horizontal (H) and nonhorizontal (NH)—and for all mergers (A). The results for individual industries are not shown, since that would have required a separate table of this kind for each of the fourteen industries (where there were sufficient observations for individual industry analysis; those results are available on request from the authors). Instead we report here only figures for all industries together, as well as summary results pertaining to individual industries (based on the binomial probability test).[19]

The nature of the information contained in the table is best explained by considering the figures in a particular row (e.g., row 4). These figures show that for all mergers, the average pretax profitability on net assets of the group of all quoted acquiring firms (i.e., firms that undertook acquisitions

Table 8–4. Comparison of Premerger Characteristics of Acquiring and Acquired Companies

Variable	Merger Type	Group 1	Number of Companies N_1	Mean Value $\bar{X}_1$	Group 2	Number of Companies N_2	Mean Value $\bar{X}_2$
						All Industries Results	
Size							
In net assets	A	AG	290	10.05	AD	290	7.91
	H	AG	137	9.85	AD	137	8.04
	NH	AG	153	10.22	AD	153	7.79
Profitability							
Pretax return on	A	AG	226	15.39	AD	226	13.90
net assets	H	AG	113	14.43	AD	113	13.32
	NH	AG	113	16.34	AD	113	14.48
Profits Variability							
Coefficient of varia-	A	AG	240	0.32	AD	240	0.50
tion of net income	H	AG	117	0.42	AD	117	0.37
	NH	AG	123	0.23	AD	123	0.63
Growth							
Growth of net assets	A	AG	241	11.99	AD	241	6.08
	H	AG	117	10.17	AD	117	6.55
	NH	AG	124	13.72	AD	124	5.63
Leverage							
Stock measure	A	AG	240	18.53	AD	240	15.73
	H	AG	117	18.04	AD	117	16.47
	NH	AG	123	18.99	AD	123	15.04

Notes: Period of comparison is five years prior to merger except for size, which is measured in the year prior to merger.

AG—acquiring companies.
AD—acquired companies.
C—control group companies.
MAG—control group companies matched with acquiring companies.
MAD—control group companies matched with acquired companies.

during the period 1967–1969 was 15.4 percent; the corresponding average profitability of the firms they acquired was 13.9 percent. The observed difference of 1.5 percent was statisticlly significant at the 5 percent level (as indicated by the t-value of 2.28). This result, however, pertains to all industries together and, for reasons explained earlier, may therefore be subject to aggregation bias.

This fear is to a certain extent borne out by the figures given in the next three columns. They show that in only nine of the fourteen individual industries was the average profitability of acquiring firms greater than that of the firms they acquired (i.e., in five industries, the acquired firms

Difference in Mean Values $\bar{X}_1 - \bar{X}_2$	Statistical Significance t-Value	Summary of Individual Industry Results		
		Number of Industries with Positive $\bar{X}_1 - \bar{X}_2$	Total Number of Industries	Proportion Positive and its Significance
2.14**	17.38	14	14	1.00**
1.81**	10.07	14	14	1.00**
2.43**	14.53	14	14	1.00**
1.49*	2.28	9	14	0.64
1.11	1.37	9	14	0.64
1.87	1.84	9	14	0.64
−0.18	−1.63	5	14	0.36
0.06	0.45	5	14	0.36
−0.40*	−2.26	3	14	0.21*
5.91**	5.90	14	14	1.00**
3.61**	2.91	11	14	0.79*
8.08**	5.23	14	14	1.00**
2.79*	2.43	11	14	0.79*
1.57	0.99	10	14	0.71
3.95*	2.40	11	14	0.79*

A—all mergers.
H—horizontal mergers.
NH—nonhorizontal mergers.
** Indicates (two-tail) significance at the 10 percent level or better.
 * Indicates (two-tail significance at the 5 percent level (5.732 percent level in the case of the binomial probability test) or better.
 In indicates the natural logarithm.

were more profitable than the acquiring). If there was no difference between the average profitability of the two groups of firms, one would expect that in about half the industries, the acquiring firms would be more profitable than the acquired, and in the other half, the acquired would be relatively more profitable. The last column shows that this null hypothesis is not rejected by the data at the 5 percent level of significance.

Therefore, to the extent that the concept of industry is economically and statistically meaningful, as there is every reason to believe it is (despite the coarseness of the two-digit industrial categories used in this study), one cannot conclude that the observed differences in the average profitability of the two groups of firms are statistically significant at the 5 percent level, notwithstanding the result for all industries together. Considered in economic terms, the observed differences are of very little quantitative significance in view of the very large degree of variability in the profitability of firms in each group: the typical standard deviation of profitability in an industry is of the order of 12 percent.

Continuing with the discussion of the profitability variable, the next two rows show that the differences in the average profitability of the two groups of firms are relatively larger in the case of nonhorizontal mergers than in the case of horizontal mergers (the figure for all mergers in row 4 shows the combined result for the two categories). However, these differences are not large enough to alter the above conclusion with respect to the economic and statistical significance of profitability as a discriminator between the two groups of firms (even if only nonhorizontal mergers are considered).

The interpretation of the other results in Table 8–4 is quite straightforward. For the size variable, for each of the two merger types and for both merger types together, the mean differences between the groups are both economically and statistically significant (the latter at the 1 percent level). Further, with respect to statistical significance, both the binomial probability test and the t-test for aggregate data for all firms yield a similar result. The acquiring companies are on average several times larger than the companies that they acquire. The results for the growth variable are similar to those for size: the acquiring companies grow on average nearly twice as fast as the companies they acquire, and the observed differences are statistically highly significant in both tests. It is worth noting that acquirers involved in nonhorizontal merger activity are, on average, faster growing (13.7 percent as against 10.2 percent) than other acquirers.

The stock measure of the leverage variable also yields unambiguous results for all mergers and for nonhorizontal mergers. Taken together these results suggest that acquiring companies are appreciably more highly levered, on average, than acquired companies.

The results of the profits variability test are somewhat more complex. They show that in the case of horizontal mergers, there is little difference in the volatility of the profits of the average acquiring company, compared with the average acquired company. However in the case of nonhorizontal mergers, the acquiring firms have on average a significantly more stable profits record (at the 5 percent level) than the firms they acquire.

To sum up, we find that acquiring companies are very much larger and have higher leverage ratios and a much faster growth rate, on average, than the acquired companies. There is, however, little difference in the average profitability of the two groups of firms. Finally, there is some evidence that for the category of nonhorizontal mergers, the firms acquired have a more volatile profits record.[20] These results are somewhat different from those obtained by Singh (1971) for acquisitions of United Kingdom quoted companies during the period 1955–1960. For this earlier period also, the acquiring companies were on the whole much bigger and had a much faster growth rate than the acquired; however, they were then appreciably more profitable on average than the companies they acquired.

Comparison of Acquiring and Control Group Companies

The nature of the differences between the premerger characteristics of the acquiring companies and the control group companies is revealed by the figures in Table 8–5. In Table 8–5 (and in Table 8–6, which compares the acquired with the control group companies), we do not give separate figures for each merger type, as this yielded similar conclusions; instead, we show additionally the results obtained for different measures of each variable. In Table 8–5 the acquiring companies are usually compared with the control group of all nonacquiring and nonacquired quoted companies in the population (indicated by letter C). However, there is evidence that firm size is correlated in an important way with some of the indicators,[21] which significantly affects the conclusions with respect to these variables. We have therefore (in both tables) also reported figures obtained by comparing the acquiring (acquired) firms with the alternative control group of matched nonacquiring-nonacquired firms (indicated as MAG or MAD). Since matching is done by size of firm within the same industry year, such a comparison should totally eliminate the influence of size (if the matching were perfect; but as noted earlier, it is not).

The most important conclusions which emerge from Table 8–5 are that the acquiring firms are much larger than the control group firms and have higher leverage ratios and a much faster growth rate. The differences between the groups are both statistically significant and quantitatively important and are larger when nonhorizontal acquirers are considered separately.

However, the results with respect to differences in profitability are apparently ambiguous. For example, we find that on each of the two statistical tests, there are highly significant differences between the two groups with respect to pretax profitability when acquiring companies are compared with the control group of all nonacquiring firms. Such differences, however, appear to arise from the fact that size and pretax profitability are negatively related, so that when the acquiring companies are compared with the control group of matched nonacquiring firms we find little difference in the average profitability of the two groups. Finally, as far as profits variability is concerned, there seems to be little difference between the groups, although the results are somewhat mixed.

Table 8–5. Comparison of Premerger Characteristics of Acquiring and Nonacquiring Companies

						All Industries Results	
Variable	Merger Type	Group 1	Number of Companies N_1	Mean Value $\bar{X}_1$	Group 2	Number of Companies N_2	Mean Value $\bar{X}_2$
Size							
In sales (t)	A	AG	208	10.47	C	858	8.61
In total assets	A	AG	230	10.13	C	1186	8.25
In net assets	A	AG	236	9.70	C	1186	7.85
Profitability							
Trading profits–sales (t)	A	AG	208	10.96	C	858	11.10
Net income–net assets	A	AG	217	15.16	C	1186	17.42
Posttax income–equity assets	A	AG	217	8.79	C	1186	9.40
Net income–net	A	AG	256	15.55	MAG	256	15.68
assets	H	AG	122	14.80	MAG	122	15.48
	NH	AG	134	16.23	MAG	134	15.87
Profits variability							
Trading profits	A	AG	217	0.42	C	1186	0.23
Net income	A	AG	217	0.34	C	1186	0.55
Net income	A	AG	268	0.31	MAG	268	0.22
	H	AG	126	0.41	MAG	126	0.25
	NH	AG	142	0.23	MAG	142	0.19
Growth							
Physical assets	A	AG	217	12.85	C	1186	9.13
Net assets	A	AG	217	12.50	C	1186	7.02
Net assets	A	AG	269	12.66	MAG	269	5.84
	H	AG	126	10.74	MAG	126	5.35
	NH	AG	143	14.34	MAG	143	6.27
Leverage							
Stock measure	A	AG	217	17.83	C	1186	12.73
Flow measure	A	AG	214	10.64	C	1166	8.50
Stock measure	A	AG	269	18.97	MAG	269	12.20
	H	AG	126	18.26	MAG	126	11.90
	NH	AG	143	19.60	MAG	143	12.47

Notes: See Table 8–4.

Comparison of Acquired and Control Group Companies

Table 8–6 shows that acquired companies on average are significantly larger (at the 5 percent level) than the control group firms when size is measured in terms of log sales. Moreover, this result holds not only for the

		Summary of Individual Industry Results		
Difference in Mean Values $\bar{X}_1 - \bar{X}_2$	Statistical Significance t-Value	Number of Industries with Positive $\bar{X}_1 - \bar{X}_2$	Total Number of Industries	Proportion Positive and its Significance
1.86**	17.38	14	14	1.00**
1.86**	17.94	14	14	1.00**
1.85**	16.81	14	14	1.00**
−0.14	−0.29	4	14	0.29
−2.27**	−4.56	2	14	0.14*
−0.62*	−2.23	5	14	0.36
−0.13	−0.24	8	14	0.57
−0.68	−0.85	9	14	0.64
0.36	0.50	9	14	0.64
0.19	1.31	8	14	0.57
−0.21	−1.30	6	14	0.43
0.09	1.70	10	14	0.71
0.16	1.38	8	14	0.57
0.04	1.87	9	14	0.64
3.72**	4.08	11	14	0.79*
5.48**	5.77	11	14	0.79*
6.82**	7.61	12	14	0.86*
5.39**	5.00	13	14	0.93**
8.07**	5.86	11	14	0.79*
5.10**	5.47	12	14	0.86*
2.14*	1.66	11	14	0.79*
6.77**	6.67	11	14	0.79*
6.36**	4.35	11	14	0.79*
7.12**	5.06	10	14	0.71

aggregate of all firms, but also for the binominal probability test based on data for individual industries. However, in view of the fact that tests on alternative measures of size (log net assets and log total assets) do not produce statistically significant results and that the information on sales was not available for a considerable proportion of companies (44 percent of taken over and 28 percent of control group firms), this conclusion must be regarded as rather tentative at this stage of investigation. More impor-

Table 8–6. Comparison of Premerger Characteristics of Acquired and Nonacquired Companies

						All Industries Results	
Variable	Merger Type	Group 1	Number of Companies N_1	Mean Value $\bar{X}_1$	Group 2	Number of Companies N_2	Mean Value $\bar{X}_2$
Size							
In sales (t)	A	AD	160	8.85	C	856	8.61
In total assets	A	AD	290	8.33	C	1186	8.25
In net assets	A	AD	290	7.92	C	1186	7.85
Profitability							
Trading profits–							
sales (t)	A	AD	160	9.31	C	856	11.10
Net income–net							
assets	A	AD	262	13.51	C	1186	17.42
Posttax income–							
equity assets	A	AD	262	7.82	C	1186	9.40
Net income–net	A	AD	238	13.90	MAD	238	17.80
assets	H	AD	121	13.51	MAD	121	16.98
	NH	AD	117	14.30	MAD	117	18.65
Profits Variability							
Trading profits	A	AD	262	0.51	C	1186	0.23
Net income	A	AD	262	0.49	C	1186	0.55
Net income	A	AD	257	0.50	MAD	257	0.31
	H	AD	127	0.38	MAD	127	0.38
	NH	AD	130	0.61	MAD	130	0.25
Growth							
Physical assets	A	AD	262	8.15	C	1186	9.13
Net assets	A	AD	262	5.96	C	1186	7.02
Net assets	A	AD	258	5.98	MAD	258	6.70
	H	AD	127	6.42	MAD	127	6.50
	NH	AD	131	5.55	MAD	131	6.89
Leverage							
Stock measure	A	AD	262	15.84	C	1186	12.73
Flow measure	A	AD	251	10.51	C	1166	8.50
Stock measure	A	AD	257	15.87	MAD	257	11.05
	H	AD	127	16.65	MAD	127	12.55
	NH	AD	130	15.10	MAD	130	9.61

Notes: See Table 8–4.

tantly, it should be noted that the control group does not simply consist of nonacquired firms; it also excludes all acquiring firms, which as Tables 8–4 and 8–5 have shown tend to be relatively big.

On the other hand, the figures point to an unambiguous conclusion with respect to profitability. Whichever measure of profitability is used, and on either of the two tests, it appears that the acquired firms are on average significantly less profitable (at the 1 percent level) than the control group

		Summary of Individual Industry Results		
Difference in Mean Values $\bar{X}_1 - \bar{X}_2$	Statistical Significance t-Value	Number of Industries with Positive $\bar{X}_1 - \bar{X}_2$	Total Number of Industries	Proportion Positive and its Significance
0.24*	2.47	11	14	0.79*
0.08	1.12	9	14	0.64
0.06	0.85	8	14	0.57
−1.80**	−3.35	2	14	0.14*
−3.91**	−8.55	2	14	0.14*
−1.58**	−5.31	2	14	0.14*
−3.90**	−5.74	2	14	0.14*
−3.47**	−4.29	3	14	0.21*
−4.35**	−3.96	2	14	0.14*
0.23	1.42	8	14	0.57
−0.06	−0.35	8	14	0.57
0.18	1.95	10	14	0.71
0.00	0.04	8	14	0.57
0.36*	2.12	10	14	0.71
−0.98	−1.77	6	14	0.43
−1.06	−1.90	5	14	0.36
−0.72	−1.11	4	14	0.29
−0.07	−0.08	4	14	0.29
−1.34	1.46	4	14	0.29
3.11**	3.62	12	14	0.85*
2.02	1.66	11	14	0.79*
4.80**	4.41	11	14	0.79*
4.10*	2.49	10	14	0.71
5.49*	3.86	10	14	0.71

firms. However, it is important to emphasize, in view of the wide variability in profitability of firms in a typical industry, that there is likely to be a large degree of overlap in the profitability figures for the two groups of firms. Thus, although profitability may be a statistically significant discriminator between the living and the dead, it may not be a very good one (this point is discussed more fully in Singh 1971).

Table 8–6 also shows that acquired firms are on average more volatile in their profits records than control group firms. Further, the data reveal the acquired firms to be somewhat slower growers than control group firms. The average differences between the groups in relation to these two characteristics are, however, quite small and in most cases statistically insignificant. On the other hand, the results for leverage suggest that acquired firms are significantly more highly geared than control group firms.

Summary of Comparative Characteristics of Acquiring, Acquired, and Control Group Companies

The results of the univariate comparisons of the average characteristics of the acquired, acquiring, and control group companies in the period immediately prior to merger may be summarized as follows:

Size	AG > AD ≥ Others
Profitability	Others > AD; Others ≥ AG; AG ≥ AD
Profits Variability	AD > Others; AD ≥ AG
Growth	AG > AD; AG > Others ≥ AD
Leverage	AG > AD > Others

In the above summary, > indicates a statistically significant and quantitatively relatively important difference between the group; similarly, ≥ connotes either a statistically insignificant (at the 5 percent level) or a quantitatively small difference.

With respect to the economic issues of the stock market selection process and its implications for firm motivation, evidence of the above results can only be regarded as a preliminary step. This is mainly because we have up to now attempted only a limited statistical analysis of the characteristics of the various groups of firms. Specifically, the analysis has been done only on a

Table 8–7. Determinants: Size Comparisons

						All Industries Results	
Variable	*Merger Type*	*Group 1*	*Number of Companies N_1*	*Mean Value $\bar{X}_1$*	*Group 2*	*Number of Companies N_2*	*Mean Value $\bar{X}_2$*
In sales	H	AGAD	76	9.69	C	858	8.61
In total assets	H	AGAD	137	9.08	C	1186	8.25
In net assets	H	AGAD	137	8.95	C	1186	7.85

Notes: Period of comparison—year prior to merger. For key to terminology adopted, see notes to Table 8–4.

univariate basis. Because of the intercorrelation between variables, it is not possible to obtain a proper profile of firms selected by the market for survival (and hence of the nature of the selection mechanism) without a multivariate analysis. Further, even the univariate investigations that have been carried out so far have been of a rather limited variety. The analysis presented here has been confined to examining the differences between the average characteristics of various groups of firms. A more refined analysis of the degrees of overlap between the groups with respect to these characteristics is also required. These investigations, which are currently being carried out, are the subject of a further paper.

TEST RESULTS ON THE DETERMINANTS
OF MERGERS

Having considered the nature of the differences between the characteristics of the acquired, acquiring, and nonmerging firms, we now proceed to present results on the specific tests on the determinants of mergers given in Chapter 2. The results for each test are presented successively in Tables 8–7 through 8–9.

Table 8–7 gives results for the size test. It shows quite unambiguously that the merging firms are on average much larger than the nonmerging ones. This conclusion holds for all industries together, as well as in thirteen of the fourteen individual industries, and is statistically highly significant on both the statistical tests used.

However, it must be stressed that this does not imply that mergers do not take place for reasons of economies of scale. All that it suggests is that the latter is unlikely to be the overriding or the single dominant motive for mergers, unless all firms in most industries are in any case below their efficient size or unless the smaller suboptimal firms that wish to merge are

		Summary of Individual Industry Results		
Difference in Mean Values $\bar{X}_1 - \bar{X}_2$	Statistical Significance t-Value	Number of Industries with Positive $\bar{X}_1 - \bar{X}_2$	Total Number of Industries	Proportion Positive and its Significance
1.08**	8.53	13	14	0.93**
0.83**	8.24	13	14	0.93**
1.10**	0.27	13	14	0.93**

Table 8–8. Determinants: High-Low Ratio of Coefficients of Variation of Profits Prior to Merger

						All Industries Results	
Variable	Merger Type	Group 1	Number of Com- panies N_1	Mean Value $\bar{X}_1$	Group 2	Number of Com- panies N_2	Mean Value $\bar{X}_2$
Trading profits	A	AGAD	240	4.20	MAGMAD	240	2.59
	H	AGAD	116	5.30	MAGMAD	116	2.81
	NH	AGAD	124	3.17	MAGMAD	124	2.37
Net income	A	AGAD	240	3.59	MAGMAD	240	3.08
	H	AGAD	116	2.64	MAGMAD	116	3.48
	NH	AGAD	124	4.49	MAGMAD	124	2.71
Posttax income	A	AGAD	240	6.39	MAGMAD	240	3.20
	H	AGAD	116	9.22	MAGMAD	116	3.87
	NH	AGAD	124	3.74	MAGMAD	124	2.58

Notes: Period of comparison—five years prior to merger. For key to terminology adopted, see notes to Table 8–4.

prevented from doing so for a variety of institutional reasons. There is, however, little direct evidence to support either of these suppositions.

Next, Table 8–8 gives results that bear on the hypothesis concerning risk spreading as a motive for mergers. Here we recall that although acquiring firms experience the same kind of profits variability as matched control group firms, they are somewhat more stable performers than acquired firms. The information given in Table 8–8 shows that there is a tendency for the average value of the high/low ratio of the coefficients of variation of profits for merging firms to be greater than the ratio for nonmerging firms

Table 8–9. Determinants: Absolute Differences in Premerger Leverage Ratios

						All Industries Results	
Variable	Merger Type	Group 1	Number of Com- panies N_1	Mean Value $\bar{X}_1$	Group 2	Number of Com- panies N_2	Mean Value $\bar{X}_2$
Leverage (net flow	A	AGAD	253	17.64	MAGMAD	253	10.57
measure)	H	AGAD	117	18.09	MAGMAD	117	9.76
	NH	AGAD	136	17.26	MAGMAD	136	11.27

Notes: Period of comparison—year prior to merger. For key to terminology, see notes to Table 8–4.

		Summary of Individual Industry Results		
Difference in Mean Values $\bar{X}_1 - \bar{X}_2$	Statistical Significance t-Value	Number of Industries with Positive $\bar{X}_1 - \bar{X}_2$	Total Number of Industries	Proportion Positive and its Significance
1.62	1.30	9	14	0.64
2.49	1.02	7	14	0.50
0.80	1.18	11	14	0.79*
0.51	0.79	10	14	0.71
−0.84	−1.54	7	14	0.50
1.78	1.43	11	14	0.79*
3.18	1.00	11	14	0.79*
5.35	0.83	6	14	0.43
1.16	0.79	11	14	0.79*

when considering nonhorizontal mergers. For each measure of profits used in calculating the ratio, the binomial probability test is significant at the 5 percent level (the average value of the ratio is greater for the nonhorizontal merging firms in eleven of the fourteen industries).

Thus, there is some evidence to indicate that risk spreading may be a motive for mergers. However, this conclusion, even in its present form, is subject to some serious qualifications. First, the test described above only shows greater relative profits variability between merging firms than between their matched control group firms and not that acquiring firms are

		Summary of Individual Industry Results		
Difference in Mean Values $\bar{X}_1 - \bar{X}_2$	Statistical Significance t-Value	Number of Industries with Positive $\bar{X}_1 - \bar{X}_2$	Total Number of Industries	Proportion Positive and its Significance
7.07**	2.75	10	14	0.71
8.33*	2.42	11	14	0.79*
5.99	1.60	8	14	0.57

Table 8–10. Determinants: Comparison of Variance of Premerger Leverage Ratios of Merging Firms with That of Control Group

Merger Type	Group 1	Number of Companies	Sample Variance	Group 2	Number of Companies	Sample Variance	Calcu-lated F-ratio	Critical F-value at 5% Level
A	AG	253	119.9	MAG	253	141.9	1.18	1.20
H	AG	117	129.1	MAG	117	121.1	1.07	1.36
NH	AG	136	112.8	MAG	136	160.6	1.42*	1.34
A	AD	253	1658.0	MAD	253	148.0	11.20*	1.20
H	AD	117	1439.4	MAD	117	129.9	11.08*	1.36
NH	AD	136	1853.6	MAD	136	163.7	11.32*	1.34

Notes: Net flow measure of the leverage ratio is used here.
Period of comparison—year prior to merger.
For key to terminology adopted, see notes to Table 8–4.

more volatile than the nonacquiring firms. Second, the evidence given earlier suggests, if anything, that acquirers are seeking out more volatile victims, so that if risk spreading were a motive, it would be for the acquired rather than the acquiring firms. Third, we should note that at a more theoretical level, risk spreading in any case is not necessarily best achieved by a more stable firm merging with a more variable one; the best strategy would also depend on the degree of correlation between the profits streams of the acquirer and its potential victims.

Nevertheless, the results of Table 8–8 could be regarded as being consistent with a risk-spreading hypothesis since important differences in profits variability ratios between pairs of merging and nonmerging firms are found only in the case of nonhorizontal mergers, where it might reasonably be argued that the risk-spreading gains from uncorrelated profit streams were more likely to occur.[22]

With respect to the leverage ratio there is also some evidence to suggest that firms may be seeking merger partners with dissimilar leverage ratios to their own. Thus as Table 8–9 shows, the average absolute difference in the leverage ratios of merging firms is significantly greater (at the 5 percent level) than for the corresponding nonmerging firms. The differences are also economically important, being on average over 7 percent when a comparison is made between all merging firms and the control group. Table 8–10 shows that as a group, acquired companies tend to have relatively extreme values of the leverage ratio compared to either acquiring companies or the nonacquired companies, which is also consistent with the view that acquirers seek out either very highly or very lowly levered companies. Moreover, as Table 8–11 shows, the potential impact upon

Table 8–11. Determinants: Contribution of Victim to Merged Company's Leverage Ratio

	All Mergers			Horizontal			Other		
	N	$\bar{x}_t$	t-ratio	N	$\bar{x}_t$	t-ratio	N	$\bar{x}_t$	t-ratio
Food	8	0.72*	6.08	6	0.82*	9.00	2	0.40	1.60
Drink	14	1.28*	5.17	10	0.94*	3.73	4	2.13*	6.18
Chemicals	22	3.16*	2.84	7	5.43*	1.94	15	2.10*	2.20
Metal manufacture	10	1.88*	2.86	2	2.85	1.18	8	1.64*	2.46
Nonelectrical engineering	28	2.91*	3.61	18	2.35*	3.15	10	3.93*	2.14
Electrical engineering	23	1.31*	3.41	12	2.01*	3.05	11	0.54*	2.60
Metal goods	9	1.53*	2.45	2	2.35	1.24	7	1.29*	1.91
Textiles	42	1.82*	2.09	21	2.66	1.57	21	0.97*	2.36
Building materials	24	2.75*	2.39	13	4.37*	2.15	11	0.83*	2.90
Paper, printing	9	4.43	1.77	7	5.60	1.80	2	0.32	1.11
Construction	10	1.82	1.74	4	0.73	1.99	6	2.55	1.49
Wholesale distribution	15	3.04*	4.66	8	3.15*	3.03	7	2.91*	3.57
Retail distribution	13	1.34	1.76	6	0.69	1.91	7	1.90	1.36
Other services	13	1.83*	3.76	5	2.90*	3.54	8	1.16*	2.64
All industries	264	2.14*	8.57	124	2.71*	5.95	140	1.63*	6.98

Notes: Net flow measure of the leverage ratio used here.

Period of comparison—year prior to merger.

x_t = absolute difference between the acquiring company's leverage ratio and the weighted average leverage ratio of the acquiring and acquired companies, in the year prior to merger.

$\bar{x}_t$ = mean value of x_t for all the mergers in the sample. This is tested against the null hypothesis that $x_t = 0$ using a one-tail t-test at the 5 percent level of significance.

For key to terminology adopted, see notes to Table 8–4.

leverage of combining the merging partners' capital structures is statistically and economically significant.

As in the case of profits variability, there are difficulties in making a straightforward interpretation of the leverage results. Earlier in the chapter, we found that acquiring firms have significantly greater premerger leverage ratios than those of the acquired firms, while the latter, in turn, were found to be more highly levered than the nonacquired and nonacquiring control group. Thus, if on average, the acquiring firms had been seeking to reduce their leverage, their most obvious partners are to be found in the control group and not in the group of companies they actually acquired. Second, it is of course the case that the impact upon leverage of an acquisition will depend upon the method of payment used to effect it.

Table 8–12. Gort's Economic Disturbance and Bargain Tests

					All Industries Results		
Variable	*Merger Type*	*Group 1*	*Number of Companies* N_1	*Mean Value* $\bar{X}_1$	*Group 2*	*Number of Companies* N_2	*Mean Value* $\bar{X}_2$
Ratio of highest price-earnings ratio to lowest price-earnings ratio							
One year prior to merger	H	AD	28	2.3	MAD	28	2.0
Two years prior to merger	H	AD	27	2.8	MAD	27	2.5
Three years prior to merger	H	AD	27	3.2	MAD	27	2.7
Mean value of highest and lowest price-earnings ratios							
One year prior to merger	H	AD	28	20.4	MAD	28	17.4
Two years prior to merger	H	AD	27	17.8	MAD	27	16.0
Three years prior to merger	H	AD	27	17.1	MAD	27	15.7

Notes: For key to terminology adopted, see notes to Table 8–4.

Table 8–13. Comparison of Three Years Postmerger Profitability of Merging Companies with Control Group Companies

					All Industries Results		
Variable	*Merger Type*	*Group 1*	*Number of Companies* N_1	*Mean Value* $\bar{X}_1$	*Group 2*	*Number of Companies* N_2	*Mean Value* $\bar{X}_2$
Trading profits–sales	A	AG	111	10.32	C	858	10.03
	A	AG	111	10.32	MAGMAD	111	9.73
	H	AG	52	10.35	MAGMAD	52	9.54
	NH	AG	59	10.30	MAGMAD	59	9.89
Net income–net assets	A	AG	225	13.78	C	1186	16.29
	A	AG	225	13.78	MAGMAD	225	13.39
	H	AG	109	12.68	MAGMAD	109	13.25
	NH	AG	116	14.81	MAGMAD	116	13.52
Posttax income–equity assets	A	AG	221	7.32	C	1180	7.62
	A	AG	221	7.32	MAGMAD	221	6.37
	H	AG	107	6.27	MAGMAD	107	5.97
	NH	AG	114	8.30	MAGMAD	114	6.73

Notes: See notes to Table 8–4.

Difference in Mean Values $\bar{X}_1 - \bar{X}_2$	Statistical Significance t-Value	Summary of Nonparametric Test Results		
		Number of Observations with Positive $X_1 - X_2$	Total Number of Observations	Proportion Positive and its Significance
0.3	0.94	15	28	0.54
0.3	0.64	14	27	0.52
0.5	1.19	14	27	0.52
3.0	1.88*	15	28	0.54
1.8	1.09	14	27	0.52
1.4	0.87	14	27	0.52

Difference in Mean Values $\bar{X}_1 - \bar{X}_2$	Statistical Significance t-Value	Summary of Individual Industry Results		
		Number of Industries with Positive $X_1 - X_2$	Total Number of Industries	Proportion Positive and its Significance
0.29	0.53	4	14	0.29
0.60	0.88	7	14	0.50
0.81	0.81	7	14	0.50
0.41	0.45	8	14	0.57
−2.51**	−4.98	2	14	0.14*
0.39	0.64	7	14	0.50
−0.57	−0.68	7	14	0.50
1.29	1.46	9	14	0.64
−0.30	−0.81	6	14	0.43
0.95*	2.52	8	14	0.57
0.30	0.56	8	14	0.57
1.57**	3.09	10	14	0.71

Table 8–14. Comparison of Five Years Postmerger Profitability of Merging Companies with Control Group Companies

| | | | | | All Industries Results | | |
Variable	Merger Type	Group 1	Number of Companies N_1	Mean Value $\bar{X}_1$	Group 2	Number of Companies N_2	Mean Value $\bar{X}_2$
Trading profits–sales	A	AG	106	10.50	C	858	10.21
	A	AG	106	10.50	MAGMAD	106	10.16
	H	AG	47	10.57	MAGMAD	47	9.81
	NH	AG	59	10.45	MAGMAD	59	10.43
Net income–net assets	A	AG	211	14.65	C	1185	16.68
	A	AG	211	14.65	MAGMAD	211	14.88
	H	AG	98	13.74	MAGMAD	98	14.93
	NH	AG	113	15.43	MAGMAD	113	14.84
Posttax income–	A	AG	208	8.94	C	1177	8.87
equity assets	A	AG	208	8.94	MAGMAD	208	8.04
	H	AG	96	7.98	MAGMAD	96	7.91
	NH	AG	112	9.77	MAGMAD	112	8.15

Notes: See notes to Table 8–4.

Before it can be concluded that the highly levered acquiring firms sought on average to reduce their leverage, we must also look at what actually happened to their leverage ratios as a result of merger. As we shall see below, the effect on average was if anything to increase rather than reduce leverage.

Finally, Table 8–12 presents some results on Gort's disturbance theory. The information given pertains to a small sample of only twenty-eight acquired firms and a corresponding number of matched nonacquired firms. The results show little difference between either the variability or the average price-earnings ratios of acquired and nonacquired companies.[23]

TEST RESULTS ON EFFECTS OF MERGERS

Profitability

Tables 8–13 through 8–16 report the postmerger profitability of the merged firms relative to that of the control group firms. The findings

		Summary of Individual Industry Results		
Difference in Mean Values $\bar{X}_1 - \bar{X}_2$	Statistical Significance t-Value	Number of Industries with Positive $\bar{X}_1 - \bar{X}_2$	Total Number of Industries	Proportion Positive and its Significance
0.29	0.50	6	14	0.43
0.35	0.51	5	14	0.36
0.76	0.74	7	14	0.50
0.02	0.02	7	14	0.50
−2.03**	−3.83	6	14	0.43
−0.24	−0.38	8	14	0.57
−1.19	−1.28	10	14	0.71
0.59	0.71	7	14	0.50
0.07	0.17	8	14	0.57
0.91	1.94	11	14	0.79*
0.07	0.10	11	14	0.79*
1.62*	2.57	10	14	0.71

in Tables 8–13 and 8–14 indicate little difference between the two groups when the control group firms are matched by industry, year, and size, except in the case of posttax profitability on equity assets.[24] In the case of this measure there is weak evidence that merging firms are more profitable in the postmerger period than the matched control group companies.

However, the most interesting point to emerge from these results is that the postmerger profitability of merging firms is not lower than that of control group firms. Earlier in the chapter it was found that although the premerger profitability of acquiring firms was about the same as that of the matched control group firms, the profitability record of acquired firms before acquisition was distinctly less favorable than that of their matched control group, which suggests that the postmerger performance of merging firms may have improved somewhat relative to that of control group firms.

This hypothesis is to some extent borne out by the results presented in Tables 8–15 and 8–16, which compare the postmerger changes in profitability for the merging companies with those for the control group.[25] For example, in relation to net income on net assets, Table 8–15 shows that there was a small decline (on average of 0.25 percentage points) in the

Table 8–15. Effects: Difference Between Post- and Premerger Profitability

All Industries Results

Variable	Merger Type	Group 1	Number of Companies N_1	Mean Value $\bar{X}_1$	Group 2	Number of Companies N_2	Mean Value $\bar{X}_2$
Trading profits–sales	A	AGAD	111	−0.87	C	858	−1.08
	A	AGAD	111	−0.87	MAGMAD	111	−1.44
	H	AGAD	52	−1.08	MAGMAD	52	−1.53
	NH	AGAD	59	−0.68	MAGMAD	59	−1.37
Net income–net assets	A	AGAD	225	−0.26	C	1186	−1.13
	A	AGAD	225	−0.26	MAGMAD	225	−1.78
	H	AGAD	109	−0.71	MAGMAD	109	−1.89
	NH	AGAD	116	0.16	MAGMAD	116	−1.67
Posttax income–	A	AGAD	221	−0.90	C	1180	−1.77
equity assets	A	AGAD	221	−0.90	MAGMAD	221	−1.82
	H	AGAD	107	−1.47	MAGMAD	107	−2.22
	NH	AGAD	114	−0.36	MAGMAD	114	−1.45

Notes: Period of comparison—difference in average profitability in three years after merger compared with that five years before merger. For key to terminology adopted, see notes to Table 8–4.

Table 8–16. Effects: Difference Between Post- and Premerger Profitability

All Industries Results

Variable	Merger Type	Group 1	Number of Companies N_1	Mean Value $\bar{X}_1$	Group 2	Number of Companies N_2	Mean Value $\bar{X}_2$
Trading profits–sales	A	AGAD	106	−0.57	C	858	−0.89
	A	AGAD	106	−0.57	MAGMAD	106	−0.80
	H	AGAD	47	−0.62	MAGMAD	47	−0.76
	NH	AGAD	59	−0.54	MAGMAD	59	−0.83
Net income–net assets	A	AGAD	211	0.63	C	1185	−0.74
	A	AGAD	211	0.63	MAGMAD	211	−0.24
	H	AGAD	98	0.47	MAGMAD	98	0.15
	NH	AGAD	113	0.78	MAGMAD	113	−0.58
Posttax income–	A	AGAD	208	0.73	C	1177	−0.54
equity assets	A	AGAD	208	0.73	MAGMAD	208	−0.06
	H	AGAD	96	0.27	MAGMAD	96	−0.06
	NH	AGAD	112	1.13	MAGMAD	112	−0.06

Notes: Period of comparison—average profitability in five years after compared with five years before merger. For key to terminology adopted, see notes to Table 8–4.

		Summary of Individual Industry Results		
Difference in Mean Values $\bar{X}_1 - \bar{X}_2$	Statistical Significance t-Value	Number of Industries with Positive $\bar{X}_1 - \bar{X}_2$	Total Number of Industries	Proportion Positive and its Significance
0.21	0.80	7	14	0.50
0.57	1.88	7	14	0.50
0.45	1.81	9	14	0.64
0.69	1.60	8	14	0.57
0.87*	2.36	8	14	0.57
1.52**	3.52	9	14	0.64
1.18	1.77	9	14	0.64
1.83**	3.36	8	14	0.57
0.87**	2.86	8	14	0.57
0.92**	2.87	8	14	0.57
0.75	1.48	9	14	0.64
1.09**	2.78	9	14	0.64

		Summary of Individual Industry Results		
Difference in Mean Values $\bar{X}_1 - \bar{X}_2$	Statistical Significance t-Value	Number of Industries with Positive $\bar{X}_1 - \bar{X}_2$	Total Number of Industries	Proportion Positive and its Significance
0.32	0.93	8	14	0.57
0.23	0.62	6	14	0.43
0.14	0.32	8	14	0.57
0.29	0.54	8	14	0.57
1.38*	3.47	10	14	0.71
0.87	1.91	7	14	0.50
0.32	0.43	7	14	0.50
1.35*	2.41	9	14	0.61
1.27**	3.61	10	14	0.71
0.79*	2.00	8	14	0.57
0.33	0.54	10	14	0.71
1.18**	3.03	8	14	0.57

Table 8–17.   Comparison of Three Years Postmerger Growth of Merging Companies with Control Group Companies

							All Industries Results
Variable	Merger Type	Group 1	Number of Companies N_1	Mean Value $\bar{X}_1$	Group 2	Number of Companies N_2	Mean Value $\bar{X}_2$
Growth of net assets	A	AGAD	225	10.62	C	1186	5.21
	A	AGAD	225	10.62	MAGMAD	225	5.04
	H	AGAD	109	8.94	MAGMAD	109	3.99
	NH	AGAD	116	12.20	MAGMAD	116	6.03
Growth of physical assets	A	AGAD	225	11.85	C	1186	8.30
	A	AGAD	225	11.85	MAGMAD	225	6.13
	H	AGAD	109	10.10	MAGMAD	109	6.47
	NH	AGAD	116	13.49	MAGMAD	116	5.80

Notes: See notes to Table 8–4.

postmerger profitability of the merging firms three years after merger compared with their profitability in the five years before merger. However, the corresponding decline in the profitability of the matched control group firms was larger (an average of 1.78 percentage points). Statistically significant relative improvements in profitability are found (at the 5 percent level) for all mergers and for nonhorizontal mergers for two measures

Table 8–18.   Comparison of Five Years Postmerger Growth of Merging Companies with Control Group Companies

							All Industries Results
Variable	Merger Type	Group 1	Number of Companies N_1	Mean Value $\bar{X}_1$	Group 2	Number of Companies N_2	Mean Value $\bar{X}_2$
Growth of net assets	A	AGAD	210	12.24	C	1181	7.65
	A	AGAD	210	12.24	MAGMAD	210	7.60
	H	AGAD	98	10.24	MAGMAD	98	7.14
	NH	AGAD	112	13.99	MAGMAD	112	8.00
Growth of physical assets	A	AGAD	211	12.24	C	1184	9.14
	A	AGAD	211	12.24	MAGMAD	211	7.88
	H	AGAD	98	10.04	MAGMAD	98	7.08
	NH	AGAD	113	14.16	MAGMAD	113	8.57

Notes: See notes to Table 8–4.

Summary of Individual Industry Results				
Difference in Mean Values $\bar{X}_1 - \bar{X}_2$	Statistical Significance t-Value	Number of Industries with Positive $\bar{X}_1 - \bar{X}_2$	Total Number of Industries	Proportion Positive and its Significance
5.41**	5.09	12	14	0.86*
5.58**	5.00	11	14	0.79*
4.95**	3.26	11	14	0.79*
6.17**	3.86	12	14	0.86*
3.55**	3.01	11	14	0.79*
5.72**	4.59	13	14	0.93**
3.63*	2.29	11	14	0.79*
7.69**	4.09	13	14	0.93**

of profitability. On the other hand, it must be noted that the results on the binomial probability test are not statistically significant.

The combined results on profitability thus provide some evidence (admittedly rather weak) that the relative profitability of merging firms improved slightly after merger; it certainly did not decline, as other investigators have concluded (Meeks 1977; Utton 1974a). Further work is being carried out to discover the reason for this difference from the results of other studies, particularly that of Meeks, who carried out a comprehensive study of mergers over roughly the same time period as we have used.

Summary of Individual Industry Results				
Difference in Mean Values $\bar{X}_1 - \bar{X}_2$	Statistical Significance t-Value	Number of Industries with Positive $\bar{X}_1 - \bar{X}_2$	Total Number of Industries	Proportion Positive and its Significance
4.59*	4.59	12	14	0.86*
4.64**	5.27	13	14	0.93**
3.09**	2.88	11	14	0.79*
5.99**	4.51	11	14	0.79*
3.10**	3.70	11	14	0.79*
4.36**	4.76	12	14	0.86*
2.96**	2.71	11	14	0.79*
4.59**	3.30	10	14	0.71

Table 8–19. Effects: Differences in Post- and Premerger Growth Rate

						All Industries Results	
Variable	Merger Type	Group 1	Number of Companies N_1	Mean Value $\bar{X}_1$	Group 2	Number of Companies N_2	Mean Value $\bar{X}_2$
Growth of net assets	A	AGAD	210	1.77	C	1181	0.59
	A	AGAD	210	1.77	MAGMAD	210	1.74
	H	AGAD	98	0.60	MAGMAD	98	1.70
	NH	AGAD	112	2.79	MAGMAD	112	1.78
Growth of physical	A	AGAD	211	0.49	C	1184	−0.01
assets	A	AGAD	211	0.49	MAGMAD	211	0.33
	H	AGAD	98	−0.54	MAGMAD	98	−0.41
	NH	AGAD	113	1.38	MAGMAD	113	0.97

Notes: Period of comparison—difference in growth rate in the five years after merger compared with the growth rate in the five years prior to merger. For key to terminology adopted, see notes to Table 8–4.

Growth

Tables 8–17 through 8–22 report corresponding results for the growth variables. A comparison of the postmerger growth performance in the three and five years after merger (Tables 8–17 and 8–18) provides strong evidence that acquiring companies continue to grow faster than control group companies after merger.

Table 8–20. Effects: Differences in Post- and Premerger Growth Rate

						All Industries Results	
Variable	Merger Type	Group 1	Number of Companies N_1	Mean Value $\bar{X}_1$	Group 2	Number of Companies N_2	Mean Value $\bar{X}_2$
Growth of net assets	A	AGAD	225	0.24	C	1186	−1.82
	A	AGAD	225	0.24	MAGMAD	225	−0.76
	H	AGAD	109	−0.63	MAGMAD	109	−1.43
	NH	AGAD	116	1.06	MAGMAD	116	−0.12
Growth of physical	A	AGAD	225	0.16	C	1186	−0.83
assets	A	AGAD	225	0.16	MAGMAD	225	−1.42
	H	AGAD	109	−0.55	MAGMAD	109	−1.20
	NH	AGAD	116	0.82	MAGMAD	116	−1.64

Notes: Period of comparison—difference in growth rate in the three years after merger compared with the growth rate in the five years prior to merger. For key to terminology adopted, see notes to Table 8–4.

Difference in Mean Values $\bar{X}_1 - \bar{X}_2$	Statistical Significance t-Value	Summary of Individual Industry Results		
		Number of Industries with Positive $\bar{X}_1 - \bar{X}_2$	Total Number of Industries	Proportion Positive and its Significance
1.18	1.08	6	14	0.43
0.03	0.02	5	14	0.36
−1.10	−0.72	6	14	0.43
1.01	0.62	6	14	0.43
0.50	0.47	8	14	0.57
0.16	0.14	8	14	0.57
−0.13	−0.08	7	14	0.50
0.41	0.24	7	14	0.50

Turning, however, to the more interesting comparison of changes in growth rates of merging and control group firms, the results shown in Table 8–19 for five years after merger and in Table 8–20 for three years indicate little difference between the two groups. As with profitability, this conclusion is important from an economic point of view in that it shows that the postmerger performance of merging firms did not deteriorate or improve relative to other firms.[26]

Difference in Mean Values $\bar{X}_1 - \bar{X}_2$	Statistical Significance t-Value	Summary of Individual Industry Results		
		Number of Industries with Positive $\bar{X}_1 - \bar{X}_2$	Total Number of Industries	Proportion Positive and its Significance
2.06	1.60	9	14	0.64
1.00	0.74	5	14	0.36
0.80	0.44	6	14	0.43
1.18	0.61	7	14	0.50
0.99	0.71	8	14	0.57
1.58	1.07	8	14	0.57
0.65	0.34	7	14	0.50
2.46	1.10	7	14	0.50

Table 8–21. Comparison of Postmerger Leverage Ratios of Merging Companies with Control Group Companies

						All Industries Results	
Variable	Merger Type	Group 1	Number of Companies N_1	Mean Value $\bar{X}_1$	Group 2	Number of Companies N_2	Mean Value $\bar{X}_2$
Three years after merger							
Net flow leverage	A	AGAD	173	17.32	C	1127	12.30
ratio	A	AGAD	173	17.32	MAGMAD	173	8.69
	H	AGAD	81	20.15	MAGMAD	81	9.21
	NH	AGAD	92	14.83	MAGMAD	92	8.23
Five years after merger							
Net flow leverage	A	AGAD	143	16.68	C	1120	12.40
ratio	A	AGAD	143	16.68	MAGMAD	143	7.48
	H	AGAD	64	19.65	MAGMAD	64	7.59
	NH	AGAD	79	14.27	MAGMAD	79	7.39
Book value leverage	A	AGAD	208	24.61	C	1177	11.31
ratio (stock	A	AGAD	208	24.61	MAGMAD	208	12.08
measure)	H	AGAD	96	24.93	MAGMAD	96	11.74
	NH	AGAD	112	24.33	MAGMAD	112	12.37

Notes: See notes to Table 8–4.

Table 8–22. Effects: Difference Between Post- and Premerger Leverage Ratios

						All Industries Results	
Variable	Merger Type	Group 1	Number of Companies N_1	Mean Value $\bar{X}_1$	Group 2	Number of Companies N_2	Mean Value $\bar{X}_2$
Three years after merger							
Net flow leverage	A	AGAD	173	1.54	C	1127	4.58
rate	A	AGAD	173	1.54	MAGMAD	173	2.11
	H	AGAD	81	3.64	MAGMAD	81	2.38
	NH	AGAD	92	−0.31	MAGMAD	92	1.92
Five years after merger							
Net flow leverage	A	AGAD	143	0.13	C	1120	4.67
ratio	A	AGAD	143	0.13	MAGMAD	143	0.59
	H	AGAD	64	1.35	MAGMAD	64	0.02
	NH	AGAD	79	−0.87	MAGMAD	79	1.05
Book value leverage	A	AGAD	208	5.63	C	1177	−1.33
ratio (stock)	A	AGAD	208	5.63	MAGMAD	208	−0.51
measure)	H	AGAD	96	6.29	MAGMAD	96	−1.26
	NH	AGAD	112	5.07	MAGMAD	112	0.14

Notes: Period of comparison—difference in leverage ratio in three and five years after merger compared with five years prior to merger. For key to terminology adopted, see notes to Table 8–4.

| | | Summary of Individual Industry Results | | |
Difference in Mean Values $\bar{X}_1 - \bar{X}_2$	Statistical Significance t-Value	Number of Industries with Positive $\bar{X}_1 - \bar{X}_2$	Total Number of Industries	Proportion Positive and its Significance
5.02*	2.26	10	14	0.71
8.64**	7.32	11	14	0.79*
10.94**	5.85	13	14	0.93**
6.60**	4.60	11	14	0.79*
4.28	0.99	11	14	0.79*
9.20**	6.79	11	14	0.79*
12.07**	5.84	13	14	0.93**
6.88**	3.93	11	14	0.79*
13.30**	14.62	13	14	0.93**
12.52**	11.41	12	14	0.86*
13.19**	7.83	13	14	0.93**
11.96**	8.36	13	14	0.93**

| | | Summary of Individual Industry Results | | |
Difference in Mean Values $\bar{X}_1 - \bar{X}_2$	Statistical Significance t-Value	Number of Industries with Positive $\bar{X}_1 - \bar{X}_2$	Total Number of Industries	Proportion Positive and its Significance
−3.04	−1.26	4	14	0.29
−0.60	−0.43	7	14	0.50
1.26	0.58	7	14	0.50
−2.24	−1.22	5	14	0.36
−4.55	−1.01	5	14	0.36
−0.46	−0.27	7	14	0.50
1.34	0.49	7	14	0.50
−1.92	−0.90	4	14	0.29
6.97**	9.98	14	14	1.00**
6.14**	7.78	13	14	0.93**
7.55**	6.88	12	14	0.86*
4.93**	4.43	12	14	0.86*

Leverage

Tables 8–21 and 8–22 present the results for the leverage ratio variables. Table 8–21 shows that the merging firms had, on average, higher leverage ratios than control group firms in the three and five years following merger. This is not surprising given the finding, discussed earlier, that the premerger leverage ratios of both acquiring and acquired firms tended to be higher than amongst the control group firms.

The findings for changes in the leverage ratio in postmerger periods relative to the premerger period, shown in Table 8–22 are rather mixed. The results for the net flow measure of leverage suggest that there is no significant difference between merging and control group firms in the average change in the leverage ratio. On the other hand, the results for the stock measure of leverage provide strong evidence that merger increases leverage. While the leverage ratio of merging firms has, on average, risen

Table 8–23. Stockholder Returns for Acquiring and Matched Nonacquiring Companies, Pre- and Postmerger

Measure	Merger Type	Number of Companies	AG	MAG	Difference AG − MAG	t-ratio
1. Stockholder return for five years preceding merger (percent per annum)	A	63	13.3	6.4	6.9*	3.97
2. Stockholder return for one year after merger (percent per annum)	A	63	51.8	33.1	18.7*	3.10
3. Stockholder return for two years after merger (percent per annum)	A	63	20.8	14.1	6.7*	2.21
4. Stockholder return for three years after merger (percent per annum)	A	63	7.6	6.4	1.2	0.55
5. Stockholders return for four years after merger (percent per annum)	A	63	11.8	10.0	1.8	0.80
6. Stockholder return for five years after merger (percent per annum)	A	63	17.9	16.4	1.5	0.77
7. 2 − 1	A	63	38.5	26.6	11.9	1.99
8. 3 − 1	A	63	7.5	7.6	−0.2	−0.05
9. 4 − 1	A	63	−5.7	−0.1	−5.6*	−2.00
10. 5 − 1	A	63	−1.5	3.6	−5.0	1.78
11. 6 − 1	A	63	4.6	9.9	−5.3*	−2.00

Notes: See notes to Table 8–4.

by about six percentage points in the five years after merger (compared with the five years prior to merger), the leverage ratio of the control group firms has, on average, slightly declined.

Stockholder Return

Table 8–23 examines the impact of mergers on the financial returns to stockholders. For this, stockholder returns[27] were calculated for a sample of sixty-three acquiring companies and their matched control group companies in the five years prior to merger and for one, two, three, four, and five years after merger.[28] The results (rows 1 to 6) show that the stockholder return is consistently higher on average, in all periods, for acquiring companies than for matched control group companies. However, the difference in stockholder return between these groups becomes less, on average, in the postmerger period. This implies that the change in stockholder return following merger is worse for acquiring firms than for control group firms. This implication is supported by the results shown in rows 7 to 11. Apart from the comparison of premerger stockholder return (five years) with stockholder return in the year after merger, the results show on average a decline in the stockholder return of acquiring companies relative to their matched control group firms. Nevertheless, it remains true that the shareholders of acquiring firms over the period as a whole were better off in terms of the return on their shares than those of the nonacquiring companies.[29]

CONCLUSION

In this chapter, we have outlined the differences in the institutional environment that has characterized the merger movement of the last two decades in the United Kingdom, as compared both with the previous merger movements in this country and with contemporary merger waves in other countries. The detailed microeconomic analysis for the peak merger years 1967–1969 has shown that there were some important differences in the average premerger characteristics of the acquired-acquiring and nonacquired-nonacquiring companies. In general, it was found easier to discriminate between the acquiring companies and the rest than between those acquired and the others. The most important distinguishing features of the acquirers, on a univariate basis, were their higher average growth, greater average leverage ratio, and bigger average size.

The test results on determinants of mergers did not yield evidence in support of there being any one single dominant motive for mergers (of those considered). This is not surprising, since there are many different reasons why firms merge. As for the effects of mergers, the United Kingdom evidence shows that the growth and profitability performance of merging companies did not deteriorate after merger. Other things being equal, this evidence is compatible with the view that although the takeover mechanism may not be particularly beneficial in terms of its effects on resource allocation, it is at least not perverse.

However, the fundamental issues involved in defining and measuring efficiency are complex in an economy that can be regarded as being in long-term disequilibrium (see Singh 1977b) and where, therefore, the ceteris paribus assumption of the conventional welfare analysis is particularly inappropriate. This and other aspects of the overall economic efficiency of mergers are discussed in Chapter 11.

NOTES

1. More specifically, the issues of industrial concentration and macroeconomic efficiency are not examined in this study. These will be discussed in forthcoming papers.
2. It should be noted that although small in number, many amalgamations are very large in size. None of the results reported in this chapter include amalgamations, but tests suggested that their exclusion did not invalidate conclusions drawn from the analysis.
3. Section 33 of the Companies Act 1967 required anyone becoming beneficially interested in one-tenth or more of the nominal value of voting equity to disclose his interest within fourteen days to the company concerned, which had to make it public in its share register within a further three days. In 1976 the law was made even more restrictive in these respects.
4. The takeover bid normally consists of a company making a bid for the shares of another company at a given price, subject to a predetermined proportion of shareholders accepting the bid by a given date. The proportion chosen has varied with the prevailing legal and stock exchange protection afforded to minority shareholders (see Weinberg 1971).
5. Singh and Whittington (1968) found that in 1954, for more than 60 percent of the firms in the four industries studied by them, the valuation ratio (i.e., the ratio of stock market valuation of a firm's ordinary shares to the book value of its assets) was less than 1; the mean valuation ratio was 0.94. However by 1960, as a result of the share price boom of 1959–1960, the mean valuation ratio had increased to 1.26, although 40 percent of the firms still had a valuation ratio below unity.
6. From 1965 to 1973 the definition was one-third of a national market. The 1973 legislation therefore tightened the net in this respect.
7. Calculated by listing the merger investments of the IRC, shown in Young & Lowe (1974: Appendix) and calculating the net assets of the seventeen companies disappearing as a result of merger, which could be identified in the databank of merger activity compiled by A. Hughes at the Department of Applied Economics, Cambridge University. Where an amalgamation was involved, the net assets of the firm ending up with the smaller share of equity in the new concern was taken as the disappearance.
8. We have not in this section considered the ways in which the stock market itself has sought to influence merger activity. While this might seem an important omission, it can be argued that for our purposes it is not. The major institution involved here is the City Panel on Take Overs and Mergers, first constituted in 1968 for surveillance on merger practices on the exchange. Its main concern, however, is with shareholder protection in bid situations rather than the extent or direction of merger activity itself. In general the evidence suggests that its impact in controlling abuses has been restricted. See further Spiegelberg (1973) and Davies (1976).

9. No comparable series is available for the distributive industries, but it seems clear that this trend was more widespread than manufacturing alone. See, for instance, the decline in all industrial and commercial quoted companies shown in Prais (1976: 91, table 5.2).

10. No straightforward inferences can be drawn from Table 8–2 due to possible aggregation errors (see below). However, nothwithstanding the aggregation problem, the hypothesis of no difference in the probabilities of acquisition in the various size quintiles is rejected at the 2 percent level. As the table suggests, there is a nonlinear relationship between size and probability of acquisition (See Singh 1975; Kuehn 1975; and Singh 1976a).

11. The highest death rate recorded in earlier periods was 2.3 percent in the years 1885–1896 during the first United Kingdom merger wave (Hart and Prais 1956).

12. These variables were dictated by the requirements of the statistical tests described in Chapters 1 and 2, rather than by the nature of the issues discussed above. Nevertheless, they do bear directly on these issues. For a discussion of these variables in connection ‚with questions of market selection processes and market discipline, see Singh (1971).

13. The price-earnings ratio is linked to Marris's (1964) valuation ratio by the following identity:

Valuation ratio = P/E multiplied by the posttax rate of return on equity assets.

14. The market rate of return was taken to be the return on the Fortune 500 industrial ordinary shares.

15. Firms making more than one acquisition are counted as separate acquirers for each of the acquisitions they make.

16. The condition of noninvolvement in takeover activity over a ten-year time span used in forming the control group was dictated by the requirements of the statistical tests of Chapter 2. It is, however, important to note that, given the very high incidence of takeover activity during the decade of the 1960s, the number of companies in the control group was relatively small. This results in the matching for size being rather inadequate, particularly in the upper size ranges.

17. Horizontal mergers were taken to be those mergers between two companies within the same two-digit industry.

18. The individual industry analysis is, in all cases, carried out for fourteen industries. Industries 37, 38, 43, 47, 49 and 70 were excluded from the individual industry analysis due to the small number of takeovers in these industries. It is worth noting at this stage why the number of observations vary in the results presented in the tables, and why the number of observations may fall short of the maximum of 290: (a) some acquiring and acquired companies did not exist throughout the period of five years prior to merger; (b) some acquiring companies did not continue to exist three (or five) years after merger; (c) "rate of return on assets" measures require balance sheet figures for six years prior to merger and so have less observations than for the other measures because companies not existing six years prior to merger are excluded in this case; (d) sales figures are universally available only after 1967; (e) coefficients of variation of profits were not calculated for those companies with zero average profit over the period; (f) leverage ratios calculated on the net flow basis were removed when negative values were obtained; (g) in tests involving ratios of post- to premerger performance, observations were removed when nonpositive values occurred.

19. This test considers whether the proportion of industries in which the difference in group means is positive is significantly different from the null hypothesis of 0.5. It would have been statistically more appropriate to analyze differences in group medians (nonparametric measure of location), but the enormous task of calculation precluded this approach being adopted.

20. There is evidence that the profits variability indicator used here is negatively related to size. Since the acquired companies are on the whole much smaller than the acquiring ones, this may explain the relatively greater variability of their profits record.

21. This conclusion is rather different from that of Singh and Whittington (1968) for the period 1954–1960. They found that size was uncorrelated with any of fourteen main

indicators, including profitability, growth, leverage, liquidity ratio, valuation ratio, and so forth, that they were investigating.

22. The available evidence is of course perfectly compatible with an alternative hypothesis that it is not the more volatile acquired firms that are seeking to reduce profits variability by merging with the more stable acquiring firms, but that the latter take over the former simply because the acquired firms are relatively cheaper to buy owing to their more variable profits record.

23. The t-test shows that the average price-earnings ratio of acquired firms (a year before merger) was significantly greater than that of nonacquired firms at the 10 percent level. However, this conclusion is not supported by the distribution-free binomial probability test, which shows that thirteen out of twenty-eight acquired firms had a lower than average price-earnings ratio.

24. The differences between the results for pretax profitability on net assets and posttax profitability on equity assets arise from the differences in the gearing ratios of the two groups of firms.

25. In this chapter all the change tests are carried out in terms of arithmetic differences in performance, but they were also done in terms of performance ratios (i.e., after/before). Since the results were essentially the same, it was decided to save space by excluding the ratio tests from our presentation.

26. It could be argued that the postmerger growth performance of merging firms is overstated to the extent that while the control group companies by definition did not grow by acquisition, the merging firms could and may have done so. However, Meeks (1977) has shown that the superior growth performance of merging firms is due as much to internal as to acquisition growth.

27. The stockholder return for a company is measured by calculating the capital gain and dividend income (including income from reinvesting dividend income in the FT 500 share index) on £100 of investment in that company's ordinary stock.

28. The analysis was also carried out for horizontal and nonhorizontal mergers separately. The results obtained were similar to those reported in Table 8–23.

29. There is considerable evidence that the shareholders of the acquired companies invariably gain from merger (because of the premium that they are paid to persuade them to accept the takeover bid: Firth 1979; Newbould 1970). This may in part explain the decline in stockholder return of the acquiring companies. It should be noted that the discussion in the text does not take into account the risk associated with the mean returns reported. Sharp and Treynor tests required for this purpose could not unfortunately be carried out in this study because of the difficulties involved in obtaining data of the necessary quality.

Chapter 9

The United States, 1962–1972

Dennis C. Mueller

BACKGROUND

The history of merger activity in the United States has been characterized by three great merger waves: the first at the turn of the century, the second in the 1920s, and the third in the 1960s. Each of these was associated with a period of sustained economic expansion and a long bull market; each came to an end when the expansion stopped and the bull market collapsed.[1] The post–World War II economic expansion has been the most gradual of all three, and the following contraction the least severe; thus, the rise and fall of merger activity in this period has been also the least pronounced. But it has nevertheless followed the same wavelike pattern of the other two. Table 9–1 presents the data for this wave.

The first two merger waves were associated with increases in both overall and industry level concentration rates. The third has witnessed

Initial research assistant work on this chapter was done by Gerald Nelson. The bulk of the work was done by Jonathan Palfrey, to whom I owe an immense debt. His ingenuity in circumventing the obstacles thrown against him by the computer center in Berlin was remarkable. What is more, he had to switch to the Warwick computer center at the eleventh hour. I can truly say that this chapter could never have been completed without his valiant efforts.

Table 9–1. Merger Activity, 1950–1975

Year	Number All manufacturing and mining	Number Large[a] manufacturing and mining	Value of Assets,[b] Large[a] manufacturing and mining	Moody's Composite Market Price per Share
1950	279	5	186	56.23
1951	235	9	202	66.98
1952	288	15	385	71.73
1953	295	26	795	72.81
1954	387	38	1479	89.04
1955	683	69	2231	117.36
1956	673	59	2111	130.55
1957	585	50	1428	125.46
1958	589	45	1173	132.02
1959	835	62	1724	163.47
1960	844	64	1734	155.46
1961	954	60	2235	185.66
1962	853	80	2660	177.87
1963	861	82	3187	202.32
1964	854	91	2577	235.08
1965	1008	91	3722	250.31
1966	995	104	4380	230.88
1967	1496	174	8956	246.54
1968	2407	225	13759	264.62
1969	2307	175	12219	262.77
1970	1351	109	6601	226.70
1971	1011	87	3141	261.43
1972	1036	87	2671	290.65
1973	1275	83	3559	285.44
1974	909	83	5119	220.35
1975	578	72	5528	
1976[c]	692	105	6590	

Source: Data are from Federal Trade Commission, Bureau of Economics, *Current Trends in Merger Activity* (1971); *Statistical Report on Mergers and Acquisitions, 1973, 1974, 1975, 1976* (1977); and *Moody's Industrial Manual.*
[a] Acquired firms with assets of $10 million or more.
[b] In millions of dollars.
[c] Preliminary.

only an increase in overall concentration. Since World War II, concentration levels have tended to rise in about the same fraction of industries as in which they have fallen, and the chief cause for those increases that have occurred would appear to be related to marketing and advertising intensities (Hamm and Mueller, 1974). Specific attempts to relate mergers in the 1960s to either market power or economy of sale efficiencies that could lead to increases in concentration have come up with negative findings (FTC, 1972; Goldberg, 1973, 1974).

Although mergers do not appear to have had an appreciable effect on

Table 9–2. Assets Held and Acquired by the 100 and 200 Largest Firms as a Percentage of All Assets

	100 Largest (1968)		200 Largest (1968)	
	Held	Acquired	Held	Acquired
1959	46.3	0.36	56.0	0.55
1960	46.4	0.25	56.3	0.45
1961	46.6	0.43	56.3	0.63
1962	46.2	0.43	56.0	0.52
1963	46.5	0.53	56.3	0.71
1964	46.5	0.43	56.6	0.52
1965	46.5	0.49	56.7	0.64
1966	46.4	0.51	56.7	0.66
1967	48.1	0.98	59.3	1.57
1968	49.3	1.27	60.9	1.70

Source: Data taken from FTC (1969): Tables 3–3, 3–7, and 3–10.
Notes: Assets held figures are for corporate manufacturing; assets acquired pertain to large manufacturing and mining firms.

industry concentration levels in recent years, they do appear to be largely responsible for increases in overall concentration. In the most careful investigation of this question to date, John McGowan (1965) estimated the contribution of mergers to the increase in concentration in the hundred largest firms to be almost three-quarters the total increase between 1950 and 1960. Studies by the Federal Trade Commission (1969) and Lee Preston (1973) suggest that the impact of mergers on overall concentration, at, say, the 200 largest firms level, has been at least as great. Table 9–2 presents FTC data covering the broad economic expansion under Kennedy and Johnson. As can be seen, both the percentage of corporate assets held by the largest 100 and 200 firms and the assets they acquired as a percent of all assets remained remarkably stable from 1959 through 1966. During this period the acquisitions of these firms appear to have just offset any tendency for overall concentration to fall due to the relatively slower growth of the largest firms. All of the increase in overall concentration over these ten years comes in 1967 and 1968, the two peak merger years.

Between 1950 and 1968 the share of corporate assets held by the largest 200 manufacturing firms increased from 47.7 to 60.9 (FTC 1969: 173). If McGowan, the FTC, and Preston are correct and this increase has largely been due to mergers, then mergers have played a significant role in transforming the structure of American Industry.

The explanation for why mergers have had a significant impact on overall concentration in the United States since World War II and not on industry level concentration can be found in the decline in importance of horizontal and vertical mergers relative to conglomerate (i.e., nonhori-

Table 9–3. Large Acquisitions in Manufacturing and Mining by Type of Acquisitions, 1948–1975 (percent, based on assets)

Type of Acquisition	1948– 1951	1952– 1955	1956– 1959	1960– 1963	1964– 1967	1968– 1971	1972– 1975
Horizontal	36.8	36.6	27.3	13.3	11.4	12.9	18.7
Vertical	23.8	11.5	20.1	23.8	8.9	6.4	6.2
Conglomerates	37.5	52.0	52.7	56.9	79.8	80.7	75.1
Product extension		45.7	33.5	37.8	49.9	36.7	24.2
Market extension		2.7	5.0	8.0	8.7	4.3	6.0
Pure conglomerate		3.6	14.2	11.1	21.2	39.6	44.9
Total	100.0	100.0	100.0	100.0	100.0	100.0	100.0

Source: FTC, Statistical Report on Mergers and Acquisitions, 1973, 1974, 1975, 1976; Current Trends in Merger Activity (1970).

zontal and nonvertical) mergers since the passage of the Cellar-Kefauver Amendment to Section 7 of the Clayton Act in 1950. This act effectively eliminated the horizontal and vertical form of merger for most companies of any size or market share (with some important exceptions), which meant that if mergers are to take place, they would have to be of the conglomerate variety. The growth in absolute and relative importance of the conglomerate form of merger is documented in Table 9–3.

United States government policy toward mergers is the toughest of any country in the world. Through a series of court decisions, it has become well-established that any merger of consequence that brings together two firms in the same industry with a combined market share of 20 percent or more is likely to be challenged and overturned (Scherer 1970: 480–82). In 1968 the Justice Department tightened this policy by announcing a set of merger guidelines that indicated that horizontal mergers bringing together firms accounting for as little as 8 percent of a market would be challenged in highly concentrated industries ($C_4 > 75$ percent) and that horizontal mergers accounting for as little as 10 percent would be challenged in less concentrated industries. Similarly tough standards were proclaimed for vertical acquisitions. Although guidelines dealing with potential entry and reciprocity were also established, policy here is less severe. In some cases conglomerate mergers have been successfully challenged, but as is obvious from the statistics in Tables 9–1 and 9–3, the bulk of these are able to escape antitrust prosecution.

It should be noted with respect to the figures in Table 9–3 that a large fraction of those mergers that the FTC classifies as "conglomerate" are either product or market extension mergers. Some of these (e.g., the Atlantic and Richfield Oil consolidation) might arguably have led to either market power or economies of scale advantages of the type traditionally described in the textbooks. But these are cetainly less likely for even this type of merger and seem fairly implausible a priori for the "pure conglomerate" merger. Thus, it must be expected that the advantages of market power and economies of scale play a less important role in explaining both the determinants and effects of mergers in the United States than in other countries, and more attention should be focused on the risk-pooling and other stock-market-related hypotheses about mergers. Indeed, the stock market's performance has been shown to be a major factor affecting the level of merger activity (Nelson 1959, 1966). The last column in Table 9–1 presents Moody's composite market price of a share of common stock. A comparison of this with the adjacent column reveals the cyclical nature of both mergers and stock market prices. Note in particular the sharp rise in stock prices and merger activity in 1955–1956 and the subsequent fall in 1957. The same occurred in the 1966–1970 period.

Contested takeovers have made up a fairly small percentage of mergers in the United States. Banks and other outsiders do not appear to have played a particularly large role in promoting mergers, at least in comparison with previous merger waves in the United States and recent experience in Europe (Markham 1955; Reid 1968: chs. 3 and 4). The driving forces behind most recent mergers in the United States would appear to be the managers of the firms involved (Reid 1968: ch. 5).

GENERAL CHARACTERISTICS OF MERGING FIRMS

In this section, we present some aggregate figures on the characteristics of the merging firms in the sample. Although in principle we attempted to gather data for both the acquiring and the acquired firms for the five years after the merger, missing data made this impossible. Thus, the entries in the tables presented here and in the tests reported below are based on the maximum number of observations it was possible to garner for each year and variable. There are a total of 287 mergers from 1962 to 1972 in our sample, of which 28 were horizontal.

Table 9–4 lists the eighteen three-digit industries from which five or more acquisitions were made by the acquiring firms. Table 9–5 lists the twenty-one three-digit industries from which five or more firms were acquired. A comparison of the two tables indicates that the base industry concentration of the acquiring firms is much higher than that of the acquired firms; seven three-digit industries had ten or more acquiring firms, but only one three-digit industry had as many as ten acquired firms. In large part this difference is explained by the possibility of an acquiring firm making more than one acquisition, while a company can be acquired only once. Table 9–6 lists the eight firms in the sample with five or more acquisitions.[2] The top three are all classified in the same industry— telephone, telegraph, and radio and TV transmitting equipment—and this accounts for this industry's heavy concentration of acquiring firm activity.

Table 9–4.   Industries in Which Acquiring Firms Engaged in Five or More Acquisitions

Industry Number	Industry Name	Number of Acquisitions
131	Crude oil	8
202	Dairy products	12
204	Milling	5
205	Bread and biscuits	5
242	Forest products	6
281	Inorganic chemicals	7
283	Drugs and pharmaceuticals	14
291	Petroleum refining	14
331	Steel	10
353	Machinery, construction, oil well drilling	11
354	Machine tools	5
361	Electrical equipment	5
363	Electrical household appliances	8
366	Telephone, radio, and TV transmitting equipment	31
371	Motor vehicles and parts	7
372	Aircraft and aerospace	11
501	Wholesale autos and parts	7
531	Retail department and discount stores	6

Table 9–5.   Industries from Which Five or More Firms Were Acquired

Industry Number	Industry Name	Number of Acquired Companies
203	Canned foods	5
262	Paper	6
284	Soap and cosmetics	8
291	Petroleum refining	5
331	Steel	10
342	Hardware	7
353	Machinery construction, oil well drilling	5
354	Machine tools	8
356	Industrial machinery	9
357	Office and business equipment	5
358	Machine service industry	7
361	Electrical equipment	5
362	Electrical industrial controls	7
364	Lamps and lighting fixtures	5
366	Telephone, radio, and TV transmitting equipment	5
367	Electronics	8
371	Motor vehicles and parts	5
382	Measuring and testing instruments	5
394	Toys and leisure time products	6
509	Wholesale scrap, waste, other durables	6
541	Retail food chains	6

Table 9–6. **Firms Making Five or More Acquisitions in the Sample**

Industry Number	Firm Name	Number of Acquisitions
366	Litton Industries	10
366	IT&T	9
366	Teledyne	9
202	Beatrice Foods	7
501	Gulf & Western	6
131	Occidental Petroleum	5
242	Boise Cascade	5
371	TRW	5

These eight firms were among the leading conglomerates of the day. Whether the intensity of their merger activity is in some way related to the character of their base industries (mature, slow growing) seems difficult to say. In some cases (e.g., Litton, Gulf and Western) the classification of home industry seems somewhat arbitrary.

Further examination of the cross-industry patterns between acquiring and acquired firms does not yield many interesting findings. Five of the fourteen acquisitions by drug and pharmaceutical firms were of soap and cosmetic companies. Half of the fourteen mergers by the petroleum companies were of firms either within the petroleum industry itself or in the technologically related agrochemical industry. Seven of the eleven acquisitions by construction and oil well drilling companies are within the two-digit machinery industry. The six acquisitions by retail and discount department stores are of other department stores or food chains. Thus, in those cases where a pattern exists, the mergers would seem to be of the horizontal or product and market extension variety, but in general such patterns do not exist.

Table 9–7 presents the mean values for some size and profitability variables in the year preceding the merger for the acquiring firms, their matched control group firms, and their base industries. In selecting a control group, each acquiring firm was assigned to a two-digit industry, and then another firm was selected from the same two-digit industry that was as near to the merging firm as possible in terms of size, but did not engage in significant merger activity during the period of study.[3] Both the acquiring firms and their size-matched control group firms are significantly greater in size than the average firm in their base industry $(X_1 - X_3)$. Indeed, the acquiring firms were so large that it was not in general possible to find other firms in the same industry of equal size that had not engaged in merger activity. The differences in size between the two samples is positive, but insignificant when based on the arithmetic mean comparison. But these differences are significant when based on the more appropriate

Table 9–7. Characteristics of Acquiring Companies, Their Size-matched Control Group Companies, and Their Industry Means, Premerger

Variable	N_1, N_2	Mean Values X_1 AG	X_2 MAG	X_3 Industry	Difference $(X_1 - X_2)$	t	t Sig. Level	Industries +/Total	Sig. Level	Difference $(X_1 - X_3)$
Size ('000,000)										
Total assets	287	507.6	424.7	206.5	82.8	1.00	31.7	17/31	72.0	301.1*
Sales	287	571.2	489.1	224.8	102.1	1.36	17.4	16/31	100.0	346.4*
Geometric means										
Total assets	287	251.2	159.6		91.6	4.38	0.0	23/31	1.1	
Sales	287	319.5	207.9		111.6	4.31	0.0	21/31	7.1	
After tax profit–assets	287	0.072	0.071	0.063	0.001	0.21	83.4	12/31	28.1	0.009*
After tax profit–sales	287	0.061	0.061	0.052	0.000	0.06	95.0	18/31	47.3	0.009*
Coefficient of variation in profit (five previous years)	277	1.05	0.39		0.67	1.59	11.2	15/30	100.0	
Growth (five previous years)										
Total assets	151	16.15	12.46		3.69		5.0*			
Sales	159	16.99	12.58		4.41		5.0*			
Leverage	287	0.188	0.148	0.154	0.040	3.88	0.0	22/31	2.9	0.034*

* Significant at 5 percent level or better.

geometric mean comparison. The difference between these two tests implies that while a few control group firms are quite large and thus pull up the arithmetic mean of this group, the "typical" acquiring firm tends to be larger on average than the paired nonacquiring firm, despite the effort to match them by size. (The differences between the two variables $X_1 - X_2$ are given in the column headed Difference $(X_1 - X_2)$. The t statistic for this difference appears in the next column to the right, the level of significance of this statistic in the second column to the right.)

Both the acquiring firms and their size-matched pairs have significantly higher profit rates than the mean profit rate for their respective industries. The difference between the two samples $(X_1 - X_2)$ is negligible and insignificant, however. Thus, there would appear to be a positive association between size and profitability over the full sample of companies. These statistics differ somewhat from other studies of the United States merger wave (e.g., Weston and Mansinghka 1971), which have found acquirng firms to have significantly lower profit rates than industry averages. This difference probably arises because while these studies have focused exclusively on the acquisition-prone conglomerates, the present includes all merging companies.

A large difference exists between the mean coefficients of variation between the two samples, suggesting that acquiring firms are more risky, but the difference between these means is not significant at conventional levels.

Both the growth rates and the leverage ratios of the acquiring firms are significantly greater than those of the nonmerging control group. This is consistent with what other observers have found in both the United States and the United Kingdom (Weston and Mansinghka 1971; Singh 1971; Kuehn 1975). Acquiring firms tend to be more aggressive and growth oriented than other firms in their industries.

The second and third from last columns in Table 9–7 present the proportion of two-digit industries for which the mean value for the acquiring firm (X_1) exceeded that for the control group companies and the significance level at which this proportion differs from a fifty-fifty split assuming a binomial distribution of possible outcomes. These statistics provide a check on the validity of the sample mean comparisons. If the differences in sample means are not simply due to aggregation biases across industries, the same pattern of results should emerge here as does when one compares sample means. For the comparisons in Table 9–7 this is the case. The arithmetic means for the size variables are not significantly different, but the geometric means are. No significant difference exists in profit rates or in the variability of profits. Acquiring firms are significantly higher levered.

Table 9–8 presents a similar set of comparisons between the acquired firms, a size- and industry-matched sample of nonacquired firms, and their

Table 9–8. Characteristics of Acquired Companies, Their Size-matched Control Group Companies, and Their Industry Means, Premerger

Variable	N_1, N_2	Mean Values			Difference $(X_1 - X_2)$	t	t Sig. Level	Industries +/Total	Sig. Level	Difference $(X_1 - X_3)$
		X_1 AD	X_2 MAD	X_3 Industry						
Size ('000,000)										
Total assets	286	55.2	55.0	136.4	0.2	0.02	98.3	11/33	8.0	−81.2*
Sales	285	69.6	70.6	168.8	−1.0	−0.10	92.0	12/33	16.3	−99.2*
Geometric means										
Total assets	286	22.7	26.2		−3.5	−1.43	15.5	9/33	1.4	
Sales	285	34.0	38.8		−4.8	−1.41	15.9	10/33	3.5	
After tax profit–assets	286	0.075	0.072	0.063	0.003	0.57	56.7	14/33	(3) 48.7	.012*
After tax profit–sales	285	0.053	0.050	0.048	0.003	0.87	38.7	18/33	72.8	.005*
Coefficient of variation in profit (five previous years)	274	0.52	0.81		−0.29	−1.07	28.5	16/33	(1) 100.0	
Growth (five previous years)										
Total assets	151	10.14	10.55		−0.41		ins			
Sales	159	10.28	10.77		−0.49		ins			
Leverage	285	0.126	0.130	0.149	−0.004	−0.42	67.5	14/33	(2) 48.7	−0.023*

* Significant at 5 percent level or better.
ins—insignificant.

Table 9–9. Characteristics of Acquiring and Acquired Companies Compared in Year Before the Merger

Variable	N_1, N_2	Mean Values X_1 AG	Mean Values X_2 AD	Differ-ence $(X_1 - X_2)$	t	t sig. level	Indus-tries +/Total	Sig. level
Size ('000,000)								
Total assets	286	505.2	55.2	450.1	9.37	0.0	31/31	0.0
Sales	285	570.3	69.6	500.7	11.71	0.0	30/31	0.0
Geometric means								
Total assets	286	249.9	22.7	227.2	23.3	0.0	31/31	0.0
Sales	285	381.1	34.0	347.1	22.6	0.0	30/31	0.0
After tax profit– assets	286	0.072	0.075	−0.003	−0.73	46.3	12/31	28.1
After tax profit– sales	285	0.061	0.053	0.008	1.62	10.5	19/31	28.1
Coefficient of varia-tion in profit (five previous years)	275	0.81	0.63	0.18	0.54	59.2	13/30	58.5
Growth (five pre-vious years)								
Total assets	151	16.15	10.14	6.01		5.0*		
Sales	159	16.99	8.79	8.20		5.0*		
Leverage	285	189	0.126	0.063	5.88	0	24/31	0.3

* Significant at 5 percent level or better.

base industries. Both the acquired companies and their control group firms are significantly smaller than the average firm in their respective industry. No significant differences in size exist between the two samples based on sample means, but a significant proportion of the acquired firms tended to be smaller than their control group pairs on an industry-by-industry comparison. Thus the acquired firms are about the same size or a little smaller than their matched pairs.

Somewhat surprisingly given their smaller size, both the acquired and control group firms have higher profit rates than their industry means. For the control group firms this must be a chance drawing, and the difference is in fact only statistically significant for the profit/assets variable. That the acquired firms are more profitable than the average firm in their industry is less puzzling. Other studies have found that acquired firms tend to be relatively healthy (see, e.g., Melicher and Rush 1974; Lynch 1971). No significant differences emerge between the acquired firms and their size-matched control group companies on the basis of any of the other variables.

Table 9–9 compares the acquiring firms with the companies they acquired. Not surprisingly, they are very much larger than the acquired firms. No difference existed in profitability on assets, but the profit-to-

Table 9–10. Characteristics of Acquiring Companies, Their Size-matched Control Group Companies, and Their Industry Means, Five Years Postmerger

Variable	N_1, N_2	Mean Values			Difference $(X_1 - X_2)$	t	t Sig. Level	Industries +/Total	Sig. Level	Difference $(X_1 - X_3)$
		X_1 AG	X_2 MAG	X_3 Industry						
Size ('000,000)										
Total assets	247	1191.3	823.0	368.7	368.3	2.13	3.4	22/31	2.9	822.6*
Sales	247	1376.3	949.2	405.0	427.2	2.09	3.7	23/31	1.1	971.3*
Geometric means										
Total assets	247	701.6	318.4		383.2	7.49	0.0	26/31	0.0	
Sales	247	883.0	399.6		484.4	7.83	0.0	28/31	0.0	
After tax profit–assets	247	0.057	0.058	0.053	-0.000	-0.03	97.9	14/31	72.0	0.004*
After tax profit–sales	247	0.049	0.053	0.045	-0.005	-1.10	27.3	15/31	100.0	0.004
Coefficient of variation in profit (five subsequent years)	266	0.29	0.52		-0.23	-2.53	1.2	13/31	47.3	
Growth (five previous years)										
Total assets	247	12.62	9.81		2.81		5.0*			
Sales	247	12.59	9.75		2.81		5.0*			
Leverage	247	0.229	0.174	0.179	0.055	5.43	0.0	24/31	0.3	0.050*

*Significant at 5 percent level or better.

sales ratio for the acquiring firms was weakly greater than that of the acquired companies. The acquiring firms grew significantly faster than the firms they acquired over the five years preceding the merger and had significantly higher leverage ratios in the year before the merger.

Table 9–10 compares the acquiring firms with their matched pairs and base industries five years after the merger. The acquiring firms have grown significantly faster than the control group firms and are now significantly larger than they on the basis of all possible comparisons.

During the five years following the mergers, the profit rates of all firms declined. This reflects the deterioration in the United States economy during the early 1970s. A large fraction of our merger sample will overlap with this period for some portion of its five-year postmerger period. The figures in Table 9–10 suggest a somewhat greater deterioration in the profitability of the acquiring firms than for other firms in their industry. While the acquiring firms had significantly higher profit rates before the merger than their industry averages, based on both assets and sales deflators, five years after the merger only their profit-assets ratio was greater than that for the industry. The difference between profit-sales ratio had now fallen to insignificance. Both measures of profitability were now higher for the control group, but neither difference was statistically significant. The mean coefficient of variation in profits for the acquiring firms dropped noticeably and was now significantly less than that of the control group. This suggests that the mergers may have reduced the inherent riskiness of the acquiring companies. The fraction of industries for which this held was not statistically different from 0.50, however, so the result may be an artifact of aggregation bias. The leverage ratios of all companies rose, and acquiring firms remained significantly more levered than both the average firm in their industries and their size-matched control group company.

RESULTS FROM THE SPECIFIC TESTS

With these general impressions of the characteristics of acquiring and acquired firms in mind, we are ready to examine the results for the specific tests developed in Chapter 2. Readers wishing detailed discussions of these tests should consult Chapter 2 and its appendix. The presentation of test results here follows the order and numbering of that appendix.

Table 9–11 presents the results for the first determinants test. The average size of a pair of merging firms is compared with the average size of a pair of randomly selected firms, matched to the acquiring and acquired firms, respectively, by industry. Here it is perhaps worth noting that the control group is not the same size-matched control group used in the

Table 9–11.   Determinants (test 1): Size Comparisons (two merging firms compared with a randomly selected pair matched by industry; figures are for year preceding the merger)

Variable	N_1, N_2	Mean Values ('000,000)		Differ-ence $(X_1 - X_2)$	t	t Sig. Level	Indus-tries $+/Total$	Sig. Level
		X_1 AGAD	X_2 MAGMAD					
Geometric means								
1.1 Sales	285	386.2	286.8	99.4	3.40	0.1	18/31	47.3
1.2 Total assets	286	293.5	216.3	77.2	3.25	0.1	20/31	15.0
1.3 Plant and equipment	285	93.2	70.4	22.8	2.45	1.5	13/31	47.3
Arithmetic means								
1.1a Sales	285	639.9	538.4	101.5	1.28	20.0	18/31	47.3
1.2a Total assets	286	560.4	476.5	84.0	0.97	33.4	17/31	72.0
1.3a Plant and equipment	285	252.7	208.9	43.8	0.89	37.2	15/31	100.0

comparisons in Tables 9–7 through 9–10 and in all subsequent tests, but a random sample matched only by industry. The merging firms are on average larger than their randomly selected matched pairs. The differences are statistically significant for the geometric means; not so for the arithmetic means. Since the size distribution is likely to be log normal, the former comparison is most legitimate. The industry-by-industry comparisons suggest that the significance of this difference may be due to aggregation bias. Under no circumstance can we accept the hypothesis that the merging firms tend to be smaller than a random pair from the same industries. Thus, the hypothesis that mergers take place among relatively small firms to achieve the efficiency advantage of size must be rejected.[4] Merging companies are on average either as big or bigger than firms drawn at random from their respective industries.

It is of course true that economies of scale, as traditionally defined, are more plausible with respect to horizontal mergers than for conglomerate and vertical integration mergers. The three size comparisons of test 1 were repeated, therefore, for the subsample of twenty-eight horizontal mergers that we have. For all three measures of size, the geometric mean of the merging sample exceeded that of the randomly selected control group, although in no case was the difference statistically significant.

The second set of tests compares acquired and acquiring firms to their size-matched pairs on the basis of risk. The first row in Table 9–12 compares the relative variability in profits for a merging pair with that for their size-matched nonmerging pairs. No statistical difference exists, nor does any statistical difference emerge in the spread of their leverage ratios (row 2). There is a greater variance in the leverage ratios across the sample

Table 9–12. Determinants (test 2): Risk Comparisons

Variable	N_1, N_2	Company Type		Mean Values		Difference $(X_1 - X_2)$	$t(F)$	$t(F)$ Sig. Level	Industry +/Total	Sig. Level
				X_1	X_2					
2.1 Coefficient of variation in profit (high-low)	284	AG, AD	MAG, MAD	7.22	6.25	0.97	0.32	74.9		
2.2 Leverage ratio (mean absolute difference)	277	AG, AD	MAG, MAD	0.138	0.148	−0.010	−0.81	41.8		
2.3 Leverage ratio (variance)	286	AG	MAG	0.018	0.013	0.005	(1.36)			
2.4 Leverage ratio	287	AG	MAG	0.19	0.15	0.04	3.88	0	22/31	2.9
2.5 Leverage ratio (variance)	284	AD	MAD	0.015	0.013	0.002	(1.13)			
2.6 Leverage ratio	285	AD	MAD	0.13	0.13	−0.00	−0.42	67.5	8/21	38.3

Table 9–13. Determinants (test 3 and 4): Premerger High-Low and Mean Value P/E Ratios, Acquired Companies Versus Matched Sample

Variable	N_1, N_2	Mean Values		Differ- ence $(X_1 - X_2)$	t	t Sig. Level	Indus- tries +/Total	Sig. Level
		X_1 AD	X_2 MAD					
3. Ratio of high to low P/E in years (geometric means)								
3.1 $(t - 1)$	218	1.59	1.76	−0.27	−4.11	0	6/33	0
3.2 $(t - 1, t - 2)$	218	1.57	1.72	−0.25	−4.40	0	8/33	0.5
3.3 $(t - 1, t - 2, t - 3)$	218	1.55	1.71	−0.16	−4.85	0	8/33	0.5
4. Mean P/E in years								
4.1 $(t - 1)$	218	17.1	19.7	−2.6	−0.80	42.3	15/33	72.8
4.2 $(t - 1, t - 2)$	218	19.8	18.7	1.1	0.33	73.9	15/33	72.8
4.3 $(t - 1, t - 2, t - 3)$	218	18.5	18.5	0	−0.01	99.5	18/33	72.8

of acquiring firms, however, compared with the matched nonacquiring firm sample (row 3). The mean leverage for the acquiring firms is significantly greater than for the nonacquiring firms (row 4), as we observed in the previous section. Thus, acquiring firms are extreme both in the average level of their leverage and in its variability across firms. The same cannot be said for the firms they acquired. Both the mean leverage ratios and the variance across the sample were insignificantly different for the matched samples of acquired and nonacquired firms (rows 6 and 5).

In Table 9–13 the results for both the disturbance theory and the bargain theory are presented. The disturbance theory is resoundingly rejected. The dispersion in P/E ratios for acquired firms is significantly less than that of their size-matched counterparts. If anything can be concluded from this test, it is that acquired firms appeared relatively attractive because there was *less* speculation as to their future performance than for firms that were otherwise similar.

No support is found for the bargain theory (4.1–4.3). Some drop in the average P/E ratio for an acquired firm relative to the control group does occur in the year immediately preceding the merger, but the differences in sample means are insignificant in all three comparisons.

Tables 9–14, 9–15, and 9–16 present the results for three sets of tests of the effects of the merger on the merging companies' profitability. The first, Table 9–14, compares the change in profitability of the merging firms with that of their two control group companies between three years after and five years before the merger. The after merger data were cut off at three years to preserve observations. Eleven of the twelve mean profit rate differences are negative, indicating again that the typical postmerger period was one of declining economic activity. The first three rows of Table

Table 9–14. Effects (test 5): Difference in Profitability, Three Years After the Merger and Five Years Before, Merging Firms Against Control Group

Variable	N_1, N_2	Mean Values X_1 AGAD	Mean Values X_2 MAGMAD	Differ- ence $(X_1 - X_2)$	t	t Sig. Level	Indus- tries +/Total	Sig. Level
5.1a Pretax profit– equity	247	−0.094	−0.010	−0.084	−0.83	40.9	16/30	85.6
5.2a Pretax profit– assets	247	−0.059	−0.021	−0.038	−0.92	36.1	16/30	85.6
5.3a Pretax profit– sales	246	−0.041	−0.012	−0.029	−0.89	37.4	18/30	36.2
5.1b Posttax profit– equity	278	0.006	−0.005	0.011	2.30	2.16	17/30	58.5
5.2b Posttax profit– assets	280	−0.008	−0.011	0.003	1.40	16.2	17/30	58.5
5.3b Posttax profit– sales	279	−0.004	−0.007	0.003	1.52	12.8	21/30	4.3

9–14 indicate that the control group firms suffered smaller declines in before tax profits in the postmerger period than the merging firms. None of the differences are statistically significant, however. The last three rows present the after tax profit rate comparisons. All of these favor the merging firms. All three *t*-values are greater than 1, although only the posttax profit/equity comparison is statistically significant. These results would seem to imply that the mergers may have achieved tax savings for the companies involved, even though they did not produce any real gains in performance. Care should be taken in assessing these conclusions, however, for the sample was somewhat larger for the second set of tests than for the first, and thus the result could have been brought about by a change in sample composition. Here it should also be noted that the superior performance of the merging firms holds up consistently across industries only for the posttax profit/sales ratio.

Table 9–15 compares the change in profitability for the merging company between the three years following and five years before the merger, with the weighted average change in profitability of the merging company's home industry. The test is analogous to the previous test, except that the industry of a merging firm is used as the benchmark rather than the control group company. As before we see that the pretax profit rates of the merging firms are lower after the merger than before for all three profit deflators. Two of the three pretax profit rates also decline for the matched industries sample, but in all cases the industries do better after the merger than the merging firms do. All *t* values are above 1, but no comparison is significant at the usual confidence intervals.

Table 9–15. Effects (test 6): Postmerger Profitability of Merging Firms Compared with that of Their Base Industries

Variable	N_1	Mean Values		Differ-ence $(X_1 - X_2)$	t	t Sig. Level	Indus-tries $+/Total$	Sig. Level
		X_1 AGAD	X_2 Industry					
6.1a Pretax profit–equity	237	−0.098	0.030	−0.128	−1.22	22.5	14/29	100.0
6.2a Pretax profit–assets	237	−0.061	−0.012	−0.049	−1.14	25.4	11/29	26.5
6.3a Pretax profit–sales	236	−0.042	−0.008	−0.034	−1.01	31.3	14/29	100.0
6.1b Posttax profit–equity	268	0.005	0.008	−0.002	−0.63	53.1	16/29	71.1
6.2b Posttax profit–assets	270	−0.008	−0.007	−0.001	−0.98	32.6	9/29	6.1
6.3b Posttax profit–sales	269	−0.004	−0.006	0.002	1.32	18.7	17/29	45.8

As before, the performance of the merging firms improves relative to their industries when posttax profit rates are used. Two of the comparisons still favor their base industries, however, and none of the comparisons is significant at even the 10 percent level. Thus, on the basis of the comparisons presented in Table 9–15, it would seem safe to conclude that the merging firms probably did somewhat worse than their base industries following merger relative to their performance before merger. At best, one might argue they did about as well.

In Table 9–16 the actual profitability of the merging firms after the merger is compared with what their profits would have been had they followed industry trends. In all cases the projected performance of the merging companies exceeds their actual performance. These differences are somewhat less pronounced for after tax profits than for before tax profits, as the previous two tests would lead one to expect. But unlike for the previous two tests, the inferior performance of the merging firms holds up across all six comparisons. The pattern is also consistent across industries. Indeed, although the differences in sample means are insignificant for the comparisons of after tax profit to assets and sales, the projected profit rates for the merging firms are higher than the actual profit rates of these firms in such a substantial fraction of industries that one feels safe in concluding on the basis of both before and after tax profit rates that the merging firms did worse after merger than they would have done had they simply performed up to their industries' levels.

On the basis of the results reported in Tables 9–14, 9–15, and 9–16, it seems safe to conclude that the mergers led to an unmistakable deteriora-

Table 9–16. Effects (test 7): Postmerger Profitability of Merging Firms Compared with the Projected Profitability of the Control Group Based on Industry Trends

Variable	N_1, N_2	X_1 AGAD	X_2 Projected AGAD	Differ-ence $(X_1 - X_2)$	t	t Sig. Level	Indus-tries +/Total	Sig. Level
7.1a Pretax profit–equity	241	0.229	0.294	−0.065	−2.37	1.8	1/29	0
7.2a Pretax profit–assets	245	0.105	0.150	−0.045	−1.15	24.9	1/29	0
7.3a Pretax profit–sales	244	0.089	0.126	−0.038	−1.17	24.4	1/29	0
7.1b Posttax profit–equity	257	0.126	0.191	−0.065	−2.66	0.8	1/28	0
7.2b Posttax profit–assets	277	0.059	0.060	−0.002	−0.66	50.7	5/29	0.1
7.3b Posttax profit–sales	273	0.050	0.051	−0.001	−0.23	81.8	3/29	0

The header spans *Mean Values* over columns X_1 AGAD and X_2 Projected AGAD.

tion in the operating performance of the merging companies and, for some, to partially offsetting tax savings. This does not appear, however, to have fully offset the reduction in gross profitability caused by the mergers.

Tables 9–17, 9–18, and 9–19 compare the growth rates of the merging firms before and after merger. The first comparison is with a weighted average of the growth rates of the two matched control group firms. The general pattern is as one might expect: a slowdown in the growth rates of both sets of firms corresponding to the general slowdown in economic activity. The merging companies experienced a greater slowdown in growth rates than their control group firms, however, as measured by all four total size statistics (sales, total assets, net plant and equipment, and employment). For the employment variable, the number of observations available was fairly small, and the comparisons were insignificant. For the other three size variables, the comparisons were generally significant based on both a comparison of arithmetic and geometric means. Although the comparisons were fairly consistent across industries for the two asset measures, this was not the case for the sales variable. In general, however, it seems reasonable to conclude that the merging firms experienced some slowdown in their rate of growth in total size following merger from what it was before. The number of observations on leverage ratio changes was small, and no significant differences between the two samples emerged.

The comparisons in Table 9–17 were also made using data for the growth rates of both samples over the three years following the merger. Although the growth rate numbers are now somewhat less meaningful, the sample

Table 9–17. Effects (test 8): Differences in Growth Rates (arithmetic means and geometric means) Between Five Years After and Five Years Before the Merger, Merging Firms Against Control Group

Variable	N_1, N_2	Mean Values		Differ-ence $(X_1 - X_2)$	t	t Sig. Level	Indus-tries $+/Total$	Sig. Level
		X_1 AGAD	X_2 MAGMAD					
Arithmetic means								
8.1 Sales	132	−3.62	−0.38	−3.23	−2.12	3.5	11/23	100.0
8.2 Total assets	124	−3.91	0.53	−4.44	−2.95	0.4	7/22	13.4
8.3 Net plant	121	−4.49	−0.43	−4.05	−2.36	1.9	7/21	18.9
8.4 Leverage ratio	40	0.77	−0.48	1.25	0.26	79.3	8/15	100.0
8.5 Employees	33	−5.25	−2.02	−3.23	−1.48	14.4	2/12	3.9
Geometric means								
8.1a Sales	115	0.79	1.01	0.78	−1.84	6.7	10/23	67.8
8.2a Total assets	106	0.84	1.08	0.77	−2.01	4.6	4/22	0.4
8.3a Net plant	94	0.63	0.97	0.65	−2.12	3.5	6/19	16.7
8.4a Leverage ratio	3	1.35	0.83	1.62	0.28	80.8	1/3	100.0
8.5a Employees	14	0.46	0.63	0.73	−0.63	53.2	4/7	100.0

sizes are larger. The exact same pattern of results emerges in these comparisons as reported in Table 9–17, with the exception that the pattern holds up better across industries. Thus, the conclusion that the merging firms experienced some slowdown in growth rates seems fully warranted.

This same conclusion emerges from a comparison of the changes in growth rates for the merging firms and a weighted average of the changes in growth rates for the base industries of the two merging firms (Table 9–18). Each of the comparisons for the four size variables indicates a significant slowdown in the growth rate of the merging firms relative to their home industries. This pattern holds up consistently across industries. Again, we find a fairly substantial increase in the growth in leverage of the merging companies, but a high variance so that the difference

Table 9–18. Effects (test 9): Differences in Growth Rates (arithmetic means) Between Five Years After and Five Years Before the Merger, Merging Firms Against Their Matched Industries

Variable	N_1, N_2	Mean Values		Differ-ence $(X_1 - X_2)$	t	t Sig. Level	Indus-tries $+/Total$	Sig. Level
		X_1 AGAD	X_2 MIND					
9.1 Sales	133	−3.56	1.41	−4.97	−3.96	0.0	8/23	21.0
9.2 Total assets	125	−3.85	0.71	−4.56	−3.79	0.0	6/22	5.2
9.3 Net plant	124	−4.33	−0.37	−3.96	−2.98	0.4	4/22	0.4
9.4 Leverage ratio	108	1.62	0.02	1.59	0.58	56.0	14/22	28.6
9.5 Employees	58	−5.75	−2.00	−3.75	−2.75	0.8	5/17	14.3

Table 9–19. Effects (test 10): Differences in Projected Size Variables (arithmetic means) Between Five Years After and One Year Before the Merger (based on industry growth rates)

Variable	N_1, N_2	Mean Values		Differ-		t	Indus-	
		X_1 AGAD	X_2 Projected AGAD	ence ($X_1 - X_2$)	t	Sig. Level	tries +/Total	Sig. Level
10.1 Sales	278	1088.8	950.3	138.6	1.67	9.6	15/30	100.0
10.2 Total assets	279	988.4	856.7	131.7	1.37	17.2	17/30	58.5
10.3 Net plant	277	422.7	394.3	28.4	0.48	63.0	16/30	85.6
10.4 Leverage ratio	205	0.237	0.240	−0.003	−0.21	83.4	16/28	57.2
10.5 Employees	219	45.4	40.2	5.2	1.00	31.7	14/24	54.1

between sample means is not significant. The same conclusions are reached from a comparison of geometric means, except that the difference for the employment variable is insignificant ($t = 0.97$), so these results are not presented here.

In Table 9–19 the actual size variables of acquiring firms five years after merger are compared with what they would have obtained had they grown at the industries' average growth rates. Although the growth rates of the acquiring firms slowed somewhat following the mergers from what they were before, they continued to grow faster than their base industries. Thus, the actual size of acquiring firms five years after merger exceeded that which they would have obtained if they and the firms they had acquired had simply grown at the average growth rates of their industries. Although the differences are persistent across all four size variables, only the sales comparison is significant at the 10 percent level. And for this variable there is an even split in the number of industries for which projected sales are larger than the actual sales of the merged companies and the number for which they are smaller. The projected leverge ratio for the merged company is slightly higher than the leverage ratio actually achieved, but the difference is far from significant.

Combining our conclusions from Tables 9–17, 9–18, and 9–19 with those of Tables 9–14, 9–15, and 9–16, we see a consistent pattern of deterioration in the performance of the merging firms based upon both growth in size and profitability measures.

Tables 9–20 and 9–21 present the results for tests 11 and 12, in which the rates of return on holding a share of the acquiring firm's stock over the period of the merger are compared with those of the control groups. For each test the rate of return on a share of the acquiring firm's stock was computed under the assumption that the stockholder bought in the year before the merger and sold (1) at the end of the year of the merger, (2) one year after, (3) two years after, and (4) three years after. From these rates

Table 9–20. Effects (test 11): Differences in Rates of Return on a Share of Common Stock Between the Five Years Preceding a Merger and Various Postmerger Intervals (acquiring firms versus control groups)

Years[a]	N_1, N_2	Mean Values		Differ-ence $(\bar{X}_1 - \bar{X}_2)$	t	t Sig. Level	Indus-tries +/Total	Sig. Level
		$\bar{X}_1$ AG	$\bar{X}_2$ MAG					
t	219	11.73	2.93	8.79	2.61	0.9	18/27	12.2
$t, t + 1$	219	2.48	−1.43	3.91	1.43	15.5	18/27	12.2
$t, t + 1, t + 2$	218	−4.42	−6.11	1.70	0.69	48.8	13/27	100.0
$t, t + 1, t + 2,$ $t + 3$	216	−7.29	−7.73	0.44	0.19	84.8	13/27	100.0

[a] The assumption is made that an individual bought a share in the year prior to the merger and sold at the end of the year (t) of the merger, ($t, t + 1$) the first year after the merger, and so forth.

of return are then subtracted the rates of return from holding the same stock from five years before the merger to one year before.

Table 9–20 compares the mean value rates of return for the acquiring firms with those of their control group companies matched by size and industry. During the year of merger (row 1), holders of the acquiring firms' stocks earned a substantially higher rate of return on their common shares than did the control group companies. The difference is significant at the 1 percent level and holds up over two-thirds of the sample's industries. After an additional year elapsed, the difference in mean rate of return for the two samples fell by one-half (from 8.79 to 3.91). This difference was no longer statistically significant at conventional levels, but the t-value was still well above one. The result was again found in two-thirds of the sample indus-tries. After the elapse of still another year the difference between the two sample means fell again by more than one-half and became unambiguously insignificant. The sample split fifty-fifty into industries in which the acquir-ing firms did better than their matched pairs and industries where they did worse. Three years after the merger (row 4) there was no distinguishable difference between the two sample means.

The declining pattern of differences between the two sample means sug-gests that the market overevaluated the likely benefits of the mergers at the time they took place. Gradually, as knowledge of the mergers' effects became known, the acquiring companies' rates of return began to follow the same pattern as those of the nonmerging control group companies.

A continual drop in the rates of return on both the acquiring and control group firms is observable in Table 9–20 as distance from the time of merger increases. This is again attributable to the preponderance of early 1970s observations in our postmerger sample years and the declining business and stock market environment that then prevailed. This cyclical observation suggests an alternative explanation for the pattern of results in Table 9–20. A large percentage of the mergers in our sample took place during the period 1965–1968, when business conditions and the stock market were advancing. And a large fraction of these were undertaken by a group of so-called "conglomerates" that were viewed with much favor by the stock market at this time. The larger rise in return observed on the acquiring companies' stocks in the year of the merger may not reflect, therefore, a direct market reaction to the announcement of a specific merger, but rather the generally favorable attitude toward these firms that prevailed at that time and the bullish stock market conditions. By extension, the subsequent decline in the relative advantage of the acquiring firms may not represent the market's reaction to information directly related to the merger-caused performance of the companies, but the market's growing disenchantment with the conglomerates over the early 1970s. Most likely, the results reflect some combination of specific information changes with regard to certain mergers and a general reevaluation of the likely future performance of some merger-oriented companies.

Regardless of what caused the converging trend in the two samples' performances, the results in Table 9–20 imply rather clearly that the stockholders of acquiring companies did not fare any better, over the long run, than did stockholders of otherwise similar nonacquiring companies. Stockholders who got out at the time the mergers took place or were announced—or perhaps simply at the stock market peak—did do noticeably better. But those that stayed with the acquiring firms over the long pull did the same as the control group's stockholders.

Table 9–21 compares the results for the acquiring firms with those of their respective industries. The first noticeable result in the table (row 1) is that the home industries of the acquiring firms fared much better relative to the acquiring companies than did the size-matched firms just examined. Since the size-matched companies are much bigger than the average firm in their respective industries, this finding suggests that smaller firms out-performed the larger companies, at least during the peak stock market years when a majority of the mergers took place.

The rate of return a shareholder of an acquiring firm earned during the year of the merger was nearly 5 percent below that of the average return earned on other stocks in the acquiring firm's base industry, a difference that was significant at better than the 5 percent level. Once again both sample means declined as distance from the merger year increased. Their difference remained relatively constant, however (between 4 and 5 percent), and the level of statistical significance was very near 1 percent over the other three time periods. Thus one can fairly safely conclude that the acquiring firms' stockholders did significantly worse than the typical stockholder of a firm in their base industry in the year of the merger and that this difference in relative performance persisted over the next three years.

Table 9–21. Effects (test 12): Differences in Rates of Return on a Share of Common Stock Between Five Years Preceding a Merger and Various Postmerger Intervals (acquiring firms versus their industry means)

| | | Mean Values | | Differ- | | t | Indus- | |
Years*	N_1, N_2	$\bar{X}_1$ AG	$\bar{X}_2$ Industry	ence $(\bar{X}_1 - \bar{X}_2)$	t	Sig. Level	tries +/Total	Sig. Level
t	230	7.95	12.71	−4.76	−2.22	2.8	9/27	12.2
t, t + 1	230	−1.37	3.45	−4.83	−2.57	1.1	10/27	24.8
t, t + 1, t + 2	230	−8.29	−3.72	−4.57	−2.56	1.1	9/27	12.2
t, t + 1, t + 2, t + 3	228	−11.28	−7.30	−3.98	−2.43	1.6	10/27	24.8

*The assumption is made that an individual bought a share in the year prior to the merger, and sold at the end of the year (t) of the merger, (t, t + 1) the first year after the merger, and so forth.

Test 13 was run, but the projected profit rates for both samples seemed unreasonably high. A programming error was suspected, but none was discovered. Given our uncertainty as to their reliability, we have not reproduced these results here. But the differences and significance levels corresponded to those in Table 9–21.

The results for rates of return on a share of common stock are consistent with those reported earlier for changes in profitability (Tables 9–14 through 9–16). The performance of the acquiring firms was better when compared with the matched sample than against the home industries. The negative findings for returns on common stocks further strengthen the conclusion that the mergers had no beneficial effects on the acquiring firms. The price of a firm's common shares should reflect the market's evaluation of the future performance of the company, while reported profits reflect only the current performance. Thus, the lack of a superior performance by the acquiring firm's shares relative to nonacquiring firms over the period including the merger and the three subsequent years indicates that the mergers not only failed to produce improved operating performances over this period but that they failed to produce expectations that superior results would be forthcoming in the future.

It is possible that the mergers, although failing to increase rates of return on common shares, did reduce risk and thereby increased risk-adjusted rates of return. To test this hypothesis we were limited in Berlin to annual observations of four or five years before and after the mergers. Given the large number of studies in the United States using large samples of quarterly and monthly data, it did not seem worthwhile to compute σ's and β's using these small samples. We limit ourselves, therefore, to a brief review of the existing literature as it pertains to the effects of mergers on stockholder risks.

Several writers have demonstrated theoretically that diversification via merger is inferior to the purchase of mutual funds or the creation of "homemade mutual funds" within the individual's own portfolio (Levy and Sarnat 1970; Smith 1970; Azzi 1978). Simulations of conglomerate diversification have confirmed this theoretical finding (Smith and Schreiner 1969). Indeed, those companies that engaged in the most amount of diversification via mergers had higher market risk (β's) than randomly selected industrial firms (Weston, Smith and Shrieves 1972; Melicher and Rush 1973; Joehnk and Nielsen 1974). Nor did conglomerate mergers lead to a reduction in market-related risk (Lev and Mandelker 1972; Joehnk and Nielsen 1974; Dodd and Ruback 1977). The only study finding any support for a risk reduction via merger hypothesis was by Joehnk and Nielsen (1974), who found that industrial firms engaging in a single diversifying merger experienced a significant reduction in their market-related risk (β's).

More relevant for our purposes are those studies that have examined the impact of mergers on risk-adjusted rates of return on common stocks. Weston, Smith and Shrieves (1972) estimated risk-adjusted rates of return on a sample of forty-eight conglomerates and found that these companies outperformed a sample of mutual funds over the period 1960–1969. Their choice of time period would appear to have added some upward bias to their results for the conglomerates, however. The conglomerates were much more volatile stocks than the mutual funds (their β's were double those of the funds), and the time period coincided with a long stock market upswing. This conjecture is confirmed in a study by Melicher and Rush (1973). They estimate the risk-adjusted returns on a sample of conglomerates for both the tail end of the 1960s stock market advance (June 1966–February 1969) and the beginning of the 1970s stock market decline (March 1969–December 1971). The conglomerates achieve higher monthly returns and risk-adjusted returns than a sample of industrials over the first period but lower returns over the second. Over the entire period their performance is the same.

These conclusions are quite compatible with the results reported here. To the extent that firms engaged in merger activity outperformed non-merging companies in our study, they did so in the year of the merger. A large fraction of these years will be in the late 1960s stock market boom years, for which Weston, Smith and Shrieves (1972) and Melicher and Rush (1973) found superior conglomerate performances. The Melicher-Rush findings of inferior conglomerate performance in the first years of the recession are consistent with our findings of deteriorating market performance of the merging firms' stocks with increasing time from the merger. Thus, it would not appear that our findings would be overturned by the calculation of risk-adjusted return statistics.[5]

CONCLUSIONS

The pattern of results emerging from this series of tests is both internally consistent and consistent with the bulk of findings to date on mergers in the United States. To be sure, some differences between our results and other studies exist, but these do not appear to be of such magnitude to cast serious doubt on our ability to draw conclusions on the basis of the existing knowledge of the determinants and effects of mergers. In this section we summarize these conclusions, drawing on both our own results and those of others where the latter seem relevant.

Acquiring firms are noticeably different from other firms in their industries. They are definitely bigger, faster growing, and more highly levered. Whether they are more or less profitable than other firms is more difficult to say. Two studies that looked only at a sample of 1960s conglomerates found them to have lower profit rates than otherwise comparable but nonmerging firms (Weston and Mansinghka 1971; Melicher and Rush 1974). The present study found the acquiring firms to be more profitable than the average firm in their respective industries, but equally profitable to nonmerging firms matched by industry and size. The present study includes horizontal and vertical acquisitions as well as conglomerates and firms making one or two conglomerate acquisitions as well as the heavy acquirers. It also covers a later period than the Weston-Mansinghka and Melicher-Rush studies, and thus some of the firms may exhibit higher profit rates because of earlier acquisitions of firms with higher profits than themselves. These and other studies have found acquiring firms to be bigger and more highly levered than otherwise comparable companies, as did the present study. Thus, these characteristics can be taken as well established.

The companies that were acquired between 1962 and 1972 were smaller than the average firm in their industry, but indistinguishable in all other respects from size-matched nonacquired firms. These findings are similar to those of Melicher and Rush (1974), but differ somewhat from those of Stevens (1973). Stevens found that acquired firms were less levered and more liquid than nonacquired companies.

Of the several possible hypotheses of the determinants of mergers, only a reduction in leverage or an increased capacity to issue more debt emerged as possible causes of mergers. Economies of scale motives were rejected because the merging companies were if anything bigger than nonmerging firms. Economic disturbances and the bargain theory were similarly rejected. Of the different tests for risk reduction, the only statistically significant result we came up with was that acquiring firms had significantly higher leverage ratios than size-matched nonacquirers. Combining this with our finding that the acquired companies had significantly lower leverage ratios than the acquiring firms, we cannot reject the hypothesis that the mergers were motivated to reduce the riskiness of the acquiring companies' debt-equity position and/or to allow for an expansion of debt outstanding. This interpretation is broadly consistent with the findings of Stevens (1973) and Melicher and Rush (1974).

The results for the effects tests paint a surprisingly consistent picture. Mergers led to a reduction in the profitability of the merging firms and a slowdown in their rate of growth in size. Some tax savings appear to be generated through merger, but not enough to offset the deterioration in operating performance of the merging companies. This deterioration in operating performance of the acquiring companies was also reflected in a deterioration in the relative performance of their common shares. Stockholders who purchased common shares in a firm making an acquisition one year before the acquisition and sold them three years thereafter did either no better or significantly worse than shareholders holding reasonable alternative shares over the same time periods.

Our findings resemble those of several other studies that have found that mergers do not improve the profitability of the merging companies and lead to no increase or even declines in the rates of return on the acquiring companies' shares, with or without adjustment for risk (see in particular Hogarty 1970b; Melicher and Rush 1973; and for a survey, Mueller 1977).

Our results for the United States, along with the many other studies of mergers in this country, raise several questions as to why these mergers take place, what their possible social advantages are, and what their social costs are. Since these questions arise with respect to the other countries' results also, we shall address them in our overview of the full set of studies (Chapter 11).

NOTES

1. The literature and statistics on the first two merger waves have been surveyed by Markham (1955) and Reid (1968: chs. 3 and 4). The recent wave is described by Reid (1968: ch.5) and Steiner (1975: ch.1). The evidence linking stock market and merger activity is discussed by all three of these writers, and is most persuasively developed by Nelson (1966).
2. The number of acquisitions listed here is only the number for which we have data on the acquired firm. Typically, these firms made many more acquisitions than those for which we have data.
3. This implies that the control group firms may have made one or more small acquisitions over the period for which we did not have data on the acquired firm or that they engaged in larger acquisitions outside of the 1962–1972 period.
4. A significant bias exists in the sampling procedure in favor of the acceptance of this hypothesis. The control group firms were all drawn from the COMPUSTAT tape. The acquired firms and occasionally an acquiring firm were often taken out of Moody's when not available on the COMPUSTAT tape. Since the typical firm that is in Moody's but not on

the COMPUSTAT tape is smaller than the average COMPUSTAT firm, the merging firm sample is biased downward in size. This is apparent in the size comparisons of Table 9–8. The geometric means of the size variables for the acquired firms bordered on being statistically smaller than their "size-matched" pairs drawn from the COMPUSTAT tape.

5. This conclusion is further borne out by an exmination of the several other studies that have estimated the returns to common shares for merging companies. Space precludes a full review of these studies here, but see Mueller (1977).

Chapter 10

A Cross-National Comparison
of the Results

Dennis C. Mueller

CHARACTERISTICS OF THE
MERGING FIRMS

In this chapter we review the basic results from each country study and attempt to derive general conclusions as to the determinants and effects of mergers in Western developed countries. We seek here to determine whether common tendencies exist across all countries and, if they do, to examine the implications of our findings for the various theories that have been put forward to explain the determinants and effects of mergers.

Table 10–1 summarizes the basic comparisons of the characteristics of the acquiring and acquired firms as reported in each country's study. The inequality signs are meant to indicate statistically significant differences. Thus, $\simeq$ implies no statistically significant difference, $>$ a positive and significant difference, and so forth. The table does not attempt to summarize all of the comparisons of size, profitability, and the other variables presented in the earlier chapters, but instead tries to generalize over the several measures of each characteristic used. In some cases, however, inconsistencies existed from one measure to another. To allow for these, and to indicate possibly weak statistical significance, we have used the symbols $\geq$ and $\leq$. When one of these is used (e.g., $\geq$), one can safely reject

Table 10–1. Summary of Characteristics of Acquiring and Acquired Firms

Country	Size			Profitability		
	AG versus MIND or C	AG, AD	AD versus MIND or C	AG versus MAG or C	AG, AD	AD versus MAD or C
Belgium	AG > C	AG > AD	AD ≈ C	AG < C	AG ≈ AD	AD ≤ C
Federal Republic of Germany	AG > MAG	AG > AD	AD ≥ MAD	AG ≈ MAG	AG ≥ AD	AD < MAD
France	AG > MIND	AG > AD	AD < MIND	AG ≥ MAG	AG ≥ AD	AD ≤ MAD
Netherlands*	AG > C	AG > AD	AD ≈ C	AG ≤ MAG	AG ≈ AD	AD ≈ MAD
Sweden	AG > MIND	AG > AD	AD < MIND	AG ≈ MAG	AG ≥ AD	AD ≈ MAG
United Kingdom	AG > C	AG > AD	AD ≥ C	AG ≈ MAG	AG > AD	AD < MAD
United States	AG > MIND	AG > AD	AD < MIND	AG ≈ MAG	AG ≈ AD	AD ≈ MAD

Country	Profit Variability			Leverage			Growth		
	AG versus MAG or C	AG, AD	AD versus MAD or C	AG versus MAG or C	AG, AD	AD versus MAD or C	AG versus MAG or C	AG, AD	AD versus MAD or C
Belgium	AG ≤ C	AG ≈ AD	AD ≈ C	AG ≈ C	AG ≥ AD	AD < C	AG > C	AG > AD	AD ≈ C
Federal Republic of Germany	AG < MAG	AG < AD	AD < MAD	AG > MAG	AG ≈ AD	AD ≈ MAD	AG ≈ MAG	AG ≥ AD	AG < MAD
France	AG ≈ MAG	AG ≤ AD	AD ≈ MAD	AG ≈ MAD	AG ≈ AD	AD > MAD	AG ≈ MAG	AG ≈ AD	AD ≈ MAD
Netherlands*	AG ≤ MAG	AG ≤ AD	AD ≥ MAD	AG ≈ MAG	AG ≈ AD	AD ≈ MAD	AG ≈ MAG	AG > AD	AD ≈ MAD
Sweden	AG ≈ MIND	AG ≤ AD	AD ≈ MIND	AG ≈ MIND	AG ≈ AD	AD ≈ MIND	AG ≈ MAG	AG > AD	AD ≈ MAD
United Kingdom	AG ≈ MAG	AG ≤ AD	AD ≥ MAD	AG > MAG	AG > AD	AD > MAD	AG > MAG	AG > AD	AD ≤ MAD
United States	AG ≈ MAG	AG ≈ AD	AD ≤ MAD	AG > MAG	AG > AD	AD ≈ MAD	AG > MAG	AG > AD	AD ≈ MAD

* Based on separate calculations for purpose of these comparisons.

AG = acquiring firm. MAG = matched AG. MIND = matched industry.
AD = acquired firm. MAD = matched AD. C = control group.

≈ = about equal.
≥ = greater than or equal.
≤ = less than or equal.

the complementary inequality (e.g., <), but one should probably reserve judgment as to whether a statistically significant relationship in the implied direction holds.

The first set of comparisons are of the size of the acquiring and acquired firms. These results are quite consistent across all countries. Acquiring firms are larger than randomly selected firms from their industries, larger than the average firm in their industries, and larger than the firms they acquire. In all countries save the United Kingdom and West Germany, the acquired firms are smaller than the average firm in their industries or appear to have been drawn at random from their industries.

In Belgium and the Netherlands the acquiring firms were somewhat less profitable than the control group companies; in France, slightly more so. In the other four countries the two groups appeared to be roughly equal in profitability. In contrast, the acquired firms tended to be either as or less profitable than the control group companies. Thus, the acquiring companies turned out to be as profitable or more profitable than the firms they acquired. No evidence of defensive acquisitions is thus found in any of our countries. In France, West Germany, and the United Kingdom the results are consistent with a "failing firm" hypothesis, although the hypothesis that the companies were actually failing was not tested.

Dramatic differences in the variability of profits were not observed across the seven countries. Where differences existed between acquiring firms and their control group companies—Belgium, West Germany, and the Netherlands—the acquiring firms had less volatile profits. No clear pattern emerged between the acquired companies and their control samples. In general, bigger firms have less variable profit rates than smaller ones, however, and this was true in our studies. Thus, in four of the seven countries profits were less variable for the acquiring companies than for the companies they acquired. In all countries, the acquiring firms were either as highly levered as or more levered than the control group firms. In France and the United Kingdom the acquired firms also tended to be somewhat more highly levered, but in Belgium the reverse occurred. In all cases the acquiring firms were either as highly levered as or more highly levered than the companies they acquired.

A fairly consistent pattern of growth rate differences holds up across all countries. Acquiring firms grow as fast or faster than the size-matched or control group nonacquiring firms. Acquired firms grow as fast as their control group companies, except in the United Kingdom where they grow a bit more slowly and in West Germany where they grow considerably more slowly. Acquiring firms thus are generally faster growing than the companies they acquire. The latter proposition holds for every country but France, where acquiring and acquired firms grow at roughly equal rates.

Table 10–2. Summary of Determinants Tests

Country	Test 1 Size	Coefficient of variation in profits	Test 2, Risk Leverage (mean abs. difference)
Belgium	AG AD > MAG MAD AG AD > MIND	AG AD ≥ MAG MAD	AG AD ≃ MAG MAD
Federal Republic of Germany	AG AD > MAG MAD	AG AD ≤ MAG MAD	AG AD ≤ MAG MAD
France	AG AD ≃ MIND	AG AD ≃ MAG MAD	AG AD ≤ MAG MAD
Netherlands	AG AD ≃ MAG MAD	AG AD ≃ MAG MAD	AG AD ≃ MAG MAD
Sweden	AG AD ≃ MIND	AG AD ≤ MAG MAD	AG AD ≃ MAG MAD
United Kingdom	AG AD > MAG MAD	AG AD ≃ MAG MAD	AG AD > MAG MAD
United States	AG AD > MAG MAD	AG AD ≃ MAG MAD	AG AD ≃ MAG MAD

Notes: See Table 10–1.

With respect to three characteristics, a consistent pattern has emerged across all countries. Acquiring firms tend to be large, fast growing, highly levered companies relative to the firms they acquire and often relative to randomly selected control group companies. Less consistency exists for the profit variables. Profitability seems to be positively related to size in some countries, while profit variability is inversely related to size, so that a pattern of higher profit levels and lower profit variability of acquiring firms vis-à-vis the firms they acquire is discernable. Exceptions to these patterns exist in some countries for some comparisons, but no alternative pattern emerges within any one country.

THE DETERMINANTS OF MERGERS

Economies of Scale

The first determinants test attempted to see whether merging firms were smaller than randomly selected pairs of companies matched by industry, as might be expected if the companies merged because they were of less than minimum efficient size in some way. The economies of scale motive was consistently rejected (see Table 10–2). Merging companies were on average as big or bigger than randomly selected pairs of companies matched by industry.

Risk

Several tests of the riskiness of the acquiring and acquired firms were conducted. The first three tests yielded conflicting results across coun-

Leverage (AG variance)	Leverage (mean AG)	Leverage (AD variance)	Leverage (mean AD)	Test 3 Disturbance theory high-low P/E	Test 4 Bargain theory mean P/E
AG > MIND AD ≃ MAG	AG ≃ MIND	AG > MIND AD ≃ MAD	AD ≃ MIND AD < C	AD < MIND	AD ≥ MIND
AG ≃ MAG	AG > MAG	AD ≃ MAD	AD ≃ MAD		
AG ≃ MAG	AG ≃ MAG	AD ≃ MAD	AD > MAD		AD ≃ MAD
AG ≃ MAG	AG ≃ MAG	AD ≃ MAD	AD ≃ MAD	AD ≥ MAD	AD ≃ MAD
AG > MIND	AG ≃ MIND	AD > MIND	AD ≃ MIND	AD > MAD	AD ≃ MAD
AG ≤ MAG	AG ≃ MAG	AD > MAD	AD ≥ MAD	AD ≃ MAD	AD ≥ MAD
AG > MAG	AG > MAG	AD ≃ MAD	AD ≃ MAD	AD < MAD	AD ≃ MAD

tries. In West Germany and Sweden there was less variability in pre-merger profits for merging firms than for nonmerging firms; in Belgium, somewhat more. In France, the Netherlands, the United Kingdom, and the United States no significant difference was observed.

Similar ambiguities were observed when comparing the absolute differences in leverage ratios between merging firms to their size-matched pairs and the variability in leverage in the acquiring firm sample. The acquiring firms were in all countries as highly levered or more highly levered than their size-matched nonacquiring pairs. The same was true for the acquired firms. A greater variability in leverage ratios across the sample of acquired firms was also observed in Belgium, Sweden, and the United Kingdom, while the reverse was never observed. Thus, the leverage ratio does appear to be related in some way to a propensity to merge. The failure of a consistent pattern to emerge for test 2.2, which looks at the absolute spread in leverage ratios between the two merging firms, casts doubt on the hypothesis that a reduction in leverage or a capacity to issue more debt was a cause of the mergers, however. Instead, it would appear that leverage is in some other way related to mergers. If we interpret high leverage as symbolic of aggressive management and a tendency to pursue growth, then it would appear that acquisitions are made by aggressive managers and that the firms they acquire have a wider dispersion of leverages than similar unacquired firms. In France and the United Kingdom, the acquired firms also tended to be more highly levered than the control group firms, however.

Economic Disturbances and the Bargain Theory

The economic disturbance theory was supported in Sweden and Holland and rejected in Belgium, the United Kingdom, and the United States. The bargain theory was rejected in every case. Although stock price movements per se may lead to some mergers, it is difficult to garner a strong case for this hypothesis from the results presented here. The causes of merger must be sought in the real economic variables that affect company performance and their impacts on stock prices.

THE EFFECTS OF MERGERS

Profitability

Tests of the changes in profitability following the merger do not provide a consistent picture across all countries (see Table 10–3). In four countries— Belgium, the Federal Republic of Germany, the United Kingdom, and the United States—the merging firms realized a slightly superior performance based on after tax profits than the size-matched control group companies. In Belgium and the United States the merging firms did not perform better than the average performance of their base industries. Thus, it would appear that in these two countries, the superior performance of the merging companies may reflect a relatively weaker performance by the size-matched control group firms rather than a relative improvement in the merging companies' own performance. In West Germany the merging firms did better than their matched industries but not much better than the control group firms, suggesting the possibility that it was the larger size of the merging companies rather than the mergers themselves that accounted for the merging companies' superior performance to their matched industries. In the United Kingdom, the merging firms did relatively better than both the size-matched and randomly drawn control group samples. In the United States the differences in profits appeared in only the after tax figures, suggesting that no improvement in real operating performance occurred as a result of the mergers. Thus, the inference that mergers have led to improved profitability in these four countries emerges with considerable qualification, particularly when one notes that the differences in profitability observed are generally quite small and/or statistically insignificant. Nevertheless, there is some evidence of improved after tax profitability of merging companies in the four countries.

In the other three countries—France, Holland, and Sweden—there was evidence of a relative decline in the profitability of the merging firms following the mergers. As in the first four countries, the differences in

Table 10–3. Summary of Effects Tests

Country	Tests 5, 6, 7 Profitability pretax	Tests 5, 6, 7 Profitability posttax	Tests 8, 9, 10 Growth in size	Tests 11, 12, 13 Rates of return on a share of common stock	Tests 14, 15 Sharp and Treynor tests
Belgium		AG AD ≳ MAG MAD AG AD ≈ MIND	AG AD ≈ MAG MAD AG AD ≈ MIND	AG ≤ MAG AG ≥ MIND	
Federal Republic of Germany		AG AD ≈ MAG MAD AG AD ≳ MIND	AG AD ≈ MAG MAD AG AD < MIND		
France		AG AD ≲ MAG MAD AG AD ≲ MIND	AG AD ≈ MAG MAD AG AD ≈ MIND	AG ≈ MAG	
Netherlands	AG AD ≈ MAG MAD AG AD ≈ MIND	AG AD < MAG MAD AG AD < MIND	AG AD < MAG MAD AG AD < MIND	AG ≈ MAG AG ≈ MIND	AG ≤ MAG
Sweden	AG AD > MAG MAD AG AD ≥ C	AG AD ≤ MAG MAD	AG AD ≈ MAG MAD AG AD ≈ MIND	AG ≈ MAG AG ≈ MIND	AG ≈ MAG
United Kingdom	AG AD > MAG MAD AG AD ≥ C	AG AD > MAG MAD AG AD > C	AG AD ≈ MAG MAD AG AD ≈ C	AG ≤ MAG	
United States	AG AD ≈ MAG MAD AG AD ≤ MIND	AG AD ≳ MAG MAD AG AD ≈ MIND	AG AD < MAG MAD AG AD < MIND	AG ≈ MAG AG < MIND	AG ≈ MAG*

*Based on survey of studies in the United States.

Notes: See Table 10–1.

sample means were not particularly large, however, and the levels of significance were generally low. No consistent pattern of either improved or deteriorated profitability can therefore be claimed across the seven countries. Mergers would appear to result in a slight improvement here, a slight worsening of performance there. If a generalization is to be drawn, it would have to be that mergers have but modest effects, up or down, on the profitability of the merging firms in the three to five years following merger. Any economic efficiency gains from the mergers would appear to be small, judging from these statistics, as would any market power increases.

Growth in Size

Further evidence concerning the efficiency effects of mergers is contained in the growth in size comparisons. If mergers result in an increase in economic efficiency, costs should fall, leading to a fall in prices and an expansion of sales. This occurred in not one single country. In the Netherlands and the United States a slowdown in the growth rates of the merging firms was observed in the postmerger period relative to the change in growth rate performance of the control group companies. In all other countries there was no statistically significant change in growth rates between the merging and control group samples from before and after the mergers. These results clearly suggest that no improvements in economic efficiency took place as a direct result of the mergers, which led to price declines and expansions in sales. It should be noted, however, that in the United Kingdom and the United States, the acquiring firms were growing faster in both the pre- and postmerger periods than their size-matched pairs. Tests 8, 9, and 10 merely establish that no relative increase in growth at the time of the merger took place. In the United Kingdom there was no change at all (as in Belgium, West Germany, France, and Sweden); in the United States and Holland there was a relative decline in growth rates.

Rates of Return on a Share
of Common Stock

It is possible that the mergers led to either market power or efficiency gains, but that the three to five year periods we had to observe the merging companies following the mergers were too short to reflect these changes in either profitability or growth rates. (Singh, 1971, argued that more than five years are needed before the effects of a company's reorganization become apparent.) The tests of the effects of a merger on the rate of return of an acquiring firm's common shares should get around this problem. Under the usual assumptions made in the finance literature, the capital market is an efficient evaluator of each company's prospects. The current price of a company's common shares should reflect all the information about a company's future performance that is generally available. At the time of the merger, any change in expectations about the future profits of the company as a result of merger should produce a change in the price of the acquiring company's shares. This change in price should in turn lead to a corresponding change in the rate of return from holding an acquiring company's shares.

Evidence of a rise in expectations about the acquiring firm's future at about the time of merger was present in four countries—France, the Netherlands, the United Kingdom, and the United States. In each of these countries, the holders of common shares of the acquiring firms experienced a significantly higher change in the rate of return on these shares between the premerger period and the immediate postmerger period than did holders of the common shares of the size-matched control group firms. In each of these four countries, the differences between the two samples' mean values diminished, however, as additional time elapsed following the merger. Three years after the mergers took place, there was no statistically significant difference between the rates of return earned on common shares for the three samples from France, the Netherlands, and the United States. In the United Kingdom the differences had flip-flopped; the nonacquiring, size-matched companies now exhibited a significantly higher rate of return performance than did the acquiring firms. This superior performance by the nonacquiring firms was still in evidence in the United Kingdom after five years had elapsed from the time of the mergers.

Thus, in those cases where mergers appear to have led to an increase in the expected profitability of the merging firms at the time of the mergers, this expectation was eliminated or reversed in the first few years after the mergers took place. It is very difficult to reconcile this pattern of rate of return changes with the hypothesis that future profitability increases resulting from the mergers were expected, but not yet realized in the companies' operating statistics. Some increases in profitability did appear to be expected at the time of merger, but these expectations seemed to sour as more information concerning the mergers became available. In Sweden there was also a deterioration in the performance of the acquiring firms' different control samples as time from the merger elapsed. Here the acquiring companies went from doing as well as the control groups in the year of the merger to doing somewhat worse three years after.

A suggestion that horizontal mergers might, after the passage of a very long period of time, result in profit increases was present in Holland. In the subsample of horizontal mergers, a gradual improvement in the relative performance of the merging companies' common shares was observed.

This pattern ran counter to the results for conglomerate mergers in the Netherlands and for the full samples in France and the United States, as just discussed. Separate testing of the horizontal and nonhorizontal sub-samples in the United Kingdom did not yield this pattern of change either, so these results for the Netherlands must be regarded as an intriguing suggestion that something else may be going on, at least for horizontal mergers. In both Holland and the United States the merging companies did less well against their base industries than they did against the size-matched control group firms, casting further doubt on the hypothesis that future profitability increases were expected. Indeed, in the United States acquiring firms experienced significantly lower increases in returns on common shares than the average firm in their industry in the year of the merger, and in each successively longer postmerger period.

In Belgium the acquiring firms did somewhat better than their base industries and worse than the size-matched control group firms on the basis of changes in rates of return on common shares. This is almost the direct reverse of the results for actual profitability changes in Belgium. Taken together it seems hard to argue that these results suggest significant present or future increases in profitability as a result of the mergers in Belgium.

IMPLICATIONS FOR THE THEORY OF THE FIRM

In Chapter 2 we set out several hypotheses about the determinants and effects of mergers. We are now in a position to assess these hypotheses in light of the results from mergers that we have gathered from our individual country studies. In so doing we shall also relate our results to other studies, where they seem relevant.

Mergers and the Profit Motive

It is difficult to reconcile the bulk of the evidence gathered here with a straightforward, textbook treatment of mergers as attempts to increase profits by improving economic efficiency or increasing market power. The finding that merging firms are as big or bigger than randomly selected firms drawn from the same industries does not sustain an economies of scale motive. The generally neutral or negative effect of mergers on profitability and growth further suggests that mergers have not led to efficiency gains in the countries we studied. A decline in the rate of growth of sales would be expected if mergers increased market power. Such declines were observed in the Netherlands and the United States, but in neither of these countries was there evidence of an increase in operating profits. Thus, if market power did increase, it would appear to be offset on average by efficiency *declines*.

At least two other studies in the United States have detected a slow-down in the internal growth rates of acquiring firms following their acquisitions (Hogarty 1970a; Lev and Mandelker 1972). This slowdown is sometimes thought of as a "shakedown" or "digestion" effect of the mergers (Lev and Mandelker 1972: 97). By this is implied some reduction in operating efficiency, leading apparently to higher prices or lower quality and thereby a reduction in sales. The possibility of a reduction in sales due to a rise in price to exploit increased market power would be equally consistent with the findings of these other studies, however. Certainly these results do not imply immediate improvements in efficiency and reductions in price following a merger.

The most widely cited study purporting to find an increase in profits resulting from mergers in the United States is by Weston and Mansinghka (1971). They found that a sample of sixty-three conglomerates started the decade 1958–1968 with profit levels significantly lower than nonacquiring control group samples but ended it with profit rates equal to the control group firms. Weston and Mansinghka do not allow for the rise in profit rates that would occur simply because the conglomerates acquired companies with higher profit rates than themselves. The tests reported in the present study avoid this shortcoming by projecting the performance of the newly formed firm on the weighted averages of the performances of the merging companies. The Weston-Mansinghka study also stops at a peak year in economic activity just before a recession during which one expected that the highly levered conglomerates would fare poorly (Reid 1971). A parallel study by Melicher and Rush (1974), which looked at the conglomerates' performance into the downswing of the early 1970s, concluded that the merging firms earned no higher profits than the nonmerging control group companies.

The largest single study of mergers prior to the present investigation is undoubtedly Geoffrey Meeks' (1977) investigation of more than 1000 United Kingdom mergers over the post–World War II period. He concluded that these mergers were typified by "a mild decline in profitability" (p. 25). This conclusion is somewhat more negative than that reached by the authors of the United Kingdom component of the present study. Closer perhaps to the present United Kingdom results, and to the overall results of our cross-national comparison, are the findings of K. Cowling and his colleagues (1979), which are based on a series of detailed case studies. Although they found some evidence of improved economic efficiency, and some evidence of enhanced and exploited market power, the typical merger probably did not result in either.

Any increases in profits that are expected to result in future years from a merger should be reflected as higher returns on the common shares of the acquiring firm at whatever point they are recognized. In the seven country studies, we found no evidence that such future profit increases were expected for as far as three years after the mergers took place. Indeed, one of the most interesting common patterns that emerged, in five of the six countries for which the tests were run, was that the market appeared to revalue the mergers downward in a fairly continuous manner as more and more information about the mergers became available. This same pattern has appeared in several other studies of the United States. Mandelker (1974) investigated some 241 mergers over the period 1941 to 1962 and observed a gradual downward drift in the rate of return performance of the acquiring companies' shares from just before the mergers to forty months afterwards. The same downward drift was observed in a follow-up study by Langetieg (1978). Langetieg pinpointed the beginning of this downward trend more accurately than Mandelker, however. The deterioration in the performance in the acquiring companies' shares begins approximately six months prior to the mergers themselves, at precisely the same time that the shares of the to-be-acquired firms begin to rise rapidly in value. Thus, the acquiring company shares begin to decline at the point when news of the merger appears to reach the market. Dodd and Ruback (1977) examine the stock market's reaction to tender offers. The immediate reaction is favorable. In the month that the tender offer is made, the shares of the successful bidding firms rise by 2.83 percent. Judging from the performance of the acquired companies' shares, this would also seem to coincide with the market's obtaining news of the merger. Starting six months after the tender offer's first announcement, at roughly the time when the consolidations take place, the returns on the acquiring companies' shares begin to decline, however. This decline continues for the next four and a half years and cumulates to 8.6 percent, totally wiping out all immediate gains to the bidding companies' shareholders at the time of the offer and in the first few months thereafter. The net cumulative change in the bidding companies' share performance from the month before the bid to five years after is −3.1 percent.

This general decline in return performance for acquiring companies resembles both our findings for the United States when the acquiring companies were compared to size and industry-matched nonacquiring companies and the overall pattern of our international comparisons study. Nevertheless, it is difficult to determine how general these findings are. An interesting pattern does seem to emerge for the United States, however. Those studies that have drawn the most postive conclusions about the effects of mergers on the welfare of the acquiring firms' stockholders have based their conclusions on the returns earned up to the mergers or up to a stock market peak (see, in particular, Weston, Smith, and Shrieves

1972; Halpern 1973; and Kummer and Hoffmeister 1978). Those studies that have drawn the most negative conclusions regarding the effects of mergers on the welfare of the acquiring firm's stockholders have extended their analysis beyond the stock market peaks and/or beyond the date that the merger is announced or consummated (see, e.g., Hogarty 1970b; Melicher and Rush 1973; and Langetieg 1978).[1]

The study from outside the United States that is most analogous to this literature is Firth's analysis (1979) of 228 successful takeover bids in the United Kingdom. As with the studies of Mandelker, Langetieg, and Dodd and Ruback and the general pattern of results reported here, Firth found that the decline in the rate of return performance of the acquiring firm's shares ran from just before the merger is announced to afterwards. Unlike the other studies, however, Firth finds that the adjustment appears to be complete within a few months. Thus, Firth reaches the conclusion that the market is able to evaluate the apparently negative consequences of a merger announcement within a couple of months, a conclusion that does not seem consistent with our United Kingdom results, not to mention those of the other countries. (Kummer and Hoffmeister, 1978, make the same claim, but do not report return results going beyond a single month past the takeover.) Firth's finding that the stockholders of acquiring firms are made worse off as a result of the mergers and, more generally, that the merger's effects are inconsistent with a profit- or stockholder-welfare-maximizing theory of the firm is, however, consistent with the results of our study.

Mergers and the Market for Control

One of the most popular explanations for mergers in recent years has been the hypothesis that they replace inefficient management and discipline managers to pursue stockholder-welfare-maximizing policies. Several studies in the United States have found that acquired firms generally (Halpern 1973; Mandelker 1974; Asquith 1979), and takeover targets in particular (Smiley 1976; Kummer and Hoffmeister 1978), have significantly worse common share performance in the premerger period than the average firm in the market. The latter has also been found by Firth (1979) for the United Kingdom. On the other hand, Langetieg (1978) found that the acquired firms, while performing badly relative to the market, were not performing badly relative to a matched control group; and Dodd and Ruback (1977) found no evidence of negative preoffer performance among their tender offer firms prior to the bids. Several studies have specifically tested and rejected a failing firm hypothesis (see, e.g., Boyle 1970; and Melicher and Rush 1974). The existing literature gives an ambiguous answer to this question.

Some evidence suggesting that mergers were a mechanism for eliminating bad management or for rescuing failing firms was noted in our seven country studies. In Belgium, France, West Germany, and the United Kingdom the acquired companies had profit rates somewhat lower than the control group samples. In Belgium, the acquiring firms also had lower profits than the matched samples, however, and did not differ significantly in profitability from the companies they acquired. It is thus hard to argue that the stockholders of the acquired companies were being rescued by more competently managed companies. While the acquiring companies in France were somewhat more profitable than the firms they acquired, the two experienced a decline in their profitability relative to the control groups after the mergers. Thus, evidence fully consistent with the market control thesis, in the sense (1) that below average performing companies are (2) acquired by firms performing better than themselves, and (3) that the two together show an improvement in performance, can be claimed only for the Federal Republic of Germany and the United Kingdom.

Previous studies of United Kingdom takeovers by Singh (1971) and Kuehn (1975) also obtained results consistent with the market for corporate control hypothesis. But Singh (1971, 1975) found evidence at least as strong of selection on the basis of size (the small disappear) as profitability, suggesting that the market for corporate control might not provide much discipline over managerial pursuit of growth. These earlier studies' conclusion that this market, to the extent that it works at all, does so with considerable slippage and uncertainty would also appear valid for the present study. There is much overlap between the samples of acquired and nonacquired firms before the mergers, and much overlap of the acquiring and nonacquiring samples after the mergers. The relatively poor showing of the acquiring companies' common shares in the postmerger period in the United Kingdom also suggests that any gains from taking over inefficiently run companies in this country were insufficient to offset the premiums that had to be paid to acquire them. Firth (1979) reached an even stronger conclusion. He found the decline in the rate of return performance of the acquiring companies following a merger sufficiently large to more than offset the gains to the acquired companies' stockholders.

The conclusion that mergers increase economic efficiency, as evidenced by profit *and* growth increases, was rejected in every one of our seven countries. This finding, along with the other results just discussed, leads to considerable skepticism about a strong version of the market for control thesis that says that mergers are motivated to and in fact do achieve efficiency gains by displacing inefficient managements. But a weak version of the hypothesis—that a company whose profits and/or share price falls relative to other comparable companies has a greater probability of being acquired—does appear to be valid at least in some countries.

Risk Spreading, Economic Disturbance, and Bargain Theories

None of the other theories that have been put forward to explain mergers fared particularly well. The bargain theory was resoundingly rejected and the economic disturbance hypothesis was rejected and accepted an equal number of times. Leverage differences would appear to have something to do with whether or not firms merge, but no systematic pattern emerged across countries. In two countries acquiring firms were more highly levered than nonacquiring firms; in none was the reverse true. In three countries there was a greater variance in leverage ratios across acquired firms; in none was the reverse true. In two countries the acquired companies were more highly levered than nonacquired firms, but in one other country the reverse was true.[2] Thus, it is difficult to conclude that any specific explanation of mergers based on the leverage characteristics of the acquiring and/or acquired firms gets unqualified support. Leverage characteristics do vary systematically with merger activity in some countries, but not to such a degree across all countries to warrant considering these differences as a primary explanation for why mergers take place.

Thus, it does not seem possible to conclude that risk reduction in any broader sense is a major objective behind mergers. None of the (admittedly somewhat crude) tests that we employed suggested that it was. Nor have studies that focused on this objective in the United States, where it would seem mostly likely to be important if it is anywhere, concluded that risk reduction was a primary motive behind mergers (see, e.g., Evans and Archer 1968; Smith and Schreiner 1969; Weston, Smith, and Schrieves 1972; Melicher and Rush 1973; Joehnk and Nielsen 1974; Lev and Mandelker 1972; and Mason and Goudzwaard 1976).

CONCLUSIONS

Our cross-national comparisons of merger statistics have produced some consistent patterns across all countries and some inconsistencies requiring further theorizing and/or data. With respect to the determinants tests, none of the hypotheses examined received consistent confirmation across the seven countries. One conclusion one might draw from these results is that Peter Steiner's (1975) "eclectic" theory of mergers holds; that is, since no single hypothesis explains all mergers, a variety of hypotheses must be assumed to govern. Although the seemingly tautological nature of this hypothesis is somewhat disturbing, it is perhaps the only hypothesis fully warranted by the results reported in this study.

On the effects side, the rather consistent lack of evidence that mergers led to or were expected to lead to significant increases in profits is inconsistent with all the neoclassical theories of mergers. Some form of managerial motive for mergers—as, say, in the pursuit of growth—is left as a sort of residual explanation for why mergers might take place. Certainly these theories would appear to be prime candidates for inclusion in any eclectic set under consideration.

Perhaps the most important findings of our study are the patterns of results we did not observe rather than those we did. At the outset, we expected differences to emerge between the United States and the six European countries, given the much heavier incidence of horizontal merger activity in the European countries. Similarly, we anticipated different results for the United Kingdom and the United States, where the stock market is a highly developed institution, and for the other five countries, where it plays a much smaller role in providing capital and disciplining managers. The failure of important differences to emerge across these countries in a way that can be related to these institutional differences is a significant result with potentially important implications for national and multinational merger policies. We take up these implications in the following chapter.

NOTES

1. I believe that this conclusion can be legitimately drawn from Dodd and Ruback's results, too, but it is not the one they themselves draw. For further discussion see Mueller (1977).
2. Stevens (1973) also isolated leverage as a significant discriminating characteristic between acquired and nonacquired firms for a sample of eighty U.S. companies. He found the acquired firms to have lower leverage ratios, a result found here for Belgium but not the United States.

Chapter 11

Competition Policy in the 1980s: The Implications of the International Merger Wave

Alan Hughes, Dennis C. Mueller, and Ajit Singh

The merger wave that struck both Europe and the United States in the 1960s was of sufficient force and potential economic impact to have set off an intense debate within the international community over merger policy (Cairncross et al. 1974; EEC 1971; OECD 1972, 1974). A primary objective of this study was to investigate over a diverse cross-section of countries the possible causes and consequences of this merger activity. Having done so, we are now in a position to survey the possible policy implications of our results and place them within the context of the broader debate over competition policy that is taking place.

In carrying out this task, two features of the world economy must be kept in mind: the widespread increase in industrial concentration, which accompanied the international merger wave, and the macroeconomic background against which it took place. Rising concentration produced pressure for the exercise of strong antitrust policies toward mergers with the objective of preventing further increases in the share of economic activity in the hands of the largest firms. Of the major industrial countries, only the United States had specific legislation controlling mergers in 1964 (Edwards 1964). By the late 1970s, almost all the leading economies had introduced, or, like the EEC, were considering the introduction of such legislation (OECD 1972). The macroeconomic environment in which the increase in concentration occurred produced equally strong pressures to pursue permissive or promotional policies toward mergers. The massive expansion in world trade, which characterized the long postwar boom, took place in an international community committed to policies of domestic full employment, and to an open multilateral system of trade and payments. Attempts to maintain and improve international competitiveness in these conditions have included, in a number of countries, the pursuit of active, interventionist industrial policies including the direct and indirect promotion of mergers (Cairncross et al. 1974; EEC 1970; Griffiths 1977; Maunder 1979; Vernon 1974; Young and Lowe 1974). Both these opposite tendencies have been reinforced by the simultaneous emergence of high rates of unemployment and inflation in the world economic crisis of the 1970s (Cornwall 1979; McCracken et al. 1977; Mandel 1979). These developments increased the pressures both for state intervention to help unemployment, and for antitrust controls to fight against inflation. They also led to increased pressures for the adoption of less open trading policies (World Bank 1978). In this setting, an assessment of the contribution that mergers on balance have made in the past, and might make in current circumstances, to improvements in economic welfare is urgently needed.

Our discussion of merger policy is organized in four sections. The first sets out the kinds of merger policies in force or under discussion in the major Western economies. The second attempts to draw the implications of our own analysis for the future development of merger policies. Since many of the factors behind the debate over merger policy arise from the problems of unemployment and industrial disequilibrium, it is inevitable that a discussion of merger policy go beyond our own static, microeconomic results. We therefore present, along with the results of our more dynamic tests involving growth, a brief review of some of the evidence bearing on the macroeconomic and dynamic issues most relevant to the current policy debate. The last section then draws together our final reflections on merger policy, emphasizing both the importance of considering merger policy in relation to other aspects of economic policy, and the issues arising from considering national merger policies in an international economy.

FOUR POLICY ALTERNATIVES

One can isolate four distinct approaches to merger policy that have been tried by different countries, are currently in effect, or are being proposed and debated. Actual merger policies in particular countries fall along a continuous spectrum rather than into any distinct groups, of course. But the division proposed here is useful, we hope, for heuristic purposes, and it reflects the divergent *conceptual* approaches to merger policy. We list them from most permissive to most restrictive.

1. *The pro-merger approach.* The government takes an active, entre-
preneurial role seeking out merger partners, encouraging companies
to merge, providing tax and other advantages to mergers.
2. *The tradeoff approach.*[1] The government adopts an essentially neutral policy toward mergers, and weighs the gains in efficiency against
the losses from increased market power from those mergers falling
within certain ranges of size or market share that are thought likely
to have significant welfare effects.
3. *The competitive structure approach.* The government prohibits *all*
mergers that will have an adverse effect on the competitive structure
of the economy without taking into account any possible efficiency
gains from the merger.
4. *The antimerger approach.* The government bans *all* mergers by
companies above a certain size of other companies above a certain
size, unless the merging firms can demonstrate large, net social
benefits from the merger.[2]

Although there is not a strict relationship between one's views regarding the causes and effects of mergers and the choice among the four
policies, the more one feels that mergers' effects are of net benefit to
society the closer one will come to advocating the first policy. This attitude
toward mergers was characteristic of the European countries up through
the mid-sixties. Not only did they not have legislation controlling mergers,
but the governments of several countries, such as France, played an active
role in encouraging them.

Over the last decade, most of the European countries have introduced
legislation to control mergers, and in several countries revisions of the
statutes to strengthen them further are under consideration. These laws
shifted the center of gravity of European merger policy away from policy 1
and toward policies 2 and 3. (For a discussion of present and proposed
European merger legislation, see George and Joll 1975; OECD 1974; HMG
1978.)

The United Kingdom exemplifies this trend, although it started somewhat earlier in that country with the introduction of a merger control
policy for the first time in 1965. That policy was designed as a version of
policy 2 and was aimed at the selective investigation of major mergers with
"The background presumption as set out in Ministerial Statements by
successive Governments . . . that more often than not mergers are beneficial but that a small proportion may be against the public interest and may
therefore need to be prevented" (HMG 1978, p. 23). In practice, for most of
the late sixties and mid-seventies, this policy has operated side by side
with others aimed at promoting mergers as part of an industrial strategy to
regenerate British industry (Hughes 1978). Only about 3 percent of the

mergers that could have been referred to the Monopolies and Mergers Commission were referred (HMG 1978, p. 24). United Kingdom policy therefore fell between options 1 and 2. The recent Green Paper from which the above quotation is drawn suggests reforms designed both to raise the rate of references and to transfer the onus of proof of benefit more toward the merging companies themselves. These suggestions, coupled with the current conservative administration's withdrawal from direct state intervention in industry, mark a move more firmly toward an active version of policy 2.

Policy 2 accepts that mergers may alter market structure and affect competitive behavior, but it also recognizes the possibility of diverse positive effects of mergers on economic efficiency. Thus, policy 2 is concerned with determining the *net* welfare consequences of mergers, the tradeoff between monopoly welfare loss and economic efficiency gain, where the latter may be broadly interpreted (Williamson 1977). To operate policy 2, antitrust authorities must balance benefits and detriments through either a judicial or an administrative procedure. The underlying model takes a neutral position regarding the existence of economic and social benefits of merger and their possible magnitude. It assumes implicitly that sensible case study assessments can be made of the net effect of the benefits and losses that a merger may induce.

In contrast, policy 3, the competitive structure approach, aims at the preservation of competitive market structures as an end in itself. It is concerned with the prevention of mergers that may inhibit competition whatever other effects on economic performance they may have. The more emphasis placed on concentration change, and the more one is convinced mergers have negligible or adverse efficiency effects, the more one will favor this approach. In its strong form it confines the antitrust authorities (whether legal or administrative) to an assessment of the anticompetitive effects of merger, or to an administration of bans on mergers between firms accounting for more than a particular share of a market. In a weaker form, this approach may combine an assessment of competitive effects with an exemption procedure in the hands of a body other than the antitrust authority, usually a government minister. Thus some objective higher than competition as an end itself may be recognized, but its attainment is not the province of the antitrust authorities, and the discretion to make tradeoff calculations is taken out of their hands.

The competitive structure approach may be based on an overtly political or philosophical argument in favor of particular market structures, and the producer behavior thought to be associated with them. Certain market structures and kinds of behavior are by implication deemed to be socially efficient. It may alternatively, or in addition, be based on the argument that the accumulated economic evidence suggests that mergers, on balance, reduce social welfare; and that costly tradeoff analyses by the anti-trust authorities of improbable, or slight, benefits against known and unwanted, anticompetitive structural changes are themselves otiose, socially wasteful, and should not be undertaken (Crew and Rowley 1971). In general terms, the structural approach may be described as concerning itself exclusively with the microeconomic efficiency losses of merger. It is believed that the competitive process to be found in relatively unconcentrated market structures is the best safeguard of technical and allocative efficiency in the usual Paretian equilibrium sense. Problems of macroeconomic performance that remain after the establishment and maintenance of competitive behavior are deemed to be outside the province of competition policy, and are to be ameliorated by the use of other policy weapons.

United States antitrust policy is based on the philosophical under-pinnings of the competitive structure approach. Section 7 of the Clayton Act has effectively constrained horizontal and vertical mergers to the point where no increases in industry concentration, let alone realized market power, appear to result from mergers in the United States. Yet mergers have continued to take place in the United States, and they have prevented a reduction in overall concentration from occurring or have even led to increases. Given the United States' attitudes toward big business and the economic and political power associated with bigness, debate in the United States has begun over whether something akin to policy 4 should not be introduced. The key difference between policies 3 and 4 is where the burden of proof resides to justify a merger. Policy 3 requires the government to demonstrate that a merger is likely to have an anticompetitive effect (but that is all that must be demonstrated) before a merger can be stopped. Policy 4 would ban a merger unless the merging companies could demonstrate an improvement in economic efficiency. Thus, policy 3 comes much closer to a laissez-faire approach to mergers where all are presumed beneficial unless they can be shown to have results on the structure of the economy that are anticompetitive. Policy 4 presumes their effects on competition will be adverse unless the companies demonstrate otherwise.

In Europe, West German policy toward mergers comes closest to what we have defined as policy 3. Advance clearance is required if the merging companies have turnover of above 1 billion DM; and advance notification of the merger if the market share of one of the parties is currently or would become greater than 20 percent. In these respects, the present West German policy resembles United States antimerger policy, that is, essentially policy 3. But the West German law does allow the merging firms to appeal a decision of the Cartel Office to the Minister of Economics on the grounds that the merger is on some other grounds in the public interest. Thus, although it mostly resembles policy 3, the West German law contains an element of tradeoff policy.

The other European countries' policies toward mergers fall in between these extremes. The French Anti-Cartel Act of 1977 would appear to have contemplated a merger policy along the lines of our policy 2, but has yet to be effectively implemented. Both Holland and Sweden appear to be heading toward merger policies of the tradeoff kind.[3]

THREE ALTERNATIVE INTERPRETATIONS OF THE STUDY'S RESULTS AND THEIR POLICY IMPLICATIONS

What does the evidence presented in the preceding chapter suggest as an appropriate direction for merger policy to take? In Chapter 10 an attempt was made to draw some general conclusions as to the determinants and effects of mergers. But our results may not suggest the same conclusions to all observers. We shall, therefore, present three possible conclusions one might draw from the seven individual country studies, commenting in passing on the policy implications of each interpretation. We confine our attention throughout this section to the implications of our own static, microeconomic tests. Macroeconomic and dynamic considerations are taken up in the following section.

Mergers Increase Market Power

In Europe the predominant form of merger has been the horizontal merger, and mergers were found to have had a significant impact on the levels of both industry and overall concentration over the period under investigation. The larger average size of merging companies relative to nonmerging companies in a majority of the countries seems less consistent with a straightforward economies-of-scale explanation, than with the argument that the merging companies are in pursuit of market power. *Ceteris paribus*, the bigger a pair of firms engaging in a horizontal merger are, the bigger their merger's impact on concentration. Since the normal presumption in economics is that higher levels of industry concentration facilitate tacit and overt collusion (Stigler 1964; Cowling and Waterson 1976), it could be argued that the mergers of the 1960s and early 1970s created the potential for higher prices and allocative welfare losses.

Our test for the creation of enhanced market power from mergers requires a rise in profits and a fall in sales following the merger.[4] Clear reductions in sales were observed in only two countries: the Netherlands and the United States. In the former, the profits of the merging firms fell as well; in the United States the weak evidence of profit increase that was observed seemed to be related to tax savings. Studies of the market power consequences of mergers in the United States have typically rejected mergers as a source of increased market power, as might be expected given their conglomerate nature (FTC 1972; Goldberg 1973). One possible bias of our testing procedure against finding that mergers had anticompetitive consequences should be mentioned. All the effects tests measure the postmerger impact of a merger by comparing the profit changes of the merging firms to the comparable changes for control groups either drawn from the same industry, or projected using the industry changes. If the rise in concentration that mergers produce fosters enhanced collusion, then the profit levels of the size-matched control group companies, or of the entire industry, might be raised as a result of the mergers. Thus, it could be argued our choice of control group would disguise the industrywide impact of mergers on monopoly profit levels, while isolating a relative efficiency or cost effect of mergers.[5] Similar charges could be leveled against our sales and other rate-of-return tests. Although this could be a problem in principle, it does not appear to be one for the European countries over the period studied. This objection requires that profits as a whole rise over time. As was argued in Chapter 1, the predominantly horizontal nature of merger activity has at least in part been offset by the massive expansion in international trade and investment flows induced by the formation of the EEC and the GATT (Meyer 1978). Thus, for example, Caves (1979) concludes, from a recent survey of cross-section industry studies in a wide range of economies, that imports have significant negative effects on price–cost margins. In some economies the introduction and enforcement of stricter controls on restrictive trade practices has also been a factor ameliorating the growth of monopoly power due to concentration change (Edwards 1967; Elliott and Gribbin 1977; O'Brien et al, 1974, 1979). Certainly there is little direct evidence that monopoly profits have risen over the period of the international merger wave. Neither post- nor pretax profit rates show any convincing upward trend in the major industrial economies. In fact, as shown in Chapter 1, the evidence is, if anything, to the contrary. In the samples of countries analyzed here, this general downward trend in profit rates is reflected in the declines shown for the control group companies for several of the profits measures used in the United Kingdom, the United States, Germany, France, and Belgium. These trends are undoubtedly dominated by forces that have little to do with merger activity. Nevertheless, it is difficult to see in them the upward shift in profits due to mergers necessary to bias our monopoly power tests, or to suggest rising monopoly power over time.

It is still possible, despite these data, that mergers have resulted in market power increases, but that increased profits have been camouflaged by increased outlays of other sorts at the discretion of managers leading to higher "costs." Two possibilities are suggested by the literature. One is the

Table 11–1. Advertising Expenditure as a Percentage of GNP in the United Kingdom and the United States (Selected Years, 1956–1976)

	Total Advertising Expenditures (% of GNP)	
	U.K.	U.S.
1956	1.07	1.99[a]
1960	1.42	2.29
1965	1.37	2.36
1970	1.26	2.07
1971	1.19	1.99
1972	1.27	1.95
1973	1.35	1.99
1974	1.20	1.92
1975	1.03	1.90
1976	1.09	1.88

Sources: For the United Kingdom, Henry (1977). For the United States, Statistical Abstract of the United States (1977, Table 1445); OECD (1976, 1979).

Notes: The data for the United Kingdom refer to total public and private expenditure on advertising in the press, radio and TV. The data for the United States refer to total national and local advertising expenditures.

[a] The figure shown for the United States is for 1955.

discretionary forms of nonprice rivalry in which companies engage in oligopolistic industries. Chief among these is probably advertising. Table 11–1 suggests, however, that for the United Kingdom and the United States at least, the period of the merger wave saw no increase in advertising's importance relative to GNP. (Advertising expenditures are related to the trade cycle, and the particularly low figures for the United Kingdom for 1975 and 1976 reflect this. Even ignoring them, however, an apparently downward trend remains [Henry 1977].)

The other place where increased monopoly profits might disappear is into higher salaries for managers and other expenditures providing direct benefits to managers. Ideally, we would require time-series data changes in these benefits over time and their relation to merger activity. Instead, we have cross-section data, which are less satisfactory for our purposes but nonetheless show that for the United States executive compensation is higher in more concentrated industries (Williamson 1963), and in managerially controlled counterparts when both possess monopoly power (Palmer 1973). In the United Kingdom the effects of merger on size and profitability imply increases in top executive salaries of about £1000 on average, a 7-percent increase when compared with average executive salaries in the late 1960s (Meeks 1977; Cosh 1975). There is, however, no evidence for the United Kingdom that concentration affects the determination of executive remuneration (Cosh 1975). Clearly, the impact of executive remuneration alone upon profit levels must in any case be very small. A major role for discretionary effects must therefore depend on other kinds of expenditures (Marris 1964; Williamson 1964), and on effects on the rest of the corporate wage and salary bill. As far as the latter are concerned, there is only weak evidence that the labor force in concentrated industries earns monopoly rents as a result of producer market power.[6]

The extent to which profits are utilized to pursue other managerial goals has never been systematically explored. There are suggestions that these may be large, however (Williamson 1964; Mueller 1972; Grabowski and Mueller 1975), and one can conjure up the idea of managers pursuing growth via mergers, which increase market power and monopoly rents, which are used to pursue additional mergers, and so on.[7] The welfare implications of this, however, are less clear cut than those of the conventional analysis of monopoly; they are best discussed with the managerial hypothesis below. All that remains favoring the hypothesis that mergers adversely affected market power is the widespread increase in domestic concentration levels that *ceteris paribus* should have created the *potential* for monopoly profits. That all other things were not equal seems clear. Nevertheless, the increases in market and overall concentration that occurred lend support for the tougher policy options 3 and 4, if one considers deconcentrated market structures as desirable in and of themselves. The case for these policy options is further strengthened to the extent that one discounts the evidence that mergers have improved economic efficiency (to be reviewed next).

Mergers Improve Economic Efficiency

Perhaps the strongest reason for suspecting that mergers improve efficiency, in the conventional allocative or technical economic sense, is that the waves occurred during a period of rapid trade expansion, increasing international competition, and falling profit rates. Many observers thought that mergers should and did take place as part of a necessary structural adjustment to the competitive process. The policies of several countries were predicated on this assumption.

To the extent that mergers represent a kind of stock market "natural selection" process, efficiency will improve for two reasons: first, "bad" management teams are replaced by "good" teams, and, second, all managers have a greater incentive to perform "well" in the sense of doing what is necessary to avoid takeover. Takeover is usually assumed to be most successfully averted by profit or stockholder welfare maximizing behavior (Marris 1964; Meade 1968). General improvements in efficiency as a result of the takeover threat cannot be observed by intercompany comparisons. Nevertheless, comparisons of the acquiring, nonacquiring, and acquired companies can shed light on the nature of the selection process. As noted earlier, detailed multivariate analyses of this process carried out for the United Kingdom (Singh 1971, 1975) suggest that even when it works in the predicted direction, it does so only in a rather limited way and then only for smaller firms. Our univariate, micro-investigation also failed to lend much support to the hypothesis that mergers improved efficiency. We did find that the profits of the merging companies rose relatively (or, more accurately, did not fall as far) in four of the countries studied. This relative improvement was also coupled with evidence that acquiring firms were as profitable or more profitable than the firms they acquired, whereas in general the latter were underperforming prior to being acquired. Although consistent with efficiency gains from the market for corporate control, we would not place too much weight on this evidence. Of the four sets of recorded profitability gains, three were either economically or statistically insignificant, and the other, for the United States, was a post-tax phenomenon only. In addition, such gains as occurred failed to impress the capital markets sufficiently to improve the stock price performance of the acquiring firms.[8] Finally, we could find no evidence that internal growth rates *improved* as a result of merger (although we did find that acquiring firms were historically faster growing than others). These results provide little support for an active tradeoff or promotional policy toward mergers as contained in options 1 and 2. We are left with the third interpretation of our results that mergers neither systematically improved microeconomic efficiency nor increased monopoly power.

Mergers Have neither Improved Efficiency at the Microeconomic Level nor Increased Market Power

In no country did we find the growth in sales of the merging companies stimulated following mergers, as we expected if mergers improved efficiency. Two countries showed a relative decline in sales. In no country was there uncontradicted evidence that the market expected future increases in efficiency or market power as reflected in the returns on the shares of the acquiring firms, even if one allows the market as much as three years to evaluate the mergers. In five countries there was a downward trend in the relative performance of the acquiring firms' common shares following the merger. In two countries this trend proceeded so far that the stockholders of the acquiring firms were relatively worse off three years after the merger. In light of our discussion of profit changes we cannot argue that there were significant operating efficiency gains from mergers. Thus, as in the previous chapter, we reach the conclusion that mergers have not had much of an impact on market power and/or efficiency in the seven countries studied, or in any one country in particular.

This uniformity in the neutral microeconomic effects of mergers in the seven countries could be regarded as the most remarkable finding of our study. We did not expect it at the outset. Differences in the effects of mergers were thought likely to arise because of differences in stock market institutions and bank involvement in mergers between countries, and because of variations in the extent of conglomerate mergers between the United States and Europe. In the latter we expected to find mergers producing large increases in profits and stockholder welfare, and we assumed our task would be to separate these between market power and efficiency increases. That this was not necessary, and that all countries' results looked pretty much the same on the effects side, suggests that common forces may be working to explain mergers in all countries. We have suggested one common force—the managerial motive—in the previous chapter, and in Chapter 1 we suggested the unifying forces of international competition and world trade. But one need not accept these explanations in order to accept the conclusion that the effects of mergers were neither to worsen competition within industries significantly, nor to improve economic efficiency as conventionally defined. This is the third and most easily defended interpretation of our findings at the microeconomic level. Before considering the other aspects of efficiency that are essential to an analysis of mergers, we first consider the implications of this neutral finding for current policy discussion.

This interpretation of our results—that mergers do not have substantial effects on either market power or economic efficiency, and are perhaps not motivated by these ends—is compatible in varying degrees with all four policies. Since some mergers have undoubtedly increased efficiency, and others have increased market power—and even though neither of these effects seems to dominate our results—the natural policy to adopt would appear to be a case-by-case examination of the benefits and costs of each merger, as contemplated by policy 2. Indeed, the only objection that one can make to this policy concerns its possible administrative costs. Policy 1, as a passive acceptance of mergers if not an active promotion of them, can be reconciled with this interpretation of our results on the grounds that business should be free to engage in any form of investment or reorganization it wants to so long as there are no adverse social consequences from these activities. The lack of evidence of significant adverse effects from mergers, coupled with a laissez-faire philosophy toward business behavior, would lead to a passive form of policy 1.

The same empirical results, coupled with a presumption in favor of maintaining deconcentrated market structures, lead to the competitive structure approach. Ironically, a laissez-faire economic philosophy can also be seen to underlie this approach. The market is presumed to be an efficient allocator of resources so long as decisionmaking within the economy is decentralized and markets are deconcentrated. Government intervention is needed only to the extent necessary to preserve this form of economic structure. The absence of evidence of significant efficiency gains from mergers, plus a belief that a deconcentrated economic structure is most efficient or politically desirable over the long run, would lead one to favor policy 3 or 4.

The choice of merger policy, however, must involve more than just the static microeconomic efficiency–market power issues we have discussed, as was indicated earlier and is further evident even from our brief discussion of these four alternative policies. Before drawing our final conclusions about national and international merger policies, we shall review some of the evidence from our own study and elsewhere regarding these broader issues.

MERGERS AND ECONOMIC WELFARE: DYNAMIC AND MACROECONOMIC CONSIDERATIONS

The most important additional set of possible consequences of mergers might be broadly defined as their impact on macroeconomic variables: unemployment, inflation, economic growth, and the balance of payments. We had originally planned to test for the effects of mergers on at least the employment of the merging firms, but data were insufficient to allow us to compare the scant results obtained across countries. We must content ourselves, therefore, with a review of the findings available in the literature.

Mergers and Inflation

The most obvious, direct effect of mergers on macroeconomic variables is probably their impact on prices. Mergers that raise monopoly power imply higher price levels. But they do not, of course, directly imply higher rates of change of prices. Arguments that they do rely on auxiliary hypotheses, which usually revolve around the inflexibility of prices in concentrated markets (von Weizsacker 1977; Scherer 1970). If monopolistic prices are flexible upward but inflexible downward, then two possible pro-inflationary consequences may follow. Short-run anti-inflation demand management policies will be unpopular to enforce because of their relatively high unemployment cost. With this argument, mergers for monopoly steepen the Phillips curve (Goldstein 1972). In addition, the ability to pass on cost increases as a result of market dominance may weaken resistance to inflationary wage claims. The latter are themselves more likely because

Table 11–2. The Responsiveness of Price to Demand Changes in United States Industries by Level of Concentration

Four-firm Concentration	0–25	25–50	50–75	75–100
Percent of industries with prices behaving				
a. flexibly[a]	90	60	45	57
b. inflexibly	10	40	55	43
Total number of industries	10	50	56	23

Source: Nordhaus (1972) and Stigler and Kindahl (1970).

[a] Flexible means rising by more than 5 percent in booms and falling by more than 5 percent in recessions. Inflexible means moving within the 5-percent range.

of the greater strength and organization of trade unions in concentrated industries. With prices inflexible downward, there may also be ratchet effects. If monopolistic prices are relatively inflexible in both directions and generally insensitive to short-run demand changes, then there may also be a tendency to overexpansions in demand management policies, since inflationary effects are felt only with a considerable lag.

In an uncertain, imperfect world, all enterprises have some discretion over prices, and the evidence suggests that both list and transactions prices exhibit considerable inflexibility, though with no particular bias up or down.[9] There is some evidence to suggest that in the 1950s in the United States prices responded more slowly to cost changes in concentrated industries (Yordan 1961), but the reverse was true for the United Kingdom in the more relevant high-inflation period of the late 1960s (Domberger 1979). Finally, Table 11–2 suggests that the degree of responsiveness of prices to demand changes varies relatively little with concentration once the latter has risen above quite low levels. Thus, there is not much support here for the view that mergers for monopoly would steepen the price inflation/unemployment tradeoff although the speed of the response to cost changes rather than its direction or magnitude may be affected.

Estimates of relative wage flexibility are more scarce, but there is limited evidence to suggest that wages are less volatile and less sensitive to market forces (such as unemployment) in dominant firms (Hamermesh 1972). The Phillips curve would imply a higher unemployment sacrifice for a given wage reduction the wider the spread of monopolization. There is, however, little clear evidence that employment is relatively unstable in more concentrated industries (Smith 1971). Evidence on wage cost increases in concentrated industries is more widespread. The relationship between the two is generally positive but unstable over time. The interaction between unionization and concentration makes their separate influences on wage increases difficult to disentangle (Allen 1968; Scherer 1970; Weiss 1966, 1971). Whatever the relative strength of *wage* inflation in concentrated industries, there is not much evidence that it leads to persistently higher *price* rises for those sectors. Studies of France, Belgium, the Netherlands and Luxembourg in the 1960s led to the conclusion that "Concentrated industries appear to behave in the same way as unconcentrated industries . . . [M]arket structure does not appear to have any influence" (Phlips 1971). Similar conclusions appear to hold for the United States except for the periods 1953–1959 and 1963–1969. In the former period, concentrated industries tended to pass on in prices more than their increase in wage costs more than did less concentrated industries (Scherer 1970; Weiss 1966). In the 1960s, however, the position was reversed, and there was a negative correlation between price changes and concentration levels (Qualls 1974; Weiss 1975). On balance, Scherer's conclusion of almost a decade ago still seems to hold; monopoly power is unlikely to be a significant factor in the explanation of inflation rates compared to the usual macroeconomic influences, although it may influence the effectiveness of particular policy prescriptions (1970).

Mergers and Investment

Although the impact of mergers on prices following a rise in concentration is perhaps their first indirect effect that comes to mind, a great deal of literature now exists analyzing the relationship between concentration and various corporate investment outlays: capital investment, research and development (R&D), and advertising.

The link between concentration and R&D, or its direct consequence—technical progress—has been the subject of much debate. Most of the evidence on the Schumpeterian hypothesis relating size and monopoly power to research and development, inventive activity, and innovation refers to the United States. It tends to indicate that in that country neither large firms nor monopolistic structures have any particular claim to progressiveness once some threshold level of size or concentration is crossed (Kennedy and Thirlwall 1972). Similar results emerge for France (Adams 1970) but not for Belgium, where one investigator concluded that "in the large majority of Belgian firms research activity would profit from increased firm size" (Phlips 1969, 1971). The results for the United States have no straightforward implications for merger policy in the European economies. The threshold sizes of companies indicated by the threshold levels of concentration may dictate concerns bigger than the largest relevant European firms.

As far as the diffusion of new techniques—rather than their invention and innovation—is concerned, the arguments from a variety of national and international studies in favor of size and concentration are on balance reasonably convincing. It is clear, however, that the diffusion process is complex, and case study material reflects the variation in the effects of size that surround the mean (Nabseth and Ray 1974; Davies 1979; Freeman 1974). The most careful econometric study on the United Kingdom economy suggests that the most appropriate structure for rapid diffusion will vary with the nature of the innovation, but, in general, it will be characterized by the presence of a few large, comparatively equal-sized firms. The implications for rationalization by merger seem well worth further research (Davies 1979).

Insofar as mergers lead to increasing concentration, we might expect offsetting benefits to monopoly power to arise from enhanced technical progress and diffusion rates. These benefits may vary considerably across industries, however, and the evidence for the United States at least could be used to support the argument that the gains from concentration in that country may have already been exploited. Where we have direct case study evidence of the effects of merger outside the United States, the conclusions are mixed. Mergers involving the largest United Kingdom computer firms certainly seem to have improved the performance of that sector in terms of product quality and corporate profitability (Stoneman 1978). In other industries mergers seem to have led to no *systematic* tendency for improved productivity performance relative to control group firms or industry averages (Cowling et al. 1979).

Nor can one say that mergers, and the consequent increases in concentration they cause, have directly led to increased expenditures on R&D. In the United States, where industry concentration levels were not affected by the merger wave, private R&D expenditures exhibited a slight upward movement over the 1967–1975 period (OECD 1979a, p. 20 ff.). In the United Kingdom, in contrast, the intensive 1967–1969 merger period was accompanied by a precipitous decline in R&D expenditures, which persisted until 1972. Since then real, private expenditures have begun to creep back upward in the United Kingdom, but they are nowhere near their mid-1960s level. On the continent, R&D expenditures have been on an upward trend in all countries, with a break around 1973. France and West Germany exhibited the fastest increase. In Sweden, R&D expenditures have also moved upward quite rapidly over the 1967–1975 period. Since all these countries experienced heavy merger activity and concentration increases during the 1960s, and the United Kingdom perhaps more so than the others, it is difficult to relate these R&D patterns to mergers and concentration increases in any systematic way (again, see OECD 1979a, p. 20 ff.).

A similar conclusion could be drawn with regard to capital investment and the impact of mergers on overall growth. In our study, we found that the acquiring companies tended to be growing as fast or faster than the companies they acquired, or than control group companies, before acquisition. With the exceptions of the United States, and of Holland, the newly

Table 11–3. The Average Rate of Growth by New Investment of Groups of Companies Distinguished According to Their Rate of Growth by Acquisition, 1948–1971

	All Companies	Rate of Growth by Acquisition				
		Zero	Low	High	Appreciable[a]	Intensive[a]
1948–1964	7.5	6.3	6.9	8.6	7.8	11.8
	(1250)	(202)	(542)	(524)	(424)	(100)
1964–1971	9.9	7.9	9.2	11.6	10.6	14.6
	(966)	(188)	(385)	(390)	(290)	(100)

Source: G. Meeks (1977).

[a] "Appreciable" and "intensive" are subgroups of "high" (number of companies in parentheses).

merged companies experienced no change in their relative growth rates following merger. These results, of course, refer to internal growth by new investment and external growth by acquisition taken together, they therefore tell us little about the impact of merger on the creation of new capacity on its own. In the United States, the adverse overall growth effect shown in the international project is reinforced by studies that have investigated sales growth, and internal investment effects (Lev and Mandelker 1972; Hogarty 1970a). These results do not apply, however, to the United Kingdom. Throughout the postwar period, as Table 11–3 shows, merger-intensive firms have had relatively high internal investment growth rates compared to other firms. The performance of the 100 intensive acquirers is particularly notable (Meeks 1977). For the peak merger years of 1964 to 1971, Meeks fit the following cross-section regression to the individual company data underlying Table 11–3:

$$I = a + bA + e$$

where I is the rate of growth by new investment
   A is the rate of growth by acquisition
   e is the error term

In 17 out of 18 two-digit industries, the variables were positively related, and in 9 of them the relationship was statistically significant at the 5-percent level. This evidence must cast doubt on the notion that mergers have inhibited new investment in the United Kingdom. This is an important area for further research, as is the effects of mergers on overseas investment. The issue of overseas investment is particularly relevant for a country like the United Kingdom. As firms need to be a minimum size before their overseas investment can assume significant proportions, mergers by leading to larger firms may encourage foreign investment at the expense of the domestic economy. Thus even if mergers did not reduce new investment in total, they may well still have reduced *domestic* investment (Singh 1975; Blackaby 1978). The neglect of both these issues reflects the lack of emphasis in most merger investigations upon dynamic effects.

As with investment we have few, direct trade effects tests. The limited results available relate to export performance alone for the United Kingdom, and they suggest neutral or adverse effects arising from merger (Newbould 1970; Newbould and Luffman 1978). There are a number of pieces of indirect evidence relating to industrial structure. Enterprise concentration seems unrelated to manufacturing trade performance in either the United Kingdom or West Germany in the 1960s (Maroof 1976), although plant size variables do appear in the United Kingdom to be positively correlated with industry export/sales ratios, and negatively correlated with import penetration ratios (Maroof, 1976). A more disaggregated study for the engineering industries of West Germany, France, and the United Kingdom in the early 1970s, however, could find no evidence of substantial structure/trade performance links (Saunders 1978). All these studies focused in the main on static cross-section relations. From the point of view of mergers and mergers policy, changes over time and the influence of mergers on trends in trade performance are required. None are currently available.

This brief review of literature on the wider effects of mergers on productivity, inflation, balance of payments, and so forth can be no more than suggestive. The evidence is limited, scattered, and far from systematic. However, since these broader consequences of mergers must be central to the formulation and implementation of a mergers policy in the real world, the issues raised point to an urgent agenda for future research.

THE CHOICE OF A NATIONAL MERGER POLICY IN THE INTERNATIONAL ECONOMY

The 1970s saw a general slowdown of Western growth and rising unemployment and inflation rates. On top of this overall pattern, there is still a wide spectrum of differences in the levels of inflation, balance-of-payment positions, and other key economic variables in the Western countries. Despite the relative uniformity across countries of the empirical evidence on the determinants and effects of mergers presented in the earlier chapters, an overall evaluation of this evidence, together with the factors discussed in the previous section, can suggest a diversity of policy responses. The emphasis placed on the specific effects of mergers will vary with the particular national economic context. Even if there were complete agreement on the micro and macro, static and dynamic effects of mergers, the appropriate policy would depend on the weight given to particular effects. For instance, even with agreement over the effects of mergers on productivity or capital investment, the importance of mergers to a country's economic welfare would depend on whether there was substantial unemployment and a chronic balance-of-payments deficit as in the United Kingdom and the United States, or moderate unemployment and a balance-of-payments surplus as existed until very recently in the Federal Republic of Germany. Moreover, the choice of merger policy should not be made independently of other policy formation. For instance, the case for an aggressive antimerger policy along the lines of policy 3 or 4 would be much stronger if the Western governments were to move in an increasingly protectionist direction. As advocates of import controls recognize, such controls are a necessary but not sufficient condition for industrial regeneration (CEPG 1978). It is certainly arguable that a much stronger domestic competition policy would be a useful supplement to a policy of protection (Hughes and Singh 1978). On the other hand, given a continuing commitment to open international trading policies, there may well be policy combinations favoring options 1 and 2. For instance, in small economies such as Sweden, Belgium, and the Netherlands, a high degree of specialization and concentration seems inevitable for successful competitive performance, and a less severe view of the structural impact of mergers may be appropriate. In open trading economies, such as the United Kingdom, policies to regenerate industry by relying on state–business planning agreements or more dirigistic planning methods are less compatible with severe policy options, such as 3 or 4, than with options 1 or 2 (Hughes 1978).

The possibility that merger policies vary among countries, however, raises the specter of clashes of national policy interests. For one generalization across countries does seem possible. Merger activity is likely to continue at fairly high levels, be it in waves or as a continual flow, in whatever form it is allowed to take place in the respective countries. Evidence in favor of this generalization is present in the United States merger history, where the closing of the loophole in the Clayton Act that allowed large horizontal and vertical mergers to take place merely diverted merger activity into conglomerate mergers. The same shifting in the direction of merger activity in Europe can be seen toward the end of the sixties and into the seventies as opportunities for horizontal mergers disappeared, and as antimonopoly statutes appeared and started to be enforced. With this in mind, it can be seen that an uncoordinated choice of merger policies across countries can have an effect on the intra- and international pattern of merger activity. If one country adopts a tough, anti-merger policy along the lines of policy 3 toward domestic mergers, companies based within its borders will be induced to make not only more conglomerate-type mergers, but more mergers across national borders. Countries wishing to adopt a tradeoff policy of weighing each merger's positive and negative effects may find the administrative burdens of this policy significantly increased, if the tougher antimerger policies of their neighbors lead to a large increase in the number of companies seeking to make acquisitions within their boundaries. In these circumstances, the antitrust authorities may well be forced to pursue discriminatory policies against mergers by foreign multinationals. Indeed, many countries already have legislation to control inward mergers.[10]

In addition to possible clashes in national merger policies, differences in policy choices may lead members of the EEC into conflict with community legislation. EEC policy toward mergers has two quite distinct goals. The first has been to remove obstacles to international mergers (especially those arising from differences in company law and taxation) so as to allow the benefits of increased scale and specialization to be more readily achieved without the risk of national monopolization, thought more likely to arise from intranational merger.[11] The second has been to preserve "undistorted competition" as one of the EEC's fundamental aims (Markert 1975; Thompson 1974; Cairncross et al. 1974).

To meet the latter objective, the proposed EEC merger law adopts a stance similar to that of West Germany in placing a premium on competition per se. Mergers are to be prohibited, if they meet certain size or market share criteria and can be shown to hinder effective competition in a substantial part of the common market (which could be a *national* market) such that trade between member states would be affected. Exemption from prohibition in the presence of an adverse competitive effect will be granted only if the merger is indispensable to the achievement of an objective given priority treatment in the common interest of the community. The priority of community law in conflicts with national law (Mathijsen 1975) could clearly raise problems where there are differences in the philosophy behind, or severity in the implementation of, merger legislation at the national level. If national policies were more severe than the EEC proposals, the problem would not be serious, but this has not so far been the case. In the United Kingdom, for instance, it is clear that in principle a merger could be cleared by the authorities, by reference to its impact on the United Kingdom national interest, but could fall afoul of the proposed EEC regulation because it affected trade flows to the detriment of some other EEC members. Jurisdictional conflicts of this kind are unlikely to be easily resolved, and the comment of the recent Green Paper on United Kingdom mergers and monopoly policy on this issue conveys adequately the difficulties involved (even though it is not intended to suggest that they are insuperable). After an assessment of possible conflicts, the Green Paper concludes, "Provided that the EEC regulation was sufficiently *limited in scope* (to the largest *European* mergers) and included *adequate* safeguards for *national economic interests* it was felt that in practice serious conflicts would be unlikely to occur" (HMG 1978, p. 30, emphasis added). Whether this rather sanguine assessment of the potential for a coordinated, if not unified, international policy toward mergers is realistic remains to be seen.

The results reported in this study should be of some help in sorting out the various policy alternatives at the national and international levels. The relative uniformity of results across countries, particularly regarding the effects of mergers, suggests that we are dealing with fundamentally the same phenomenon in all countries, at least at the static microeconomic level of analysis. This conclusion buttresses the case for a common policy toward mergers across the several countries. But the qualitative nature of our results can also be used by those favoring a different policy toward mergers than other countries choose, based on either macrodynamic economic considerations or the political philosophy of the country. Neither the static costs of monopoly welfare losses from a promerger policy nor the efficiency losses from a tough antimerger policy appear significant.

While we feel we have obtained answers to some of the questions raised in current debate over merger policy, we have asked only the most basic questions about the causes and consequences of mergers. Much remains to be done, as we have tried to indicate in this chapter. Our study is but the first stage of research on international merger questions. We hope it has opened the door to further cross-national comparative research on mergers. If others march through this door, we should be able to answer the remaining unresolved issues concerning the determinants and effects of mergers.

NOTES

1. This policy is named after Williamson's (1968, 1977) pioneering analysis of it.
2. This policy could be considered a tough variant of the tradeoff approach with the onus of proof of benefit on companies rather an onus of proof of detriment placed on the antitrust authority. It could also be regarded as tougher than the competitive structure approach insofar as it assumes adverse competitive or structural effects and requires the demonstration of major positive offsetting benefits.
3. The institutional form of the actual or proposed merger policies vary greatly among the countries. This reflects cultural differences and past competition policy developments. All of them, nevertheless, accept the possibility of trading off benefits and losses. For discussions of the proposed changes in France, Sweden, and the Netherlands, see OECD (1978, No. 1 & 2).

4. "Rise" and "fall" predictions are made ceteris paribus, of course. Actual measurements were made against the control group samples. Throughout our discussion of the effects of mergers, terms such as "rise" and "fall" are to be understood in these relative terms.

5. Thus, this bias exists only with respect to testing for market power effects. The test for efficiency improvements is not biased.

6. Although concentration and wages are correlated in several countries (Scherer 1970; Phlips 1971; Jenny 1975), these correlations appear to be explained by higher quality levels of the workers hired in the high-concentration industries (Weiss 1966, 1970; Scherer 1970).

7. This "hypothesis" would suggest that high concentration produces mergers, a relationship that Gort found existed (1969).

8. If one is willing to interpret our results as implying that stockholders of acquiring companies are not only no better off following mergers but also no worse off, one could conclude that welfare has improved. The stockholders of acquired companies are usually better off as a result of mergers because of the premia paid for their shares. The conclusion that stockholders of acquiring companies are no worse off as a result of mergers cannot be drawn for the United Kingdom and United States, however. If one allows the market three years to evaluate the mergers, stockholders of acquiring companies in these two countries are worse off. The downward trends for France, Holland, and possibly Sweden also suggest that stockholders of acquiring firms will actually be worse off on average in these countries with enough time allowed to elapse after the merger.

9. See Means (1972), Coutts, Godley, and Nordhaus (1978), Moore (1972), Stigler and Kindahl (1970), and Nordhaus (1972). There is a great deal of literature on administered prices, which we shall not attempt to review here. Comprehensive surveys are in Scherer (1970), Nordhaus (1972), and Kottke (1978).

10. Indeed, even countries without domestic merger control policies have maintained other policies aimed at preventing foreign takeovers, e.g., France until recently, and Australia (OECD 1972–1974).

11. In this connection, EEC policy would be aimed against the use of domestic merger policies to discriminate between mergers on the basis of the nationality of the partners involved, at least of those of EEC member status.

Bibliography

Aaronovitch, S., and M. C. Sawyer. 1974. *Big Business*. London: Macmillan.

Adams, W. 1970. "Firm Size and Research Activity in France and the United States." *Quarterly Journal of Economics* 84 (August): 386–409.

Alberts, W., and J. Segall. 1966. *The Corporate Merger*. Chicago: University of Chicago Press.

Allen, B. 1968. "Market Concentration and Wage Increases: US Manufacturing, 1947–64." *Industrial and Labour Relations Review* 21 (April): 353–66.

Asquith, P. 1979. "Mergers and the Market for Acquisitions." University of Chicago. Mimeo.

Auquier, A., and R. E. Caves. 1979. "Monopolistic Export Industries, Trade and Optimal Competition Policy." *Economic Journal* 89 (September): 559–81.

Azzi, C. 1978. "Conglomerate Mergers, Default Risk, and Homemade Mutual Funds." *American Economic Review* 68 (March): 161–72.

Bain, J. S. 1966. *International Differences in Industrial Structure: Eight Nations in the 1950's*. New Haven: Yale University Press.

Baumol, W. J. 1967. *Business Behavior, Value and Growth*. Rev. ed. New York: Macmillan.

Baumol, W. J., and B. G. Malkiel. 1967. "The Firm's Optimal Debt-Equity Combination and the Cost of Capital." *Quarterly Journal of Economics* 81 (November): 547–78.

Beesley, M. E. 1968. "Economic Effects of National Policies towards Mergers and Acquisitions." In B. W. Denning, ed., *Corporate Long Range Planning*. London: Longman.

B. E. Q. B. 1977. "Industrial and Commercial Companies: Profitability and the Cost of Capital." *Bank of England Quarterly Bulletin* (June).

Bergson, A. 1973. "On Monopoly Welfare Losses." *American Economic Review* 63 (December): 853–70.

Berry, R. A. 1969. "A Note on Welfare Comparisons between Monopoly and Pure Competition." *Manchester School* 37 (March): 39–57.

Blackaby, F. T., ed. 1979. *De-Industrialisation*. London: Heinemann.

Blair, J. M. 1972. *Economic Concentration: Structure, Behavior and Public Policy*. New York: Harcourt, Brace and World.

Boyle, S. E. 1970. "Pre-merger Growth and Profit Characteristics of Large Conglomerate Mergers in the United States 1948–68," *St. John's Law Review* (special ed.) 44 (Spring): 152–70.

Brenner, M., and D. Downes. 1975. "A Critical Evaluation of the Measurement of Conglomerate Performance, Using the Capital Asset Pricing Model." Research Program in Finance, Working Paper No. 35, Graduate School of Business Administration, University of California, Berkeley, May.

Brooks, D., and R. Smith. 1963. *Mergers Past and Present*. London: Acton Society Trust.

Bull, A., and A. Vice. 1961. *Bid for Power*. London: Eleh Books.

Cairncross, A., et al. 1974. *Economic Policy for the European Community*. London: Macmillan.

Caves, R. E. 1979. "International Cartels and Monopolies in International Trade." In R. Dornbusch and J. A. Frenkel, eds., *International Economic Policy*. London: Johns Hopkins University Press.

CEPG. 1979. *Economic Policy Review 5*. Cambridge, England: Department of Applied Economics.

Chandler, A. D. 1966. *Strategy and Structure*. New York: Anchor Books.

Channon, D. F. 1973. *The Strategy and Structure of British Enterprise*. London: Macmillan.

————. 1978. *The Service Industries*. London: Macmillan.

Coase, R. A. 1972. "Industrial Organisation: A Proposal for Research." In V. R. Fuchs, ed., *Policy Issues and Research Opportunities in Industrial Organisation*. New York: National Bureau of Economic Research.

Cochran, W. G. 1964. "On the Performance of the Linear Discriminant Function." *Technometrics* 6 (May): 179–90.

Cockerill, T. A. J. 1977. "Economies of Scale, Industrial Structure and Efficiency: The Brewing Industry in Nine Nations." In A. Jacquemin and H. W. de Jong, eds., *Welfare Aspects of Industrial Markets*. Nijenrode Studies in Economics No. 2. Leiden: Martinus Nijhoff.

Cornwall, J. 1979. *Modern Capitalism*. London: Martin Robertson.

Cosh, A. D. 1975. "The Remuneration of Chief Executives in the United Kingdom." *Economic Journal* 85 (March): 75–94.

Coutts, K.; W. A. H. Godley; and W. D. Nordhaus. 1978. *Industrial Pricing in the United Kingdom*. Cambridge: Cambridge University Press.

Cowling, K., and D. C. Mueller. 1978. "The Social Costs of Monopoly Power." *Economic Journal* 88 (December): 727–48.

Cowling, K.; P. Stoneman; J. Cubbin; J. Cable; G. Hall; S. Domberger; and P.

Dutton. 1979. *Mergers and Economic Performance*. Cambridge: Cambridge University Press.

Cowling, K., and M. Waterson. 1976. "Price-Cost Margins and Market Structure." *Economica* 43 (August): 267–74.

Crew, M. A., and C. K. Rowley. 1971. "Anti-Trust Policy: The Application of Rules." *Moorgate and Wall Street* (Autumn).

Curzon, G., and V. Curzon, eds. 1977. *The Multinational Enterprise in a Hostile World*. London: Macmillan.

Dalton, J. A., and S. L. Levin, eds. 1974. *The Anti-Trust Dilemma*. Lexington, Mass.: D. C. Heath & Co.

Davidow, J. 1977. "Some Reflections on the OECD Competition Guidelines." *Anti-Trust Bulletin* 22 (Summer): 441–58.

Davies, P. L. 1976. *The Regulation of Take-Overs and Merger*. London: Sweet and Maxwell.

Davies, S. 1979. *The Diffusion of Process Innovations*. Cambridge: Cambridge University Press.

Davis, O. A., and A. B. Whinston. 1967. "Piecemeal Policy in the Theory of Second Best." *Review of Economic Studies* 34 (July): 323–31.

Dewey, D. 1961. "Mergers and Cartels: Some Reservations about Policy." *American Economic Review* 51 (May): 255–62.

Dodd, P., and R. Ruback. 1977. "Tender Offers and Stockholder Returns: An Empirical Analysis." *Journal of Financial Economics* 5 (December): 351–73.

Domberger, S. 1979. "Price Adjustment and Market Structure." *Economic Journal* 89 (March): 96–108.

Dyas, G. P., and H. T. Thanheiser. 1976. *The Emerging European Enterprise*. London: Macmillan.

Edwards, C. D. 1967. *Control of Cartels and Monopolies: An International Comparison*. New York: Oceana Publications.

Elliott, D., and J. D. Gribbin. 1977. "The Abolition of Cartels and Structural Change in the UK." In A. Jacquemin and H. W. de Jong, *Welfare Aspects of Industrial Markets*. Leiden: Martinus Nijhoff.

EEC. 1970. *Industrial Policy in the Community*. Brussels: Commission of the European Communities.

———. 1971– . *Reports on Competition Policy* (periodic publication). Brussels and Luxembourg.

Evans, J. L., and S. H. Archer. 1968. "Diversification and the Reduction of Dispersion: An Empirical Analysis." *Journal of Finance* 23 (December): 29–40.

Federal Trade Commission. 1969. *Economic Report on Corporate Mergers*. Washington, D.C.

———. 1972. *Economic Report on Conglomerate Merger Performance: An Empirical Analysis of Nine Corporations*. Washington, D.C.

———. 1979. "Tables and Graphs on Aggregate Concentration." Washington, D.C. Mimeo.

Firth, M. 1979. "The Profitability of Takeovers and Mergers." *Economic Journal* 89 (June): 316–28.

Flemming, J. S.; L. D. D. Price; and D. H. A. Ingram. 1976. "Trends in Company Profitability." *Bank of England Quarterly Bulletin* (March, June).

Franko, L. G. 1976. *The European Multinationals*. London: Harper and Row.

Freeman, C. 1974. *The Economics of Industrial Innovation*. Hammondsworth: Penguin Books.

Galbraith, J. K. 1967. "A Review of a Review." *The Public Interest* 9 (Fall): 109–18.

George, K. D. 1972. "The Changing Structure of Competitive Industry." *Economic Journal* (supp.) 82 (March): 353–68.

George, K. D., and C. Joll, eds. 1975a. *Competition Policy in the UK and the EEC*. Cambridge: Cambridge University Press.

———. 1975b. "A Review of the Main Economic Issues." In K. D. George and C. Joll, *Competition Policy in the UK and the EEC*. Cambridge: Cambridge University Press.

George, K. D., and T. S. Ward. 1975. *The Structure of Industry in the EEC: An International Comparison*. Cambridge: Cambridge University Press.

Goldberg, L. G. 1973. "The Effect of Conglomerate Mergers on Competition." *Journal of Law and Economics* 16 (April): 137–58.

———. 1974. "Conglomerate Mergers and Concentration Ratios." *Review of Economics and Statistics* 56 (August): 303–309.

Goldstein, M. 1972. "Anti-Inflationary Demand Management in the United States: A Selective Industry Approach." *International Monetary Fund Staff Papers* 19 (July): 344–94.

Gort, M. 1969. "An Economic Disturbance Theory of Mergers." *Quarterly Journal of Economics* 83 (November): 624–42.

Gort, M., and T. F. Hogarty. 1970. "New Evidence on Mergers." *Journal of Law and Economics* 13 (April): 167–84.

Grabowski, H. G., and D. C. Mueller. 1972. "Managerial and Stockholder Welfare Models of Firm Expenditures." *Review of Economics and Statistics* 54 (February): 9–24.

———. 1975. "Life-cycle Effects on Corporate Returns on Retentions." *Review of Economics and Statistics* 57 (November): 400–409.

Greer, D. F., and F. Rhoades. 1976. "Concentration Policy and Productivity Changes." *Southern Economic Journal* 43 (October): 1031–44.

Gribbin, J. D. 1974. "The Operation of the Mergers Panel Since 1965." *Trade and Industry* 17 (January): 70–73.

Griffiths, R. T., ed. 1977. *Government Business and Labour in European Capitalism*. London: Europotentials Press.

Hahn, F. H. 1973. "The Winter of Our Discontent." *Economica* 40 (August): 322–30.

Halpern, P. J. 1973. "Empirical Estimates of the Amount and Distribution of Gains to Companies in Mergers." *Journal of Business* 46 (October): 554–75.

Hamermesh, D. 1970. "Wage Bargains, Threshold Effects, and the Phillips Curve." *Quarterly Journal of Economics* 84 (August): 501–17.

———. 1972. "Market Power and Wage Inflation." *Southern Economic Journal* 39 (October): 204–12.

Hamm, L. G., and W. F. Mueller. 1974. "Trends in Industrial Market Concentration, 1947–1970," *Review of Economics and Statistics* 56 (November): 511–20.

Hannah, L. 1974a. "Take-Over Bids in Britain Before 1950." *Business History* 16 (January): 65–77.

———. 1974b. "Mergers in British Manufacturing Industry 1880–1918." *Oxford Economic Papers* 26 (March): 1–20.

———. 1976a. *The Rise of the Corporate Economy.* London: Methuen.

———, ed. 1976b. *Management Structure and Business Development.* London: Macmillan.

Hannah, L., and J. A. Kay. 1977. *Concentration in Modern Industry.* London: Macmillan.

Harberger, A. 1971. "Three Basic Postulates for Applied Welfare Economics." *Journal of Economic Literature* 9 (September): 785–97.

Hart, P. E., and S. J. Prais. 1956. "The Analysis of Business Concentration: A Statistical Approach." *Journal of the Royal Statistical Society* (series A, general) 119, pt. 2: 150–81.

Hart, P.; M. Utton; and C. Walshe. 1973. *Mergers and Concentration in British Industry.* Cambridge: Cambridge University Press.

Henry, H. 1977. "Advertising Expenditure 1960–76." *Advertising Quarterly* 52 and 53 (complete issues).

HMG. 1969. *Mergers.* London: HMSO.

———. 1978. *Review of Monopoly and Mergers Policy: a consultative document.* Cmnd. 7198. London: HMSO.

Hill, T. P. 1979. *Profits and Rates of Return.* Paris: OECD.

Hindley, B. 1972. "Recent Theory and Evidence on Corporate Merger." In K. Cowling, ed., *Market Structure and Corporate Behavior,* pp. 1–17. London: Gray-Mills.

Hjalmarsson, L. 1977. "Monopoly Welfare Gains and the Costs of Decentralization." In A. Jacquemin and H. W. de Jong, *Welfare Aspects of Industrial Markets.* Nijenrode Studies in Economics No. 2. Leiden: Martinus Nijhoff.

Hogarty, T. F. 1970a. "Profits from Mergers: The Evidence of Fifty Years." *St. John's Law Review* (special ed.) 44 (Spring): 378–91.

———. 1970b. "The Profitability of Corporate Mergers." *Journal of Business* 43 (July): 317–27.

Horowitz, I. 1970. "Employment and Concentration in the Common Market." *Journal of the Royal Statistical Society* ser. A (1933): 463–79.

Horst, T. 1972. "Firm and Industry Determinants of the Decision to Invest Abroad: An Empirical Study." *Review of Economics and Statistics* 54 (August): 258–66.

Hovers, J. 1972. "Overname in theorie en praktijk." Ph.D. thesis, Katholieke Hogeschool Tilburg, The Netherlands.

Hughes, A. 1976. "Company Concentration, Size of Plant, and Merger Activity." In M. Panic, ed., *The UK and West German Manufacturing Industry, 1954–72.* London: National Economic Development Office, HMSO.

———. 1977. *Birth, Death and Survival in the U.K. Manufacturing Quoted Sector 1948–72.* Cambridge, England: DAE. Mimeo.

———. 1978. "Competition Policy and Economic Performance in the UK." In *Competition Policy.* London: National Economic Development Office, HMSO.

Hughes, A., and A. Singh. 1974. "Take-overs, Mergers and Centralisation of Capital: Some International Aspects." Cambridge: Department of Applied Economics. Cambridge University. Mimeo.

———. 1978. "Takeovers Economic Efficiency and a Disequilibrium Industrial

Economy: The Uneasy Case for an Aggressive Anti-Trust Policy in the UK."
Paper presented at the European conference on Industrial Organisation, Nuren-
burg. Cambridge: Department of Applied Economics, Cambridge University.
Mimeo.

Hymer, S., and R. E. Rowthorn. 1970. "The Multinational Corporation: the Non-
American Challenge. In C. P. Kindleberger, ed., *The International Corporation*. Cambridge, Mass.: Harvard University Press.

Intriligator, M. 1971. *Mathematical Optimization and Economic Theory*. Englewood Cliffs, N.J.: Prentice-Hall, Inc.

Jacquemin, A., and H. de Jong. 1976. *Markets, Corporate Behaviour and the State*.
The Hague: Nijhoff.

————. 1977. *European Industrial Organisation*. London: Macmillan.

Janssen, P. 1971. "Groot en klein in de Nederlandse Industrie." The Hague:
Stichting Maatschappij en Onderneming.

Janus, P. R. 1975. "Concentratie en deconcentratie in nijverheiden delfstoffen-
winning." Voorburg: Centraal Bureau voorde Statistiek.

Jenny, F. and A.-P. Weber. 1972. "Concentration et politique des Structures
Industrielles." Paris: Economie et Planification, Documentation Française.

————. 1974. *Concentration et Politique des Structures Industrielles*. Paris: La
Documentation Française.

————. 1975. "French Antitrust Legislation: An Exercise in Futility?" *Antitrust
Bulletin* 20 (Fall): 597–639.

————. 1976. "Profit Rates and Structural Variables in French Manufacturing
Industries." *European Economic Review* 7 (February): 187–206.

————. 1978. "The Determinants of Concentration Trends in the French Manufacturing Sector." *Journal of Industrial Economics* 26 (March): 193–207.

Jensen, M. C. 1972. "Capital Markets: Theory and Evidence." *The Bell Journal of
Economics and Management Science* 3 (Autumn): 357–98.

Joehnk, M. D., and J. F. Nielsen. 1974. "The Effects of Conglomerate Merger
Activity on Systematic Risk." *Journal of Financial and Quantitative Analysis* 9
(March): 215–25.

Johnson, H. G. 1968. "The Economic Approach to Social Questions." *Economica* 35
(February): 1–21.

Jong, H. W. de. 1971a. "Concentration in Benelux." In H. Arndt, ed., *Die Konzentration in der Wirtschaft*. Berlin: Duncker and Humbolt.

————. 1971b. *Ondernemingsconcentratie*. Leiden: H. E. Stenfert Kroese, N. V.

————. 1972. *Dynamische Concentratietheorie*. Leiden: H. E. Stenfert Kroese, N.
V.

————. 1976. "Theory and Evidence Concerning Mergers: An International Comparison." In A. Jacquemin and H. W. de Jong, eds., *Market Corporate Behaviour
and the State*. Leiden: Martinus Nijhoff.

Katzenbach, E. 1978. "Effectivere Fusionskontrolle," *Wirtschaftswoche* 32 (April
8).

Kennedy, C., and A. P. Thirlwall. 1972. "Technical Progress: A Survey." *Economic Journal* 82 (March): 11–72.

Klundert, Th. van de. 1970. *Grondslagen van de Economische Analyse*. Amsterdam: J. H. de Bussy.

Kottke, F. 1978. "Statistical Tests of the Administered Price Thesis: Little to Do about Little." *Southern Economic Journal* 44 (April): 873–82.

Kuehn, D. 1975. *Takeovers and the Theory of the Firm*. London: Macmillan.

Kummer, D. R., and J. R. Hoffmeister. 1978. "Valuation Consequences of Cash Tender Offers." *Journal of Finance* 33 (May): 505–16.

Langetieg, T. C. 1978. "An Application of a Three-Factor Performance Index to Measure Stockholder Gains from Merger." *Journal of Financial Economics* 6 (December): 365–83.

Larner, R. J. 1966. "Ownership and Control in the 200 Largest Non-Financial Corporations, 1929 and 1963." *American Economic Review* 56 (September): 777–87.

Lev, B., and G. Mandelker. 1972. "The Microeconomic Consequences of Corporate Mergers." *Journal of Business* 45 (January): 85–104.

Levy, H., and M. Sarnat. 1970. "Diversification, Portfolio Analysis and the Uneasy Case for Conglomerate Mergers." *Journal of Finance* 25 (September): 795–802.

Lintner, J. 1971. "Expectations, Mergers and Equilibrium in Purely Competitive Securities Markets." *American Economic Review* 61 (May): 101–11.

Locksley, G., and T. Ward. 1979. "Concentration in Manufacturing in the EEC." *Cambridge Journal of Economics* 3 (March): 91–97.

Lovell, M. 1978. "The Profit Picture: Trends and Cycles." *Brookings Papers on Economic Activity* 3: 769–88.

Lynch, H. H. 1971. *Financial Performance of Conglomerates*. Boston: Harvard Business School.

Macrosty, H. 1907. *The Trust Movement in British Industry*. London: Longmans.

Mandel, E. 1979. *The Second Slump*. London: New Left Books.

Mandelker, G. 1974. "Risk and Return: The Case of Merging Firms." *Journal of Financial Economics* 1 (December): 303–35.

Manne, H. G. 1965. "Mergers and the Market for Corporate Control." *Journal of Political Economy* 73 (April): 110–20.

Markert, K. 1975. "E. E. C. Competition Policy towards Mergers." In K. D. George and C. Joll, *Competition Policy in the UK and the EEC*. Cambridge: Cambridge University Press.

Markham, J. 1955. "Survey of the Evidence and Findings on Mergers." In *Business Concentration and Public Policy*. New York: National Bureau of Economic Research.

Maroff, F. 1976. "UK and West German Trade in Manufactures." In M. Panic, ed., *The UK and West German Manufacturing Industry, 1954–72*. London: National Economic Development Office, H.M.S.O.

Marris, R. 1964. *The Economic Theory of Managerial Capitalism*. Glencoe, Ill.: Free Press.

———. 1968. "Review of J. K. Galbraith: The New Industrial State." *American Economic Review* 58 (March): 240–47.

Marris, R., and A. Wood. 1971. *The Corporate Economy*. London: Macmillan.

Mason, R. H., and M. B. Goudzwaard. 1976. "Performance of Conglomerate Firms: A Portfolio Approach." *Journal of Finance* 31 (March): 39–48.

Mathijsen, P. 1975. "Competition Policy Laws which Apply to Member States." In K. D. George and C. Joll, *Competition Policy in the UK and the EEC*. Cambridge: Cambridge University Press.

Maunder, P., ed. 1979. *Government Intervention in the Developed Economy.* London: Croom Helm.

McClelland, W. G. 1972. "The IRC 1966–71: An Experimental Period." *Three Banks Review* (June): 23–42.

McCracken, P. et al. 1977. *Towards Full Employment and Price Stability.* Paris: OECD.

McGowan, J. J. 1965. "The Effect of Alternative Anti-Merger Policies on the Size Distribution of Firms." *Yale Economic Essays* 5 (Fall): 423–74.

———. 1971. "International Comparisons of Merger Activity." *Journal of Law and Economics* 14 (April): 233–50.

Meade, J. E. 1968. "Is 'The New Industrial State' Inevitable?" *Economic Journal* 78 (June): 372–92.

Means, G. C. 1972. "The Administered-Price Thesis Reconfirmed." *American Economic Review* 62 (June): 292–306.

Meeks, G. 1977. *Disappointing Marriage: A Study of the Gains from Merger.* Cambridge: Cambridge University Press.

Melicher, R. W., and D. F. Rush. 1973. "The Performance of Conglomerate Firms: Recent Risk and Return Experience." *Journal of Finance* 28 (May): 381–88.

———. 1974. "Evidence on the Acquisition-Related Performance of Conglomerate Firms. *Journal of Finance* 29 (March): 1941–49.

Mennel, W. 1962. *Takeover.* London: Lawrence and Wishort.

Meyer, F. V. 1978. *International Trade Policy.* London: Croon Helm.

Modigliani, F., and R. A. Cohn. 1979. "Inflation, Rational Valuation and the Market." *Financial Analysts Journal* (March): 24–44.

Moon, R. W. 1968. *Business Mergers and Take-Over Bids.* 3rd ed. London: Gee & Co.

Moore, M. 1972. "Stigler and Kindahl on Inflexible Prices." *Canadian Journal of Economics* 5 (November): 486–93.

Moyle, J. 1971. *The Pattern of Ordinary Share Ownership 1950–70.* Cambridge: Cambridge University Press.

Mueller, D. C. 1969. "A Theory of Conglomerate Mergers." *Quarterly Journal of Economics* 83 (November): 643–59.

———. 1977. "The Effects of Conglomerate Mergers: A Survey of the Empirical Evidence." *Journal of Banking and Finance* 1 (December): 315–42.

Müller, J. 1976. "The Impact of Mergers on Concentration: A Study of Eleven West German Industries." *Journal of Industrial Economics* 25 (December): 113–32.

Müller, J., and R. Hochreiter. 1975. *Stand und Entwicklungstendenzen der Konzentration in der Bundesrepublik Deutschland.* Göttingen: Verlag Otto Schwarz and Co.

Nabseth, L., and G. Ray. 1974. *The Diffusion of New Industrial Processes.* Cambridge: Cambridge University Press.

Neale, A. D. 1970. *Anti-Trust Laws of the U.S.A.* Cambridge: Cambridge University Press.

Neild, R. R. 1979. "Managed Trade between Industrial Countries." Cambridge: Department of Applied Economics, Cambridge University. Mimeo.

Nelson, R. L. 1959. *Merger Movements in American Industry 1895–1956*. Princeton, N.J.: Princeton University Press.

———. 1964. Testimony in U.S. Congress, *Hearings on Economic Concentration*. Pt. I. Washington, D.C.

———. 1966. "Business Cycle Factors in the Choice Between Internal and External Growth." In W. Alberts and J. Segall, eds., *The Corporate Merger*. Chicago: University of Chicago Press.

Newbould, G. D. 1970. *Management and Merger Activity*. Liverpool: Guthstead.

Newbould, G. D., and G. A. Luffman. 1978. *Successful Business Policies*. Farnborough: Gower Press.

Nordhaus, W. D. 1972. "Recent Developments in Price Dynamics." In O. Eckstein, ed., *The Econometrics of Price Determination*. Washington, D.C.: Federal Reserve System.

———. 1974. "The Falling Share of Profits." *Brookings Papers on Economic Activity* 1: 169–208.

O'Brien, P., et al. 1974. *Competition in British Industry*. London: G. Allen Unwin.

OECD. 1972– . *Annual Reports on Competition Policy in OECD Member Countries*. Paris.

———. 1974. *Mergers and Competition Policy*. Paris.

———. 1976. *Main Economic Indicators Historical Statistics 1960–75*. Paris.

———. 1977a. *Restrictive Practices of Multinational Enterprises*. Paris.

———. 1977b. *Towards Full Employment and Price Stability*. Paris.

———. 1979a. *Trends in Industrial R & D*. Paris.

———. 1979b. *Main Economic Indicators*. Paris, August.

Palmer, J. 1973. "The Profit Performance Effects of the Separation of Ownership from Control in Large US Industrial Corporations." *Bell Journal of Economics and Management Science* 4 (Spring): 293–303.

Parry, T. G. 1973. "The International Firm and National Economic Policy." *Economic Journal* 83 (December): 1201–21.

Payne, P. L. 1967. "The Emergence of the Large Scale Company in Great Britain 1870–1914." *Economic History Review* 20 (December): 519–42.

Peltzman, S. 1977. "The Gains and Losses from Industrial Concentration." *Journal of Law and Economics* 20 (October): 229–63.

Penrose, E. T. 1959. *The Theory of the Growth of the Firm*. New York: Wiley.

Phlips, L. 1969. "Concentration Dimension et Recherche Dans L'Industrie-Manufacturiere Belge," *Recherches Economiques de Louvain* 1 (February). Rptd. in condensed form in *European Economic Review* (1970).

———. 1971. *Effects of Industrial Concentration*. Amsterdam: North Holland Publishing Company.

Pickering, J. F. 1978. "The Abandonment of Major Mergers in the UK." *Journal of Industrial Economics* 27 (December): 123–31.

Poeche, J. 1977. "The Possibilities and Limitations of an International and Interregional Anti-Trust Policy." In G. Curzon and V. Curzon., *The Multinational Enterprise in a Hostile World*. London: Macmillan.

Posner, R. A. 1969. "Oligopoly and Anti-Trust Laws: A Suggested Approach." *Stanford Law Review* 21 (February): 1562–1606.

———. 1975. "The Social Costs of Monopoly and Regulation." *Journal of Political Economy* 83 (August): 807–27.

Prais, S. J. 1976. *The Evolution of Giant Firms in the United Kingdom*. Cambridge: Cambridge University Press.

Preston, L. E. 1973. "Giant Firms, Large Mergers and Concentration, Patterns and Policy Alternatives, 1954–68." *Industrial Organization Review* 1, no. 1: 35–46.

Pryor, F. L. 1972. "An International Comparison of Concentration Ratios." *Review of Economics and Statistics* 54 (May): 130–40.

Reid, S. R. 1968. *Mergers, Managers and the Economy*. New York: McGraw-Hill.

———. 1971. "A Reply to the Weston/Mansinghka Criticisms Dealing with Conglomerate Mergers." *Journal of Finance* 26 (September): 937–46.

Richardson, G. B. 1961. *Information and Investment*. Oxford: Oxford University Press.

Rowley, C. K. 1973. *Anti-Trust and Economic Efficiency*. London: Macmillan.

Rowley, C. K., and A. T. Peacock. 1975. *Welfare Economics*. London: Martin Robertson.

Rowthorn, R. E., with S. Hymer. 1971. *International Big Business*. Cambridge: Cambridge University Press.

Rumelt, R. P. 1974. *Strategy, Structure and Economic Performance*. Boston: Graduate School of Business.

Rydén, B. 1972. *Mergers in Swedish Industry*. Stockholm: Almgvist, Wiksell.

Sampson, A. 1973. *The Sovereign State*. London: Hodder and Stoughton.

Samuels, J. and D. Smyth. 1968. "Profits, Variability of Profits and Firm Size." *Economica* 35 (May): 127–39.

Sargent, Florence P. 1961. *Ownership, Control and Success of Large Companies*. London: Sweet and Maxwell.

Saunders, C. 1978. *Engineering in Britain, West Germany and France: Some Statistical Comparisons*, Sussex European Papers, No. 3. Brighton: University of Sussex.

Scherer, F. M. 1969. "Market Structure and the Stability of Investment." *American Economic Review* 59 (May): 72–79.

———. 1970. *Industrial Market Structure and Economic Performance*. Chicago: Rand McNally.

———. 1973. "Investment Variability, Seller Concentration and Plant Scale Economies." *Journal of Industrial Economics* 22 (December): 157–60.

Scherer, F. M.; A. Beckenstein; E. Kaufer; and R. D. Murphey. 1975. *The Economics of Multiplant Operation: An International Comparisons Study*. Cambridge, Mass.: Harvard University Press.

Scott, J. 1979. *Corporations, Classes and Capitalism*. London: Hutchinson.

Servan-Schreiber, J. J. 1967. *Le Défi Americain*. Paris: Denoel.

Sharpe, W. 1970. *Portfolio Theory and Capital Markets*. New York: McGraw-Hill.

Shepherd, W. G. 1967. "What Does the Survivor Technique Show About Economies of Scale?" *Southern Economic Journal* 34 (July): 113–22.

Singh, A. 1971. *Takeovers: Their Relevance to the Stock Market and the Theory of the Firm*. Cambridge: Cambridge University Press.

———. 1975. "Takeovers Economic Natural Selection, and the Theory of the Firm:

Evidence from the Post-war United Kingdom Experience." *Economic Journal* 85 (September): 497–515.

———. 1976a. "Review of Kuehn." *Journal of Economic Literature* 14 (July): 505–06.

———. 1976b. "Monopoly Capital Revisited: The Role of Centralisation by Merger." Forthcoming in H. Magdoff, ed.

———. 1977a. "U.K. Industry and the World Economy: A Case of Deindustrialisation." *Cambridge Journal of Economics* 1 (June): 113–36.

———. 1977b. "The Structural Transformation of British Industry: An Alternative View." Cambridge: Department of Applied Economics, Cambridge University. Mimeo.

———. 1979. "North Sea Oil and the Reconstruction of the U.K. Industry." In F. T. Blackaby, ed., *De-Industrialisation*. London: Heinemann.

———. 1980. "Third World Industrialisation and the Structure of the World Economy." In D. Currie and W. Peters, *Contributions to Economic Analysis*. London: Croom-Helm.

Singh, A., and G. Whittington. 1968. *Growth, Profitability and Valuation*. Cambridge: Cambridge University Press.

———. 1975. "The Size and Growth of Firms." *Review of Economic Studies* 42 (January): 15–26.

Smiley, R. 1976. "Tender Offers, Transactions Costs and the Firm." *Review of Economics and Statistics* 58 (February): 22–32.

Smith, D. S. 1971. "Concentration and Employment Fluctuations." *Western Economic Journal* 9 (September): 267–77.

Smith, K. V., and J. C. Schreiner. 1969. "A Portfolio Analysis of Conglomerate Diversification." *Journal of Finance* 24 (June): 412–27.

Smith, V. L. 1970. "Corporate Financial Theory Under Uncertainty." *Quarterly Journal of Economics* 84 (August): 451–71.

Spiegelberg, R. 1973. *The City*. London: Quartet Books.

Steer, P., and J. Cable. 1978. "Internal Organization and Profit: An Empirical Analysis of Large UK Companies." *Journal of Industrial Economics* 27 (September): 13–30.

Steindl, J. 1965. *Random Processes and the Growth of Firms*. London: Griffin.

Steiner, P.O. 1975. *Mergers: Motives, Effects, Control*. Ann Arbor: University of Michigan Press.

Steinherr, A., and H. Peer. 1975. "Worker Management and the Modern Industrial Enterprise: A Note." *Quarterly Journal of Economics* 89 (November): 662–69.

Stevens, D. L. 1973. "Financial Characteristics of Merged Firms: A Multivariate Analysis." *Journal of Financial and Quantitative Analysis* 8 (March): 149–58.

Stigler, G. J. 1950. "Monopoly and Oligopoly by Merger." *American Economic Review* 40 (May): 23–34.

———. 1964. "A Theory of Oligopoly." *Journal of Political Economy* 72 (February): 44–61.

———. 1966. "The Economic Effects of the Antitrust Laws." *Journal of Law and Economics* 9 (October): 225–258.

Stigler, G. J., and J. K. Kindahl. 1970. *The Behavior of Industrial Prices*. New York: NBER.

Stoneman, P. 1978. "Merger and Technical Progressiveness: The Case of the British Computer Industry." *Applied Economics* 10 (June): 125–39.

Stout, D. K. 1979. "De-Industrialisation and Industrial Policy." In F. T. Blackaby, ed., *De-Industrialisation*. London: Heinemann.

Sutherland, A. 1969. *The Monopolies Commission in Action*. London: Cambridge University Press.

———. 1970. "The Management of Merger Policy." In A. Cairncross, ed., *The Managed Economy*. London: Allen and Unwin.

Teh-wei, Hu. 1973. *Econometrics: An Introductory Analysis*. Baltimore: University Park Press.

Thompson, D. 1977. "The Competition Policy of The European Economic Community." In G. Curzon and V. Curzon, *The Multinational Enterprise in a Hostile World*. London: Heinemann.

U.N. 1974. *Multinational Corporations in World Development*. London: Praeger.

U.S. Senate. 1969. *Hearings before the Anti-Trust Sub-Committee of the Senate Committee on the Judiciary*. Vol. 3. Washington, D.C.

Utton, M. A. 1974a. "On Measuring the Effects of Industrial Mergers." *Scottish Journal of Political Economy* 21 (February): 13–28.

———. 1974b. "Aggregate vs Market Concentration: A Note." *Economic Journal* 84 (March): 150–55.

———. 1975. "British Merger Policy." In K. D. George and C. Joll, *Competition Policy in the UK and the EEC*. Cambridge: Cambridge University Press.

Van Hoorn, J., Jr. 1971. "The Effects of Taxation on Industrial Concentration in Belgium, France, Great Britain, Italy, the Netherlands, Austria, Switzerland and the United States." In H. Arndt, ed., *Die Konzentration in der Wirtschaft*. Berlin: Duncker and Humbolt.

Vernon, R., ed. 1974. *Big Business and the State*. London: Macmillan.

Weinberg, M. A. 1971. *Takeovers and Mergers*. London: Sweet and Maxwell.

Weiss, L. 1965. "An Evaluation of Mergers in Six Industries." *The Review of Economics and Statistics* 47 (May): 172–81.

———. 1966. "Concentration and Labor Earnings." *American Economic Review* 56 (March): 96–117.

———. 1971. "Quantitative Studies of Industrial Organization." In M. D. Intriligator, ed., *Frontiers of Quantitative Economics*. Amsterdam: North Holland Publishing.

———. 1975. "The Role of Concentration in Recent Inflation." In . Y. Brozen, ed., *The Competitive Economy*. Morristown, N.J.: General Learning Press.

von Weizsacker, C. C. 1977. "Inflation and Competition." In A. Jacquemin and H. de Jong, *Welfare Aspects of Industrial Markets*. Leiden: Martinus Nijhoff.

Weston, J. F. 1970. "The Nature and Significance of Conglomerate Firms." *St. John's Law Review* (special ed.) 44 (Spring): 66–80.

Weston, J. F., and S. K. Mansinghka. 1971. "Tests of the Efficiency Performance in Conglomerate Firms." *Journal of Finance* 26 (September): 919–36.

Weston, J.; K. Smith; and R. Shrieves. 1972. "Conglomerate Performance Using the Capital Asset Pricing Model." *The Review of Economics and Statistics* 54 (November): 357–63.

Whittington, C. 1971. *Prediction of Profitability and Other Studies in Company Finance*. Cambridge: Cambridge University Press.

Williamson, O. E. 1963. "Managerial Discretion and Business Behavior." *American Economic Review* 53 (December): 1032–57.

———. 1965. *The Economics of Discretionary Behavior*. Englewood Cliffs, N.J.: Prentice-Hall.

———. 1968. "Economies as an Anti-Trust Defense: The Welfare Trade-offs." *Amerian Economic Review* 58 (March): 18–36 (rptd. with correction in C. K. Rowley, ed., *Readings in Industrial Economics*. London: Macmillan, 1972).

———. 1970. *Corporate Control and Business Behavior*. Englewood Cliffs, N.J.: Prentice-Hall.

———. 1974. "The Economics of Anti-Trust: Transaction Cost Considerations." *University of Pennsylvania Law Review* 122 (June): 1439–96.

———. 1975. *Markets and Hierarchies: Analysis and Anti-Trust Implications*. New York: Macmillan.

———. 1977. "Economies as an Anti-Trust Defense Revisited." In A. P. Jacquemin, and H. W. de Jong, eds., *Welfare Aspects of Industrial Markets*. Nijenrode Studies in Economics No. 2. Leiden: Martinus Nijhoff.

Windle, H. R. 1977. "Restrictive Practices by Multinational Corporations: the Design for Multilateral Action." In G. Curzon and V. Curzon, *The Multinational Enterprise in a Hostile World*. London: Macmillan.

Winter, S. G., Jr. 1964. "Economic Natural Selection and the Theory of the Firm." *Yale Economic Essays* 4 (Spring): 225–72.

———. 1971. "Satisficing, Selection and the Innovating Remnent." *Quarterly Journal of Economics* 85 (May): 237–61.

World Bank. 1978. *World Development Report*. Oxford: Oxford University Press.

Wouterse, J. 1970. "Kenmerken van Ausierijpe Andernemingen." Ph.D. thesis, Nederlandse Economische Hogeschool, Rotterdam.

Wright, J. F. 1962. "The Capital Market and the Finance of Industry." In G. D. N. Worswick and P. H. Ady, eds., *The British Economy in the Nineteen Fifties*. Oxford: Clarendon Press.

Yamane, T. 1960. *Mathematics for Economists*. Englewood Cliffs, N.J.: Prentice-Hall.

Yordon, W. J., Jr. 1961. "Industrial Concentration and Price Flexibility in Inflation: Price Response Rates in 14 Industries 1947–58." *Review of Economics and Statistics* 43 (August): 287–94.

Young, S., and A. V. Lowe. 1974. *Intervention in the Mixed Economy*. London: Croom Helm.

About the Editor

Dennis C. Mueller is Professor of Economics at the University of Maryland. Previously, he taught at Simon Fraser University and Cornell University and held research positions at the Brookings Institution and the International Institute of Management, Science Center Berlin. In 1972–1973, he held a postdoctoral fellowship at the Center for Study of Public Choice, Virginia Polytechnic Institute and State University. Professor Mueller received a B.S. in mathematics from Colorado College and a Ph.D. in economics from Princeton University.

List of Contributors

J. R. Cable
University of Warwick

Andrew Cosh
Cambridge University

Jan-Olof Edberg
Studieförbundet Näringsliv
and Samhälle

Alan Hughes
Cambridge University

Frédéric Jenny
ESSEC

Anne-Marie Kumps
Facultés Universitaires Saint-
Louis

Dennis C. Mueller
University of Maryland

J. P. R. Palfrey
University of Warwick

Henk Peer
Katholieke Hogeschool Tilburg

J. W. Runge
Philips GmbH.

Bengt Rydén
Studieförbundet Näringsliv
and Samhälle

Ajit Singh
Cambridge University

André-Paul Weber
ESSEC

Robert Wtterwulghe
Facultés Universitaires Saint-
Louis

About the
Science Center Berlin

The Wissenschaftszentrum Berlin (Science Center Berlin), a non-profit corporation, serves as a parent institution for institutes conducting social science research in areas of significant social concern.

The following institutes are currently operating within the Science Center Berlin:

1. The International Institute of Management,
2. The International Institute for Environment and Society,
3. The International Institute for Comparative Social Research.

They share the following structural elements: a multinational professional and supporting staff, multidisciplinary project teams, a focus on international comparative studies, a policy orientation in the selection of research topics and the diffusion of results.

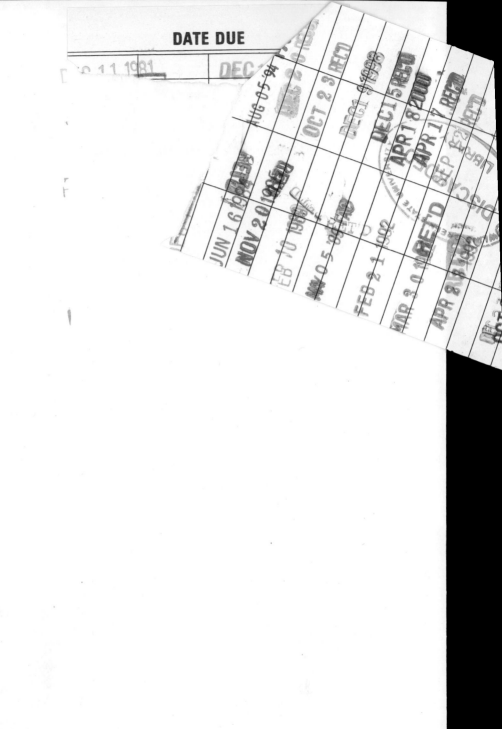